GAME OF QUEENS

GAME
OF
QUEENS

THE WOMEN WHO MADE
SIXTEENTH-CENTURY EUROPE

SARAH GRISTWOOD

BASIC BOOKS
NEW YORK

Published in the United States by Basic Books, an imprint of Perseus Books, LLC, a subsidiary of Hachette Book Group, Inc.

Books published by Basic Books are available at special discounts for bulk purchases in the United States by corporations, institutions, and other organizations. For more information, please contact the Special Markets Department at Perseus Books, 2300 Chestnut Street, Suite 200, Philadelphia, PA 19103, or call (800) 810-4145, ext. 5000, or e-mail special.markets@perseusbooks.com.

Designed by Jack Lenzo

Library of Congress Cataloging-in-Publication Data
Names: Gristwood, Sarah, author.
Title: Game of queens : the women who made sixteenth-century Europe / Sarah Gristwood.
Description: New York : Basic Books, 2016. | Includes bibliographical references and index.
Identifiers: LCCN 2016038073 (print) | LCCN 2016038268 (ebook) | ISBN 9780465096787 (hardback) | ISBN 9780465096794 (e-book)
Subjects: LCSH: Queens--Europe--History--16th century. | Women heads of state--Europe--History--16th century. | Europe--Politics and government--1492-1648. | BISAC: HISTORY / Modern / 16th Century. | HISTORY / Europe / Western. | BIOGRAPHY & AUTOBIOGRAPHY / Women. | BIOGRAPHY & AUTOBIOGRAPHY / Royalty.
Classification: LCC D226.7 .G75 2016 (print) | LCC D226.7 (ebook) | DDC 940.2/209252--dc23
LC record available at https://lccn.loc.gov/2016038073

10 9 8 7 6 5 4 3 2 1

CONTENTS

�֍

Chronology   viii
Family Trees   xiii
Dramatis Personae   xvi
Preface   xxv
Author's Note   xxxi

PART I 1474–1513

1. Entrance: The Netherlands, 1513   3

2. 'Lessons for My Daughter':
   Spain and France, 1474–1483   10

3. Youthful Experience:
   The Netherlands and France, 1483–1493   15

4. 'Fate Is Very Cruel to Women':
   Spain, Savoy, and France, 1493–1505   21

5. Princess Brides: England and Scotland, 1501–1505   30

6. Repositioning: The Netherlands,
   Spain, England, and Scotland, 1505–1512   35

7. 'False Imputations': France and the Netherlands, 1513   42

8. Flodden: Scotland and England, 1513   50

PART II 1514–1521

9. Wheel of Fortune: France and the Netherlands, 1514–1515   59

10. 'A Splendid New Year's Gift': France, 1514–1515   64

11. 'One of the Lowest-Brought Ladies':
    Scotland and England, 1515–1517   71

12. 'Inestimable and Praiseworthy Services': The
    Netherlands and France, 1516–1519   81

13. The Field of Cloth of Gold: Calais, 1520   87

14. Repercussions: The Netherlands and France, 1520–1521   95

PART III 1522–1536

15. 'Wild for to Hold': England and Scotland, 1522–1524   107

16. Pavia: Italy, France, the Netherlands, and Spain, 1525   116

17. 'A True, Loyal Mistress and Friend': England, 1525–1527   123

18. New Pieces on the Board: Scotland,
    the Netherlands, Hungary, Italy, and France, 1526–1528   132

19. 'Ladies Might Well Come Forward':
    The Netherlands and England, January–June 1529   139

20. The Ladies' Peace: Cambrai
    and England, July–December 1529   145

21. Exits and Entrances:
    The Netherlands, France, and Italy, 1530–1531   149

22. 'Thus It Will Be': England, 1530–1531   155

23. 'A Native-Born Frenchwoman': England, 1532–1535   159

24. 'Inclined Towards the Gospel':
    France and the Netherlands, 1533–1536   164

25. 'To Doubt the End': England, 1536   169

PART IV 1537–1553

26. Daughters in Jeopardy: England and Scotland, 1537–1543   181

27. Pawns and Princesses:
    The Netherlands and France, 1537–1543   188

28. New Winds: England and France, 1544–1547   197

29. Accommodations: France, 1548–1550   200

30. 'Device for the Succession': England, 1547–1553   204

PART V 1553–1560

31. 'Herculean Daring': England, 1553–1554   211

32. 'Not One Year of Rest':
    Scotland and the Netherlands, 1554–1558   222

33. Sisters and Rivals: England, 1555–1558   226

34. 'If God Is with Us': France, 1558–1560   232

35. 'Maidenly Estate': England, 1558–1560   239

36. Trouble in Scotland: Scotland, 1558–1560   245

PART VI 1560–1572

37. 'Rancour and Division': France, 1560–1561   251

38. 'Two Queens in One Isle': Scotland and England, 1561–1565   258

39. Challenge and Conciliation: France, 1562–1565   268

40. 'Majesty and Love Do Not Sit
    Well Together': Scotland, 1565–1567   274

41. 'Daughter of Debate':
    The Netherlands, France, and England, 1566–1571   285

42. The Massacre of Saint Bartholomew's
    Day: France, 1572–1574   293

PART VII 1572 On

43. Turning Points: England and France, 1572–1587   309

44. Prise: Fotheringhay, 1587   312

Postscript   317

Acknowledgments   325
Notes and Further Reading   327
Illustration Credits   333
Index   335

CHRONOLOGY

❊

1474   December 11   Isabella I becomes queen regnant of Castile, succeeding her half brother, whose putative daughter La Beltraneja, however, also claimed the throne.

1479   January 20   Isabella's husband, Ferdinand, becomes King of Aragon, succeeding his father. He and Isabella exercise effective joint rule as the 'Catholic Kings' of Spain.

1482   March 27   Mary, ruling duchess of Burgundy, dies, to be succeeded by her young son Philip.

1483   August 30   Charles VIII becomes king of France, succeeding his father, Louis XI. Charles' sister Anne de Beaujeu becomes regent in all but name during the thirteen-year-old's minority.

1486   February 16   Maximilian I (Maximilian of Austria), widower of Mary of Burgundy, is elected Holy Roman Emperor.

1491   December 6   Anne, the ruling duchess of Brittany, is forced to marry the French king Charles, beginning what would become a permanent attachment of Brittany to France's interests.

1492   January 2   Ferdinand and Isabella conquer Granada and end the Moorish rule of southern Spain.

        March 31   Ferdinand and Isabella expel the Spanish Jews at the demand of Grand Inquisitor Tomás de Torquemada.

        April 17   Ferdinand and Isabella sign an agreement with Italian navigator Christopher Columbus, allowing him to claim any new lands discovered on their behalf.

1498   April 7   Louis XII becomes king of France, succeeding his kinsman Charles VIII.

1504   November 26   Juana 'the Mad' becomes titular queen regnant of Castile, succeeding her mother, Isabella. Her father, Ferdinand, and husband, Philip of Burgundy, contest control of the country.

1506   September 22   Philip of Burgundy dies, leaving his widow, Juana, to spend most of her life in incarceration, and leaving control of Castile to Ferdinand of Aragon. Philip's own Netherlands territories pass to his six-year-old son Charles.

1507   March 18   Margaret of Austria is appointed regent of the Netherlands for her nephew Charles.

1509   April 21   Henry VIII becomes king of England, succeeding his father, Henry VII. He immediately marries Katherine of Aragon.

1513   September 9   The Battle of Flodden between England and Scotland sees James IV of Scotland die, to be succeeded by his infant son James V, whose mother, Margaret Tudor, is left as regent.

1515   January 1   François I becomes king of France, succeeding his cousin and father-in-law, Louis XII.

1516   January 23   The death of Ferdinand leaves Aragon to his grandson Charles, already ruler of the Netherlands. On March 14 it is announced that Charles will assume rule of all Spanish territories, nominally sharing that rule with his incarcerated mother, Juana, official queen regnant of Castile.

1517   October 31   Martin Luther posts ninety-five theses on the door of the Palast Church at Wittenberg, condemning corrupt practices in the Catholic Church.

1519   June 28   Charles V is elected Holy Roman Emperor following his grandfather Maximilian.

1521   January 3   Pope Leo X (the first pope from the Florentine banking family, the Medicis) excommunicates Martin Luther.

        April 8   Charles V gives control of his Habsburg Austrian lands to his brother Ferdinand (who also acts as his regent in the Holy Roman Empire) and keeps control of his Spanish, New World, and Netherlands territories.

        April 18   Luther appears before the Diet (or Assembly) of Worms, but refuses to recant.

1525   February 24   Battle of Pavia sees the crushing defeat of the French by Charles V's army, and capture of King François.

1526   August 29   Battle of Mohács sees an Ottoman army under Suleiman the Magnificent defeat Hungarian forces, and the subsequent reorganization of Hungary. The Turkish threat to the east becomes an ever-greater factor in European politics through the following decades.

1527   May 6   Rome is plundered by Imperial troops, Pope Clement VII (a second Medici pope, uncle of Catherine de Medici) is forced to flee. This has serious consequences for the papal inquiry into the validity of the marriage of Henry VIII to Katherine of Aragon.

1529   August 3   Ladies' Peace of Cambrai signed by Margaret of Austria (on behalf of her nephew Charles V) and Louise of Savoy (on behalf of her son François I).

October 1   The Marburg Colluquy, a discussion between Martin Luther and the more radical Swiss reformer Ulrich Zwingli, illustrates important theological differences between different branches of the new Reforming faith. Nonetheless, the following year 1530 sees the 'Protestant' princes of Germany form the Schmalkaldic League, a defensive alliance against the overlordship of Holy Roman Emperor Charles V.

1531   January 3   Mary of Hungary is requested by her brother Charles V to assume regency of the Netherlands, following the death of their aunt Margaret of Austria.

1533   January   Henry VIII of England secretly marries Anne Boleyn, who is crowned queen June 1 before the birth of their daughter, Elizabeth, on September 7.

1534   March 23   First Act of Succession secures the English succession to King Henry's children by Anne Boleyn and declares Princess Mary a bastard. In November the Act of Supremacy declares Henry the 'only supreme head on earth' of the English Church.

1536   January 7   Katherine of Aragon, Henry VIII's first wife, dies.

May 19   Anne Boleyn, Henry VIII's second wife, executed.

May 30   Henry VIII marries his third wife, Jane Seymour.

October 13   The Pilgrimage of Grace protests against Henry VIII's break with Rome and the Dissolution of the Monasteries but is harshly repressed.

1542   April 15   James V of Scotland dies, to be succeeded by his infant daughter Mary; beginning the slow rise to power of James' widow, Marie de Guise.

1545   December 13   Pope Paul III convenes the Council of Trent, the twenty-five sessions of which would be held off and on until 1563. The ecumenical council both consolidated the doctrines of the Catholic Church and condemned those of Protestantism. This can be seen as the start of the Counter Reformation.

1547   January 28   Henry VIII dies, to be succeeded as king of England by his son Edward VI.

March 31   Henri II becomes king of France, succeeding his father, François I.

1553   July 6   The early death of Edward VI sees the throne pass for a mere nine days to Lady Jane Grey before being seized by Edward's half sister, Mary Tudor. Crowned as Mary I, she sets about returning England to the Catholic faith.

1555   May 25   Jeanne d'Albret becomes queen regnant of Navarre.

October 25   Mary of Hungary resigns regency of the Netherlands.

1556   January 16   Charles V abdicates the crown of Spain to his son Philip II, to whom he had already handed over the Netherlands the previous October.

1558   November 17 Elizabeth I becomes queen of England, succeeding her half sister, Mary.

1559   April 3   Treaty of Cateau-Cambrésis, orchestrated by Christina of Denmark, ends sixty-five years of intermittent warfare (much of it centring on rival claims to the Netherlands).

May 2   John Knox returns to Scotland from exile. In Geneva, where he had worked closely with John Calvin, he had published the pamphlet *The first blast of the trumpet against the monstrous regiment of women*.

July 10   François II (husband to Mary, Queen of Scots) becomes king of France, succeeding his father, Henri II. The Guise family rises to power.

1560   December 5   Charles IX becomes king of France, succeeding his brother François II. His mother, Catherine de Medici, assumes power during his minority, in rivalry to the Guises.

1561   August 9   Mary, Queen of Scots, returns to her country to assume active rule.

1562   March 1   The Massacre of Vassy, the killing of French Protestants by the Duc de Guise's men, triggers the start of the French Wars of Religion.

1564   July 25   Maximilian II becomes Holy Roman Emperor, following his father, Ferdinand.

1567   February 10   Lord Darnley, second husband to Mary, Queen of Scots, is murdered.

May 15   Mary marries Lord Bothwell, widely held responsible for Darnley's murder.

July 24   Mary is forced by her rebellious nobles to abdicate in favour of her infant son James VI.

	September 5 The Duke of Alba, arriving in the Netherlands to put down iconoclastic riots, establishes the 'Council of Troubles'. Margaret of Parma resigns her regency, and Alba's harshness signals the start of the long Dutch Revolt against Spanish rule.
1568	May 16 Mary, Queen of Scots, flees south over the border into England, to begin almost twenty years of captivity.
1571	October 7 The Battle of Lepanto gives a league of European Catholic powers a great naval victory against the Ottoman Turks.
1572	June 9 Jeanne d'Albret dies, to be succeeded as ruler of Navarre by her son Henri.
	August 24 Celebrations for Henri of Navarre's marriage to Catherine de Medici's daughter, intended to heal religious divides, instead herald the terrible anti-Protestant slaughter of the Massacre of St Bartholomew's Day.
1574	May 30 Henri III becomes king of France, succeeding his brother Charles IX.
1581	July 26 Seven northern (and largely Protestant) provinces of the Netherlands formally declare independence from Spain.
1587	February 8 Mary, Queen of Scots, is executed at Fotheringhay.
1588	August 8 The approach of the Armada fleet, sent by Philip of Spain against England, provokes Elizabeth I's address to the troops at Tilbury. Much of the fleet is destroyed by adverse weather.
1589	August 2 Henri of Navarre becomes Henri IV of France, succeeding his kinsman and brother-in-law Henri III. This ends the line of Valois kings and brings in the Bourbon Dynasty.
1603	March 24 Elizabeth I dies, leaving the throne of England to James VI of Scotland, son of Mary, Queen of Scots.

England and Scotland

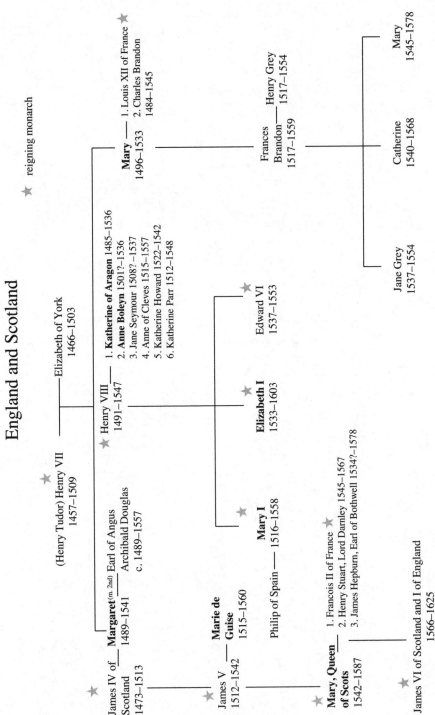

★ reigning monarch

(Henry Tudor) Henry VII 1457–1509 —— Elizabeth of York 1466–1503

★ Henry VIII 1491–1547 —— 1. **Katherine of Aragon** 1485–1536
2. **Anne Boleyn** 1501?–1536
3. Jane Seymour 1508?–1537
4. Anne of Cleves 1515–1557
5. Katherine Howard 1522–1542
6. Katherine Parr 1512–1548

Mary 1496–1533 —— 1. Louis XII of France
2. Charles Brandon 1484–1545

Frances Brandon 1517–1559 —— Henry Grey 1517–1554

Margaret (m. 2nd) 1489–1541 —— Earl of Angus Archibald Douglas c. 1489–1557

James IV of Scotland 1473–1513

Edward VI 1537–1553 ★

Elizabeth I 1533–1603 ★

Jane Grey 1537–1554

Catherine 1540–1568

Mary 1545–1578

Marie de Guise 1515–1560

Mary I 1516–1558 ★ —— Philip of Spain

James V 1512–1542

Mary, Queen of Scots 1542–1587 ★ —— 1. Francois II of France ★
2. Henry Stuart, Lord Darnley 1545–1567
3. James Hepburn, Earl of Bothwell 1534?–1578

James VI of Scotland and I of England ★ 1566–1625

France

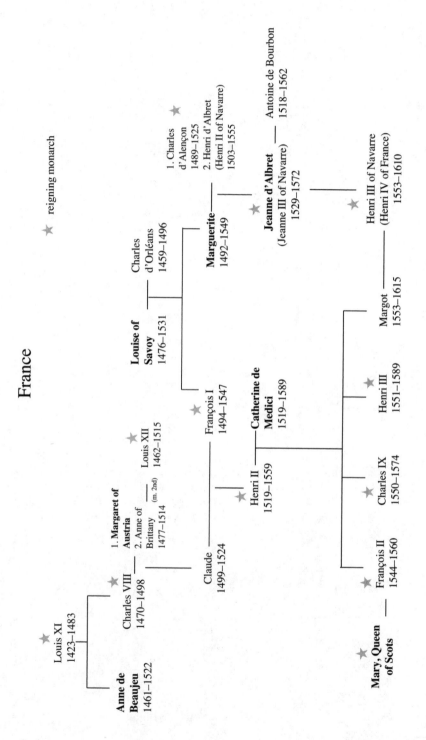

★ reigning monarch

Louis XI
1423–1483

Charles VIII
1470–1498

Anne de
Beaujeu
1461–1522

1. Margaret of
Austria
2. Anne of
Brittany   (m. 2nd)
1477–1514

Louis XII
1462–1515

Claude
1499–1524

François I
1494–1547

Louise of
Savoy
1476–1531

Charles
d'Orléans
1459–1496

Marguerite
1492–1549

1. Charles
d'Alençon
1489–1525
2. Henri d'Albret
(Henri II of Navarre)
1503–1555

Antoine de Bourbon
1518–1562

Jeanne d'Albret
(Jeanne III of Navarre)
1529–1572

Henri III of Navarre
(Henri IV of France)
1553–1610

Henri II
1519–1559

Catherine de
Medici
1519–1589

François II
1544–1560

Mary, Queen
of Scots

Charles IX
1550–1574

Henri III
1551–1589

Margot
1553–1615

Spain and the Habsburg Empire

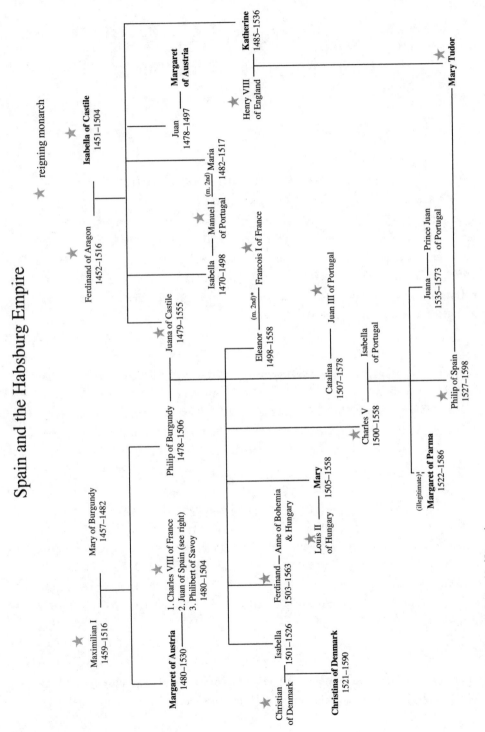

reigning monarch

Maximilian I
1459–1516

Mary of Burgundy
1457–1482

Isabella of Castile
1451–1504

Ferdinand of Aragon
1452–1516

Margaret of Austria
1480–1530

1. Charles VIII of France
2. Juan of Spain (see right)
3. Philibert of Savoy
1480–1504

Philip of Burgundy
1478–1506

Juana of Castile
1479–1555

Juan
1478–1497

Margaret
of Austria

Isabella
1470–1498

(m. 2nd) Maria
1482–1517

Manuel I
of Portugal

Katherine
1485–1536

Henry VIII
of England

Isabella
1501–1526

Ferdinand
1503–1563

Anne of Bohemia
& Hungary

Mary
1505–1558

Louis II
of Hungary

Eleanor
1498–1558

(m. 2nd)*

Francois I of France

Catalina
1507–1578

Juan III of Portugal

Charles V
1500–1558

Isabella
of Portugal

Mary Tudor

Christian
of Denmark

Christina of Denmark
1521–1590

(illegitimate):

Margaret of Parma
1522–1586

Juana
1535–1573

Prince Juan
of Portugal

Philip of Spain
1527–1598

* Eleanor first married Manuel I of Portugal

DRAMATIS PERSONAE
GAME OF QUEENS: WHO'S WHO

※

SPAIN AND THE HABSBURG EMPIRE
ISABELLA I OF CASTILE (1451–1504)

Queen regnant of Castile from 1474, Isabella's marriage to **Ferdinand II of Aragon (1452–1516)** united the two main Spanish kingdoms. They famously ruled together as the mighty Catholic monarchs, producing only a short-lived son but several influential daughters. On Isabella's death, Castile was inherited by their eldest surviving daughter, **Juana 'the Mad' (1479–1555)**, but Ferdinand proved reluctant to lose his power in that kingdom.

MAXIMILIAN I, HOLY ROMAN EMPEROR (1459–1519)

After his marriage to **Mary of Burgundy (1457–1482)**, ruling duchess of what would later be known as the Netherlands, Maximilian's ambition was to unite as much of Europe as possible in the hands of his Habsburg family. The marriage of his son **Philip of Burgundy (1478–1506)** to Ferdinand and Isabella's daughter Juana produced (among other children) the future 'Charles V'.

MARGARET 'OF AUSTRIA' (1480–1530)

Maximilian and Mary of Burgundy also had a daughter, Margaret. Contracted to the young French king Charles VIII, she was sent off as a toddler to be raised in that country. When that alliance fell through, she married Isabella and Ferdinand's son and heir, Juan, and then, after his early death, the Duke of Savoy. But when he too died, she returned to the Netherlands, which she ruled as regent for many years, on behalf of her nephew Charles, with a twelve-year-old Anne Boleyn as one of her maids.

CHARLES V (1500–1558)

Charles inherited the hereditary Austrian lands of his paternal grandfather, Maximilian (besides the elective title of Holy Roman Emperor Maximilian also held);

the Burgundian inheritance of his father, Philip (the Netherlands); and the Castile of his mother, Juana, and the Aragon of his maternal grandfather, Ferdinand (to say nothing of any lands in the New World). He found the inheritance personally wearing and would indeed cede the Austrian lands, power in eastern Europe, and eventually leadership of the Holy Roman Empire to his younger brother, **Ferdinand (1503–1564)**. But this concentration of territories into the hands of one family established the Habsburg dominance of the sixteenth century.

MARY 'OF HUNGARY' (1505–1558)

Another sibling of Charles V and Ferdinand, Mary was married to the king of Hungary until the battle of Jarnac made her a youthful widow. She had then to hold Habsburg power on Ferdinand's behalf against the advance of the Ottoman Turks. Niece to Margaret of Austria, who raised her, she then became Margaret's successor as regent of the Netherlands. Mary's three sisters all became queens consort: **Eleanor (1498–1558)** of first Portugal and then France; **Isabella (1501–1526)** of Denmark, Norway, and Sweden; and **Catherine (Catalina, 1507–1578)** of Portugal, which she would come to rule as regent.

CHRISTINA OF DENMARK (1521–1590)

Daughter to Isabella and her husband, Christian of Denmark, Christina, after her father's deposition, was raised by Isabella's aunt Margaret of Austria and sister Mary of Hungary. Married to the dukes first of Milan and then of Lorraine, she was considered as a possible bride for Henry VIII of England. She was a determined player on the European political scene, attempting to regain her father's Scandinavian kingdoms, and key negotiator of the important peace of Cateau-Cambrésis.

MARGARET 'OF PARMA' (1522–1586)

The illegitimate daughter of Charles V, Margaret too was raised by Mary of Hungary, whom in 1555 she in turn succeeded as regent of the Netherlands, on behalf of her half brother, Philip of Spain. Her son, Alexander Farnese, Duke of Parma, was Philip's great general.

PHILIP II (1527–1598)

Philip 'of Spain' was also hereditary ruler of the Netherlands as well as the increasingly important New World territories. Early in his life, his marriage to Mary Tudor also made him king consort of England; late in it, he also inherited Portugal, through his mother. He is, of course, famous or infamous for the armada that in 1588 he sent against Elizabeth of England.

FRANCE

ANNE DE BEAUJEU (A.K.A. ANNE OF FRANCE, 1461–1522)

Eldest daughter of the French king **Louis XI (1423–1483)**, Anne acted as regent of France in all but name during the minority of her younger brother, **Charles VIII (1470–1498)**. A powerful and influential figure, author of an advice manual for noblewomen that has been compared to Machiavelli's *The Prince*, she helped to raise both Margaret of Austria and Louise of Savoy.

ANNE OF BRITTANY (1477–1515)

Inheriting the independent duchy of Brittany from her father in 1488, Anne's hope was to preserve the independence of Brittany in the face of pressure from France. After some months of armed conflict, however, she found herself forced in 1492 to marry the young French king Charles VIII, who with the help of his sister, Anne de Beaujeu, kept her largely powerless. By the terms of the marriage, she was forced on Charles's death to marry his successor, the next king of France, **Louis XII (1462–1515)**.

LOUISE OF SAVOY (1476–1531)

Initially just a poor relation of Anne de Beaujeu, Louise's status rose steadily as several French kings in succession died without heir, until the closest in line to the throne was François, her son by the Count d'Angoulême. After **François I (1494–1547)** became king in 1515, Louise was widely regarded as the power behind his throne.

MARGUERITE OF NAVARRE (A.K.A. MARGUERITE D'ANGOULÊME, 1492–1549)

Besides François, Louise also bore a daughter, Marguerite. The three were so close they were known as 'the trinity', and neither of Marguerite's two marriages (to the Duc d'Alençon and to Henri II of Navarre) impeded her devotion to her brother or her sway over his court. An author, intellectual, and reformer of the Catholic Church, Marguerite may have been a role model for the young Anne Boleyn.

BONNIVET (GUILLAUME GOUFFIER, SEIGNEUR DE BONNIVET, 1488?–1525)

Soldier and nobleman Bonnivet was raised in company with the future François I, whose tutor was Bonnivet's elder brother, Artus Gouffier. Made admiral of France in 1515, François's favour placed him in charge of a number of important military and diplomatic campaigns. He has also been identified as the predatory hero of sections of Marguerite of Navarre's *Heptameron*.

CATHERINE DE MEDICI (1519–1589)

Daughter of the great Florentine banking family, with all too bitter a personal experience of the wars of the early sixteenth century, Catherine was married to the future **Henri II (1519–1559)**, a marriage that made her queen consort of France. But it was only after Henri's death in 1559 that she became the powerful figure behind the three of her sons who successively occupied the French throne, **François II (1544–1560)**, **Charles IX (1550–1574)**, and **Henri III (1551–1589)**.

GUISE (FRANCIS, DUC DE GUISE, 1519–1563, HENRI, DUC DE GUISE, 1550–1558, AND THE GUISE FAMILY)

Catherine de Medici's chief rivals for power in France were the members of the powerful Guise family. As uncles to the young Mary, Queen of Scots, the soldier Duke Francis and his brother, the Cardinal of Lorraine, exercised particular influence over Mary and her husband, the French king François II. After Francis was assassinated in 1563, his son Henri became the leader of the Catholic faction in the French Wars of Religion.

JEANNE D'ALBRET (1528–1572)

The daughter of Marguerite 'of Navarre', **Jeanne d'Albret** in 1555 inherited her father's Navarrese kingdom. Reared in her mother's reforming tradition, in 1560 she publicly converted to the Protestant faith and became the first great heroine of the Reformation. Her marriage to **Antoine de Bourbon (1518–1562)** produced a son, **Henri of Navarre (1553–1610)**, who eventually became Henri IV of France.

SCOTLAND

MARGARET TUDOR (1489–1541)

Elder sister to Henry VIII, Margaret was married to **James IV (1473–1513)**, the King of Scots, only to see him killed by her brother's army at Flodden, leaving her regent for her baby son, **James V (1512–1542)**. Determined to hold on to power, Margaret was nonetheless insecure about her ability to wield it alone and made two more disastrous marriages,

ANGUS (ARCHIBALD DOUGLAS, SIXTH EARL OF ANGUS, 1489?–1557)

Margaret Tudor married Angus as her second husband in 1514, perhaps for the support of his powerful Douglas clan. The marriage soon turned sour, and Angus would be one of Margaret's chief rivals for control of her son, the young king. The marriage did, however, produce a daughter, **Lady Margaret Douglas (Countess of Lennox, 1515–1578)**, whose bloodline produced the future monarchs of a united British Isles.

ALBANY (JOHN STUART, SECOND DUKE OF ALBANY, 1481?–1536)

Raised in France, and married to a French heiress, Albany was nonetheless a grandson of the fifteenth-century king of Scotland James II. He was thus an obvious choice to replace Margaret Tudor as regent for her infant son, James V. He acted with considerable ability as regent of Scotland from 1515, but never altogether came to terms with the country.

MARIE DE GUISE (1515–1560)

A French noblewoman from the powerful Guise family, Marie in 1538 married James V of Scotland. He died in 1542, however, just days after the birth of their only child, and from that time Marie's life was dedicated to trying to preserve the Scottish throne for her daughter, Mary.

ARRAN (JAMES HAMILTON, SECOND EARL OF ARRAN
AND DUKE OF CHÂTELHERAULT, 1519?–1575)

Arran's descent from an earlier Scottish king, James II, left him convinced he had the right to take a leading part in Scottish affairs. Vacillating (or perhaps pragmatic), he nonetheless contended for power with Marie de Guise after James V's death and would be a thorn in the side of her daughter, Mary Stuart.

JAMES STEWART (FIRST EARL OF MORAY, 1531/2–1570)

The illegitimate son of James V, Lord James had, prior to the return of his young half sister, Queen Mary, established himself in a position of power in Scotland, a position he had no desire to relinquish. A committed Protestant, he moved from being Mary's adviser to one of the agents of her downfall (and regent for the son who replaced her).

MARY STUART (MARY, QUEEN OF SCOTS, 1542–1587)

Queen of Scotland from her earliest infancy, Mary nonetheless spent most of her youth in France, awaiting marriage to Catherine de Medici's eldest son, François. After his early death, however, she returned to Scotland in 1561 and set about trying to rule that turbulent country. Her mistakes are notorious, and all male—Rizzio, Darnley, Bothwell. But just as significant in her final downfall and execution at Fotheringhay is the fact that her bloodline made her a Catholic rival for Elizabeth Tudor's English throne.

DARNLEY (HENRY STUART, OR STEWART, LORD DARNLEY, 1545–1567)

The son of Lady Margaret Douglas, Margaret Tudor's daughter, Darnley had thus a claim to the English throne. This may be the rationale behind his marriage in 1565 to Mary, Queen of Scots. His personality soon showed Mary, however, that the marriage had been misguided, while his murder at Kirk o'Fields besmirched her reputation and led indirectly to her overthrow.

BOTHWELL (JAMES HEPBURN, FOURTH EARL OF BOTHWELL, 1534/5–1578)

The direct cause of Mary's downfall was her third marriage, to the Earl of Bothwell, made in May 1567 while Bothwell was still widely suspected of Darnley's murder. Mary's hand may, however, have been forced by Bothwell's abducting and raping her. Fleeing abroad after her defeat and deposition, he died a prisoner in Denmark, reputedly insane.

JAMES VI (1566–1625)

Son to Mary, Queen of Scots, and Lord Darnley James (like several of his predecessors on the Scottish throne), James VI was crowned while still in his cradle, his mother having been forced to abdicate the throne. Reared in the harsh traditions of the Scottish reformed church, he was taught to see Mary as an example of bad management and perhaps womanly weakness. He was, however, on good terms with Elizabeth I, on whose death in 1603 he became also James I, king of England.

ENGLAND

HENRY VII (1457–1509)

The first Tudor monarch won the crown of England at the battle of Bosworth in 1485. His marriage to the Yorkist heiress Elizabeth united the Yorkist and Lancastrian claims, ending the Wars of the Roses, but there seems, even on the Yorkist side, to have been no thought that Elizabeth of York could herself assume the crown. Marrying his heir, Prince Arthur, to Ferdinand and Isabella's daughter Katherine was a coup for his fragile new dynasty.

KATHERINE OF ARAGON (1485–1536)

Youngest daughter to Ferdinand and Isabella of Spain, wed first to Henry VII's eldest son, Arthur, Katherine then (after Arthur's early death) famously and controversially married Arthur's younger brother, Henry VIII. It was a love match that endured for more than the first decade of Henry's reign, but it foundered on her failure to give him a son.

HENRY VIII (1491–1547)

Most widely known for his six wives, and for the break with Rome to which his desire for a male heir led him, Henry was also a Renaissance monarch. Rival to François I and Charles V, he was anxious to play a role on the wider European stage. His elder sister, Margaret, was already married to the King of Scots when he came to the throne in 1509, but he arranged the marriage of his younger sister, **Mary (1496–1533),** to Louis XII of France and tolerated her second marriage to his own favourite **Charles Brandon (Lord Lisle, Duke of Suffolk, 1484–1545).**

WOLSEY (THOMAS, CARDINAL 1473?–1530)

A meteoric rise through the ranks of the church brought Wolsey, a butcher's son, from humble origins to a preeminent position in the government of Henry VIII. Lord Chancellor of England, and a cardinal after 1515, he exercised a controlling hand over the diplomacy of much of Henry's early reign, but fell—as dramatically as he had risen—over his failure to get Henry his divorce from Katherine of Aragon.

CROMWELL (THOMAS, 1485?–1540)

A protégé of Wolsey's, Cromwell survived his master's fall and—from even more humble origins—rose to have his finger in even more of the nation's pies. A layman committed to religious reform, he was nonetheless also given unique powers over the nascent Church of England, which he used to mastermind the Dissolution of the Monasteries. Cromwell first supported and then fell out with Anne Boleyn and was instrumental in her downfall. His own downfall, however, came through another of Henry's wives, when the king turned against his fourth wife, Anne of Cleves, a marriage Cromwell had promoted.

ANNE BOLEYN (1501?–1536)

Anne was born in comparative obscurity. She was reared, however, first under the tutelage of Margaret of Austria and then at the French court. Despite her disgrace and death on the scaffold, England's Protestantism and the reign of her daughter, Elizabeth, are her enduring legacies.

EDWARD VI (1537–1553)

Henry VIII's third wife, Jane Seymour, at last gave him the longed-for son, but Edward survived only six years after inheriting his father's throne at the age of nine. The zealous Protestantism of his reign culminated in the boy king's attempt to will the throne not to either of his half sisters, Elizabeth and Mary, but to his second cousin **Lady Jane Grey (1537–1554)**, a granddaughter of Henry VIII's younger sister, Mary.

MARY TUDOR (1516–1558)

Daughter to Katherine of Aragon and Henry VIII, Mary Tudor suffered acutely from the breakup of her parents' marriage, refusing to follow her father's move toward the Reformed faith. She endured years of real hardship before, in 1553, the death of her younger brother Edward brought her to the throne. Once on it, however, her efforts to restore Catholicism, and her marriage to Philip of Spain, brought her the sobriquet 'Bloody' Mary.

ELIZABETH TUDOR (1533–1603)

Anne Boleyn's daughter had an equally difficult path to the English throne, for all that her long reign has her remembered as our greatest monarch. History tells of her long rivalry with her kinswoman Mary Stuart, across the Scottish border, but it is less often that we think to see her in relation to other European female rulers.

DUDLEY (ROBERT, FIRST EARL OF LEICESTER, 1532–1588)

Son of the man who promoted Lady Jane Grey to the throne, Robert Dudley nonetheless became Elizabeth I's great favourite—some said lover—and the longest-running contender for her hand in marriage. Her reputation as well as his suffered when his wife Amy Dudley died in suspicious circumstances, but he remained her close adviser and friend.

BURGHLEY (WILLIAM CECIL, FIRST BARON BURGHLEY, 1520–1598)

The great statesman of Elizabeth Tudor's reign, Cecil became principal secretary of state immediately upon her accession and subsequently Lord Treasurer. Like his rival Dudley, he was a committed Protestant, urging the queen to aid her co-religionists in Europe, and was a particularly determined enemy to the Catholic Mary, Queen of Scots.

REFORMERS

MARTIN LUTHER (1483–1546)

The German theologian and former monk is credited with having launched the Protestant Reformation when in 1517 he reputedly nailed his ninety-five theses—or complaints of corrupt practices within the Catholic Church—to a church door in Wittenberg. His refusal to recant did indeed spark a great divide in Europe, but in fact Luther's ideas (which still shared some key points of Catholic doctrine) would be superseded in many territories by a new and more severe generation of largely Swiss reformers.

JOHN CALVIN (1509–1564)

Best known as leader of the Protestant Church in Geneva, Calvin was born in France but fled after a clampdown in 1534 forced a distinction between those seeking only reform of the Catholic Church and those at odds with its central tenets. The doctrines of what became known as Calvinism include the belief that the fate of each human soul is predestined and the absolute sovereignty of God in its salvation, without reference to ritual or good works.

JOHN KNOX (1513/6?–1572)

The Scottish reformer and firebrand—once sentenced to row the French galleys as a prisoner for his part in a rebellion—found life in English and European exile only hardened his virulent anti-Catholicism. An outspoken critic of the Catholic Mary, Queen of Scots, his most famous work, *The First Blast of the Trumpet Against the Monstrous Regiment of Women*, set him also at odds with the Protestant Elizabeth Tudor.

PREFACE

✳

The Queene is queint, and quick conceit,
Which makes hir walke which way she list,
And rootes them up, that lie in waite
To work hir treason, ere she wist
Hir force is such, against her foes,
That whom she meetes, she overthrows.

—NICHOLAS BRETON, *THE CHESSE PLAY* (1593)

IN THE EASTERN LANDS WHERE chess was first played, all the human figures were male, with the king flanked by his general or chief counsellor, his vizier. It was as the game spread through Europe, after the Arabs invaded in the eighth century, that the queen first appeared, but still as a comparatively impotent figure, able to advance only one diagonal square at a time. It was in the Spain ruled by Isabella of Castile that the chess queen took on the almost unbounded power of movement we accord her today.

Two books written in Spain in the last years of the fifteenth century describe these new powers, referring to 'lady's chess' or 'queen's chess'. True, in 1493 the Italian translator of Jacobus de Cessolis's *Game of Chess* queried whether the queen could really assume the knight's powers, 'because it is uncharacteristic of women to carry arms, on account of their frailty'. Two decades earlier, William Caxton's English translation had stressed above all else the queen's 'shamefastedness' and chastity.

But the translators can never have met the 'warrior queen' Isabella, herself an impassioned player. It is likely that it was largely the example of Isabella and the real-life ruling women who had come before her that finally provoked an echo on the board.*

---

* In Russia, where change came later, it was only in the eighteenth century, during the rule of Catherine the Great, that the chess queen really overtook the vizier. By the same token, the

The allegorical significance of the game was obvious to contemporaries: it was, as many an illustration can testify, this that had made it a staple of courtly love play. But the change of moves would not be without controversy. The new game became known as mad queen's chess—*scacchi de la donna* or *alla rabiosa* in Italian, *esches de la dame* or *de la dame enragee* in French. But it was here to stay.

FROM THE ACCESSION OF ISABELLA of Castile to the throne in 1474 to France's Massacre of Saint Bartholomew's Day almost a century later (a horror that ruptured loyalties across the continent) was an Age of Queens. The period saw an explosion of female rule scarcely equalled in even the twentieth century. These years saw the birth of the new Reformed religion as well as the dawn of the world we know today, and for much of them large swaths of Europe were under the firm hand of a reigning queen or a female regent. This was a sisterhood that recognised both their own bonds as women and their ability to exercise power in a specifically feminine way.

This book will follow the passage of power from mother to daughter, from mentor to protégée: from Isabella of Castile to her daughter Katherine of Aragon and from Katherine to her daughter, Mary Tudor; from the French dowager Louise of Savoy to her daughter, writer and reformer Marguerite of Navarre; and from Marguerite not only to her own daughter, Jeanne d'Albret, but to her admirer Anne Boleyn and thence to Elizabeth Tudor.

As the century wore on, the daughters of the first powerful women would come to find themselves at the forefront of the great religious divides that racked the sixteenth century. Most, though not all, attempted to exercise a measure of religious toleration before those hopes foundered on other, more extreme, opinions.

Religion helped bring many of them into prominence; religion, in the end, would drive them apart and bring to an end the Age of Queens. But the sheer scale on which the women of the sixteenth century exercised power (as well as the challenges they faced) remains both a spectacle and a source of warning right up to our own day.

THROUGHOUT THE CENTURY THE HABSBURGS would prove doughty, if unexpected, promoters of female authority. With some notable exceptions, the Habsburg empire—which in the course of the century came to stretch

---

chess queen's initial appearance in the early part of the millennium had also coincided, if that is the word, with a brief boom in female authority.

from the Mediterranean to the English Channel, from the glories of the Alhambra to the grey skies of Antwerp—knew women as regents rather than as queens regnant. Nonetheless, the Netherlands in particular passed from the hands of a ruling duchess into those of an almost unbroken succession of authoritative female governors, each the niece of her predecessor, that endured for sixty years.

The Habsburgs' great rival in Europe, France, subscribed to the Salic Law, which forbade a woman from inheriting the throne. It had, nonetheless, a formidable tradition of women exercising rule on behalf of an absent husband or underage son. Oddly enough, at the start of this era England was perhaps the least female friendly of all the European powers.

England had no Salic Law, yet when Henry Tudor became Henry VII of England, he subsumed into his own claim the blood rights of two women, his mother, Margaret Beaufort, and his wife, Elizabeth of York. No one, including the women themselves, seems to have found his action extraordinary. Yet it was England, of course, that saw a woman, Anne Boleyn, tip a nation into religious revolution. It was England that, in Anne's daughter, would go on to produce perhaps the most admired female ruler in history.

That, in a sense, is an impetus for this book. I have now written about two royal Elizabeths—Elizabeth of York and Elizabeth I—and I want to join up the dots: What lessons had England learned in those seventy years to accept a queen regnant as a possibility? (And, as a corollary, why did it then cease to do so?) It is in Europe that the answer may lie.

THE FEMALE RULERS OF EUROPE themselves recognised bonds of sisterhood stretching across the borders—and sometimes even running contrary to the interests—of their countries. They consciously invoked their status as women to conduct business in a different way. The year 1529 saw the famous 'Ladies' Peace' of Cambrai, a halt in the long war between Spain and France, struck between Margaret of Austria, the Habsburg emperor's aunt and regent, and Louise of Savoy, mother to the French king. The princes might fear loss of honour if making peaceful overtures, but, as Margaret wrote, 'ladies might well come forward' in such an undertaking.

This was an ideal that would echo through their century. There were a number of attempts, however abortive, to revive the idea of a ladies' peace over subsequent decades.* Sixteen years before Cambrai, in fact, on the eve

---

* And beyond, as witness, for example, the 1915 Women's International Peace Conference that hoped to end the First World War.

of the battle of Flodden that cost her her husband, the Scottish king, Margaret Tudor had wished she might meet with her sister-in-law Katherine of Aragon, ruling England while her husband, Henry VIII, was away: 'If we shall meet, who knows what God by our means may bring to pass?' Mary Stuart always hoped England and Scotland could find lasting peace, if only she and Elizabeth Tudor could meet.

The line of descent from mother to daughter, whether physical or spiritual, runs like an artery through sixteenth-century Europe. And the connections between them form a complex web. Margaret 'of Austria', born daughter to the ruling Duchess of Burgundy, was sent as a toddler to the French court, where she fell under the influence of the formidable Anne de Beaujeu, and then as a teenager to the court of Castile, where she became Isabella's daughter-in-law and sister-in-law to Katherine of Aragon. She was then, as an adult, herself instrumental in raising Anne Boleyn.

But the powerful women in the later decades of the 'long sixteenth century' found themselves in a very different climate from that which their predecessors had enjoyed. Elizabeth I at the end of this story has many affinities with Margaret of Austria at the beginning. But while Margaret of Austria had lived in four realms by her early twenties, Elizabeth Tudor never set foot outside her own land. Neither woman bore a living child, yet Margaret would become known as 'La Grand Mère de l'Europe', while Elizabeth's preferred identity was famously that of virgin.

The Reformation had driven fault lines across the continent, while conversely giving to some of these women a fame more enduring than they might otherwise have enjoyed. This book was born, though I didn't realise it, when as a teenager I read Garrett Mattingly's classic *The Defeat of the Spanish Armada* and noted his passing comment that in 1587, the year of the execution of Mary, Queen of Scots, it was sixty years since the parties of religion had begun to form, the old versus the new, 'and always by some trick of Fate one party or the other, and usually both, had been rallied and led by a woman'.

IN THE SO-CALLED GYNOCRACY DEBATE, concerning women's fitness for authority, two writers influenced the political thinking of the times to a degree that requires special mention here. One, of course, was Niccolò Machiavelli, whose *The Prince* was first privately distributed in 1513. The second is Christine de Pizan, French-Italian poet, preceptress, and, some would argue, early feminist: the first woman to become a professional writer. Her work of the early fifteenth century, *The Book of the City of Ladies*, had lost none of its relevance by the sixteenth century (or even, perhaps, the twenty-first), as the interest demonstrated by a number of women in this story goes to prove. Anne de Beaujeu and Louise of Savoy inherited copies of Christine's work, while Margaret of Austria's three-volume set would have passed on to her niece Mary of Hungary. Anne of Brittany and Margaret of Austria also owned suites of tapestries based on the *City of Ladies*, as did Elizabeth Tudor.

All too aware of the clerical portrayal of women as Eve's daughters, weak and essentially untrustworthy, Christine gives into the mouth of Justice a refutal of 'certain authors' who 'criticise women so much', pointing out that there is 'little criticism of women in the holy legends and the stories of Jesus Christ and his Apostles', whatever Christ's later servants might say.

Machiavelli—who portrayed fickle Fortune as a woman—saw war as a prince's first duty as well as pleasure. By contrast, Christine's model of the virtuous ruler downplays the ruler's role as warlord (a practical problem for the female ruler, leaving aside the question of any innately pacific tendencies) and stresses the 'prudence' that in the Aristotelian concept was the entry point of all the other virtues. Prudence was a virtue attributed to the majority of these women, and *The Book of the City of Ladies* made a point of describing a number of women from ancient or more recent French history who had successfully governed nations or territories.

The continuity of experience—the repetition of tropes and patterns through the century—is something of a theme of this book. Most can be allowed to manifest themselves through the course of the narrative, but one is so insistent as to require special note: the question of how frequently debate about these powerful women centres around their bodies.

These are women each of whom would prove to have a role beyond the usual consort's function of a breeding machine, but nonetheless the story abounds with questions of debated virginity and fertility—of women most easily attacked through querying their chastity or their desirability. Questions, even, as to whether the division of a sovereign's body natural and body politic might not be the best way to allow female rule. This was perhaps the idea behind Elizabeth I's famous speech at Tilbury: 'I know I have the body of a weak and feeble woman, but I have the heart and stomach of a king'.

Though the forceful women of fifteenth-century Italy are sadly beyond the scope of this story, Caterina Sforza may be the most striking of 'the ones that got away' (as well as another suggested as a model for the new chess queen). Machiavelli, who encountered Caterina when sent on an embassy, described how, besieged and with her children taken hostage, Caterina pulled up her skirts and showed the besiegers 'her genital parts', telling them she had the means to make more children if necessary. Caterina was perhaps unique even among contemporaries, but nonetheless the stress on a powerful woman's physicality is something that endures today.

MODERN COMPARISONS ARE OFTEN INVIDIOUS and will largely be excluded from the main body of this text. Nonetheless, at this of all moments, they cannot be ignored completely. A decade ago, as I write—on 19 January 2006, to be precise—the *New York Times* paid an international group of women a backhanded compliment. It was, it said, 'the most interesting and accomplished group of female leaders' ever assembled, 'with the possible exception of when Queen Elizabeth I dined alone'.

A good deal has changed in the past ten years concerning women's role on the international stage. But a lot has *not* changed, and that includes the visibility of much of women's history. Elizabeth and her kinswomen apart, the female rulers of sixteenth-century Europe are not always familiar to the general reader of the English-speaking countries. In the attempt to change that, this book must be regarded as an opening gambit. But one thing at least it can hope to do: prove that Elizabeth I could dine in some extraordinary company.

AUTHOR'S NOTE

✠

In a book with sixteen protagonists, four are called some version of 'Margaret' and another four of 'Mary'. I therefore make no apology for distinguishing them as clearly as possible, even at the cost of some consistency. Thus, while Margaret of Austria keeps her natal title despite her three marriages, Marguerite 'of Navarre' is so described even before her marriage to the king of that small country. It is the title under which she is most familiar, the title under which her writings are still published today. Also in the interest of clarity, spelling, punctuation, and capitalisation have sometimes been modernised.

PART I
1474–1513

'Since you have given women letters and continence
and magnanimity and temperance, I only marvel that
you would not also have them govern cities, make laws,
and lead armies. . . .'

The Magnifico replies, also laughing:

'Perhaps even that would not be amiss. . . . Do you not
believe that there are many to be found who would
know how to govern cities and armies as well as men
do? But I have not laid these duties on them, because I
am fashioning a Court Lady, not a Queen'.

—BALDASSARE CASTIGLIONE,
THE BOOK OF THE COURTIER (1528)

ENTRANCE
The Netherlands, 1513

✳

The girl who arrived at the court of the Netherlands in the summer of 1513 was herself a courtier's daughter, bred to know the steps of that dangerous dance—a life where assets were exchanged for attendance, where favour was won by flattery. She knew how the pageantry of a Christmas masque could spell out a message, how a family's fortune could rise or fall on a ruler's whim, and knew that in the great chess game of European politics, even she might have a part to play.

No one, of course, had yet any idea just how great a part that would be.

She arrived as the latest of the eighteen maids of honour waiting upon Margaret of Austria, the regent of the Netherlands. Just twelve years old, she had been handed over to a stranger (one of the regent's esquires) and escorted from her manor home in the Weald of Kent to make the rare journey across the sea. She would have been keyed up to a pitch of excitement, but scared, too, surely. Perhaps no arrival in her life—not even her arrival at the Tower of London more than twenty years later—would be quite as alienating as this one.

Twelve years old . . . or about that, anyway. We do not know the date of Anne Boleyn's birth with certainty. We deduce it, in fact, partly from the knowledge that she came to Margaret of Austria's court in 1513 and that twelve was the youngest age at which a girl would normally take up such duties.

'I find her so bright and pleasant for her young age that I am more beholden to you for sending her to me than you are to me', Margaret wrote to Anne's father. The tribute meant more for the fact that Margaret had herself served a European-wide political apprenticeship unparalleled in even the sixteenth century. At thirty-three, after six years ruling the Netherlands on behalf of her father, Maximilian, and his grandson and her nephew Charles, she was a figure of international authority.

To follow the early career of Margaret of Austria is to read a *Who's Who* of sixteenth-century Europe. And Margaret in turn would come to play a significant role in the lives of two of the most controversial queens in English history.

'Whatever you do, place yourself in the service of a lady who is well regarded, who is constant, and who has good judgement', one of Margaret's own mentors, French governor Anne de Beaujeu had advised, in a manual of instruction for her daughter. If Anne Boleyn was to learn the lesson that a woman could advance ideas, exercise authority, and control her own destiny, she could hardly have fallen into better hands.

Controversial German scholar Cornelius Agrippa dedicated *On the Nobility and Excellence of the Feminine Sex* to Margaret of Austria. Agrippa said the differences between men and women were merely physical—'The woman hath that same mind that a man hath, the same reason and speech, she goeth to the same end of blissfulness, where shall be no exception of kind'—and that the only reason women were subordinate was lack of education and masculine ill will.

In schoolgirl French, the chosen language of Margaret of Austria's court, Anne Boleyn wrote to her father of her own determination to make the most of her opportunities. She wrote with a distinctly idiosyncratic grammar and spelling (she would strive, she wrote in that letter, to learn to speak French well 'and also spell'), but under a tutor's eye. Margaret's court was a centre both of power and of pleasure, but it was also Europe's finest seminary. French diplomat Lancelot de Carles would later describe how the young Anne 'listened carefully to honourable ladies, setting herself to bend all her endeavour to imitate them to perfection and made such good use of her wits that in no time at all she had command of the language'.

PORTRAITS OF THE WOMAN ANNE Boleyn met in 1513 display a subtle mixture of messages. Since the end of her third and last marriage, Margaret of Austria had made a point of having herself painted always in a widow's coif and with only the white of the headdress and sleeves of her costume to relieve the inky black. At first sight, no more sombre figure could be imagined. But appearances can be deceptive. To appear as a widow was on the surface a statement of self-abnegation, almost of weakness, a plea for pity. But in fact, it allowed a woman both moral and practical authority; it was the only role that allowed her to operate independently, as neither a child nor a chattel.

Black, in heraldic language, was the colour of trustworthiness, or *loyauté*. Margaret of Austria had a name for reliability, but one Italian visitor noted that besides 'a great and truly imperial presence', she had 'a certain most pleasing way of laughing'. Black fabric, needing so much expensive dye and so much labour to produce its depth of colour, was the luxury material of the sixteenth century, and in the portrait now in Vienna, the pale fur on Margaret's sleeves is costly ermine. The court to which Anne Boleyn had come—whether at the summer palace of Veure (La Veuren) or at Margaret's main base of Mechelen—was one of culture and of luxury.

Among the illustrated books Anne Boleyn could have seen in Margaret's library was the already famous *Très Riches Heures du Duc de Berry* (a legacy from Margaret's last husband) as well as newer books decked with flowers in the margins. Anne would later exchange notes with Henry VIII in the margins of just such a book.

Erasmus was just one of the artists and thinkers Margaret of Austria welcomed to Mechelen. Outwardly a large but, by palace standards, unostentatious brick-built house, Margaret's home was a place where devotional works jostled with Renaissance nudes. A *mappa mundi* that Van Eyck had made for her great-grandfather Philip the Good sat beside more recent acquisitions.

One was what Margaret's inventories describe as *ung grant tableau* (a large picture), *qu'on appelle, Hernoul-le-fin*, what is now called the Arnolfini portrait. This had, said her inventories of 1516, 'been given to Madame by Don Diego'. Don Diego de Guevara, a Spaniard who had come into the service of Margaret's family, was another courtier with a young female relation to place in the ducal household, and the Arnolfini portrait (*fort exquis*, exquisite, as one of Margaret's later inventories describes it) may have been a token of his gratitude—and a sign of just how highly these places were sought.

Walls were hung with blue and yellow damask, with green taffeta, or with Margaret's legendary collection of the tapestries for which the Netherlands was famous. Later, after the conquistador Cortés returned from Mexico, Margaret's collection would include Montezuma's feather cloak on the walls, Aztec mosaic masks, and a stuffed bird of paradise. As a northern pioneer of the kind of cabinet of curiosities beloved by Italian patrons, she employed a curator and two assistants to look after her collection.

Those in charge of young girls, Anne de Beaujeu wrote, should 'make sure they serve God, hear the Mass every day, observe the Hours and other devotions, pray for their sins, go to confession, and frequently give alms. And to console them and enliven their youth, and the better to maintain their love for you, you must sometimes let them frolic, sing, dance, and

amuse themselves happily but honestly, without groping, hitting, or quar-
relling'.* A *fille d'honneur* had no specific duties, which makes it all the likelier that Anne would have witnessed and perhaps participated in Margaret
of Austria's pleasures. Margaret kept close by her a paint box, covered in
purple velvet and disguised as a book, that she herself used frequently.
Music was another important recreation; her choir was legendary, and she
herself was a notable keyboard performer (and a composer of songs). The
masses, motets, and chansons in her music books were by the composers
Anne herself later favoured, her interest in music a bond with Henry VIII.

Margaret also played chess for recreation, with a set of chalcedony and
jasper or one of silver and gilt. (Her godmother, Margaret of York, who
owned Mechelen before her, had kept volumes on chess in the study she had
hung with violet taffeta.) But Margaret of Austria played the same game
also on a wider stage, as, in the years ahead, Anne Boleyn too would do.

THE THRIVING MERCHANT-LED COMMUNITY OF the Netherlands also had
a tradition of social mobility; even the Arnolfini portrait features not an
aristocratic but an aspirational merchant couple. This too, perhaps, was not
without its effect on Anne. The Boleyns themselves, one might say, were an
example of English social mobility.

Not that Anne came from such humble stock, as has often been
claimed. There was indeed merchant money in the Boleyn family, but it
was Anne's great-grandfather who had made his family fortune and become Lord Mayor of London. In the go-getting Tudor age, many great
families had connections closer than that with trade, and Anne was better
born than two of Henry's other wives. Her mother, indeed, was a scion of
the mighty Howard family, eldest daughter of the Earl of Surrey, later the
Duke of Norfolk.

Anne Boleyn's father, Thomas, had himself a connection to the Irish
earldom of Ormonde, and his mother was heiress to half the Ormonde
fortune. But Thomas's career in royal service began as a comparatively im-
pecunious young man on the make. He rose rapidly, however, and was present when Katherine of Aragon married Henry VII's heir in 1501, one of
the escorts who took the king's eldest daughter, Margaret Tudor, to marry
the Scots king in 1503. By the time Henry VIII came to the throne in 1509,
Thomas Boleyn was just into his thirties, perhaps a little too old to be one

---

* The English ambassador often saw Margaret's nieces and nephews playing outdoors, around a
  bonfire, or, in winter, with a sled rigged like a ship.

of the king's close cronies but nonetheless, as an accomplished man at the joust as well as a linguist and clever courtier, the sort Henry was glad to have about him.

In 1512 Thomas was sent on his first diplomatic mission, to the court of Margaret of Austria, and Anne Boleyn's appointment there was proof of how well, in the course of a ten-month stay, the two had gotten on. There is a record of their shaking hands on a bet that they could advance in their negotiations in ten days, both wagering different types of horse: her Spanish courser against his hobby. In that letter to Thomas about Anne's progress, Margaret told him that if the young girl continued as well as she was doing, then 'on your return the two of us will need no intermediary other than she'.

BEYOND A GENERAL, FAINTLY SEXUALISED reference to her cosmopolitan gloss and Frenchified ways, Anne's early experience abroad does not perhaps feature as strongly as it should in our understanding of her. She is more usually placed against a background of Hever, the lovely, fortified manor house in the Weald of Kent bought and remodelled by her great-grandfather and inherited by her father, Thomas, in 1505. Hever indeed is where she had spent most of her childhood. There, preparing to go abroad for what was always likely to be a stay of years, she would have walked around the ravishing springtime orchards and gardens, taking, with an intelligent adolescent's intensity, a last look.

But though Mechelen too had, under Margaret's rule, fine gardens aplenty, the contemporary image of court life dwelled on the snares and tares amid the plants. The Tudor rising classes both feared and needed the court. It was the only place where real secular preferment might be won, but also the place where any slip of the tongue or tactics, any overweening ambition or misplaced allegiance, could be quite literally fatal. This was the world into which Anne Boleyn had been sent by her relations, aimed like any arrow.

On the one hand, she was there as her family's agent and ambassador, as surely as her father was England's. On the other, what would this long separation do to her relations with that family? She would at times be in company with her father, and other family members, in the decade ahead, when their careers brought them, too, across the Channel. But for long periods, she must have often been forced back on her own resources. In later years she was perceived as not showing a proper womanly reliance on the guidance of her family—the wider Howard clan—but after this decade on largely her own recognisance, why should she?

At the court where Margaret of Austria consulted with her council every day, Anne, with the wits, the determination, and above all the power of observation de Carles noticed, surely learned more than the French tongue. She might have observed a woman exercising power—and perhaps even, within careful confines, enjoying her sexuality.

There was another lesson Anne Boleyn could have learned in Margaret's glamorous, cultivated sphere. The Netherlands (the old Burgundian) court was home to all the pageantry and parade of courtly love: that great game of sexual role-playing that dominated upper-class Europe for three centuries and still influences us today.*

This too was a game Anne learned how to play.

'Sir', Anne wrote to her father, 'I understand from your letter that you desire me to be a woman of good reputation [*toufs onette fame*] when I come to court'. But the lessons she could learn at Mechelen were many and varied.

The English court had long borrowed its best ideas from Burgundy. On the one hand, Margaret maintained a strict etiquette. Anne and her fellow maids would have been guarded carefully. On the other, Margaret wrote a poem for her young attendant ladies, warning them against taking the game too seriously:

> *Trust in those who offer you service,*
> *And in the end, my maidens,*
> *You will find yourselves in the ranks of those*
> *Who have been deceived.*

A girl's best defence lay in wit and confidence. 'Fine words' were a game that two could play. It was, of course, a game in which Anne Boleyn became the expert and which no one in Europe played more significantly.

Margaret, for all her widow's wear, allowed those around her to play at the game of courtly love, to an extent that could indeed be misunderstood by those from a less flexible culture. But as events would shortly prove,

---

* The duchy of Burgundy had come to comprise not only the southerly territory we think of as Burgundy today, but also much of modern Belgium and Holland. Since the original 'Burgundy' was indeed almost immediately to be yielded to France under the terms of Margaret of Austria's marriage treaty, it will be more convenient to speak at once of 'the Netherlands'. These Netherlands would themselves be split into the Catholic Spanish Netherlands and the seven independent Protestant provinces before the end of the sixteenth century.

Margaret knew when it was time to stop playing. Anne Boleyn should have taken heed.

Fifteen years later, Europe would hear of Anne Boleyn as the rival to Katherine of Aragon, queen of England and Margaret of Austria's onetime sister-in-law. Theirs was a struggle in which the power of personality (and of personal appeal) was just another side of the coin to questions of policy.

Anne's time at the court of the Netherlands, and later of France, gave her that cosmopolitan polish that so captivated Henry VIII. But it also made her Katherine's match in another sense. To watch a woman exercising power, in a way still unfamiliar to England, gave Anne a taste of the kind of European training Katherine herself had enjoyed as daughter to Isabella, the queen regnant of Castile.

The story of Anne Boleyn and Katherine of Aragon, and of their daughters, was part of a much larger European picture. In the years ahead, the royal women of the British Isles would be woven, or would sometimes weave themselves, into a web of rivalry and mutual reliance with Habsburg, Valois, and Medici women every bit as colourful as they. But to understand *that*, it is necessary first to look briefly at the decades that had gone before.

2

'LESSONS FOR MY DAUGHTER'
SPAIN AND FRANCE, 1474–1483

✳

I t was 13 December 1474, the day after Isabella of Castile received news of the death of King Enrique, her half brother. She entered the great church of Castile's capital, Segovia, dressed in plain mourning white; she emerged, after the Mass, decked with jewels and blazing with colour. On the very porch, on a hastily built platform draped in brocade, she was proclaimed as Castile's queen. Isabella would become the first, and more famous, of two women who would set a precedent for the female rulers of the sixteenth century.

As the procession wound its way through the streets, Isabella of Castile rode on horseback, with nobles on foot bearing the train of her gown. Ahead of her went one lone horseman holding a drawn sword, pointing upward, the traditional symbol of kingship. When he heard the news in distant Zaragosa, even Isabella's husband, Ferdinand of Aragon, was shocked that she had taken to herself the symbolic sword. His advisers had assured him he could tame his wife 'by satisfying assiduously the demands of conjugal love'. But all the same, Ferdinand protested in horror that he had never heard of a queen who usurped this masculine attribute.

After five years of marriage, Ferdinand should have known his Isabella better. She had, after all, broken with precedent in herself arranging their marriage. The heir to a neighbouring kingdom edging the Pyrenees, he was a useful ally in Isabella's battle for her own disputed throne.

Isabella had not been born to inherit Castile. There were two male heirs ahead of her, first her half brother, Enrique, and then her full brother, Alfonso. But when Enrique succeeded to the throne with no sign of a child to follow him, and when Alfonso died suddenly, in the course of Enrique's reign, Isabella's position changed. It was then that she had made her alliance with Ferdinand, with the terms of the marriage ensuring that she would continue to outrank him in Castile. He was an experienced soldier who could fight her battles as well as sire her children. A match made on practical grounds, it was nonetheless to become one of the most famously successful partnerships in Christendom.

Ferdinand's potential as stud was already proven, though when Isabella took the throne the couple had only a daughter, Isabella, named after her mother, not a son. His abilities as a soldier would also prove useful, since Isabella was not the only candidate for queen regnant of Castile.

Her sister-in-law, Enrique's wife, had eventually borne a daughter, though rumour said this Juana was sired by a lover called Béltran rather than by Enrique. That gave Isabella the chance to stake her own claim above that of the child, 'La Beltraneja', who would, eventually, retire defeated to a convent, still only in her teens. In 1470s Spain (as in England some seventy years later), the twists of heredity decreed that it would be two women disputing a throne—and worth querying whether a woman trying to challenge a man would still have won her victory. But Isabella had also received the sanction of one theoretician, Fray Martin de Cordoba, in his *Jardin de nobles doncellas*: 'Some people, My Lady . . . take it badly when a kingdom or other state comes under the rule of a woman. But, as I will explain below, I disagree, since, from the very beginning of the World to the present, we see that God always gave women responsibility for humanity's salvation, so that life would emerge from death'.

But the struggle against the supporters of La Beltraneja—the War of the Castilian Succession—went on for another five years, and it was almost the end of the 1470s before Ferdinand and Isabella could feel sure of Castile. By this time Isabella had also borne a son, Juan. Three more daughters 'of Aragon' would follow: Juana, Maria, and Katherine.

The crusade was now to drive out the Moors, who had for many years colonised Spain's southern tip. Contemporaries varied in their opinions as to whether Ferdinand or Isabella was the most significant partner in their alliance after Ferdinand succeeded his father in 1479. Despite the marriage agreement, Ferdinand had more authority in Isabella's kingdom than she did in his. (Ferdinand's Aragon was, unlike Castile, governed by a variant on the Salic Law that prohibited female rule, though it did, unlike that prevailing in France, allow inheritance through the female line.) But her territory was by far the larger and richer, and a Venetian diplomat said that she was the one most spoken of.* Ferdinand and his advisers took some time to

---

* The Concordia de Segovia, weeks after Isabella took the throne of Castile, decreed that her arms would precede his on all chancery documents; his signature, however, would come first, a typical, and effective, compromise. The Concordia was not, however, without critics, who

accept this unusual situation, but in the end the pair did much to live up to their famous slogan, that they would 'command, govern, rule, and exercise lordship as one'. Their motto was *Tanto monta, monta tanto, Isabel como Ferdinand* (To stand as high, as high to stand, Isabel as Ferdinand).

Famously, Isabella of Castile accompanied her own armies to the battlefield—clad in armour and mounted on a warhorse—if not actually into the fray. She was an efficient organiser of supplies and provisions and of armaments too, recruiting thousands of workmen to build roads along which the guns could pass. A mobile hospital comprising six huge tents was another of her innovations, but her contribution was significant, too, in two other ways. The first was the talismanic importance she had for her soldiers, so that her presence was said to spur on the Castilian troops to certain victory. (Interestingly, the troops cried out for 'King' Isabella.) The second was as a tactician, but Isabella's role can be hard to assess with certainty, since in military matters she was careful to defer to her husband, at least publicly.

Isabella did not hesitate to take her daughters with her from one siege to another, but it was still her son, Juan, and he alone, who was given the training of a future ruler. Isabella (like Elizabeth Tudor after her) may have regarded herself as an exception to the usual role allocated to women as opposed to seeking a general expansion of that role. But nonetheless, as the fifteenth century drew toward its close, hers was a formidable example of female monarchy.

IN 1483 ANOTHER WOMAN CAME to join Isabella at the forefront of European politics, Anne de Beaujeu, ruling France on behalf of her thirteen-year-old brother, the new king. France had a tradition of royal women assuming responsibility on behalf of a male relative. Christine de Pizan's *City of Ladies* had been written, at the beginning of the century, as an argument that an earlier French queen, Isabeau of Bavaria, should be allowed to act as regent during her husband's bouts of insanity. (The *City of Ladies*, moreover, figured the Virgin Mary as exercising a regent's powers on behalf of her heavenly son.)

Born in 1461, Anne de Beaujeu (also known as Anne of France) could never herself have succeeded to the throne, because France subscribed to the Salic Law. Instead, she had at thirteen been married off to a brother of the Duc de Bourbon, a gentle soul twenty-one years older than herself.

---

held that Ferdinand—himself the great-grandson of an earlier Castilian king—should now be Castile's ruler, 'because he is a man'.

Anne at twenty-two had escaped damage from the inbreeding that weakened so many of her family. Her father, Louis XI, had called her 'the least foolish of women', refusing to admit that there could be a clever one. And on his death he broke with tradition by giving her (and, nominally, her husband) charge of the young king Charles VIII, in preference to the normal combine, which would have entailed his widow, the boy's mother, as guardian and his male relatives forming a regency council. Instead, Louis's widow, Queen Charlotte, was forbidden to have any contact with her son.

Though the Salic 'Law' debarred women from inheriting, or even transmitting, a claim to the throne, in one sense it actually favoured female authority in a limited sphere. As one contemporary writer, Jean de Saint-Gelais, put it, the person of an underage king should be placed in the hands 'of those nearest to him who are not entitled [*non capables*] to succeed'. It might seem less dangerous to give a measure of authority to a woman, since there could be no question of her snatching the final authority of monarchy itself, than to a male relative.

Anne de Beaujeu, 'Madame la Grande', was a controversial figure, a true daughter to the father she revered.* Louis had—not without cost to his people—done much to increase the power and the territories of the French crown. But Anne was likewise undoubtedly able, working within the confines of a position that was not always easy.

One contemporary called her a 'virago', 'a woman truly superior to the female sex . . . who did not cede to the resolution and daring of a man'. She would have been born to the height of sovereignty 'had nature not begrudged her the appropriate sex'.

Time and again, exceptional women would be praised as being hardly women at all and would sometimes seem themselves to accede to the verdict. Christine de Pizan described herself when widowed as metamorphosed into a man to provide for her family. But it was also noted of Anne de Beaujeu that one of her most effective techniques was not to flaunt her position, being content usually to operate from behind the scenes.

She was also a notable chess player. The volume of advice *Enseignements* (*Lessons for my daughter*) that Anne wrote later in life warns a girl, 'You should have eyes to notice everything yet to see nothing, ears to hear everything yet to know nothing, and a tongue to answer everyone yet to say nothing prejudicial to anyone'. Keep your own counsel about 'that which

---

* Many of the women in this story would, at the least, find it prudent in public to invoke their father's, rather than their mother's, legacy.

can affect your honour', unless 'it is something that strains your heart to conceal', and then confide only inside the family.

Anne advocates the virtues urged on women, piety and docility, but less for their own sake, if you look closely, than as a technique. Perhaps this is why *Enseignements* has been compared to Machiavelli's *The Prince*. The perfections and the ploys urged on women and on men may be different ones, but each volume comes from the pen of a writer who sees virtue as a tool.*

In the century ahead, France would see several notable instances of a woman's authority coming from women who had directly or indirectly profited from Anne de Beaujeu's example. Both Anne and Isabella of Castile are cited when successful women rulers are discussed in Baldassare Castiglione's famous *Book of the Courtier* (published in Venice in 1528), for both would prove to have an influence that extended far outside their own lands.

---

* Whether these supposed womanly virtues do not, however, in themselves constitute a limitation on women remains an issue up to our own day.

3
YOUTHFUL EXPERIENCE
The Netherlands and France, 1483–1493

More immediately, both Anne de Beaujeu and Isabella of Castile would be mentors to another significant woman, Margaret of Austria. Margaret would grow up to be the third example of a successful female ruler cited by Castiglione. But Margaret was only a child when, in 1483, she, like another young girl, Louise of Savoy, with whom as an adult she would sit across a conference table, came into Anne de Beaujeu's care.

Margaret's mother, Mary, the ruling Duchess of Burgundy, had inherited that territory from her own father, Charles 'the Bold', in the cold early spring of 1477. The nineteen-year-old Mary had faced huge challenges. As soon as her father died, French king Louis XI laid claim to a significant part of his lands, while the city-states of Flanders seized the chance to claim ever more autonomy. But Mary had support, in the form of her stepmother, Charles's widow, Margaret of York, sister to English king Edward IV and the future Richard III. Together, the two women had acted to resist the French invaders. They reached an accommodation with the Netherlands parliament, the Estates-General (though not before the latter had arrested and brutally executed some of the two women's most trusted advisers). And they were able to bring about Mary's long-planned marriage to Maximilian, archduke of Austria and son of the Holy Roman Emperor.*

* The ancient title of Holy Roman Emperor, though it had been for the last century held by members of the Habsburg family, was an elective office for which the rulers of Europe could compete. Created for Charlemagne in the year 800, it carried special responsibility to, and prestige within, the Catholic Church, a secular counterpart to the pope's religious authority. It also, crucially, carried with it not only overlordship of the conglomeration of ecclesiastical and temporal principalities that made up Germany but also an ever-shifting degree of influence in certain other areas, most notably Italy. The empire was not abolished until the Napoleonic era.

The marriage took place the same summer and was blessed with two healthy children, Margaret 'of Austria' and her brother, Philip. But in March 1482, Mary of Burgundy died after a riding accident.

On a domestic level, Mary left her children to the care of her stepmother, Margaret of York. Duchess Mary had written of her stepmother that she had always held 'our person and our lands and lordships in such complete and perfect love and goodwill that we can never sufficiently repay and recompense her', and the younger Margaret, goddaughter to the elder, would come to feel the same way. But the ducal family of Burgundy was royal in all but name, and for royal children—and especially royal girls—things were never that easy.

Duchess Mary had willed her lands to her children, with the regency to be held by her husband, Maximilian, during their minority. But the degree to which Netherlanders were prepared to accept foreign Habsburg dominance would be a growing source of conflict. The city of Ghent, indeed, wrested away from Maximilian the right to raise young Philip, the new Duke of Burgundy. As for little Margaret of Austria, two days before Christmas 1482, the Treaty of Arras made peace between France and Burgundy, promising her in marriage to thirteen-year-old Charles VIII, soon to be king of France under his sister Anne's care. Territories like Mâcon now became the property of France as Margaret's dowry, on the condition that she should not make any further claims on her mother's lands. She, of course, was too young to object. Her father—ambitious, aggressive, and intensely hostile to France's expansionism—was furious at seeing the lands given away. But Maximilian had now been cut off from power in his dead wife's lands by a regency council appointed to take control during his son's minority.

Just a year after her mother's death, resplendent in adult black velvet and pearls, the three-year-old Margaret was sent off toward France, escorted to the border by a great retinue. Only a tiny handful, however, would be allowed to remain with her as she was carried through France on a triumphal progress. Margaret was met at the border by Anne de Beaujeu, whose status, as a mere daughter during her father's reign, was still lower than Margaret's. The three-year-old Margaret was given a ceremonial entry into Paris, where just two months earlier Anne herself had been denied one.

On 22 June 1483, at the Loire château of Amboise that would become her principal residence, Margaret of Austria met and was formally engaged to her prospective husband, to whom, indeed, she was officially married the next day. She was now Dauphine of France. But two months later, on

30 August, old King Louis XI died. Margaret became, nominally, France's queen, and Anne de Beaujeu became effectively its ruler, not merely guardian of the young king, but also the country's regent in all but name.

Anne de Beaujeu's assumption of power met with resistance; one of her concerns was that the disgruntled French nobles should try actually to kidnap the young king. Conversations reported between France's princes spoke of sending Anne back home to her household duties. But slowly she won most of the dissenting voices around, to ratify a status quo that, while declaring that in his early teens Charles VIII was sufficiently mature not to require a regency, left Anne and her husband in control of his person.*

One noble not won around, however, was the Duc d'Orléans, who might otherwise have expected to lead a regency council. A kinsman of the king, he was moreover married to Anne's humpbacked younger sister, Jeanne. The match had been made in cynicism by the old king, who hoped thus to keep the ambitious d'Orléans without heir, saying callously that 'any children they have will not cost them much to keep'.

In the winter of 1484–1485, offering to free the young King Charles from his sister Anne's 'clutches', d'Orléans launched a rebellion. Anne de Beaujeu and the royal forces successfully put it down, always with the young king as their figurehead, to mask the unpalatable thought of a woman's leading a military campaign. D'Orléans's wife, Jeanne (like Anne de Beaujeu herself a daughter of the dead King Louis), sided with her sister against her husband, while their mother, Queen Charlotte, King Louis's widow, sided with d'Orléans. But it was time to curb the ambitions of the d'Orléans clan through any means available. One such means was marriage, made easier by the fact that Anne de Beaujeu was raising not only Margaret of Austria but also a number of other aristocratic girls whose families were bound to her by ties of influence or family.

ONE SUCH GIRL WAS THE eight-year-old Louise of Savoy, later Margaret of Austria's adversary and ally, now a mere pawn to be deployed against the d'Orléans clan. Louise had been born in 1476 as daughter to a younger son of the Duke of Savoy, a man his contemporaries knew as *Monsieur sans Terre*, Mr Lackland. With her mother dying when she was seven, Louise (and her younger brother, Philibert) went to be brought up by Anne de Beaujeu, a cousin on her father's side as well as her aunt by marriage on her mother's.

---

* A device that would subsequently be used by several other French-educated queens.

But in this extensive family, Louise of Savoy was very far from being an important member, certainly treated in a very different way than Margaret of Austria, the young queen. While Margaret's household accounts record a queenly entourage—twenty ladies and six lords in waiting, chaplain, treasurer, physician and secretaries, ponies and parrots, falcons and hounds, clothing even for her dolls—those around her would have had a significantly lesser status. Louise was given eighty livres a year to buy a court gown for state occasions. Who would have guessed Margaret and Louise would one day be meeting as equals across the conference table?

Louise of Savoy had since she was two been nominally betrothed to Charles d'Angoulême, a junior scion of the d'Orléans family almost twenty years older than she. Being tied to the penniless Louise, however, was—another humiliation for her—a way for French king Louis to clip the d'Orléans wings. When in 1487 d'Angoulême followed the example of his kinsman d'Orléans by joining another rebellion—this attempt so abortive it was known as the Mad War—he was ordered, by way of curbing his ambitions, to proceed with the marriage to the ten-year-old Louise on terms very favourable to the young bride. The ceremony went ahead on 16 February 1488, and a surviving letter from Louise's peripatetic father, making a rare appearance at her side, displays the eleven-year-old's concerns.

Her father wrote jocularly to his own new wife that Louise had been questioning him about the wedding night in a way that showed her eagerness. But in fact, a look at the context of the phrase reveals a darker story: 'My daughter says that she is still too narrow, and she does not know whether she might die of it; so much so that she asks every day how big and how long his thing is, and whether it is as big and long as her arm, which shows that she is already itching to be at the business of you other old married women'.

When she was finally sent to live with her husband, in his châteaux in the Loire Valley and Cognac, Louise of Savoy had to come to terms with the fact that Charles d'Angoulême's establishment was ruled by his mistress, the daughter of one of his officials, Jean de Polignac, and that his illegitimate children by several women would be brought up with Louise's own. D'Angoulême's mistress, however, appears to have taken his young wife under her wing, and Louise accepted the friendship; Anne de Beaujeu's lessons in discretion and pragmatism had been well learned. There were, after all, compensations. Louise had been reared in a family that valued books, and the cultured Charles possessed a notable two hundred or more volumes—romances, theological texts, Boethius and Ovid, and the works of the ubiquitous Christine de Pizan—while his court was home to artists, notably illuminator Robinet Testard and a number of men of letters, such as the Saint-Gelais brothers.

But there was one lesson learned by every aristocratic girl: that to raise her status in her husband's household, Louise of Savoy needed a male heir. Just three years into her marriage, still a young teenager but already concerned, she turned to a saintly hermit to pray for her fertility. He reassured her not only as to her prospects of bearing a son, but (she later said) as to that son's own glorious prospects.

The following year, 1492, Louise gave birth to a mere girl, Marguerite, but in 1494 there followed the all-important boy. As Louise's *Journal* later had it, 'François, by the Grace of God, King of France, my pacific Caesar took his first sight of the light of day at Cognac, about ten hours after midday 1494, the 12th day of September'.*

CHANGE HAD ALSO MEANWHILE COME, by now, for the most prominent of Louise of Savoy's playmates. In 1491 Margaret of Austria's secure and indulged prospect as queen of France came to an abrupt end.

The important dukedom of Brittany had, three years before, been inherited by a young ruling duchess (just as Margaret's mother, Mary, had inherited the duchy of Burgundy). Anne of Brittany was not yet twelve when she had inherited, but she was nonetheless determined to rule. In pursuit of that aim, she had undergone a proxy marriage ceremony with Margaret of Austria's father, Maximilian, decades her senior but delighted thus to be striking a blow against the hated French, one that would give the Habsburgs, with territory both to France's east and to its west, something of a stranglehold on that country.

But Anne de Beaujeu, still a dominant force in France, had other plans for Brittany. She was determined to annex the duchy, whether by force of arms or in some other way.

Anne of Brittany was persuaded—or forced by the French troops encircling her borders—to renounce Maximilian and marry Charles VIII, but it was noted that the ceremony had no show of joy about it. (Hardly likely, perhaps, after the bride had allegedly been forced to parade naked in front of her groom's advisers to demonstrate her fitness for childbearing.) Charles's existing marriage to Margaret of Austria would be annulled, a not unusual arrangement when a match made between two minors was as yet unconsummated.

---

* The journal was less a diary as we know it than a note—possibly compiled for astrological reasons—that at some later point in her life recorded all the significant events that had happened on particular days of the year.

Margaret of Austria had been dumped for a bigger heiress, basically—the victim of France's quarrel with her father, Maximilian. She was nonetheless kept in France for another two years; there was, after all, the question of what would happen to the dowry lands she had brought with her. Eventually, in May 1493 by a new treaty, Maximilian won them back, but meanwhile Margaret had been moved out of royal Amboise and into conditions she clearly found humiliating. She had become attached to Charles VIII—and he to her—and now felt isolated. A desperate letter survives from Margaret to Anne de Beaujeu, pleading against the removal of a cousin and companion: 'All the pastime I have, and when I have lost her I do not know what I shall do'.

Anne of Brittany too would become passionate about her unenthusiastic husband, Charles, but found herself sidelined with no voice in the affairs of her duchy, receiving ambassadors only with Anne de Beaujeu by her side. Anne herself and her husband enjoyed less influence than they once had and were increasingly spending time on their estates. Nonetheless, when the time came for Charles to go off to war in Italy, it was once again Anne de Beaujeu who was recalled to power, with Anne of Brittany left in her charge. There was perhaps always a concern as to what the young queen-duchess—who never gave up her dream of Brittany's independence—might do if left unsupervised.

But Anne of Brittany had quickly given Charles VIII a son, and when, finally, the thirteen-year-old Margaret of Austria was sent home, the future of France at least seemed ensured. Margaret took with her a farewell gift made by Anne of Brittany's most skilful embroideress. The two women kept up a connection, but Margaret remained lastingly angry toward the country that had rejected her. On the way home she cracked a bitter joke when offered wine from that year's worthless vines (*sarments*). They fitted in well, she said, with the king's oaths, or *serments*.

Margaret of Austria had already experienced something of the twists and turns of Fortune that loomed so large in the late medieval mind. 'Always remember that, as Saint Augustine says, you cannot be certain of even a single hour', Anne de Beaujeu wrote. For the moment, Fortune seemed to be favouring Louise of Savoy, now the mother of an important son—but perhaps she too had learned that it was not easy for a woman to control her own destiny.

4

'FATE IS VERY CRUEL
TO WOMEN'

Spain, Savoy, and France, 1493–1505

✳

Both Margaret of Austria and Louise of Savoy were now young women, looking to find their place in the world. But Margaret's future was not yet clear. In June 1493, at Cambrai (the scene of several important later encounters), she met again her godmother and stepgrandmother, Margaret of York, for whom she had been named. The next few years would be spent in the older Margaret's company. But another marriage was always going to be on the board.

In 1493 Margaret's father, Maximilian, succeeded his father as Holy Roman Emperor. Margaret, like her brother, Philip, was now to be used to cement his great project: an anti-French alliance. Philip was to marry Juana, daughter of the rulers of Spain, Ferdinand and Isabella; Margaret was to marry Juan, their heir. The grand scheme comprised plans for the youngest daughter of the Spanish monarchs, Katherine of Aragon, later to marry the heir to the English throne, thus cementing another useful alliance.

On 5 November 1495, at Malines, Margaret of Austria underwent a proxy marriage with her Spanish prince. The discussions over whether she should set sail for Spain before Juana arrived in Flanders resemble, in a modern scenario, nothing so much as the exchange of hostages. Nonetheless, in late January 1497 she was under way.

The weather was so bad her ship had to take refuge on the English coast and dock in Southampton, to the delight of the English king, Henry VII, who sent letters urging her to lodge in the town long enough for him to visit and for her to avoid the 'movement and roaring of the sea'. Perhaps she wished she had, for in the Bay of Biscay her ship ran into storms so severe that Margaret composed her own rueful epitaph:

> Here lies Margot, the willing bride,
> Twice married—but a virgin when she died
> (Cy-gist Margot la gentil' damoiselle
> Qu'ha deux marys et encor est pucelle)

Safely landed in Spain, Margaret met her new mother-in-law, Isabella of Castile. It was a chance to witness a woman exerting regal force in the most direct way.

Margaret met a woman who as her years advanced would be most at ease in the rough habit of a Franciscan monk but who, in public, could appear decked in rubies the size of a pigeon's eggs. Isabella commissioned a female professor of Latin to remedy the defects in her own education but nonetheless educated her own daughters as consorts, not as rulers.

Five years earlier, in 1492, a single triumphant year had seen Isabella of Castile riding into the palace of the Alhambra, victorious at last over the Moors, who had long occupied southern Spain; her expulsion of the Jews; and the discovery of the New World by her protégé Christopher Columbus. But even more significant, perhaps, would be Isabella's work in supporting, but also, crucially, in reforming, the Catholic Church in Spain.

Back in 1478 Isabella had applied to the pope for permission to launch the Inquisition in Spain. Her and Ferdinand's officers acted with such harshness that the pope felt impelled to intervene; they were replaced with the now infamous Tomás de Torquemada, who soon established not only an authoritarian spiritual rule but also an efficient network of tribunals across all the territories of the Catholic kings. This was the impetus that fuelled action against Moor and Jew. Isabella's Castile had been frontline territory, with Islam on its very boundaries. But her efforts would prove to be something of a preemptive strike, explaining why Protestantism would never make any real incursion into the Spanish peninsula.

The impetus for change did come from Isabella herself. She would boast that in her eagerness to root out other, heretical, strands of faith, 'I have caused great calamities and depopulated towns, lands, provinces and kingdoms'. The human cost of her actions was high; one priest who observed the expulsion of Jews whose families had lived in Spain for centuries recorded the emigrants collapsing, giving birth, dying by the roadside, 'so that there was no Christian who was not sorry for them'. Nonetheless, there would, after her death, be moves for Isabella's canonisation.

This was to be the spirit, and the lesson, her daughters carried abroad with them, as they were married off to spread the influence of Isabella and

Ferdinand's dynasty. And Margaret of Austria, as she arrived in Spain, would have a chance to meet at least some of her new sisters-in-law.* The eldest of them—named Isabella for the mother whose heir she was—had years before been married to the heir to the king of Portugal. Her young spouse had been killed in a riding accident after they had been married a mere seven months, however, and after years of family pressure Isabella had been persuaded in 1497 to marry Manuel, who had replaced her first husband as Portugal's king. As Margaret of Austria arrived in the country, Isabella was departing,† while Juana had of course already left for the Netherlands.

But Margaret of Austria certainly met her youngest sister-in-law, who, however, was preparing eventually to leave the Spanish court. The marriage of Katherine of Aragon to the English heir Prince Arthur was becoming ever more pressing. In July 1498, Spain's ambassador in England wrote that 'the Queen and the mother of the King [Elizabeth of York and Margaret Beaufort] wish that the Princess of Wales [Katherine] should always speak French with the Princess Margaret [of Austria] who is now in Spain, in order to learn the language, and to be able to converse in it when she comes to England. This is necessary, because these ladies do not understand Latin, and much less, Spanish'.

Margaret had been warmly welcomed in Spain, despite a certain clash of cultures; seventeenth-century Jesuit and author Pedro Abarca in *Reyes de Aragon* wrote that although Margaret was allowed all her habitual servants, freedom, and diversions, she was warned not to treat grandees 'with the familiarity and openness usual with the houses of Austria, Burgundy, and France but with the gravity and measured dignity of the kings and realms of Spain'.

But just months after his marriage to Margaret—in the autumn of 1497—the frail, oversolemn Juan had died, and Margaret ('so full of sorrow', as she described herself, 'that there was no room for any more griefs') lost the baby she was carrying. Her court poet Jean Lemaire in *Couronne Margaritique* later wrote that she endured a labour of twelve days and nights without food or sleep.‡

---

* Again, it will often be convenient to speak of 'Spain', although official unification of the Spanish kingdoms would not happen until the eighteenth century.
† The third daughter, Maria, would, when Isabella also died early, be called upon to step into her dead sister's shoes and in her turn also marry Manuel.
‡ Lemaire would eventually move from Margaret's service to that of Anne of Brittany—an example of how, intentionally or otherwise, interaction between women could be maintained by their officers.

Margaret told her father that Queen Isabella had never left her and she would have died but for her mother-in-law's care. Ferdinand and Isabella wrote to Maximilian that Margaret was 'as strong and full of courage as you would wish her to be, and we try to console her. . . . [W]e have and will have as much care of her as we would have if her husband were alive'. A generous reaction, given that many contemporaries believed Juan had been killed by overindulgence in 'the pleasures of marriage' with the hot-blooded Margaret.

Margaret of Austria had now no real role in Spain, any more than she had had in France after Charles VIII abandoned her. Again, however, Margaret stayed on for a time in her new country, where she had found great popularity. Her departure was delayed while her father-in-law and her father haggled over her dowry, her future marriage possibilities, her best deployment in the ongoing tug of war with France, and finally over the route and timing of her journey. But early in 1499—crossing by land the France of which she had once been called queen—she returned to Flanders, nineteen years old and cheated of married life once again.

She arrived just in time to stand godmother (alongside her own godmother, Margaret of York) to her brother Philip of Burgundy's son by Juana of Aragon, eventual heir to both Spain through his mother and to his father's Netherlands territories. For the Habsburg Dynasty, the birth of baby Charles was a triumph, but on a personal level the marriage of Philip and Juana was a disaster. Not perhaps for the husband, who had from the first treated his wife with a contempt bordering on cruelty, but for Juana, who responded to this harsh treatment with a devotion to Philip so slavish— and, if hostile reports are to be believed, so hysterically jealous—that it became the chief grounds for the allegations of her insanity.

Probably Margaret's personal sympathies were torn, and she was in any case soon given her own residence at the castle of le Quesnoy, away from the court. Politically, however, in March 1501 Spanish ambassador Fuensalida reported with disgruntlement that Madame Margaret 'simply follows her brother's fancies in all things'. When later asked by the Spanish to mediate between the warring couple, she sent word to Ferdinand that there was nothing she could do. As the Spanish ambassador reported ominously, 'She is returning to her own lands now because she is not able to suffer here the things that she sees going on'.

But Margaret of Austria was never going to remain in the Netherlands forever. Discussions about yet another marriage, conducted by her father and brother, had begun while she was still in Spain, with mention of the

Duke of Milan, the king of Scotland, that of Hungary and even that of France, since Margaret's childhood husband, Charles VIII, had now died and a new king sat on the French throne. But in the end, the choice for Margaret's next husband fell on the young Duke of Savoy, Philibert, the brother of Margaret's erstwhile playmate Louise of Savoy.

The duchy of Savoy was the gateway to Italy—stage for much of the competitive fighting between the great European powers—and so the match gave Margaret of Austria's relatives access to a strategically vital territory. Moreover, while Philibert was technically a vassal of Maximilian's, his French upbringing at Anne de Beaujeu's hands meant he was very much under the sway of that country, and this was something Margaret's father and brother may have been eager to change.

Margaret showed no eagerness to remarry. But in fact, though this third marriage would prove to be the least important on the great European stage, it would be the one that gave her the most happiness.

Philibert, a party-loving daredevil just a few months younger than she, shared with Margaret's brother the sobriquet 'the Handsome'. The marriage contract was signed at Brussels on 26 September 1501, and Margaret of Austria set off in October (accompanied for the first half league by Margaret of York, the last time they would meet). At the beginning of December, she met Philibert near Geneva and was received enthusiastically. For the first time, Margaret had a partner who shared her own vitality. Touring the duchy together, they settled down at the castle of Pont l'Aine, near Borg, only in the spring of 1503.

But there was another side to Philibert's gaiety. His time occupied by hunting, jousting, and dancing, he had no interest in attending to the business of the duchy. That had been dealt with by his illegitimate half brother, René, that is, until the advent of Margaret, who had no intention of leaving the 'Bastard of Savoy' his authority. Whether her hostility was justified, she used every weapon at her disposal against him, even involving her father to get René stripped of the letters of legitimacy that gave him, as a bastard, the right to his property.

Her motives may have been political—she had, after all, her family's interests to follow—or they may have been personal. Perhaps past experiences had soured her of (usually masculine) authority. Perhaps, even, she had seen from her sister-in-law Juana's fate what happened when a royal wife abnegated public responsibility. Either way, the Bastard wound up declared a traitor, taking refuge in France, where he was welcomed by his half sister, Louise of Savoy.

While Philibert hunted, Margaret of Austria took up the reins of government, telling him not to worry his pretty head about it, effectively. She summoned the council, appointed officers, discussed foreign policy with her brother when he visited, and approved his plans for a continued rapprochement with France.

She never neglected the parties or the hunting—there is an account of her appearing at one masque as queen of the Amazons, with a crimson headdress and jewelled cuirass and (one thinks of Isabella of Castile) naked sword in hand. But her experience in Savoy was the final stage of her political apprenticeship—a rehearsal for activities on the wider European stage to which fate was about to return her.

The summer of 1504 was a scorchingly hot one, when even Philibert was unable to hunt. So in the first days of September, he returned to his avocation with even more enthusiasm. After a frenetic morning pursuing a wild boar, he flung himself down in the shade, gulping from a fountain—only to be seized by a sudden chill. Back at the palace, the doctors were summoned, but despairing. Margaret ordered her valuable pearls to be ground up for medicine, but to no avail. Philibert died on the morning of 10 September, and the story goes that Margaret's attendants had to restrain her from flinging herself out of the window.

She did fling herself into the rebuilding of the family church at Brou, where he was buried, having it carved all over with her self-invented motto: 'FORTUNE. INFORTUNE. FORT. UNE'. It can translate to imply that 'fate is very cruel to women' or, conversely, that *Fortune. Misfortune. Strengthens. One*, the *e* of *une* making it clear that it is a woman in question.[*] In the years ahead, Margaret of Austria's palace at Mechelen would feature wooden busts of herself and Philibert, with Margaret, though she commissioned them after his death, wearing the loose hair of a bride rather than the widow's cap.

She was twenty-four and cheated of married life for yet a third time. Her father and brother were at first anxious to marry her off yet again, but after three such ill-fated attempts at matrimony, Margaret declared herself 'much disinclined to make another trial'.

But besides her husband, she had lost her newfound role. Or had she? Philibert was succeeded by an eighteen-year-old half brother whose youth made it seem, for a while, as though Margaret might still manage to hold on

---

[*] Margaret's insistence on keeping Philibert's heart with her was behaviour not wholly unlike that which would have her sister-in-law Juana declared insane.

to a measure of power. The new young duke, however, reneged on the deal, leaving Margaret furious.

If he thought that 'by such unmannerly treatment he can reduce us and put his intentions through, he has the wrong idea', she wrote later. 'For all that we are a woman, our heart is of a different nature'.*

IN FRANCE LOUISE OF SAVOY too was now a youthful widow. The little Dauphin—that son Anne of Brittany had born to Charles VIII of France at the start of their marriage—had died in 1495, and Louise's husband Charles d'Angoulême fell sick of fever and died on his way to the Dauphin's funeral. Resisting, like a striking number of these women, any attempt to marry her off again, Louise had concentrated on keeping control of her son, François.

As the boy's leading kinsman, the Duc d'Orléans had claimed that Louise of Savoy could not take guardianship of her two children, being herself a minor, since France set twenty-five as the age of legal majority for women. But the young widow argued that in Cognac, where François was born, women were allowed to exercise rights of guardianship at fourteen. The royal council had decided more or less in her favour, with the Duc d'Orléans (so long as Louise did not remarry) given merely a supervisory role.

Louise of Savoy settled down in Cognac to administer her extensive lands. There she set about raising her two children in the strong-minded and scholarly tradition she had herself learned in Anne de Beaujeu's household. 'Also, my daughter, if at some point in the future God takes your husband, leaving you a widow, then you will be responsible for your children, like many other young women; have patience, because it pleases God, and govern wisely', Anne wrote in her *Enseignements*. Louise's motto (borrowed from Lorenzo de Medici and written on the wall of her room at Angoulême) was *Libris et liberis* (Books and children).

Her daughter, Marguerite, had the same teachers as her son. Both learned Spanish and Italian from their mother and Latin and biblical history from two humanist scholars. A miniature shows Marguerite and her brother playing chess. But there was no doubt which of the two children occupied more of their mother's attention.

Louise of Savoy has been blamed for her exclusive focus on François, but Marguerite herself would share that obsessive interest, and perhaps it was inevitable, as the childlessness of successive short-lived French

---

* Impossible not to think, in comparison and contrast, of the 'heart and stomach of a king' and Elizabeth I at Tilbury.

kings brought François ever closer to the throne. When in 1498 Charles VIII suddenly died, after hitting his head on the lintel of a doorway, the throne passed to Louis, Duc d'Orléans, cousin to Louise's husband, d'Angoulême—and Louis was himself still childless, the cynical predictions about his marriage to the crippled Jeanne having proved all too accurate.[*]

After Charles VIII's death, his widow, Anne of Brittany, threw herself into hysterical mourning, but immediately also took steps to resume her rights in her duchy. Her first marriage contract had stipulated that if King Charles died, the only person she could remarry was the next king of France, a way to continue France's annexation of Brittany. The new king, Louis XII, accordingly took steps to set aside his existing wife, the barren Jeanne, on the grounds of nonconsummation. Jeanne was asked to undergo a humiliating physical examination, a papal decree was granted, and Jeanne retired to a convent, eventually to be canonised a saint.

But while the marriage of Louis and Anne of Brittany was politically necessary for both sides, even this did not guarantee a solution to the problem of the succession. The groom was thirty-six and in poor health, while Anne's repeated pregnancies by Charles had yet produced no heir.

Unless or until a son was born to King Louis and his new queen, Louise of Savoy's boy, François, was heir presumptive. Under these circumstances, Louise had to battle to be allowed to continue rearing François herself. She did have to bring her son rather closer under Louis's eye, to Amboise on the Loire, where François and the gang of young men placed around him could, as he grew, enjoy the hunting and mock tournaments so much to his taste. She also had to submit to the surveillance of Louis's trusted man the Seigneur de Gié, whose aggressive conception of his duties made the family at times feel like prisoners. Louise's children slept in her bedroom, and an officer was present at the *lever*, the ceremonial rising of the young heir. One day when Louise declared her children were still sleeping, an official went so far as to break down the door.

Anne of Brittany went on enduring repeated pregnancies, and Louise's journal makes no bones about her feelings. In 1502: 'Anne, Queen of France, on the twenty-first of January Saint Agnes Day, gave birth at Blois to a son; however, still-born, he was no threat to my César's rise to power'. There continued to be no sign of a living boy. In 1499 Louise and her children were at Romorantin when Queen Anne had joined their seclusion to avoid

---

[*] One seventeenth-century chronicler reported that 'for a moment', Anne de Beaujeu contemplated seizing the crown herself.

the plague and there gave birth to a daughter, Claude. Was the idea of a match between this royal daughter and Louise's son, François, also born at Romorantin?

Perhaps neither mother wanted the match: Anne of Brittany because she secretly hoped to marry Claude, Brittany's heiress, to the imperial Habsburgs and thus maintain her duchy's independence. (Anne had always kept in touch with Margaret of Austria.) Louise of Savoy may have reflected that Claude came from a family with a poor record of fertility and was—like so many of her inbred clan, like Louis's first wife, Jeanne—mildly deformed. Louise and Anne of Brittany were always at enmity, although in 1504 they had briefly collaborated to rid themselves of the overbearing Seigneur de Gié.

But in 1505, when Louis XII fell desperately ill, it made imperative what had long been discussed: the betrothal of twelve-year-old François, the heir, to King Louis's seven-year-old daughter, Claude. Louis's will gave guardianship of Claude to her mother, Anne, but gave Louise a seat with her on the regency council, with both women swearing to execute the will with their hand on a piece of the True Cross.

King Louis recovered, but the betrothal ceremony went ahead, though the juvenile spouses then separated to grow up. The following spring another formal ceremony acknowledged François as Louis's heir.

Margaret of Austria and Louise of Savoy were both at this point youthful widows. But while Margaret was again plunged into uncertainty, Louise's path lay clear ahead.

5
PRINCESS BRIDES
England and Scotland, 1501–1505

A princess's fate was to be married for her family's benefit and her own happiness or otherwise a matter of fortune. Across the Channel, in England and in Scotland, two other royal girls were feeling the force of that lesson.

The year 1501 had finally seen the arrival of Katherine of Aragon in England and her marriage to its heir, Prince Arthur, celebrated with extraordinary festivities. Isabella of Castile and her husband had displayed some qualms at sending their youngest to distant England, where the Tudor regime was still a fragile new arrival, but Isabella was not the woman to let sentiment stand in the way of dynastic advantage.

Any foreign princess faced a terrifying prospect, arriving exhausted and travel worn on the shores of a foreign land after a long and dangerous journey, knowing your entire future depended on your pleasing the man (or boy) you were about to meet and that, at best, you faced a future of juggling your loyalties toward him and your responsibilities to your native country. It must have taken all the festivities—the tournaments and the tumblers, the pageants and the parades between the river palaces—to pin the ritual smile on Katherine of Aragon's face. And she may, as Isabella's daughter, have been taken aback to discover the limitations on a royal Englishwoman's power.

True, Henry VII's mother, Margaret Beaufort—'My Lady the King's Mother'—exercised a good deal of influence, but the same could not be said of his wife, Elizabeth of York. Both Margaret Beaufort and Elizabeth of York, moreover, had been required to set aside their own blood rights to let Henry ascend his throne. There was no thought that a woman could rule in England as she could in Castile, though Katherine could not have known how this assumption would come to haunt her.

In January 1502 the young couple set out for Ludlow, Arthur's seat as Prince of Wales. But less than five months after the wedding came tragedy. On 2 April 1502, Prince Arthur died after a short illness, leaving his parents devastated and his wife in the most painful uncertainty. Another royal bride widowed early, she was another princess left stranded in a foreign country without an obvious role to play.

BUT MARRIAGE ABROAD WAS THE princesses' lot, and at the English court one of Katherine of Aragon's new Tudor sisters-in-law was preparing for that destiny. Margaret Tudor had been born in 1489, the eldest daughter of Henry VII and Elizabeth of York. She was not yet four when her elder brother, Arthur, at six was sent off to Ludlow to assume his role as Prince of Wales, and Margaret was reared with her younger siblings, Henry and Mary. The royal children grew up largely at Eltham Palace, outside London, and Desiderius Erasmus, the great humanist from the Netherlands, brought by English scholar Thomas More to pay his respects in 1499, portrays them as happy, though his report makes it clear the eight-year-old Henry ('already with a certain royal demeanour') expected and was given precedence over the two girls.

There had already been discussions of Margaret Tudor's future. In 1498 the Spanish ambassador reported to Ferdinand and Isabella on the proposed marriage between the eight-year-old Margaret and the twenty-five-year-old James IV of Scotland but added that there were many 'inconveniences' involved. Henry VII said that his wife and his mother, Margaret Beaufort, had joined forces to protect little Margaret: 'The Queen and my mother are very much against this marriage. They say if the marriage were concluded, we should be obliged to send the Princess directly to Scotland, In which case they fear the King of Scots would not wait, but injure her, and endanger her health'.

Wait . . . as in wait to consummate the marriage, and here Margaret Beaufort knew all too well what she was talking about. She herself had been married at twelve and a mother at thirteen, the birth permanently damaging her slight physique. If the granddaughter named for her had inherited Margaret Beaufort's small stature, this was a real and vivid concern. Nonetheless, 25 January 1502 (just weeks after Arthur and Katherine set out for Ludlow) saw the formal celebration at Richmond Palace of Margaret Tudor's marriage to the king of Scotland. Representatives of both countries signed the three agreements that made up the optimistically named Treaty of Perpetual Peace, aimed at ending dispute between the ever-squabbling neighbours and arranging the details of Margaret's match and her ten-thousand-pound dowry.*

The following day, after Mass was celebrated in the new royal chapel, a proxy wedding ceremony was performed in the queen's great chamber, with the Earl of Bothwell standing in for the absent King James. Henry, his wife, Elizabeth, and Margaret herself were asked whether they knew of any impediment and whether Margaret was acting 'without compulsion and of her own free will'. She affirmed that 'if it please my Lord and Father the King and my Lady Mother the Queen', she was content—a full and unqualified affirmation, in the eyes of the sixteenth century.

After the business was concluded and the trumpets sounded out, Queen Elizabeth 'incontinently' (as a contemporary chronicle of the proceedings describes it) took her daughter by the hand, and, two queens together, they 'dined both at one mess covered'—a covered dish to indicate their regal status. Jousts and a supper banquet followed, and *Te Deum* was sung at St Paul's. The next morning the twelve-year-old Queen of Scots came into her mother's great chamber and 'by the voice of' the officer of arms gave thanks to all the noblemen who had jousted for her and distributed prizes 'by the advice of the ladies of the court'. Praise went to one young gentleman, Charles Brandon, of whom more would be heard a few years down the line. It was agreed Margaret should be sent north not later than September 1503, but for the moment she was to be left in her mother's charge.

There is a story that Prince Henry wept with rage when he realised his sister, as a queen, now outranked him. But Henry was about to become much more important in the scheme of things. Barely two months after Margaret Tudor's wedding came news of her brother Arthur's death in Wales—and worse was to follow.

As Margaret's sombre mourning clothes were softened by sleeves of white and then of orange, she would have known her mother was pregnant again. Elizabeth of York had thought to put her childbearing years behind her, but with Arthur gone there was an heir but no spare. In February 1503, just days after bearing a short-lived daughter, Queen Elizabeth died.

Margaret Tudor had, that coming summer, to travel north toward her new life without her mother behind her. On 8 July she set out north—'richly

---

* Sixteenth-century Scottish historian John Leslie said there was also mooted another possibility, that if Henry's male line should ever die out, Margaret's heirs would succeed to the English throne. If so, well and good, for 'England would not accress unto Scotland but Scotland would accress unto England', said Henry prophetically. But at the time, with two of Henry's sons alive and well, that must have seemed unlikely.

dressed, mounted upon a fair palfrey', 'very nobly accompanied, in fair order and array'—to be crowned queen of Scotland in Edinburgh. She was not yet fourteen years old.

She met her thirty-year-old husband at Haddington, just inside Scotland, and the account written by the 'Somerset Herald' shows, with unusual clarity, the stages of two people getting to know each other under these trying circumstances. As James IV was brought to what was now Margaret's great chamber, she met him at the door, and the two 'made great reverences, the one to the other, his head being bare, and they kissed together'. The greeting to the rest of her party being done, they 'went aside, and communed together by long space'.

Returning the next day, James found Margaret playing cards in her room, and she kissed him 'of good will'. When bread and wine were brought to him, he served her before himself and played for her on the clarichords and the lute, 'which pleased her very much'. The next day, seeing the stool where she was seated for supper 'was not for her ease', he gave her his chair. A letter back to her father, Henry, in England, in the early days of Margaret Tudor's marriage, breathes homesickness and the uncertainties of an adolescent trying to negotiate her own path through the power plays of a foreign court. 'I would I were with your Grace now, and many times more', she told her father, as many another princess must have wished to do. All the same, it sounds as if, by the standards of the day, Margaret had been lucky.

KATHERINE OF ARAGON'S SITUATION, by contrast, was all the worse for the death of her kindly mother-in-law, Elizabeth of York, though for a brief time it seemed that might open new, if controversial, possibilities. King Henry was now a widower, just as his son's wife, Katherine of Aragon, was now a widow. Marriage between the two looked for a moment like a good way of resolving the equation and keeping Katherine's dowry and the Spanish connection—good to Henry, anyway. But Katherine's mother, Isabella of Castile, was horrified when she heard the rumours: such a marriage between father and daughter-in-law would be 'a very evil thing—one never before seen, and the mere mention of which offends the ears—we would not for anything in the world that it should take place'.

Instead, in June 1503, the seventeen-year-old Katherine of Aragon was betrothed to Arthur's eleven-year-old brother, Prince Henry, amid some confusion as to whether she was betrothed as Arthur's widow in the fullest sense or as the virgin survivor of an unconsummated marriage. But there was another extended row between Henry VII and Ferdinand over the question of Katherine's dowry, with Katherine caught between her father's and her father-in-law's diplomacy. Events in Spain, moreover, were about to make Katherine less attractive as a marital possibility.

In November 1504 Isabella of Castile died, with questions over what would happen to her country. From the English perspective, this meant that an alliance with Katherine now represented an alliance only with her father's Aragon rather than one also with the more important Castile, and in June 1505 Prince Henry was instructed by his father to repudiate his betrothal to her. While her sister-in-law Margaret Tudor seemed comparatively secure in Scotland, Katherine was left once again without clear prospects in a strange land.

6

REPOSITIONING

The Netherlands, Spain, England, and Scotland, 1505–1512

✵

There were those on the other side of the Channel whose place on the political board would be affected even more directly by the death of Isabella of Castile. One would prove to be Katherine of Aragon's former sister-in-law, Margaret of Austria, and another was Katherine's sister Juana.

Juana was heir to her mother, Isabella, but from the first Juana showed little sign of taking the reins of power into her own hands. The tussle was thus between Juana's husband, Philip of Burgundy (Margaret's brother), and Juana's father, Ferdinand of Aragon, Isabella's widower, who was reluctant to relinquish the larger part of the lands he had coruled for many years.

News of her inheritance caught Juana with her husband in the Netherlands, but the couple set about making preparations for a return to Spain. Storms forced Philip and Juana to make harbour on the coast of England, which gave Katherine of Aragon the thrilling possibility of seeing her sister, but in fact Philip purposely kept Juana away from Henry's court until he himself was firmly established as the star visitor, which left Katherine only a few hours to spend with the sister she was likely never to see again.

But in Spain, in September 1506, Philip of Burgundy died of a sudden fever, while the comportment of his widow, Juana, made it easy for her male relatives to outmanoeuvre her. Juana would shortly be declared incapable—insane—though the diagnosis is now suspect. Indeed, Juana herself had written to her father that while the Castilians 'want to make out that I am not in my right mind . . . if I did fly into passions and failed to keep up my proper dignity, it is well known that the only cause of my doing so was jealousy'. It is however possible her husband forced her to write the letter.

Juana would be no player in the game of queens. Most of her life would be spent incarcerated, and it remains unsure to what degree this was inevitable. Certainly, she was effectively the victim of a stitch-up, in which her husband had been at least as complicit as her father. A deal was struck whereby Castile would be controlled by Juana's father, Ferdinand, during the minority of her six-year-old son, Charles.

But what of the Netherlands Charles had also inherited on his father's death and where Philip and Juana had left him when they sailed to Spain? Regency of the Netherlands would pass to Charles's other grandfather, Maximilian, but Maximilian resided in his own, Austrian, lands. Instead, with the approval of all involved, he devolved his powers onto his Netherlands-born, recently widowed (and thus fortuitously available) daughter, Margaret of Austria.

In the weeks before Philip of Burgundy's death, Maximilian's agent had been describing how he 'daily pressed [Margaret] during a whole month' to consent to marriage with England's Henry VII. Maximilian had been assuring the English king that he himself would travel to Savoy to persuade her. But now her family had found another use for her, and at twenty-seven Margaret had found the part she was born to play.

When fate, and her brother's death, placed the government of the Netherlands in her hands, she took to the role with ability. Margaret of York had died in 1503, but Margaret of Austria set up court in her godmother's old home of Mechelen, where council meetings were held twice a week, though most of the 150 people who made up her household lived around the city.[*]

Sworn in as governess-general in March 1507, Margaret took her nephew Charles on a tour of his domain—promising on his behalf to preserve the rights and privileges of each of the seventeen provinces, receiving their oath of fidelity, and convening the Estates-General to raise a tax with which to redeem Charles's mortgaged lands, since Philip had left his territories in very poor array. A good deal of her time was occupied in international diplomacy and the pursuance of her father's policies.

Her own hand in marriage was still a pawn Maximilian was attempting to play. But Margaret of Austria continued to resist all blandishments, still resolutely refusing to marry Henry VII of England, though her father assured her that she would be able to return to her own domains for three or four months of every year and thus 'will not feel yourself a prisoner in England . . . with a headstrong man'. She was persuaded to write Henry a

---

[*] There she was to raise not only her nephew Charles but his three sisters; Charles's younger brother, Ferdinand, however, was raised by the grandfather for whom he was named, in Spain; while a youngest sister, Catalina, born after Juana had returned to Spain, shared her mother's captivity.

number of flattering letters and thus keep up her father's alliance with England that way.

THE DEATH OF PHILIP OF Burgundy brought potential benefits for another woman, too. Henry VII now sought a marriage with the widowed Juana, unperturbed, so the Spanish ambassador reported, by any thought of insanity, 'especially since I have assured them [the English] that her derangement of mind would not prevent her from bearing children'. As Juana's sister, Katherine of Aragon had become involved, at Henry's request, in the negotiations.

Katherine, of course, had every reason to long for Juana's presence at Henry's side, which might not only help her free herself from limbo but also relieve her endless money worries. The disputes about her dowry had dragged on, and she sent frantic pleas to her father that she was spending not on frivolities but on necessities. (The Spanish ambassador de Puebla was famous for eating at court to save money.) It was at this point that she was able to deliver to her father-in-law a 'letter of credence', making her officially ambassador for her father, Ferdinand.

But in fact, Ferdinand was never going to give Henry VII the controlling hand in Spanish affairs he might have had as Juana's husband. And Katherine of Aragon's minor triumph notwithstanding, the desperate tone of her letters in these last years of Henry VII's reign is more pathetic than anything later in her story.

MARGARET TUDOR'S LIFE IN SCOTLAND, by contrast, continued for some time on the same gracious note with which it had begun, and for that she had probably her husband to thank. James was a complex character—devout and romantic—determined someday to go on crusade, but meanwhile amusing himself with a variety of studies, which included the practise of dentistry.*

But James IV was also an ardent practitioner of the amatory arts, and from the very first Margaret had to cope with evidence of his infidelity. In the autumn James took her (and her ladies, and her musicians, and the eighteen wagons of 'gear') on a tour of her traditional dower land, starting at the romantic lochside palace of Linlithgow. When they moved on to Stirling, however, Margaret found that this dower castle was being used as a nursery for the king's half-dozen illegitimate children.

---

* He paid those who allowed him to take out their teeth rather than the reverse, a practice that might endear him to many today.

But James's long devotion to his mistress Janet Kennedy may have made it easier for him to show restraint in other directions. It was more than three years after her arrival in Scotland that in 1507, by now seventeen, Margaret gave birth to a son. James was ecstatic—and not forgetful of Margaret, who after the birth lay dangerously ill. James went on pilgrimage to Saint Ninian's shrine on the Galloway coast to pray for her recovery—on foot, seven days for a 120-mile journey. At exactly the moment he knelt at the tomb, Margaret's fever abated . . . or so it was reported through all the Christian countries.

Tragically, just over a year later, the baby died—but Margaret Tudor was already again pregnant. When she gave birth to a baby girl in July 1508, however, the baby died the same day. It was, of course, too soon to know how closely events in England would be replicating this story. But Margaret's fertility or lack thereof had implications in England, too, for since the death of Prince Arthur, she had been second heir to the English throne.

Margaret Tudor was, like so many princesses, the living pledge of an international alliance, and the Anglo-Scottish accord had at first seemed to being going well. But by 1508 James IV was receiving embassies from Louis XII of France, whose alliance with Maximilian against the growing power of Venice did not include England. James was, moreover, irritated when his father-in-law arrested his cousin the Earl of Arran for passing through his kingdom without official permission. Henry VII sent north, to kiss and make up, an able new young English official by the name of Thomas Wolsey. Margaret was tasked with winning Wolsey an audience, since her husband declared ominously that he was too busy 'shooting guns and making gunpowder'. After five days, however, she managed it, albeit with an inexperience in the smooth ways of diplomacy that had her contradicting any Scot who said her father in England had done anything wrong.

When on 21 April 1509 Henry VII died, Margaret Tudor (pregnant once again) was now direct heir to the English throne. While James and the new king Henry VIII confirmed the Treaty of Perpetual Peace, Margaret's baby, born in October at Holyrood, was christened Arthur, a name with such significance in recent and legendary English history. This Arthur would die at a year old, but, of course, there was by that point every reason to hope that Henry VIII and his new queen would have children of their own.

WHEN HENRY VII OF ENGLAND died, his son Henry VIII instantly marked his accession by marrying Katherine of Aragon, his brother's widow. Henry wrote to Margaret of Austria in the Netherlands, truly or falsely, that this was by a dying Henry VII's 'express command'. The wedding took place fast and privately, but the joint coronation less than a fortnight later was to be huge and public. That ceremony took place on 24 June 1509, and though a sudden shower forced the drenched queen to shelter under the awning of a draper's stall, Katherine's dreary years were at an end—for the moment, anyway.

Her world had gone from darkness into light. It was, on the surface, a fairy-tale piece of romanticism. Katherine at twenty-four still had the sunny good looks noted when she first came to England; she was described by ambassadors as being 'buxom' (amiable) and lively, inclined to smile even in adversity. Interestingly, however, letters between Katherine of Aragon and her father, Ferdinand, before the marriage suggest also a more pragmatic agenda behind the love match and a more active role for Katherine. Ferdinand urged his daughter to use 'all your skill and prudence' so as swiftly to 'close the deal'.* And Katherine, once safely wed, told Ferdinand that she loved her new husband so well, first because he was the 'so true son of your highness', who desired to serve Ferdinand 'with greater love and obedience' than even a blood son might do. This identification of Katherine of Aragon with Spain's interests was a potential source of danger. But for the moment, this marriage gave the young Henry a partner more experienced in the ways of the world than he.

Perhaps there was a hint of trouble to come when in January 1510 Katherine suffered her first miscarriage—but this was in itself a not uncommon occurrence. More worrying in hindsight, with knowledge of both Katherine's and her daughter Mary's gynaecological history, was the fact that her doctors seem to have convinced Katherine she had miscarried only one of twins and was still pregnant, though even the Spanish ambassador reported she had resumed her menstrual cycle. She remained in seclusion, preparing for childbirth, until forced to emerge, discreetly, in the spring. By that time, however, she was able to announce that she was pregnant once again.

On the morning of New Year's Day 1511, indeed, Katherine gave birth to a boy, christened Henry amid great rejoicing. After just seven weeks, the baby died—but again, such misfortunes were not uncommon in the sixteenth century. Certainly, Katherine of Aragon's relationship with Henry was still strong, strong enough that by 1513 she had been able to influence her husband and steer his country in the direction of an alliance with the

---

* More appealingly, Ferdinand told his daughter that 'to be well married is the greatest blessing in the world . . . and source of all other kinds of happiness'—an indirect tribute to Isabella of Castile.

Habsburgs and with her natal family. She had obviously not forgotten her connexion with Margaret of Austria, who had been one of the godparents of that short-lived male baby.

MARGARET OF AUSTRIA'S ROLE AS governor of the Netherlands had not always been easy; indeed, she wrote that she often wished herself back in her mother's womb. She had to tread carefully around her father. 'I know that it is not my business to interfere in your said affairs, as I am an inexperienced woman in such matters, nevertheless the great duty I have towards you emboldens me to beg of you . . . to take care whilst there is still time', she wrote on one occasion. ('Rude and ungracious' was how he described the advice so carefully hedged around.) She had, moreover, to stand up for the needs of the Netherlands themselves as distinct from her father's grandiose policies. But she had scored an early victory for those Netherlands when she succeeded in overturning a trade agreement with England highly detrimental to their interests, the 'Malus Intercursus'.

Five years before Anne Boleyn arrived in the Netherlands, moreover, Margaret of Austria had been a major player in the League of Cambrai, trusted in 1508 to represent her father, the emperor Maximilian, and her former father-in-law Ferdinand in negotiating an alliance with the French to aid the papacy against the encroachments of Venice.

Maximilian wrote advising her to engage all the houses on one side of Cambrai,* leaving the other to the French king's representative. Meanwhile, French king Louis was himself writing chattily to remind her of how he had played with her when she was a little girl at Amboise. Even the pope, another partner in this alliance against the encroachments of the Venetian republic, had been in the habit of sending Margaret devotional objects and relics of great value, while even Henry VII had ordered his ambassador to speak to Margaret about English interests. As her court poet Jean Lemaire put it, 'Madame Margaret has seen and experienced more at her youthful age . . . than any lady on record, however long her life'.

Commentators spoke of her 'courteous and caressing manners'. Though Margaret wrote to her ambassador in England that the negotiations gave her a headache and that she and her opponent frequently 'got into each other's hair', she was willing to bring all her various abilities to the fight. Was it at Margaret of Austria's court that Anne Boleyn learned that her

---

* Cambrai was the border-town scene of Margaret's own later triumph and a name that comes up time and again in this story.

gender—femininity, sex itself—could be a weapon? Could it be a gambit in the great game that would set her against another woman, another queen, as surely as black and white face off across the chess board?

But the League of Cambrai did not long endure, after the pope decided that France itself represented more of a threat than Venice. The year 1511 saw the pope organising a Holy League against France, to which he recruited Maximilian and Ferdinand, Venice and Henry VIII. Margaret's father had written that French perfidy would teach her a lesson. 'We have more experience of the French than you have . . . and we would rather you were deceived by their fair speeches than ourselves, so that you would take more care in future'.

Faced with one long-running problem—the revolt of the Duke of Guelders, striving to win back the independence of his territory—at the end of 1510 Margaret had written in agitation to her father, 'You know I am a woman and that it is not my place to meddle in war. . . . I beseech you my lord to have good advice over all this'. Yet a few months later: 'My Lord, I am readying myself . . . in order to march before our army. The army makes a very good sight, together with the artillery'. Her father told her that she had fought 'with the courage of a man and not that of a woman'.

The year 1512 was a particularly wearing one, with Guelders getting the backing of the French and Margaret having no money to fight either her own or her father's various campaigns. But in 1513 the new anti-French coalition was confirmed, and Margaret was as central to the process as the very name, the Treaty of Mechelen, suggests. Margaret (in contrast to her former sister-in-law Juana) was at the very heart of European diplomacy.

7

'FALSE IMPUTATIONS'

France and the Netherlands, 1513

✳

'**A** woman', Castiglione wrote, 'has not so many ways of defending her-self against false imputations as has a man'. Margaret of Austria was one of several women about to prove the truth of that dictate. The first six years of Margaret's regency had left her looking like a woman with her hands very firmly on the reins. Anne de Beaujeu's perfect pupil, you might say—the sort Anne meant when she wrote that noblewomen were, 'and should be, a pattern, and an example for others in all things'.

But a great deal of Anne de Beaujeu's advice centred on one particular theme: 'Suffer no man to touch your body, no matter who he is. . . . [N]ot one in a thousand escapes without her honour being attacked or deceived, however "good" or "true" her love. Therefore, for the greatest certainty in such situations, I advise you to avoid all private meetings, no matter how pleasant they are'.

Even the slightest slip could incur blame. Or, as Anne de Beaujeu had written in an uncomfortable prophecy, 'There is no man of worth, however noble he may be, who does not use treachery, nor to whom it does not seem good sport to deceive or trick women of rank. . . . [T]here is no man so per-fect who, in matters of love, is truthful or keeps his word'. The truth of that was about to be proved by Margaret of Austria herself—but perhaps also in France, by the daughter of Anne de Beaujeu's protégé, and Margaret's former playmate, Louise of Savoy.

The early years of Louise's daughter, Marguerite, are inevitably known chiefly through accounts of her brother, François, on whom centred all the hopes of the family 'trinity'.* But Marguerite's marriage had long been

---

* When the fourteen-year-old François had been taken out of his mother's care to live at court, Louise had wailed in her *Journal* that his departure had 'left me all alone'—for all that

discussed. While still a child she had been offered as a bride for the future Henry VIII, but declined, since it was felt that England's heir merited a daughter of the king of France, not merely a cousin.

As François's likely accession and marriage to King Louis XII's daughter Claude were established, England had come back with a counteroffer: the suggestion that Marguerite might indeed marry the younger Henry—if Louise of Savoy would marry his father, the widowed Henry VII. But Louis of France feared this double alliance might admit too much English influence into his country. When the English then suggested that Marguerite herself might marry the ageing Henry VII, she is reputed to have given a spirited refusal: 'When my brother becomes king I will marry a man who is young, rich, and noble—without having to cross the Channel!' But in fact, in 1509 Marguerite had been married off to the personally unimpressive Charles, Duc d'Alençon, thus settling a long-standing territorial dispute between the Alençon house and Marguerite's house of Angoulême.

IN 1513 IT WAS NOT Marguerite of Navarre but the English who crossed the Channel, and for matters not of love but war. In theory at least, England's efforts were always directed at regaining the power and the territories it had held on the continent for much of the Middle Ages and lost only in the fifteenth century. But in fact war was recognised as the main business, as well as pleasure, of the ruler—Machiavelli had very explicitly said as much—and Henry VIII was delightedly flexing his muscles as a warrior king when his alliance with the pope and the emperor Maximilian against France brought him abroad at the head of a mighty army.

The fall of the town of Thérouanne, near the border of France and the Netherlands, that August was followed by a siege and triumphant capture of the wealthy walled city of Tournai. And when the treaty she struck between her father, Maximilian, and Henry VIII brought Henry across the English Channel, Margaret of Austria was there. Her father, quixotically, had declared his intention of serving as a volunteer in the English army. When he asked her to join him at the besieged town of Tournai, she replied that she would do so if it were really necessary, 'but otherwise, it is not fitting for a widow to be trotting about and visiting armies for pleasure'. Was she protesting too much? Maybe.

Marguerite had remained with her. Hard not to think of Henry VIII, though the father of a healthy daughter, considering himself childless in the years ahead.

Later, Margaret of Austria did take her nephew Charles to meet her
father and Henry VIII at Lille and went on to Tournai with notable consequences. Though they might not be considered worthy of record in the
chronicles of great European events, the small drama played out in the summer of 1513 and the months that followed is worth anatomising not only for
the insight it gives into the protagonists (Henry VIII included) but as a test
case of the way a powerful woman could be manipulated through her sexuality—the way in which, particularly where women were concerned, the
personal became part of the political story.

Tudor chronicler Edward Hall described how Henry received Charles
and Margaret outside Tournai and brought them into the town 'with great
triumph. The noise went that the Lord Lisle made request of marriage to
the Lady Margaret . . . but whether he proffered marriage or not she favoured him highly'. 'Lord Lisle' was the recently ennobled Charles Brandon,
a man on the make and one with already a colourful marital history.

Born of gentry stock, Brandon had been raised up in the court. His father died at Bosworth, on the battlefield that gave Henry VII his crown and
bearing Henry's standard. This sacrifice on the father's part ensured favour
for the son. A star of the tiltyard, he first jousted publicly on the occasion of
Katherine of Aragon's marriage to Henry VIII and had, crucially, quickly
become the boon companion of the younger man. Contracted in youth to
one of Elizabeth of York's gentlewomen, he made her pregnant before repudiating the match in order to marry her wealthy widowed aunt instead. He
had sold many of the aunt's lands before getting that marriage annulled on
the grounds of consanguinity and returning to marry the younger lady—
who then died in 1510, leaving Brandon free. Made a Knight of the Garter
in April 1513, he was created Viscount Lisle in May, when he was also betrothed to the eight-year-old Elizabeth Grey, heir to the Lisle barony.

He had raised fifteen hundred men for the 1513 campaign and at the
siege of Tournai led a successful assault on one of the city gates, in reward
for which Henry had handed to him the keys of the surrendering city.
Margaret of Austria's agent with the English army reported to her that he
was 'a second king'—someone she would, in any case, have been watching
carefully.

Margaret and her nephew Charles spent ten days with the English
force—ten days of 'great solace'. (In celebration of the victory, Margaret was
presented with a six-piece tapestry depicting Christine de Pizan's *City of
Ladies*.) It is likely Anne Boleyn too was there in Margaret of Austria's train
and observing the phenomenon that was the young Henry VIII. Spectators

reported that one evening Henry danced 'from the time the banquet finished until nearly day, in his shirt [that is, without his doublet]' with Margaret and with Margaret's 'damsels'.

But Margaret of Austria may not have had eyes only for Henry. What she saw in those ten days were Brandon and King Henry answering all comers at the joust, Brandon and King Henry dressed identically in purple velvet decked with gold, Brandon coming in disguised with the king in the masque that followed a banquet of a hundred dishes. On 20 October Margaret and her nephew returned to Lille, but talk of their visit to Tournai continued during the months ahead.

When Brandon was created Duke of Suffolk, it may have been tribute to his prowess in France, but such a leap, for such a man, attracted a great deal of international comment. Erasmus was among those shocked. Some said Brandon had been so dramatically elevated to make him a more fitting match for Margaret: 'Gossip has it that Maximilian's daughter Margaret is to marry that new duke, whom the King has recently turned from a stableboy into a nobleman'. In May Brandon and Henry were once again defenders at a tournament, bearing the motto 'Who can hold that will away'—perhaps suggesting that Brandon might be about to make a foreign journey.

If Brandon had indeed pretensions to Margaret of Austria's hand, it looked as though Henry was encouraging them. But the king at least found it prudent to express annoyance, writing to Margaret to promise signal punishment of the rumourmongers. He acknowledged, however, 'that the common report is in divers places that marriage is contemplated between you and our very dear and loyal cousin and councillor the Duke of Suffolk'. Margaret's feelings can be seen in two long letters, signed simply 'M'.

'M' dared not write directly to king or duke, she said, 'because that I fear my letters to be evil kept'. *Discretion* was the watchword, for all this was a tardy slamming of the stable door, and Margaret sounds a repeated note of almost hysterical caution.

After having been some days at Tournai, Margaret had been, she declared, struck by King Henry's love for Brandon, by 'the virtue and grace' of Brandon's person ('the which me seemed that I had not much seen gentleman to approach it'). Because of 'the desire the which he always showed me that he had to do me service', she forced herself 'to do unto him all honour and pleasure'.

This seemed to be 'well agreeable' to King Henry—who indeed 'many time spake unto me, for to know if this goodwill . . . might stretch unto some effect of promise of marriage'. As Margaret tells it, it was Henry who urged that this (a love match, a woman making her own choice?) 'was the fashion of the ladies of England, and . . . was not there holden for evil'. Margaret replied that 'it was not here the custom, and that I should be dishonoured, and holden for a fool and light'.

But Henry VIII would brook no argument. Margaret of Austria was forced to find another plea: that the English were so soon to leave the country. This went down better, but Henry warned Margaret that she would surely have to marry somebody—'that I was yet too young for to abide thus; and that the ladies of his country did remarry at fifty and threescore years'.

Margaret, she insisted, had no desire to marry again—'I was too much unhappy in husbands'. But the men would not believe her. Twice more, in Brandon's presence, Henry urged Margaret to the match, telling her again that she might well be forced into a marriage. Unconvinced by her protests, 'he made me to promise in his hand that howsoever I should be pressed of my father, or otherwise, I should not make alliance of marriage [with] prince of the world, at the least unto his return, or the end of the year'.

What was going on here? Was Henry truly just playing Cupid, sportingly trying to help his crony toward this great match? Was he trying to avoid Margaret making another match, one disadvantageous to England? And what of the feelings of the two most involved?

In what sounds like a three-way conversation 'at Tournai in my chamber one night after supper, full late', Brandon told Margaret (she wrote) he would never marry, nor yet take 'lady nor mistress, without my commandment, but would continue all his life my right humble servant'. These were the tropes of courtly love, and perhaps Margaret of Austria, that child of a determinedly chivalrous court, was taken in. She promised 'to be to him such mistress all my life as to him who me seemed desired to do me most of service'. And after that, said Margaret crossly, there was no more said of the affair, nor should there have been, if it had not been for some 'gracious letters' that had not been carefully and privately kept.

She was not, after all, quite swept away—not too swept away to query whether King Henry, in his role of 'trwcheman' [sic] or go-between, had (for whatever motive) perhaps protested even more than Brandon felt or to note that many of the questions asked about the rumoured match seemed to be more concerned with Henry's part in it than with her own.

Margaret has been told, she wrote, that Brandon had been showing off a diamond ring of hers, 'which I cannot believe, for I esteem him much a man of virtue and wise'. But one night at Tournai, 'after the banquet he put himself upon his knees before me, and in speaking and him playing, he drew from my finger the ring, and put it upon his, and then showed it to me and I took to laugh'.

Margaret told Brandon he was a thief, a *laron*, and that she hadn't thought the king had thieves in his company. Brandon couldn't understand the word *laron*, so Margaret tried the Flemish word *dieffe* and begged him (once that evening, when he seemed not to understand her, and once next morning through the king) to give the ring back to her, 'because it was too much known'. She gave him one of her bracelets instead—a less incriminatingly familiar piece of jewellery.

But Brandon took the ring from her again at Lille and would not give it back, saying he would give her other, better, rings. He 'would not' understand her protests, and Margaret could only beg that the jewel would never be shown to anybody. She had been carried beyond what her prudence would allow. But all the same, at bottom the matter of the ring was or should have been a courtly game. Fun, flattering, and genuinely warming, no doubt, for a woman who was still, as Henry VIII kept reminding her, too young to have given up on love, but not in itself to be taken seriously.

The serious part came in the second letter, in which Margaret of Austria promised to show 'all the inconveniences which may happen of this thing'. She had been horrified to discover the business was being spoken of—at home, abroad, even in Germany, 'so openly as in the hands of merchant strangers'. An English merchant had dared to make wagers upon it, and though she was grateful for everything Henry had done to quash the story, 'yet I see the bruit is so imprinted in the fantasies of people . . . [that] I continue always in fear'.

The letter shows her not as the powerful fixer but as a very rattled still young woman. Nonetheless, Margaret of Austria had made her choice—power over pleasure. But the same trap that had caught even the confident and experienced Margaret of Austria may in the same year have also ensnared the more vulnerable Marguerite of Navarre.

Clever, complex, self-critical, and conflicted, Marguerite was also the author of a huge body of published writings that were highly unusual for her day in exploring, almost obsessively, a woman's inner journey. Most notable is the *Heptameron*, a collection of stories about love and lust, supposedly told to each other by a group of stranded travellers, that Marguerite wrote later in life. Though modelled (like Christine de Pizan's *City of Ladies*) on Boccaccio's *Decameron*, parts of the *Heptameron* display so many echoes of real life that the idea it is to some degree autobiographical cannot be entirely dismissed.

The near-contemporary writer Brantôme identifies Marguerite and a young nobleman called Guillaume Gouffier, Seigneur de Bonnivet, as protagonists of one particular story describing a sexual assault. And though much of Brantôme's writing is scurrilous to the point of being near pornography, he is the better a witness for the fact that both his mother and his grandmother had been Marguerite's ladies-in-waiting.

The protagonists of novella ten of the *Heptameron* are Floride and Amadour—the flowery named Marguerite and an amorous Bonnivet? In the novel Amadour had married Floride's favourite attendant, 'Aventur'ade, who died early; in real life Bonnivet married Marguerite's lady-in-waiting Bon'aventur'e, who likewise died young. Floride had known Amadour in childhood; just so had the real-life Bonnivet come into Marguerite's family circle when his elder brother had been appointed to oversee the education of her brother, François. That was in Marguerite's youth, but in 1513 Marguerite had been for four years a married woman, which made her fair game in the essentially adulterous sport of courtly love.

In December 1513 Marguerite and her husband, d'Alençon, were visiting Louise in Cognac—and the hapless d'Alençon had fallen from his horse and broken his arm—when François came to join them with Bonnivet in his train. And if the events of the *Heptameron* are in any sense autobiographical, Bonnivet was set on the path 'that leads to the forbidden goal of a lady's honour'. The protagonists of the novel have an encounter where Amadour seizes Floride's hands and takes her feet 'in a vice-like grip'. 'His whole expression, his face, his eyes had changed as he spoke. The fair complexion was flushed with a fiery red. The kind, gentle face was contorted with a terrifying violence, as if there was some raging inferno belching fire in his heart and behind his eyes'. When Floride repulses him, he claims merely to have been testing her—a familiar trope of the courtly love story.*

Marguerite had in general a difficult and a dramatic emotional history.† (One letter to her spiritual adviser tells us that in her childhood, Louise of Savoy had so 'beaten and berated' Marguerite for some 'folly and guile' that Marguerite could not believe her mother really loved her.) But the continued prevalence of sexual violence in Marguerite's writing may suggest some specific concern or trauma. The narrator of the *Heptameron*, Parlamente, warns her female listeners against men's treachery. 'A woman's love is rooted

---

* Years later, Anne Boleyn, arrested, would express the hope that Henry wished only to test her.
† Marguerite's lifelong concern with the establishment of hospitals and the care of orphaned children makes it very hard not to think of another people's princess who compensated for lack of love closest to home by loving all the world in the hope it would love her.

in God and founded on honour. . . . But most [men's] love is based on pleasure, so much so that women not being aware of men's evil intentions, sometimes allow themselves to be drawn too far'.

Perhaps, like Margaret of Austria, Marguerite of Navarre had learned a painful lesson, and there was a lesson there for Anne Boleyn too, surely, though only time would prove how well or badly she had learned it.

8

FLODDEN

SCOTLAND AND ENGLAND, 1513

✳

The same quarrel between France and its neighbours that had taken Charles Brandon across the Channel was fought out also in the British Isles (and would continue to be through the first part of the century). Where France led, its old ally Scotland would usually follow, whereas in England Katherine of Aragon had been one of the chief promoters of war against France, her Aragonese father's ancient enemy.

As the Venetian ambassador put it, 'The King is bent on war, the Council is averse to it; the Queen will have it, and the wisest councillors in England cannot stand against the Queen'. But any resumption of the centuries-old conflict between England and Scotland would set Katherine of Aragon painfully at odds with her husband's sister Margaret Tudor, wife to the Scottish king.

When Henry VIII set off on campaign in France in the summer of 1513, Katherine was left as 'Regent and Governess' of England, albeit with a council of noblemen to advise her. Her appointment might well have been controversial. Some half century before, when Henry VI's wife, Margaret of Anjou, had tried to exercise power during his incapacity, the result had been a power struggle culminating in civil war, the Wars of the Roses.

'Moreover it is a right great perversion, / A woman of a land to be a regent' ran a popular ditty, while descriptions of Margaret of Anjou as a 'great and strong laboured woman' went hand in hand with slurs on her sexual morality. But since then, the mechanics of Henry VIII's very accession had been (in the words of the Garter Herald) 'over seen by the mother of the late king', Henry VII's mother, Margaret Beaufort. Katherine's influence over her husband's policies was an accepted, if not necessarily a welcome, fact, and there was, in any case, a different tussle looming.

Scotland's 'Auld Alliance' with France set it, too, on a collision course with the 'holy alliance' of which England was a part and dragged the two island neighbours also into war with each other. Katherine herself—just as her mother, Isabella of Castile, had done—accompanied the country's army northward when the Scots took advantage of Henry's absence to invade.

Peter Martyr d'Anghiera at the Spanish court, heard that 'in imitation of her mother Isabella', Katherine gave a moving speech to rally the troops, telling them that 'they should be ready to defend their territory, that the Lord smiled upon those who stood in defence of their own'.

She wrote to the Netherlands (her letter addressed to that rising man Thomas Wolsey, there with King Henry) that she was busy 'making standards, banners and badges'. She also wrote to Margaret of Austria, asking her to send a physician to Henry. But like her mother, Isabella, before her, Katherine immersed also herself in the most fundamental preparations for war. She was organising troops and money northward—artillery, provisions, and ships—and told Wolsey also that 'my heart is very good to it'.

The Earl of Surrey in the North would be England's first line of defence, and a second wave of troops was stationed across the Midlands. But Katherine herself (taking in her luggage a light gold helmet with a crown) was prepared if necessary to command a third wave even farther to the south—this despite the fact that she was perhaps once again in the early stages of a pregnancy. Events meant her force would not be needed, but the possibility was sufficiently realistic that the Venetian ambassador in London could report that 'our queen also took the field against the Scots with a numerous force one hundred miles from here'.

Katherine of Aragon's fervour was in sharp contrast to the feelings of Margaret Tudor, whom Katherine had known a decade before, on her first arrival in England, and with whom, on a personal level, she felt considerable sympathy.

MARGARET TUDOR HAD ALWAYS TAKEN seriously the idea that it was her mission to bring about closer relations between England and Scotland, but that dream had begun to look fragile almost from the start of her brother's reign. Her husband, James IV, had been horrified by the anti-French league formed between England and its allies, including Spain, the empire, and the papacy. He wrote, and made Margaret write, to the crowned heads of Europe, beseeching them to keep the peace.

One welcome event in the spring of 1512 was the birth of another son. But Margaret Tudor's hopes of an Anglo-Scottish alliance seemed far from accomplishment—further than ever when French queen Anne of Brittany sent James her glove, with a letter begging him to be her champion.

Margaret was horrified that her husband took so seriously a gesture from the games of chivalry. Later stories report that she dreamed of seeing him hurled from a cliff, while her own jewels, under her horrified gaze, changed from diamonds into a widow's pearls.

A kind of family relations still went on—the ambassador who came north to talk to James brought a letter from Henry to Margaret. When she had recently been pregnant with her surviving boy, he and Katherine had sent the girdle of Our Lady to her from Westminster Abbey. But when, dining with the ambassador, Margaret plied him with questions about the brother she had not seen for a decade—and also about the enthusiasm husband and brother shared for building up their navies—the man assumed she had been told by her husband to get naval secrets. Small wonder the ambassador reported that she ended the meeting 'right heavy'.

The collapse of the Treaty of Perpetual Peace between England and Scotland—clearly by now inevitable—was all the more strange for the fact that Margaret Tudor and her Scottish son were still Henry VIII's heirs. Henry was in France when the Scottish herald arrived, bearing a declaration of war. Henry shouted out that James IV was a man of no faith and that he himself was, moreover, 'the very owner' of Scotland, which James held only by homage—harking back to a claim made centuries before. It would 'become him, being married to the king of England's sister, to recount the king of England his ally', Henry said. 'I care nothing but for the mistreating of my sister, that would God she were in England on a condition she cost the Scottish king not a penny'.

Presciently, James IV had not waited to hear Henry VIII's reply before he began to muster his armies. On his way to join them, he stopped to see Margaret at Linlithgow, now (like Katherine) in the early throes of another pregnancy. He dismissed her dreams of his death, her pleas that he should not go. 'It is no dream. Ye are to fight a mighty people'. If she really spoke those words, there could have been pride as well as terror there, since they had been her people too. There is a tower in Linlithgow from which, yet another romantic story says, Margaret strained her eyes southward to watch for James's return. But they also say she never even sent to search the battlefield at Flodden where, on 9 September, the armies met, so certain had she been of what would happen that day.

The loss of Scottish life was appalling—perhaps as many as ten thousand men. Katherine in England described the victory in triumphant terms to Henry, sending her husband the coat of the slain Scots king, James IV.

She would instead have sent the king himself (as a prisoner, or as a corpse?), she wrote, 'but our Englishmen's hearts would not suffer it'.

When the news of her husband's death, 140 rugged miles away, reached Margaret Tudor at Linlithgow, the twenty-three-year-old pregnant widow acted both swiftly and decisively. Though the battle had been fought well south of the border, the English armies might yet advance into Scotland, and Margaret took her eighteen-month-old son, the new James V, farther inland, to her own castle of Stirling, where the rocky crags below made the castle at least feel invulnerable. There he was crowned on 21 September, just twelve days after his father's death, in what became known as the Mourning Coronation.

After the catastrophe of Flodden, only fifteen temporal lords, and a handful of bishops, were left alive to help Margaret govern the country. A reeling council, a mere twenty-three men, hastily read and approved the will James had made before he left Linlithgow, which left Margaret as regent for their son. (Just a half century before, after all, Scotland had seen another queen consort, Mary of Guelders, acting as regent for her son, the nine-year-old James III.) Margaret was to be 'testementary tutrix' to the new James V, though she was not to act without a quorum of lords who would be permanently on hand to advise her.

In their wreck of a country, Margaret Tudor and the Scottish council acted swiftly to try to restore order. As September turned to October, royal proclamations were sent out forbidding the looting of houses and the molesting of women left (as so very many were) without a male protector. Stirling, and other fortresses, had to be strengthened, as there were hardly enough men left to garrison them.

Very quickly, though, cracks began to appear in the Scottish command. When Margaret wrote to the pope, suggesting her own candidates for several bishoprics left vacant when their incumbents died at Flodden, there was anger that she had failed to consult the lords about her choices.

More seriously, there was division over what line to pursue with England, whose troops were still, as a punitive measure, burning crops and raiding villages along the Scottish border. A number of younger lords wanted to continue the war and avenge their kinsmen. To do so, they wanted the help of their traditional ally, France. And they wanted a military leader, the obvious candidate being the man who was now (since the infant James V had, as yet, no siblings) Scotland's heir.

John Stuart, Duke of Albany, cousin to James IV, had spent his whole life in exile in France, his father having been exiled after trying to seize the

Scottish throne. Now many lords thought he should be recalled. On 26 November the council wrote to the French king, asking him to send Albany home to Scotland 'for its defence'. Margaret was to continue her role as regent and tutrix of the young king, whose person was to be 'kept as devised in the late King's will'.

Henry VIII for one was horrified, convinced that Albany might easily depose a vulnerable baby monarch, might spirit him away to the Outer Isles, and from thence who knew where, much as his own great-uncle Richard III was widely believed to have spirited away his nephews, the 'Princes in the Tower'. Henry saw himself as his Scottish nephew's natural protector. But that was not how the situation appeared to the Scots.

For Margaret Tudor herself, there must have been a clash of loyalties—familiar to many royal consorts but surely in this case worse than most, since her husband had actually been killed by her brother's troops. Yet in this task that now came upon Margaret so suddenly, Henry was the closest natural adviser she had left for the protection of herself and her son.

For their part, the Scottish lords must have looked at Margaret with double vision. On the one hand, she was their queen, wife of one beloved Scottish king and mother of their present ruler. On the other, she was the sister of the man, Henry VIII, who had caused that same king's death and brought them only defeat and disgrace. The message Henry passed north was tactfully mediated—that Margaret's sister-in-law Katherine of Aragon sent love—but the more Margaret Tudor seemed to turn toward her brother for help, the more divided the perception of her would grow.

For all her triumphalism, Katherine had expressed herself as personally sympathetic to Margaret. 'The Queen of England for the love she bears the Queen of Scots would gladly send a servant to comfort her'. Margaret wrote back, asking Katherine to put her in Henry's remembrance.

In the weeks after Flodden, Katherine did indeed send Friar Bonaventure Langley to Stirling to discuss a truce. As can be seen time and again, the personal, the feminine, was a cover for the political. One story had Margaret claiming war might have been averted had she only been able to meet with the sister-in-law she had known at the English court: 'If we shall meet, who knows what God by our means may bring to pass?' But any closeness to the queen of England could still be one strike against the queen of Scotland.

Margaret Tudor suffered other disadvantages. Unlike her European contemporaries, or Katherine, she had been raised by a woman, Elizabeth of York, who had been kept away from power by her husband, Henry VII.

Margaret struggled to occupy a position to which, Tudor-like, she did indeed lay claim, but for which nothing in her life had prepared her.

In the years ahead, she too would find herself caught in a different trap, the one that lay in wait for powerful women. The one that had entangled Marguerite of Navarre and Margaret of Austria and that (at the court not of France or the Netherlands but of England) would later have one last deadly game to play. Meanwhile, the protagonist of that legendary drama would soon be moving from the orbit of Margaret of Austria to that of Marguerite of Navarre, as the shifting landscape of the European scene sent the young Anne Boleyn her way.

PART II
1514–1521

When it comes to the government of their affairs, [widowed women] must depend only on themselves; when it comes to sovereignty, they must not cede power to anyone. And then, you must protect yourself from deceitful and presumptuous followers, especially those with whom you conduct business often, because of the suspicions that can arise.

—Anne of France (Anne de Beaujeu),
Lessons for my Daughter (1517–1521)

9

WHEEL OF FORTUNE

France and the Netherlands, 1514–1515

✳

Machiavelli envisaged Fortune as a woman. But the events immediately following the traumatic year of 1513 made it clear that no spirit of sisterhood would move Fortune to give her fellow women an easy ride. Louise of Savoy in France and Margaret of Austria in the Netherlands were both to find themselves spinning on her wheel.

On 9 January 1514 Anne of Brittany, Louis XII's queen, died just before her thirty-seventh birthday. Her funeral saw an extended parade of ceremony suitable not just for a queen but for a king as well as an outpouring of public grief, both recognition, perhaps, of the doughty part she had played in trying against the odds to preserve the independence of her duchy.

But Anne of Brittany's death was like a stone dropped in a pond. And the ripples spreading out from this stone would reach to touch Margaret of Austria's as well as Louise of Savoy's family.

Anne de Beaujeu played a prominent part in the funeral ceremonies, as did Louise of Savoy and her children. Louise's daughter, Marguerite, would assume an elder sister's role toward the two daughters Anne of Brittany had left, fourteen-year-old Claude (now Duchess of Brittany in her own right, thanks to the marriage agreement Anne had made with Louis XII before their marriage), and little Renée, who would come to absorb some of Marguerite's ideas. Louise noted in her *Journal*: 'Anne, queen of France, passing from life to death, left me the administration of her goods, her fortune and her daughters . . . a charge of which I have acquitted myself honourably and kindly; this is known to all, a recognised and demonstrable truth, and confirmed by public opinion'.

Plans were carried out as arranged. On 14 May François underwent a binding marriage ceremony with Claude, a marriage that made him Duke of Brittany. François's friend Fleuranges wrote that Claude had inherited her mother's disapproval of François and his clan: 'never a day but those two houses were bickering'. Personal compatibility was not the point, however, and François must have felt confident as he went off hunting the next day.

But the hopes of Louise and her family had been founded on the inability of the pair on the French throne to produce a son. Anne of Brittany's death—paving the way for a younger bride for King Louis XII—could yet prove worrying news for them.

HENRY VIII's YOUNGER SISTER, EIGHTEEN-YEAR-OLD Mary Tudor, had long been contracted to marry Margaret of Austria's nephew Charles. Mary had only recently been in correspondence with Margaret about the styles of dress the Flemish ladies preferred. But earlier in 1514, as Margaret of Austria urged ever more desperately that her father should push ahead with the match between her nephew and the English princess—vital to foster the peace in her Netherlands territories—her father, Maximilian, and her erstwhile father-in-law, Ferdinand, had been conspiring to keep her in the dark about very different plans.

In 1514 Ferdinand wrote to his ambassador (was he intending to show Margaret the letter?) that she was 'the most important person in Christendom, since she acts as mediator in almost all the negotiations between the princes'. And, in another letter, he wrote that 'Madam Margaret is the person on whom, more than anyone else on earth, peace or war depends'. But the flattery may have been intended to keep her in line.

He and Maximilian now proposed that instead of marrying Mary Tudor, as had been arranged to cement the alliance between England and the Habsburgs, Charles should instead marry the French king's little daughter, Renée. Ferdinand was also offering the recently bereaved Louis XII a new bride of his own, either Margaret herself or Margaret's niece Eleanor. Louis chose the nubile Eleanor, and the marriage articles were drawn up.

'Madame Margaret', Ferdinand said, 'dwells on the great difference of age between the King of France [fifty-one] and Madame Eleanor [seventeen]. Lanuza [the ambassador] is to tell her that in marriage of great kings difference of age is never taken into account. . . . Madame Margaret is mistaken if she thinks it is a disadvantage that Madame Eleanor is so thin. Thin women generally . . . bear more children than stout ones'.

As Margaret, frantic, wrote to Maximilian, it was all very well for Spain to make peace with France: they had the barrier of the mountains to protect them, and England had the sea. By contrast, the Netherlands, long the object of France's rapacity, was protected by no such freak of geography. But no holds were barred in the attempt to unite the empire, France, and Spain into one future 'family', of which Maximilian envisaged himself the head. And when England too made its own peace with France, there was yet another change of marriage plans. The proposed marriage between Louis XII and Eleanor was off; instead, he would marry the woman who had been promised to Margaret's nephew Charles: King Henry VIII of England's sister Mary.

In addition to the hastily assembled trousseau, and to the immense 'Mirror of Naples' diamond the French king had sent as a wedding gift, Mary Tudor would, of course, take a number of English ladies in her train, and the Boleyns were never going to miss such an opportunity. In August 1514, Thomas Boleyn wrote to Margaret of Austria to ask that his daughter might be released from service in order—her French, thanks to Margaret, being now so good!—to transfer to the French court. The place Margaret had given Boleyn as a great favour was now to be put aside for an even more promising opportunity.

Nonetheless, Anne's name is not on the list of those who accompanied Mary on her journey from England, and she is not recorded in France until slightly later. Her whereabouts for a few months are unknown. Margaret of Austria and her court were away in Zeeland when Thomas Boleyn's letter would have arrived, and that may have caused the delay. Or Margaret may have stalled, whether out of a reluctance to foster this Anglo-French marriage in even the smallest way or out of sheer pique.

And, as Margaret would feel acutely, Mary Tudor's was far from the only royal marriage that year.

In May Margaret of Austria's niece Mary had been summoned to Maximilian's court in Vienna, preparatory to a marriage with the son of the king of Hungary. In June Margaret was called upon to arrange, at very short notice, the marriage of her niece Isabel, not yet thirteen, to King Christian of Denmark, twenty years her senior, whose ambassadors had arrived on a Wednesday and, on the Saturday, declared their wish that the marriage should take place the next day, the day of Christian's coronation. 'But Monseigneur', Margaret wrote to her father, 'it was very difficult to arrange such a solemn function in so short a time. . . . [B]ut, anxious to please them and gratify their desires, I agreed . . . and I did my best to have everything arranged and put in order'. The bride, at least, she wrote touchingly, was a figure 'it certainly did one good to look at'. This marriage would end badly, but for the next year Isabel, like her elder sister, Eleanor (now rebetrothed to the heir of Portugal), was to be left in Margaret's care.*

---

* When Eleanor's betrothal to the heir of Portugal fell through, she would instead be married to his father, the Portuguese King Manuel himself, who had already been married to two of her Spanish aunts, Isabella of Castile's daughters. No wonder the results of Habsburg inbreeding would become notorious.

MARGARET OF AUSTRIA HAD ALSO been finding herself under pressure from events within the Netherlands. Her nephew Charles was now in his teens and beginning to resent the government of an autocratic aunt. She had long been at odds with William de Croy, the Sieur de Chievres, the nobleman who had been left as governor of the country in her brother's absence until Margaret had replaced him.

Chievres had remained tutor and mentor to her young nephew Charles, working well enough with Margaret until the Holy League against France she had helped to mould offended his own strongly French sympathies. Things came to a head over a seemingly unrelated matter. Castile—one of the territories of which Charles would be ruler—was in the grip of a nationalist movement, the Castilians concerned alike about their current government by Ferdinand of Aragon and their future under a boy being raised wholly in the Netherlands. The Castilian faction at Margaret of Austria's court was headed by one Don Juan Manuel de la Cerda, a political agitator whom Ferdinand was anxious to get into his hands. It seemed a comparatively minor matter to Margaret to have Don Juan arrested with the intention of sending him to Aragon, but she found she had gone too far.

Don Juan was a knight of the Order of the Golden Fleece, the glorious chivalric order of Burgundy to which even privileged foreign males like Henry VIII were proud to belong. Now the knights—headed by Charles as their titular leader and by Chievres—came to Margaret in a deputation, furiously brandishing the statutes that declared that one of the order could be tried only by his brother knights. Margaret was indignant and uncomprehending: 'Ah, Messeigneurs, if I were such a man as I am a woman I would make you bring your statutes to me and make you sing out passages from them!' (Perhaps she was aware that her former mother-in-law Isabella of Castile had persuaded the papacy to grant her administration of three such chivalric orders, though not without some masculine grumbling that this was 'a monstrous thing'.)

The affair ended when Maximilian (himself a former head of the order) had Don Juan brought to Germany for investigation. But Margaret of Austria had lost much goodwill among the local nobility.

Under the influence of Chievres, the Estates-General demanded that Charles should be declared of age, offering Maximilian a large sum of money if he would agree. Maximilian did not even warn Margaret he was planning to do so. No wonder her letters to him complain that he does not take her fully into his confidence, so that the foreign ambassadors seem to know more of events than she.

In the spring of 1515, letters from Charles to the various provinces of the Netherlands declared, 'It is fit and reasonable that all things which concern our rights, greatness, lordship, and even the doing of justice and our other affairs, should be conducted henceforth in our name and under our title'.

Maximilian himself wrote to Charles (and sent a copy to Margaret), 'We make no doubt, because of the honour and love you owe to our very dear daughter, your aunt, that you communicate your chief and most arduous business to her, and that you take and use her good advice'. But Maximilian himself was to find he too was no longer as important as he had been in Charles's country.

Now that Margaret of Austria was displaced, complaints about her rule came in thick and fast. She was blamed for having failed to maintain the alliance she had made with the Netherlands' trading partner England and for having used Netherlands money for alien wars—though it might be more accurate to say that she had failed entirely to stop her father from doing so—and even for having illegitimately enriched herself.

Through all this Margaret had to put on a brave face, to accompany her nephew on the extended tour that marked the handover of power. But, as she wrote to her father, she asked herself whether she should not retire south to her own lands and devote herself to her own 'small interests'. Shortly after Charles's emancipation—when Maximilian nonetheless continued to bombard her with business—she replied that she had passed on his letter to de Chievres but could do no more, 'for now I do not meddle in any business'.

In fact, time would tell that Margaret of Austria was too determined, too canny a politician, to remain long in the shadows—someone who could be circumvented, yes, but still someone around whom even the most alpha males moved carefully. After that six-month tour of the provinces with her nephew, at a meeting of the council she read aloud to Charles a memorandum refuting the accusations made against her, accusations planned, she said, 'to give you suspicions of me, your humble aunt, to withdraw from me your goodwill and confidence, which would indeed be a poor recompense for the services which I have rendered you until now. . . .

'Item.—Madame has lent her money for State affairs, and has greatly reduced the expenses of her own household. . . . For three years, far from having a pension for her services, she spent her dowry as long as it lasted'. At the end of her oration, it was agreed 'that Madame was held fully discharged from all things'. Margaret of Austria 'gracefully' retired for a time into her books, her estates, her ongoing plans for the building of her husband Philibert's tomb in Brou. But she did so without any shadow hanging over her head.

10

'A SPLENDID NEW YEAR'S GIFT'

FRANCE, 1514–1515

✳

Another royal death in France would soon prove to be another turn of the wheel of Fortune. This one meant that, while Margaret of Austria's star seemed to have fallen, that of her erstwhile playmate Louise of Savoy would rise dramatically . . . but not without some scares along the way.

The arrival in France of Mary Tudor—young, nubile, and presumably fertile—cannot have been welcome to Louise and her family, anxious lest the birth of a son to the old king should spoil François's chance of the throne. But old Louis XII seemed enchanted with his new bride and claimed to have performed great feats in the bedroom.

Perhaps no one quite believed it. François's friend the courtier and adventurer Fleuranges reported François's having told him, 'Unless people are lying very hard, I now know that the king and queen cannot possibly have children'. But there were other worrying possibilities. As the king's son-in-law and putative heir, François had led the party to welcome Mary Tudor and taken a starring role in the jousts in her honour. He got on notably well with his beautiful nineteen-year-old stepmother-in-law. Soon Louise was being warned to keep a close eye on her son, lest he himself father a male baby to supplant him. But Louise's anxieties were not to last.

Fleuranges reported sayings that the king of England had sent a filly to the king of France to gallop him off to heaven or to hell. It proved all too accurate a prophecy. Less than three months after Mary Tudor was married, on 1 January 1515 her husband, Louis XII, was dead.

Fleuranges described how the new François I put on mourning clothes and, 'coming to the palace in haste, informed all the princes and ladies of the kingdom, especially his mother, Madame Louise. It was a splendid New Year's gift, I must say . . .', Louise recorded. 'On the first day of January I lost my husband and on the first day of January my son became king of France'.

Technically, it was unclear that François was king until it was confirmed that Mary Tudor was not pregnant. But the principle of 'The king is dead—long live the king' prevailed, the more so since no one thought a posthumous baby was likely. The official period of mourning was cut short, and François was crowned at the end of the month.

FOR THE NEW DYNASTY IN France, Mary Tudor, the old king's widow, represented a loose thread. But Mary would find her own solution, another Tudor sister prepared to put passion before policy. Wolsey had urgently warned from the earliest days of her widowhood that she should give no heed to any new 'motion of marriage' that might be made to her. 'I trust the King my brother and you will not reckon in me such childhood', she replied, from her widow's seclusion, indignantly.

But there were 'motions' aplenty, rumours of the Duke of Lorraine, of François himself, putting Claude away to marry her or of her brother cementing another foreign, this time a Habsburg, alliance with her hand. It may have been this—and an awareness that disputes over her dowry would play a major part in her future, if it were negotiated between the two kings—that prompted Mary Tudor to act.

Before she left England, she had extracted an informal promise from her brother that if she married the aged King Louis, she would be allowed to choose her next husband. And she knew on whom her choice would light. Charles Brandon had escorted her to France; in January he was sent to negotiate her return to England. But there was already an acknowledged attraction between the pair, and on Brandon's arrival Mary sent for him. 'I never saw woman so weep', wrote Brandon afterward in excuse, telling Wolsey on 5 March, 'The queen would never let me be in rest till I had granted her to be married, and so, to be plain with you, I have married her heartily and lain with her'.

This was more than lèse-majesté, but the couple could rely on a measure of protection from the French, to whom this appeared as a handy way of avoiding either the expense of a queen dowager permanently in France or Mary's being used to cement some unwelcome political alliance. With Mary's brother Henry, it was a different story.

But even he was not too angry to be placated by the couple's promising to give to him Mary's dowry and any goods she had received through her marriage. (To François's fury, she sweetened the deal by smuggling back to her brother in England the fabulous Mirror of Naples.) Returning home, her marriage confirmed in a public English ceremony, Mary Tudor settled into a future of domesticity. Many of her English ladies returned home with her, but Anne Boleyn (perhaps because her command of French was so good?) remained behind.* In the early days of her French sojourn, Anne had, if later stories are to be believed, also to witness her sister Mary's brief affair with the libidinous François—and to witness, too, the detrimental effect on Mary Boleyn's reputation. The lessons in love, and in the dangers it posed for women, were coming in thick and fast.

Mary Tudor's was not the future every royal woman would choose. Louise of Savoy's *Journal* noted coolly that Mary, on the last day of March, had married Brandon, 'a person of low estate'. Temperamentally, perhaps Louise had more in common with Margaret of Austria. She too could vouch for Brandon's charms, but she received word of such an illicit love match with incomprehension, something, she wrote to Maximilian, so senseless the idea would never have entered her head.

LOUISE OF SAVOY WAS RISING forty, still in her prime, when her son, François I, inherited the French throne. There seems from the first to have been a sense that the business of government—at least in these early stages of the reign—was as much her concern as that of her son. 'A boy's best friend is his mother' might have been the motto for early modern monarchs. England had recently seen two new rulers (Edward IV and Henry VII) treat their mothers as mentors (and unlike those two, François had not even had himself to fight for his crown).

As the main officers of state were confirmed once more in their office (as François's brother-in-law, Alençon, his sister Marguerite's husband, was declared second person of the realm and Bonnivet Admiral of France), several of Louise's trusted officials were also given important places. She herself was given estates—the duchy of Angoulême, that of Anjou, the counties of Maine and Beaufort, and the barony of Amboise—that made her hugely wealthy.

Nor was the earlier governess of the French royal family Anne de Beaujeu forgotten. Her son-in-law, the Duc de Bourbon, was made Constable of France. (This would be an appointment with consequences, since the amalgamation of Bourbon's own lands with those Anne's daughter, Suzanne,

---

* There has long been debate over whether Anne Boleyn, appointed to Queen Claude's household, remained there for the duration of her stay in France or was transferred to that of Marguerite, who seems a more likely mentor. But Marguerite's involvement in her brother's court perhaps makes the distinction unnecessary, and we can assume Anne would at the very least have been acutely conscious of the doings of so charismatic a figure.

stood to inherit made a huge and potentially controversial landmass right in the centre of France.) Anne, like Louise and Marguerite but unlike François's wife, the pregnant Claude, accompanied François to his coronation in Rheims.

As Louise of Savoy's *Journal* had it: 'This day of the Conversion of St Paul 1515 my son was anointed and consecrated in the church of Rheims. For this I hold myself grateful to the Divine Mercy, by which I am amply repaid for all the adversities and inconvenience which came to me in my early years and in the flower of my youth. Humility has borne me company and Patience has never abandoned me'.

The humility was not evident to all. Charles Brandon wrote to Henry VIII of Louise: 'It is she who runs all, and so may she well; for I never saw a woman like to her, both for wit, honour, and dignity. She hath a great stroke in all matters with the King her son'.

A Venetian envoy asked the veteran Marshal Trivulzio who really held power in the land—who controlled the king? The answer was that Louise of Savoy

> lays claim to managing everything, not allowing him to act without her concurrence. . . . [I]t is his mother, with Madame de Bourbon [the still-active Anne de Beaujeu], and Boisy [François's former governor, Bonnivet's brother], who really manage everything. It is a great pity to see him under petticoat government. But what can you expect, the way he lives? He does not get out of bed until a little before noon. Then, after dressing and hearing mass, he goes straight to dinner. Immediately afterwards he withdraws to his mother. Then, after a short while with the council, he plunges into amusement which goes on incessantly until supper time.

Venice now knew to whom to apply—'the Most Christian King's most illustrious mother' was soon assuring the Venetians her son would prove 'the greatest and most faithful friend' their city had ever had.

The year before her son's accession, Louise of Savoy had been at Blois when the ceiling of her room came down. 'I think it was a sign that the whole of this house was destined to rest on me', she wrote later in her *Journal*, 'and that I was divinely appointed to have charge of it'. But in many ways, it would be a burden as well as an opportunity. When the Venetian envoy added that François's mother 'applies all her energy to accumulating money', it was a reputation that would cling to Louise. But perhaps it was also the result of what one writer called Louise's avidity for security, something Louise shared with Henry VII's mother, Lady Margaret Beau-fort. But Henry had shared his mother's closefistedness, while Louise faced the very real problem of how freely her son could spend—not least on the expensive sport of war.

On Louise of Savoy, inevitably, fell much of the task of helping to sort out the difficult relationships of François I's reign. His relationship with Charles V, as ruler of the Netherlands, seemed in the short term to be en-sured by Charles's betrothal to Louis XII's four-year-old daughter, Renée (yet another royal marriage destined never to take place). Louise hoped also to bring the pope on side by arranging the marriage of his Medici brother to her own half sister, Philiberte of Savoy.

But the three-way relationship between the French crown, the papacy, and France's own secular and religious bodies had long been an edgy one. In 1516 François, surely with Louise's advice behind the scenes, hammered out with Pope Leo an agreement known as the Concordat of Bologna, which gave François the right to nominate his own religious officials. This, how-ever, put him into conflict with the Paris Parlement and with the faculty of theology at the university, who had previously been involved in making such appointments.* The Parlement was likewise outraged that the king's sister Marguerite and her husband, Alençon, had been given an annual pension of twenty thousand livres and the lucrative right to name the head of each of France's trade guilds, as well as the duchy of Armagnac, which Parlement held to be inalienably attached to the French crown itself.

Marguerite's role in her brother's quarrels with both his Parlement and his religious authorities would have later consequences, not least for Marguerite herself. But for the moment, his generosity meant her husband, Alençon, accepted that her place would now be largely at her brother's court, where she took on many of the ceremonial duties of a queen, just as her mother accepted much of the workload of a king. In novella four of the *Heptameron*, Marguerite wrote of a young prince ('fond of the ladies, of hunting, and generally enjoying himself') whose wife, however, 'was rather difficult, and did not enjoy the same things as he did, so he always used to take his sister along as well'. Her letters to him were most often signed as François's most humble and most obedient subject and sister—or *et mi-gnonne*, darling.

---

* The Paris was by far the most powerful of France's seven Parlements—a provincial high court rather than a legislative assembly. François's voice here was Chancellor Duprat, a longtime associate of Louise.

Queen Claude was shy, plain, and afflicted with a limp, and in any case almost solidly pregnant, with deliveries in 1515, 1516, 1518, 1519, 1520, 1522, and 1523, though only two of the children would outlive their parents. But it seems Louise of Savoy—and surely Marguerite too—valued Claude for what she could do for François and they could not. Though the near-contemporary biographer the Seigneur de Brantôme would write that Claude was bullied by her mother-in-law as well as ignored by her husband, there is no evidence that she resented her treatment; she had, after all, grown up partly under Marguerite's, and Louise's, wing.

The relationship between mother and son was so close that when François ran a thorn into his leg, Louise wrote that 'true love forced me to suffer the same pain'. So her feelings about her son's natural venturesomeness were mixed. She was terrified when he had a boar captured and set loose in the courtyard at Amboise, only to kill it himself with one blow of the sword. It was infinitely worse when it became clear François was determined to pursue his ambitions for the disputed territory of Milan, to which he had a hereditary claim.

When François left for the Italian Wars, taking all the nobles of his blood with him, he announced that his mother would act as regent while he was away: 'We have decided to leave the government of our realm to our well beloved and dear Lady and Mother, the Duchess of Angoulême and Anjou, in whom we have entire and perfect confidence who will by her virtue and prudence, know how to acquit this trust'.

Though the Italian Wars would prove to be an endlessly enduring business, François's efforts of 1515 met with impressive success. In September the battle of Marignano was, said one observer, a battle of giants, in which François's force achieved an overwhelming victory over the army of Swiss mercenaries assembled by the Sforzas, the current rulers of Milan, in alliance with the Papal States. Never had there been seen so spirited and cruel a battle, François boasted to his mother. Louise, with Claude, immediately went on pilgrimage to Notre-Dame de la Guiche to give thanks for the preservation of 'him, whom I love better than myself, my boy, glorious and triumphant Caesar, subjugator of the Swiss'. On 10 October François entered Milan in triumph, the very model of a young warrior king.

When the news came of François's return from Marignano, Louise of Savoy, Marguerite, and Claude set out to meet their 'triumphant Caesar', as Louise's journal describes him. 'God knows that I, poor mother, was overjoyed to see my son safe and whole after all he had suffered and endured to

serve the common good'. By January 1516 they were with him for his triumphant entry into Marseille.

The pattern of Europe in the first half of the sixteenth century was one
of three young men feeling their oats: François I, the Habsburg Charles,
and Henry VIII of England. Each had a woman—mother, aunt, or wife—
standing behind them. And if the last years had seen several women trying to juggle the demands of power with their female destiny, then Louise
seemed to have done so most successfully.

11

'ONE OF THE LOWEST-BROUGHT LADIES'

Scotland and England, 1515–1517

❈

For Henry VIII's other sister, Margaret Tudor, things had already long been going badly. But an event like the death of Louis XII in France had an effect far outside his own country, even in distant Scotland, France's 'Auld Ally'.

As far back as the autumn of 1513, Henry in England had been receiving agents' reports that the Scots lords 'were not pleased that the Queen should have rule, as they fear she will comply too much with England'. Even when, in February 1514, Margaret managed to push through an uneasy peace with England, not everyone on her council was happy with the deal.

But when in March 1514 the summoning of the Scottish Parliament exhibited her to the people in the eighth month of her pregnancy, she was cheered to the rafters—the more so since her gracious speech left most of the real business of the session to others and allowed the Parliament to take control of all the main fortresses in the country. As the Madonna figure, the mother, the dead king's relict, she was welcome in the country. It was when she tried to overstep those bounds that there was difficulty.

On 30 April she gave birth to a second son, Alexander, Duke of Ross. In England Henry and Katherine of Aragon—who had possibly suffered a miscarriage the previous autumn—had still no living child. That Margaret Tudor's offspring would succeed to the throne of England looked more than ever likely. In the summer she emerged from her confinement, and on 12 July the Scottish nobles signed a unanimous statement in support of her regency. 'Madame', it ran, 'we are content to stand in one mind and will to concur with all the lords of the realm to the pleasure of our master the

King's grace, your grace and for the common weal'. Yet within a few weeks, the situation had changed completely.

On 14 August, at a secret ceremony, Margaret Tudor was married for a second time—to the Earl of Angus. Roughly her own age (twenty-four), he was a scion of the powerful but controversial Douglas clan, hated by most of the other nobles.

History has often chosen to see Margaret as a fool for love, seduced by a pretty face, and so it might have been. Or she may, like other women in this story, have been determined to avoid her male relations marrying her off again for their own purposes. But it is also possible that she was trying to bolster her own authority.* Throughout the last century, the Douglases, after all, had almost rivalled the Scottish crown. But if that were her motive, then she could hardly have chosen more unwisely.

On 26 August the council demanded that Margaret Tudor should summon John Stuart, the Duke of Albany, from France to become governor of Scotland—to take her place, basically. Most councillors were behind a demand that she should surrender the Great Seal and issue no further proclamations. By the middle of September, they were questioning whether it was even appropriate that she should remain in charge of her son the baby king, James V. The provisions of her husband's will had been dependent upon her not remarrying. Now that was forfeit, as Lord Home trenchantly put it: 'We have shown heretofore our willingness to honour the Queen contrary to the ancient law and custom of this kingdom. We have suffered and obeyed her authority the whiles she herself kept her right by keeping her widowhood. Now she has quit it by marrying, why should we not choose another to succeed in the place she has voluntarily left?'

The Lyon Herald was sent to inform Margaret that she was to be deposed from the regency. He addressed Margaret not as 'the Queen's Grace' but as 'My Lady the King's Mother'—the title her own grandmother and namesake, Margaret Beaufort, had borne so proudly. Margaret Tudor took it less kindly. And her new husband's grandfather and mentor, old Lord Drummond, boxed the herald's ears—a staggering breach of propriety.

Margaret dismissed Drummond's insult to the Lyon Herald and, more seriously, nominated her husband, Angus—whose own uncle called him a callow young fool—as her coregent. Angus proved the truth of the

---

* Her granddaughter Mary would be similarly convinced that it was impossible for a woman to rule alone, unsupported 'by the firmness of a man', and would choose as disastrously.

description by attacking the Lord Chancellor, who had made clear his disapproval of the match, and seizing the Great Seal. The outraged nobility stopped Margaret's dower rents, while the Lord Chancellor and his followers rode to Edinburgh and took possession of the city.

This was civil war or something like it. Margaret and Angus promptly fled with Margaret's sons into Stirling Castle: 'My party adversary continues in their malice and proceed in their Parliament usurping the King's authority as I and my lords were of no reputation reputing us as rebels' was how she put it to her brother Henry VIII.

The Scottish lords would have allowed her to keep charge of her sons if she gave up her regent's powers, but Margaret Tudor was having none of this. Her sons were 'right lifelike' (lively) she assured Henry. But she ended her letter, 'If you send not soon succours in men and money I shall be super extended'. She urged her brother to send an English army to where her husband was trying to relieve the besieged Castle of St Andrews. The army was to be proclaimed a peacekeeping force, the Scots told that 'their lands and goods shall not be hurt and they shall be recompensed double and treble'. But she was, essentially, inviting an enemy to occupy their country.

'Brother all the welfare of me and my children rests in your hands'. She warned that her adversaries were now forging her signature, and Henry should take as genuine only those letters signed not just 'Margaret R' but 'your loving sister Margaret R'. In late January 1515 Henry VIII sent word that she should flee to the border, but Margaret quailed at the practical difficulties, and at the implications for her and her son's power.

'God send I were such a woman that might go with my bairns in my arms', she wrote back. If that had been so, then 'I should not be long from you'. But she was a queen, and the death of the old French king Louis XII, while making her sister, Mary, a merry widow, had dramatically weakened Margaret's position, depriving her a family connection to the French throne.

The promise King Louis had made to his bride's brother Henry VIII to keep the Duke of Albany in France, and away from rivalry with Margaret in Scotland, had died with him. On 2 April 1515 Albany set out from the French court.

FROM THE TIME ALBANY ARRIVED back in Scotland, in answer to the council's summons, to separate Margaret from her son the king, it was, as the Venetian ambassador wrote home, François I who was likely to be blamed 'for this cruelty'. The French ambassador in London wrote to François's mother, Louise of Savoy, asking to be recalled and warning that the opinion on the London streets was that Henry VIII should declare war on France to avenge the insult to his sister.

When Albany reached Scotland, the tussle came, inevitably, over control of the young king. A cultivated man, wealthy from his marriage to a great French heiress, Albany spoke little English and less of the Scottish idiom than Margaret herself, but, nonetheless, he set conscientiously and ably about his responsibilities.

Albany was to appoint four from a selection of peers made by the council as guardians, and Margaret was then to vet his choices. When the child was to be handed over to his new mentors, it was a dramatic public scene. In the forecourt of Stirling Castle, Margaret Tudor stood holding the young king by the hand, Angus by her side, her younger son in a nurse's arms. But as the representatives of the council approached, Margaret formally called on them to declare the cause of their coming—and ordered the portcullis dropped in their faces. Requesting six days to consider Parliament's plan, ignoring her husband's urging that she should comply, she retreated into the formidable and easily defensible bulk of Stirling, while her rattled husband, Angus, withdrew to his own lands.

Albany, of course, followed, determined to take Stirling by siege, however long it took. When Margaret saw the force and the heavy artillery Albany had assembled against her, she was frightened enough to comply. Even then she caused the little king to be the one who handed over the castle's keys—a defeat with dignity. While Albany set off after Angus and his family, Margaret was taken back to Edinburgh under guard. On 2 August she signed a statement declaring her wish that Albany should indeed 'have the charge and keeping' of both her sons—forced to do so, she later declared, by Albany's 'crafty and subtle ways'.

Once again her brother Henry VIII's representative urged her to flee south, to withdraw from Edinburgh 'with all the politic ways and wisdom you can use'. This time Margaret agreed. She was now heavily pregnant with Angus's child and had already told Albany that she proposed to 'take her chamber' for the child's birth at Linlithgow. Arriving there, she claimed sickness so that Angus would be allowed to visit her. When dark came, with a handful of servants, they slipped away, riding hard despite Margaret's pregnancy. Before dawn they reached the Douglases' Tantallon Castle, close to the border.

With Albany coming in pursuit, the queen and her party had to flee again so speedily that Margaret's clothes—even her precious jewels—had to be left behind. As England's Berwick Castle came into sight, adventure descended into bathos, as its governor refused to admit them without orders, but finally Henry VIII's representative, Lord Dacre, arrived to escort Margaret instead to his own headquarters, Harbottle Castle.

This was a military stronghold and no place for a royal confinement. It was difficult even to get a midwife through the rough and bandit-infested country. But it was here, having arrived in a state of collapse, that after an extended labour, Margaret gave birth to a daughter.*

Margaret would later charge Albany that she had been forced 'for fear and jeopardy of my life' to flee into England, 'great with child and nigh my deliverance', so that eight days after crossing the border, 'I was delivered of child fourteen days afore my time to my great spoil and extreme danger'. It was certainly ten days before she could sit up long enough to read letters from her brother Henry and from Katherine of Aragon and November before, at an agonisingly slow pace, she could be moved to the more comfortable castle of Morpeth.

At Morpeth, as the household began to prepare for Christmas, Margaret was at last shown the array of gifts Henry and Katherine had tried to get to her at Harbottle—dresses, bed hangings, everything to kit her out like a queen again. When she was carried in a chair from her room to see all of the dresses laid out in the great hall, she cried out, 'Ye may see the King my brother hath not forgotten me, and that he would not that I should die for lack of clothes'. Clothes were, of course, an important signifier of status, besides any question of pleasure or practicality.

Margaret was still suffering with what seems to have been sciatica, unable to enjoy the resplendent Christmas festivities. Lady Dacre's cook prepared the invalid almond milk and broths alongside the Christmas baked meats, game, and jellies, but, wrote Sir Christopher Garnyshe, the man Henry had sent north with his gifts, 'Her grace hath such pain in her right leg that this three weeks she may not endure to sit up while her bed is a-making, and when her grace is removed it would pity any man's heart to hear the shrieks and cries that her grace giveth'. Nevertheless, he added, Margaret 'hath a wonderful love of apparel', making her attendants display the dresses Henry had sent once or twice a day.

When she did grow stronger with the first months of the New Year, it was only to hear dreadful news. Her second son, the Duke of Ross, had died in Scotland, in Albany's charge, of a childhood illness. Her hosts had

---

* This baby, Lady Margaret Douglas, would grow up to be the mother of Lord Darnley, while her half brother James would of course become father to Darnley's wife, Mary, Queen of Scots, so that Margaret was twice over the founder of the united British monarchy.

known since Christmas, but decided to spare her while she herself was so ill, the more so since, Sir Christopher recorded, she loved to speak of this little boy, praising him 'even more than she doth her elder son the King'. Sir Christopher added: 'I think her one of the lowest-brought ladies'.

Her spirits would not be raised by the fact that her husband, Angus, returning to his own lands in Scotland, then decided to remain there. He preferred to make an accommodation with Albany rather than becoming a penniless exile by accompanying Margaret as she prepared to go south to the English court.

'When it comes to the government of their lands and affairs, [widows] must depend only on themselves', Anne de Beaujeu had written. Margaret Tudor—unlike Louise of Savoy and Margaret of Austria—had not lived up to that wise advice. But then she, unlike them, had not had the benefit of Anne's example.

IN 'MUCH HEAVINESS', AS DACRE put it, Margaret Tudor nonetheless set out southward on 8 April. Ambassadors from Scotland reached London before her, but Henry VIII refused to see them until he had met his sister. From Stony Stratford she wrote to him that she was 'in right good health and as joyous of my said journey towards you, as any woman may be in coming to her brother' and that she was 'most desirous now to come to your presence and to have a sight of your person'. She reached London on 3 May, entering the city in a triumphal procession, riding a white palfrey sent by Queen Katherine.

There were, with Henry VIII's sister Mary Tudor, the Dowager of France, now three queens at the English court. It was the first time the Tudor siblings had been together since 1503, and whatever Margaret's recent experiences, the news from the other two meant that this was a time of celebration. In March, at their London house, Mary Tudor had given birth to Brandon's son, and in February Katherine of Aragon had for the first time borne Henry a living child—'a lively little daughter', as an Italian correspondent wrote to Erasmus—the princess Mary.

Venetian ambassador Giustinian wrote home bluntly that the birth of a mere girl 'has proved vexatious, for never had this entire kingdom ever so anxiously desired anything as it did a prince, it appearing to every one that the state would be safe should his majesty leave an heir male, whereas, without a prince, they are of a contrary opinion'.

But Katherine of Aragon was, of course, triumphant and Henry convinced that a living daughter was at least promise of better to come. As he told

Giustinian, 'We are both young'. Though Katherine wanted to rear the child herself, Henry insisted that instead there should swing into place the whole panoply ratified by his grandmother Margaret Beaufort, with a lady governess to take care of her from the christening and everything in accordance with tradition, right down to the ermine quilt on the baby's 'cradle of estate'.

All of May was party time, with a tournament at which Henry and men were decked out in purple velvet, embroidered with golden roses. But behind the scenes there were, of course, stresses. Both the Tudor sisters were alarmingly short of money. Mary Tudor and her husband, Charles Brandon, had already worked out that the only way to cope with expectations of the state a dowager queen of France should keep in public was for Mary to live largely in private on their country estates. Pending some arrangement about the receipt of income from her Scottish lands, Margaret Tudor was dependent on her brother's goodwill. There were rumours that her life in Scotland was over forever: Giustinian heard that Henry was to find a pretext to have her marriage to Angus annulled and marry her to the emperor Maximilian.

In fact, Henry VIII was in negotiation with Albany and the Scottish authorities, and as a first stage in the bargain Margaret's wardrobe and jewels, at least, were returned to her, including pieces of crimson satin set with diamonds and of white taffeta sewn with pearls, gold collars, and a red silk hat set with a diamond given to her by the king of France. The Scottish lords even promised to retrieve from storage in Stirling the 'furrings' her late husband, James, had given her. They promised to help Margaret's own commissioners look into the matter of her rents . . . but somehow, no money arrived. By Christmas 1516 Margaret was writing that she had no money to give presents to the servants on New Year's Day, to the detriment of her brother's honour and her own.

Of the three queens in England, even Katherine of Aragon had her problems, despite the birth of her daughter. Katherine had long been suffering for the policy of her relatives on the continent, the English alienation from Ferdinand and Emperor Maximilian that had seen Henry marry his sister into France. The Spanish ambassador found that 'strange words' were said to him as he went through the town and complained he felt like a bull at whom everyone threw darts. Katherine herself had been horrified by her father's ruthless shifts of loyalty—or (so the Spanish ambassador hoped) found it prudent to pretend she was. 'The reason the queen is behaving so strangely is that her confessor, Friar Diego, has told her to act as though she has forgotten Spain and everything Spanish in order to win the English king's love and the love of the English. She has become so accustomed to doing this that she will not change'.

In due course, political necessity had brought Ferdinand and Henry VIII back into a somewhat edgy alliance, and Katherine of Aragon had once again found herself in the position of mediator, trying to explain the one to the other. But in January 1516, just weeks before Katherine gave birth to her daughter, Ferdinand had died, his life shortened by his recklessness in 'following more the counsel of his falconers than of his physicians'. By then, however, Katherine's political stance was perhaps becoming less important than it had once been.

King Henry had always looked for support in the daily business of politics, and now he found it in the portly shape of Thomas—or, as he had become in the autumn of 1515, Cardinal—Wolsey. Wolsey's rise had been meteoric, and he was now, in his early forties, reaching the position of power he would hold for more than a decade.

Born the son of a butcher, Wolsey had been ordained a priest after studying at Oxford and entered the service of Henry VII, who appointed him royal chaplain and then Dean of Lincoln. Henry VIII on his accession appointed him his almoner, but even that did not explain what lay so close ahead. His rise in the church was dazzlingly rapid—Dean of York, Bishop of Tournai (for his work in organising Henry's army there), Bishop of Lincoln in March 1514, and Archbishop of York that September. A year later he was made Cardinal and appointed Lord Chancellor four months after that. Just six years after Henry's accession, he had a pudgy finger in every international as well as domestic pie. And already it was clear that Wolsey's view of England's interests would not always accord with Katherine of Aragon's naturally pro-Spanish policy.

Wolsey, inevitably, had been prominent in the negotiations with the Scottish lords carried out on Margaret Tudor's behalf, hammering out the arrangement by which, just a year after she arrived at her brother's court, Margaret would return north. But first, there was a dramatic scene to play. The spring of 1517 saw what came to be known as Evil May Day, on which several hundred London apprentices, whipped up into a xenophobic frenzy by an irresponsible preacher, rioted through the streets, attacking members of London's foreign community.

The riots were quickly put down and more than a dozen of the rioters hung, drawn, and quartered, but there remained several hundred more in London's gaols. Popular pity was aroused by the fact that some of the 'poor younglings' were as young as thirteen. They were brought to trial on 7 May in Westminster Hall, bound, and haltered, expecting to have to face a dreadful fate. When Wolsey asked the king for mercy on them, Henry sternly refused (as no doubt it had been agreed he would do), and then Katherine of Aragon, with both her Tudor sisters-in-law, dramatically made the same plea. Three queens on their knees before him. . . . As Henry agreed, and the tearful prisoners were set free, it was a scene straight from the pages of chivalry. An intercessory function, of course, had been traditional for queens—from the biblical Esther and Bathsheba to the Virgin Mary.

A WEEK OR SO LATER, Margaret Tudor left the city, propelled in part by her brother's reluctance to maintain her forever and partly by her own optimistic conviction that she could get back in Scotland all the power she had lost. Her hopes were the higher for the fact that, almost as she reached the Scottish border, her nemesis, Albany, was sailing back to France to visit his wife there. Before he left he had agreed with Henry VIII and Wolsey that (for the next few months, at least) Margaret would have Stirling Castle and free access to her son. Greeted at the border by her husband, Angus, and the nobleman who was carrying out Albany's duties, she must have felt optimistic about her return.

The first check came when she went, immediately, to Edinburgh Castle to find the son she had not seen for almost two years. She was denied entrance and told her son had been taken to Craigmillar because there was plague in the city. It was clear, as she finally got a limited measure of access, that some of the lords feared she might try to snatch him back to England.

But Albany was far from eager to speed back to the taxing responsibilities of Scotland. He wrote to Margaret, suggesting the lords might allow her to resume the regency. But Margaret's idea was that her husband should rule with her as coregent, and this the lords absolutely refused. She had once again been given the chance of a measure of power—and, once again, her foolish decision threw it away.

And the lords, after all, knew more than she did. While Margaret was in England, her husband, Angus, had been living with the lady to whom he had formerly been betrothed, Lady Janet Stewart, and he had been doing so on the rents from Margaret's lands—Methven and Ettrick Forest. Nor was he prepared to refund the revenues he had seized, and much of Margaret's energy over the next few years would be devoted to trying to reclaim them.

Just three months after she had arrived back in Scotland, she was writing to Henry, begging to return to England and separate from Angus.

Henry's response was to send north a friar to impress on her the importance of marriage.* The Scots lords themselves agreed with English observers that she was being badly treated, with 'no promise kept to her', as Henry's representative Lord Dacre reported. But if, as she complained, they gave her 'nothing but fair words', the same was true of her brother. Since England's best ally in Scotland was likely to be Angus's Douglas clan, Henry was determined that Margaret should remain his wife.

One moment Margaret seems to be moved more by Angus's iniquities in taking her revenues from Ettrick Forest than by his keeping a mistress. But to complain of that, after all, might meet with scant sympathy, since Katherine of Aragon was by now having to put up with her husband's relationship with one Elizabeth Blount. The revenues were a more concrete grievance.

The feuding of Margaret Tudor and her husband had vital political consequences, the more so since Albany showed no signs of coming back to Scotland, telling the Clarencieux Herald that he wished he had broken both his legs before ever he set foot in the country. In England Henry and Katherine were both horrified to hear that Margaret now sought a formal separation from Angus, which he opposed, preferring to claim a husband's right to her income.

The following autumn Margaret would be writing to her brother that she and Angus had not been together 'this half year' and that she had been forced to pawn her jewels and silver. 'I am so minded that, an [if] I may by law of God and to my honour, to part with him, for I wit well he loves me not, as he shows me daily'. Her son was kept apart from her; she was personally humiliated and living in poverty. The years ahead would show a Margaret Tudor dreaming always of regaining a measure of power, but coupling acts of energy and inventiveness with those of utter folly.

---

* This may seem ironic, considering Henry's future history.

12

'INESTIMABLE AND PRAISEWORTHY SERVICES'

The Netherlands and France, 1516–1519

In the Netherlands another Margaret, Margaret of Austria, was managing her return to power more skilfully. A series of events would mean that—whether or not she wanted—she was never going to be left long in quietude, and the first of them had come quickly.

In January 1516 Ferdinand of Aragon had died, and his grandson Charles added Ferdinand's territories to the Castile of which (in his mother Juana's enduring incarceration) he was de facto ruler. As ruler also of the Netherlands, he was faced with the task of trying to govern two separate realms, on opposite ends of the continental landmass.

It was imperative that Charles should visit Spain, and quickly, since the Spanish Cortes showed signs of resisting a ruler they had never seen and who did not speak a word of their language. To do so safely, he needed to leave the Netherlands not only at peace with their neighbours, both France and England, but in experienced hands. Maximilian, for one, had no doubt whose hands those should be, writing to Charles of the virtues of his 'so good and virtuous aunt' and writing that Charles, Margaret, and Maximilian himself were literally as one [*une mêsme chose correspondant à ung mêsme désir et affection*]. Another trinity, in effect—if not in the passion of emotion the French one shared, then at least in practicality.

In February 1517 Maximilian came to the Netherlands in person to effect a complete reconciliation of aunt and nephew and to discuss the future, since to the huge lands Charles already ruled, more might yet be added on Maximilian's death, not only his own hereditary Austrian lands, but the Holy Roman Empire of which François and Louise also dreamed. When Charles set out in 1517, he left a turbulent Netherlands (northern parts of which were in revolt against Habsburg rule) in the hands of a regency council, nominally led by Maximilian himself. But one seat on it was assigned to Margaret, moving back toward power by slow degrees.

Early in 1518 two members of the Netherlands council who had been Margaret's strong opponents both died; in July, from Saragossa, Charles granted his 'very dear Lady and Aunt' the right to sign 'all letters, acts, and documents with her own hand, which are issued for us', declaring that she 'alone' should 'provide and dispose of the appointments of this our country'. This was still not quite a full regency, but Maximilian had every reason to write to Margaret in December of his hopes that 'as your good nephew he [Charles] will increase your said authority more and more'.

But the steady accretion of territories and dignities to Charles and his Habsburg family led to a shifting in European diplomacy. Through the years ahead François I and Charles would be the great rivals, but this left England a delicate but often rewarding diplomatic game to play, adjusting the balance between the pair. In 1518, however—with the Habsburgs temporarily at peace with France—the most urgent job on England's international calendar was to improve relations between England and England's ancient enemy.

So in October 1518 there was once again an Anglo-French betrothal to be celebrated, as there had been four years before. This time the Princess Mary who was to be allied to France was not Henry VIII's sister, but his and Katherine's two-year-old daughter, who would be contracted to François I's son and heir, the seven-month-old French Dauphin. Just as Margaret of Austria, four years before, had felt betrayed when her nephew's English alliance was replaced with a French betrothal, so Katherine of Aragon too can only have been dismayed when her only daughter was promised to the old enemy of her natal country. But as Henry's wife and England's queen, her task was to put a good face on things, and she did it nobly.

In the Queen's Great Chamber at Greenwich, on 5 October, Katherine was asked, as protocol required, whether she approved this match for the toddler Mary, seated in front of her. 'With great pleasure we give our royal word', she said doughtily. Perhaps she found comfort in reflecting that any actual marriage would not take place for many years and that slips between cup and lip were a virtual certainty.

But the French representatives—led by none other than the same Bonnivet who featured in Marguerite of Navarre's writings—were received with great honour. Wolsey, two days before the official ceremony, had entertained them at York House, to a 'most sumptuous supper, the like of which,

I fancy, was never given by Cleopatra or Caligula', wrote Venetian envoy Giustinian, 'the whole banqueting hall being so decorated with huge vases of gold and silver that I fancied myself in the tower of Croesus'. George Cavendish, Wolsey's gentleman usher and biographer, noted that the aim was 'to make the French such triumphant cheer that they might not only wonder at it here, but make a glorious report in their country'. As twelve masked gentlemen and twelve masked ladies began to dance after the feast, they were revealed as Henry and his sister Mary, a neat allegory since this was also the king of England partnering the dowager queen of France. Katherine of Aragon, with the excuse of another visible pregnancy, had gone to bed early.

A meeting was to be arranged between the kings of England and France for 1519. (It would be postponed until 1520.) But meanwhile, Katherine had high hopes, as even the Venetian ambassador wrote, 'God grant she may give birth to a son'. She and Henry had spent the summer balancing the differing demands of her health: to stay away from London while the sweating sickness was there, yet during (as Henry wrote) 'her dangerous times' to move her as little as possible. Alas, the high hopes were not to be. In November 1518 Katherine was delivered of a daughter, one who was either stillborn or lived only very briefly.

Katherine of Aragon's distress was the greater for another eventuality. In the summer of 1519, Henry VIII at last got his healthy boy. But the mother of his son was not Katherine but his mistress Elizabeth ('Bessie') Blount. The king acknowledged the boy and named him Henry Fitzroy. It was proof—if any were needed, in a century that assumed the woman's 'fault'—that it was not the king but the queen who could not produce a boy. But it also perhaps gave Henry an option other than the succession of his daughter, Mary, should the vexations of gender prove more worrying than those of illegitimacy.

MEANWHILE, ON THE OTHER SIDE of the English Channel, in the great European power tussle and in another kind of succession struggle, a new factor had come into play.

The battle to become the next Holy Roman Emperor was no new thing. To avoid a prolonged interregnum, a certain amount of discreet campaigning for the next emperor went on before the death of the last. Another Habsburg to follow Maximilian was the likeliest candidate, but there was technically no reason to assume this was a done deal. Early in her son's reign, Louise of Savoy had been in touch with her kinsman the Elector of Bavaria, urging François's candidacy.

The question was a vital one. Charles feared incursions into his own hereditary German states, and even into the Netherlands, if François I won the imperial crown. More pressingly yet, François wrote that 'seeing the greatness of the kingdoms and lordships he [Charles] possesses, he might, in time, do me inestimable harm'. If Charles gained control of Germany, as well as Spain, Austria, and the Netherlands, France would be almost completely surrounded on every landward side.

And the race was about to get off the starting block. On 12 January 1519 the emperor Maximilian fell ill and died, ordering his attendants not to shed tears over so natural and inevitable an event and desiring to be buried next to Mary of Burgundy. His daughter Margaret's personal grief was expressed, as so often in her life, by a long poem. Maximilian had been, she wrote, César, her only lord and father (*mon seul seigneur et père*). But Margaret was busy. The battle for Maximilian's title (and the attempt to influence the seven electors) suddenly gained heat and intensity.

Through the summer of 1518, Margaret of Austria had been engaged in a new campaign, this time with the Fugger banking family. Even Charles himself was shocked at how much his aunt was spending on his campaign, more than a million gold guilders, on top of the half million Maximilian in his lifetime had already thrown into his grandson's cause. (The merchants of Antwerp, prudently, were forbidden at the same time to loan money to any foreign power.) Charles had, as Margaret allegorically put it, 'written to us that the horse on which he wishes to come and see us is very dear. We know well that it is dear; but as matters stand, if he does not wish to have it, there is a buyer ready to take it, and since he has broken it in, it seems a pity he should give it up, whatever it costs him'.

François I (claiming he was motivated not by personal ambition but by a desire to lead Christendom against the Turks) was also openly determined to gain the imperial crown *soit par amour, soit par argent, soit par force* (by love, by money, or by force). Troops had to be recruited and border towns reinforced, and one of Margaret's own ambassadors said that the baseness of the intrigues made the very bribers blush for shame. To counter France's attempts to do the same thing by *amour*, or sheer popularity, Margaret exchanged letters with the electors, distributed presents among their relatives and their staffs, and sent out her secretary Marnix with promises and warnings. The imperial contest cast its shadow over everything in these months—even the response of the religious establishment to a new cloud on the horizon.

The day 31 October 1517 was celebrated afterward as 'Reformation Day', the day on which German monk Martin Luther reputedly nailed a copy of his ninety-five theses, or points for disputation, to the church door in Wittenberg. Whether that is literally true, his rebuke to the church practice of indulgences gave voice to a widespread chorus of complaint.*

But at this point, Luther's own beliefs were considerably less radical than those that would later come to define 'reform'. He appeared, for example, still to believe in Purgatory, to accept that good works and penance could contribute to man's salvation, and the first reaction of the Vatican was to instruct the German Augustinian order, to which Luther belonged, to sort out among themselves this routine and not unreasonable call for reform.

In general terms, the papacy—with the Turkish threat looming in the East of Europe—already had plenty on its plate. Specifically, the pope's remonstrances to Luther were softened by his need not to antagonise Luther's protector, Frederick 'the Wise' of Saxony. The very month of the imperial election, June 1519, would prove to be the one in which Luther arrived at the University of Leipzig for the public debate that saw him pushed in a position that set him at odds with the whole Western church. But at the time, the imperial election seemed the more exciting contest.

It was, to say the least, unconvincing when François declared that there was no personal conflict between himself and Charles, that the imperial crown was a mistress for whom they were both contesting, and they could rival one another for her hand in all friendliness and chivalry. But there is an intriguing suggestion that the positions of the women—Margaret of Austria and Louise of Savoy—were less entrenched than those of the men for whom they campaigned. Both were painfully aware of the costs of the election.

François's friend Fleuranges reports an encounter between an ally of Louise's and the Spanish ambassador Naturelli, discussing the possibility of finding a third-party candidate acceptable to both sides, one who, as the Spanish ambassador put it, 'would not be profitable to one or the other but to the whole of Christendom and the unity of Germany'. Perhaps that was a quixotic thought, but both women seem to have hailed with interest the idea of their young men ceasing to lock horns, feeling that an understanding was better than an overwhelmingly costly victory. Naturelli wrote to Margaret of Austria, 'I put before Madame [Louise] all the arguments which

* Stripped of its rhetoric, the belief was that an indulgence gave the Christian the right to purchase—literally purchase, for money—the reduction of the time a soul would spend in Purgatory. The cost of the new building of St Peter's Basilica in Rome was the cue for a bull proclaiming the issue of a new indulgence in 1515. Eventually, the issue of indulgences would itself prove the doorway into a dispute about the very existence of Purgatory.

you wrote to me'. But it was of no avail. Even Henry VIII entered the lists, though he would get, in the end, not one vote, humiliatingly.

François's campaign was in the hands of his old crony Bonnivet, who ran the gamut of electioneering antics. When the election began at Frankfurt in June, he even donned disguise to try to smuggle himself in, since while the election was on, foreigners were banned from the city. His campaign was conspicuous for its lack of success, however: the pope (whose hands alone could ultimately crown an emperor) had originally promised to support François, but changed his mind. Charles was elected unanimously as 'Charles V', thanks less, perhaps, to his stronger family roots in the area than to the fact that, begged by the electors to protect them against France, he had a huge army of mercenaries surrounding the city.

Louise of Savoy recorded the event in her journal with stoicism, referring to the will of Christ. But she knew France was now dangerously close to being encircled by Habsburg territory, while the campaign had cost a fortune to both sides.

In October the Venetian Giustinian was reporting home that both Louise of Savoy and her son 'were more unpopular all over France than words could express'. Louise 'is supposed to have invested much capital throughout the country, and is intent on hoarding, for the purpose, it is said, of aiding the King in the event of any sudden need'. Bonnivet (possibly suffering from syphilis) wisely took himself for a cure before reappearing at the French court. His standing as one of François's cronies, as well as leading negotiator and fixer, was too well established for him to be permanently damaged. But it was the end of François's first heyday.

In the Netherlands, Margaret of Austria ordered bonfires, feasts, and prayers to celebrate the fact that, 'inspired by the Holy Ghost', the electors had chosen her nephew. Unanimously! As for that nephew himself, he gave credit where credit was due. On 1 July, in Barcelona, in view of her 'great, inestimable and praiseworthy services', he signed letters naming his 'very dear lady and aunt' as regent and governess of the Low Countries, to be obeyed as he would be himself. The world would see that Margaret of Austria had won.

There was, however, another great international competition in store.

13

THE FIELD OF CLOTH OF GOLD

CALAIS, 1520

✳

What was the 'Field of Cloth of Gold'? A celebration of Anglo-French amity (the official theory)? A chance for two of the young titans of Europe to compete face-to-face under an unconvincing mask of friendship? François I sought to ensure English neutrality in any war between himself and Charles V; Henry VIII was enjoying being courted by both sides. . . . All of the above, perhaps. But one thing is for sure: it was the party of the century—which meant that the ladies had a role to play.

Henry would come to his proposed meeting with the French king accompanied by his wife, Katherine of Aragon, and by his sister Mary Tudor, the former queen of France. François would bring his wife, Claude, of course, but also his mother, Louise of Savoy, and his sister Marguerite. It is a safe supposition, too, that Anne Boleyn was present. Not only were linguists at a premium, but her parents were certainly there, as was her sister and perhaps her brother, George.

It's no surprise that the Boleyns were present in force. So was anybody who was anybody. The English train comprised almost six thousand people and more than three thousand horses, and though no comparable figures survive for the French party, every effort was made to ensure that the two kings and the two countries kept equal status in every way.

Katherine of Aragon's preparations started early. She was under pressure to make an impressive display. Henry's ambassador in France wrote anxiously to him that Queen Claude, 'with the King's mother, make all the search possible to bring at the assembly the fairest ladies and demoiselles that may be found. . . . I hope at the least, Sir, that the Queen's Grace shall bring such in her band, that the visage of England, which hath always had the praise, shall not at this time lose the same'. (How did that go down with

Spanish Katherine, who despite her 'very beautiful complexion' was dubbed 'not handsome' in the cold, clear eyes of European diplomacy?)

But Katherine of Aragon had also been working in another way: working with her nephew and her former sister-in-law Margaret of Austria to provide a framework for the Field of Cloth of Gold that would present Henry with a very different European possibility—an alliance with the new emperor Charles instead of with France. As the Venetian ambassador noted, she had already 'as a Spaniard' been gratified by her nephew's success in the imperial election.

The French king's mother was all too aware of Katherine's influence. Henry and François had made a pact, months earlier, not to shave their beards before they met. Henry broke the pact 'by the queen's desire', Thomas Boleyn assured Louise of Savoy, perhaps only meaning to suggest that this was not serious; the queen had, after all, made Henry 'great instance' about getting rid of his beard on various occasions before. But Louise of Savoy took it differently. 'Is not the queen's grace aunt to the king of Spain [Charles]?', Louise pointedly asked Thomas Boleyn. She seemed to accept Boleyn's reassurances, affirming politely that 'their love is not in the beards, but in the hearts'.

But later she was asking another English ambassador whether Katherine of Aragon had 'any great devotion to the assembly', the Field of Cloth of Gold. The ambassador could only reply, lamely, that Katherine had 'none other joy and comfort in this world' than to promote anything at all that might stand with her husband's pleasure.

In fact, reports said Katherine of Aragon was making no secret of her disapproval of the planned meeting and finding a receptive audience for her complaints among the traditionally Francophobe English. 'There is no doubt that the French interview is against the will of the queen and of all the nobles', Charles was told. It was, however, dear to the heart of Wolsey, now (in the words of one Italian observer) 'the man who rules both the king and the entire kingdom'. But in a sense, the international situation played into Katherine's hands. Henry's position as the counterbalance between France and the Holy Roman Empire, the man who could make the shape of Europe, was too good not to enjoy.

As Charles V expressed a burning desire to meet his 'uncle' Henry (and his aunt Katherine), Charles's other aunt, Margaret of Austria, arranged a high-powered delegation to England, including several of her own closest men, who arrived at the start of April, pointing out that Henry could be the first European monarch with whom Charles would meet since his elevation to the imperial role. It was in Katherine of Aragon's room that, in a meeting with Henry and Wolsey, England decided to agree. Henry's anxious assurances to his wife suggest the strength of Katherine's part in the decision.

Shortly afterward, Henry VIII's ambassador in France was asking that the meeting with François I be delayed for a week. François refused, saying Henry should be at Calais no later than 4 June, on the reasonable plea that his wife, Claude, would be in the seventh month of her fifth pregnancy. But the meeting with Charles did almost fall through on the grounds of time, as his journey from Spain to England was delayed by contrary winds. As Charles wrote to Katherine from Coruna, 'We have been told of the effort and will that you have put into arranging these meetings. But as the sea is so changeable that men cannot always do what they want . . . we beg you, if there is some delay, that, as you have already done, you try to make our brother and uncle, the king of England, wait for as long as is possible'.

Charles V finally arrived on English shores on 26 May—the day after Henry and Katherine arrived in Canterbury on their way to the south coast, the day on which they should have sailed the other way. But, galloping to Dover Castle to greet his guest, Henry kept his whole mighty cavalcade waiting four more days. Charles was greeted by the archbishop in Canterbury Cathedral, then taken to the archbishop's palace next door, where a tense Katherine was waiting, royally dressed. She broke into tears after she embraced him: the representative of her family. His huge retinue—including two hundred ladies, dressed in the Spanish fashion, an evocative sight for Katherine of Aragon—was entertained for three days in Canterbury, three days of banqueting, dancing, and games of courtly love in which the Spanish noblemen excelled. (One went so far as to swoon at one lady's beauty and require to be carried out of the room by his hands and feet.) As the two trains, English and Spanish, left Canterbury for the south coast, the meeting had been a rehearsal of what lay ahead at the other, the Anglo-French, party.

Katherine and Henry set sail from Dover on 31 May and after a few brief hours' crossing landed at Calais. The encounter was to take place on the plain, the Val d'Or, between the English citadel of Guisnes and the French town of Ardres, so that each king could sleep in his own territory. Four days later they set off for Guisnes. The first meeting of the two kings was scheduled for 7 June, the Feast of Corpus Christi.

It was an extraordinary sight that greeted their eyes and one that had been months in the preparation. England had sent more than six thousand workmen, two thousand of them to work on Henry's temporary palace, a *trompe l'oeil* fantasia whose solid foundations and dazzling array of newfangled glass windows were topped off by canvas painted to look like brick. It was a combination of utter luxury and practicality. Or parsimony: as one observer noted, the whole thing could be dismantled and taken home again for reuse with no more than the cost of transportation. But there were statues of Cupid and of Bacchus, from which flowed claret cup and malmsey, or red and white wine, and silver cups stood around for the drinking. (None were stolen, it was remarked by contemporaries.)

Suites of tents—blue and gold, or gold and scarlet, topped with heraldic beasts—were linked by curtained passageways to resemble the layout of a palace. Like the rooms of a permanent palace, they were scented with flowers and furnished with tapestry, while the royal chapel was stuffed with holy relics. Katherine's oratory had in the centre a large shield bearing the arms of England and, provocative under the circumstances, maybe, of Spain.

There were other tents, some three hundred of them, striped in the Tudor colours of green and white for the kitchens and dormitories, painted or embroidered for the courtiers. Not that accommodation could be provided for everybody; even some 'knights and ladies' were forced to sleep outdoors in the hay.

The French party approached the accommodation problem differently. In Ardres work was done on the king's lodging, which was attached, by a gallery of clipped box plants, to a large banqueting pavilion, whose ceiling was made to look like the night sky. But they too also brought in master tent makers to erect fabulous creations in the field itself of stout canvas that was then covered in more luxurious fabrics, silk, velvet, and damask, in blue, violet, and crimson, with the royal livery colours of tawny, white, and black. Claude's pavilion and Louise of Savoy's were dressed with *toile d'or* and *toile d'argent*, with *fleur-de-lis* in gold thread strewn onto, respectively, violet and crimson satin, alongside the two women's own heraldic emblems, though unseasonable weather blew down many of the French tents.

In between the two camps a nine-hundred-foot tournament ground boasted an artificial tree of honour, decorated with hundreds of silk or satin flowers representing English hawthorn and French raspberry, on which the challengers could hang their emblazoned shields. But women could not play a major part in the chivalric encounters that were the first order of the day.

The two kings did not compete against each other, or not officially. There was an impromptu bout of wrestling that saw François throw Henry. (He would seize another such advantage of surprise when, disregarding the protocol that surrounded their normal meeting, he showed up in Henry's bedroom one morning, insisting that he himself would be the English king's valet.) Henry's brother-in-law Charles Brandon did not distinguish himself in the joust, having hurt his hand, but Bonnivet was one of the chief organisers of the French side.

The ladies would have their ceremonial part in the tourney. The two queens met on 11 June in a royal pavilion where they could receive the homage of the knights. Queen Claude came dressed in cloth of silver over an underskirt of cloth of gold and riding in her coronation litter made to match. She was followed by her ladies in three coaches draped in silver, and the likelihood is that the ladies included Anne Boleyn. Louise of Savoy came in black velvet and was followed by 'an infinite number of ladies' in crimson velvet, with sleeves lined in cloth of gold. She was said to have purchased 'a whole emporium' of the dazzling stuff.

Katherine of Aragon too had been buying fabric for months; she, of course, had already had her nephew's entourage to dazzle, in cloth of gold lined with violet velvet, in black 'tilsent' sparkling silk, crimson tissue 'pirled' with gold, and 'rich cloth of gold tissue'. (Even her fifty-five footmen wore white satin and green velvet, with Spanish 'feathers of arrows' embroidered on their doublets; her seven henchmen wore orange boots, black velvet cloaks, coats of green and russet velvet, and doublets of yellow.) It was noted that Katherine herself wore a headdress in the 'Spanish fashion', with the hair hanging down over her shoulder. A point was being made here, silently.

But clothes wars apart, the women came into their own away from the tourney. Etiquette decreed that the two kings should be feasted not by each other but by each other's ladies. Henry and François ate together less formally on a handful of occasions, but at the great banquets, on 10, 17, and 24 June, two kings at one board might give rise to awkward questions of precedence, and nothing could be left to chance.

Surviving reports (from French, Venetian, and Mantuan observers) record the two kings leaving their lodgings at the same time, as announced by the firing of cannon. They encountered each other briefly on the tournament ground and passed on. François (on the tenth, the first occasion) was received by Katherine of Aragon in her huge chambers to dine on gold plate under a cloth of state and surrounded by tapestries. Beyond the royal party, a long hall had been divided into two, the one for 134 ladies to dine and the other for some 200 gentlemen.

Each of perhaps three courses consisted of fifty dishes—sweet and savoury together, topped off by a 'subtlety', an elaborate and often allegorical creation in marzipan or spun sugar. Account books record that in the course of their visit, the English camp consumed almost thirty thousand fish (in which they included a dolphin), more than six thousand birds, and almost a hundred thousand eggs. After the meal there was dancing in the main hall, led by the king's sister Mary Tudor partnering a French nobleman, after which François—who like Henry was an impassioned dancer—had a masquing dance performed 'in the Italian manner'.* Henry, for his part, was being entertained by the French in a hall decked with pink brocade, with twenty-four trumpeters playing as he waded his way through a solid four hours of food before the dancing.

On the second occasion, the seventeenth, Louise of Savoy came to join her son, François, while his sister, Marguerite, partnered Henry VIII. Both kings slipped out of the hall to don their costumes for the masque: François and his companions wearing long gowns with plumes and hoods to dance 'in the Ferrarese fashion'. Henry had brought three companies of masquers with him, with fake beards and gowns described as being in the Milanese style for himself and his fellows, black velvet doctors' costumes for another group of noblemen, while yet another group boasted purses and girdles of seal skin to dress as visitors from 'Ruseland or farre Estland'. Henry loved to dress up (at home no one was supposed to admit they recognised him), and by the sound of it, François did, too. For the third and last banquet, both royal parties wore masquing costumes from the start. Nine worthies headed the English party—soldierly heroes from Alexander to King Arthur—led by Hercules with a club covered in green damask and lion's pelt made from cloth of gold.

But the whole long international encounter was as choreographed as a masque. When the two queens met at an open-air mass in the tiltyard, they each tried to insist that the other have the first chance to kiss the Gospel but wound up embracing each other instead. Contemporaries recorded the precise ceremonial, how 'the English King dined with the French Queen and the Duchess of Alençon at Ardres . . . kneeling with one knee on the ground, his bonnet in his hand, he first kissed the Queen, then Madame [Louise of Savoy], then the Duchess of Alençon [Marguerite of Navarre]'.

Even the gifts exchanged were carefully recorded: The English queen gave the French one several hobbies and palfreys with their appurtenances, presenting also a saddle and harness to Louise of Savoy. Claude gave

---

* This may mean that, in contrast to the usual practice for a formal masquing dance, men and women danced together.

Katherine of Aragon in return a litter of cloth of gold ('as well as mules and pages'). Louise of Savoy gave Wolsey a valuable jewelled crucifix, while he gave her a small cross of precious stones, with a piece of the True Cross inside it.

But behind the scenes, serious business was going on. At Guisnes, even before the kings began their joust, Wolsey had visited the French camp and arranged that he and Louise of Savoy should settle matters between England, France, and Scotland. One of the victors of these festivities was indeed Wolsey, honoured as the pope's own representative (in which capacity he could treat even François as an equal), talking to everybody. Marguerite of Navarre had begun to address him as father, while he described her as his daughter or goddaughter (*filleule d'alliance*). (Margaret of Austria would write to Wolsey as to her dear son.)

The two groups parted on 24 June, and the next day the English made their way back to Calais. Here Henry VIII waited until 10 July. François, too, stayed in the vicinity, for in that summer of 1520, the Field of Cloth of Gold was followed—as had been arranged back in May—by another meeting. Henry and Katherine of Aragon went on to the coastal town of Gravelines, on the border with the Netherlands, and there met Charles V and Margaret of Austria, who accompanied them back to Calais for a few days of more restrained festivities. (François made it known he was just a day's ride away and would come over to join in the debates without ceremony if asked. He wasn't; several of his gentlemen, however, made use of their English friends to gate-crash the parties.)

Margaret of Austria, in her brief Spanish marriage, had, of course, lived at close quarters with Katherine of Aragon. Now the two reaffirmed their girlhood bonds over a supper. Charles V showed his particular mettle: while Henry had been competitively on edge with François, and left far from sure he had gotten the best of the encounter, Charles offered him a modest air and a welcome flattery, stressing Henry's importance in keeping Europe's balance. While Wolsey was in pursuit of that 'universal peace' so long aspired to—a church-sponsored Anglo/imperial/French alliance against the infidel Turks who were menacing Europe's eastern borders—Charles wanted an alliance with England against France.

He didn't get it, or not immediately, but for all that, the Gravelines meeting, like the Field, might be considered to have gone off well. Perhaps it was a triumph for Wolsey's subtlety. He managed to seem to promise everything to everybody without technically breaking his word to anybody, for to the best of our knowledge (no exact record of the discussion survives), nothing agreed at Gravelines actually contradicted the Anglo-French agreement for a marriage between François's son the Dauphin and Henry's daughter Mary.

The mood at the French court as everyone returned home was positive, at least where François was concerned, with an allegorical book singling out the 'wise knowledge and divine way of achieving of Our Lady Concord'— Louise of Savoy. Louise herself had been putting a good face on things. The Venetian ambassador reported her telling foreign envoys that the French king and the English king had parted with tears in their eyes, that they planned to build a chapel to Our Lady of Friendship and a palace where they could meet every year.

But while spending the summer in the lovely settings of Blois and Amboise, Louise must have been more conscious than her son of the cost of the recent venture, may have been all too aware that the real winner of the summer had yet to be decided. François I or Charles V? In the end (just as had happened with the contest to become Holy Roman Emperor), it would not be the French party.

14

REPERCUSSIONS
The Netherlands and France, 1520–1521

✳

One of the winners, again, was Margaret of Austria. That autumn of 1520, she and her nephew Charles travelled from Gravelines to Maastricht, where he reappointed her his regent in the Netherlands. On 18 September he signed over to her, for life, the town and territory of Mechelen, with two hundred thousand gold florins. Together, aunt and nephew then moved on to Charles's German territories, where on 23 October, at Aix-la-Chapelle, he was crowned into the office to which he had been elected the previous year, that of 'King of the Romans' and Holy Roman Emperor-Elect.[*] The German princes swore fealty, and Charles V promised to uphold the rights of the empire (and those of the church) and was girded with Charlemagne's sword, while Charlemagne's crown was placed on his head.

Margaret of Austria had a prominent place in the cathedral, as well she deserved. She had even stripped her home at Mechelen of its tapestries and silver plate to make a good show at the coronation festivities, Fleuranges wrote in a description to Louise of Savoy.

In France, meanwhile, all the 'trinity' were at a loss. In the winter of 1520–1521, François had three accidents—a fall from a horse, a prank that ended in a fire, and a mock battle that got out of hand—and though none caused him any lasting injury, the last shave was close and made Louise palpitate over how easily she might have been wholly lost, *femme perdu*.

That was even before he went back to the Italian Wars. Power in Italy was still a huge bone of contention between France and the empire, the

---

[*] Traditionally, no prince was officially entitled to call himself Holy Roman Emperor until crowned by the pope, in Rome. But Charles's predecessor, Maximilian, had broken with this tradition, winning from the pope the right to call himself emperor-elected. Charles would eventually be crowned by the pope—the last holder of the title so to be—but not for another decade.

disputed territories of Milan and Naples, particularly. Now largely hemmed in by Charles's territories to the south, east, and north, François was alarmed by the way Charles's new imperial title also gave him an Italian foothold.

In the spring of 1521, France made several incursions into foreign territory; French aggression was followed by imperial retaliation, and it was clear that England—abandoning its position of neutrality—would be forced into the conflict. In August 1521 Cardinal Wolsey crossed the Channel to Calais to act as a mediator between Charles and François. The French sent him wine; Margaret of Austria (knowing his distaste for riding) sent him a red velvet litter, lined with green satin against which his cardinal's robes would stand out clearly. More important but less tangible, both sides had long been offering their voice to get him the papacy. But any talk of peace was unavailing. Instead, the cardinal moved on to Bruges for another round of diplomatic discussions with the emperor.

Ever pro-English, Margaret of Austria, *la bonne Angloise*, rushed to join them, supplementing the substantial presents of money made to the English suite with more domestic courtesies: a daily breakfast delivery of fresh rolls, sugar, and wine. She sent Wolsey candles to light his bedroom, while his musicians played at her parties, and the upshot was that England entered a covert alliance with Charles V. The alliance between Charles and Henry was to be cemented at a future date by *his* marriage to Henry's daughter Mary—disregarding the previous match made between Mary and the French Dauphin. Margaret of Austria was one of the two signatories on the emperor's behalf. She indeed had thrashed out the details with Wolsey. And in the summer of 1521, as Charles prepared for war with France, it was his aunt Margaret whose speech to the Netherlands' governing body raised him men and money.

THE WAR THAT DOMINATED THE next four years would be cripplingly expensive for both sides. But in France, there simply was no money. A visiting Englishman, William Fitzwilliam, wrote of how 'the King borrows of any man that hath any, and if any man refuse to lend he shall be so punished that all other shall take ensample from him. . . . They eat up all they have, to their shirts'. In this crisis both François and Louise of Savoy would turn to expedients that divided them from powerful nobles, and even, briefly, from each other.

It all tied in with the ageing Anne de Beaujeu. For all the noble girls to whom she had been mentor and surrogate mother, Anne had borne just one surviving child, a daughter, Suzanne (the addressee of Anne's *Enseignements*), who, however, herself died at the end of April 1521. This left her husband, Charles, the great Duc de Bourbon, a childless widower. Suzanne had been his kinswoman as well as wife, whose claim to the Bourbon inheritance had been united to his. But now the question was what he or his children by any second marriage could still inherit of the Bourbon lands. Charles de Bourbon came from the younger branch of the Bourbon family, Suzanne having been the last representative of the senior. Now Charles's claim might be challenged, since both Louise of Savoy and François I also had Bourbon blood in their veins through Louise's mother, while the king could reasonably claim that the terms under which the lands had been granted saw them revert to the crown on the failure of the male line.

It was perhaps just in an attempt to cut through the Gordian knot that Louise of Savoy now took an extraordinary step. She, who had always fought so hard against remarriage, sent an envoy to Bourbon, suggesting she should marry him. (That way, since she was past childbearing age, the lands should still ultimately revert to her son's crown.)

The proposal is recorded only in a seventeenth-century continuation of the chronicle originally written by Bourbon's secretary, so one can't know for sure whether Bourbon really called her 'the worst woman in the realm, the dread of all nations'. He would not marry her 'for the whole of Christendom', he added; Louise, when she heard, vowed that his words should cost him dearly. King Henry in England made a personal story out of it, telling Charles V's ambassador, 'There has been much discontent between the King Francis and the said Bourbon, since he has refused to marry Madame the Regent, who loves him very much'. More surely, Bourbon was already discontented, feeling he was not given his right place in the realm.

Trouble at home was matched by disaster abroad, in the ongoing Italian Wars. Six years earlier, the battle of Marignano had given France control of Milan, but in November 1521 the French lost the city again. To add another turn of the screw (reported one contemporary, Jean du Bellay), when the defeated general responsible for Milan's loss came to explain himself to the king, he protested furiously that the problem had been lack of money, which had lost him his mercenaries. François roared out that he had sent the money; the treasurer Semblancay answered that he had gotten the money ready to send but that it had been taken, in payment of a debt she claimed, by Louise of Savoy. It blew over, of course, but not before son had confronted mother in a scene unparalleled in their history.

IN THE NETHERLANDS, BY CONTRAST, Margaret of Austria was prepared to pawn her jewels to fund her nephew as, in the spring of 1522, he prepared to set out again toward his Spanish territories. There the 'Revolt of the Co-muneros' had seen Castilian rebels, rising up against Charles, a man they saw as a foreigner, attempt to make his incarcerated mother, Juana, once more the active head of state.* Margaret's hand is all over her nephew's policy of the first years of the 1520s, and her loyalty was not without its reward: Charles had informed the Estates-General that in his absence they would be governed by his aunt, 'who for so long has shown by her praiseworthy, memorable services and great experience, that she well knows how to honourably acquit herself of the said government and administration'. Charles also settled the question of Margaret's claim to the estates of her father, Maximilian, which she surrendered in return for 250,000 pounds, payable in ten yearly instalments.†

Margaret's task would not be easy. The Netherlands were rife with problems—financial, structural, and religious—as the years ahead would prove. Nonetheless, as a woman who sought her family's advance, and who welcomed authority, she was flying high. If there had been a contest between the mother of the French king and the aunt of the Habsburg ruler, then Margaret of Austria, and the Habsburgs, seemed again to have won.

That said, there was one cavil. The Habsburgs, even more immediately than the French monarchy, had to deal with an unexpected threat, the ramifications of which, though they can hardly have realised it, would come to dominate their century. In 1520 Martin Luther's questioning of the pope's authority had led to a papal bull, or edict, condemning him as a heretic. Luther had publicly burned the bull, along with volumes of canon law, but his very estrangement from the church had encouraged him to take his own thinking in more revolutionary directions.

Luther was moving toward the idea of justification by faith alone—that man's salvation lay purely in his faith, not in any good works he might do—though he still held aloof from the idea that the bread and wine celebrated at the Mass were merely representative of Christ's body and blood. These would be central tenets of the Reformed religion. At the same time, Luther's refutation of a papal authority imposed from distant Italy was already becoming identified with political discontent.

---

* Charles had always ruled nominally in conjunction with his mother and would continue to do so throughout her lifetime, while it appears to have been Juana herself who now elected not to join with the Comuneros in trying to overset her son.

† He had also settled his brother Ferdinand's position, by giving him control of Maximilian's hereditary Austrian lands and regency in Charles's absence of the German territories. This marked the start of the division of the house of Habsburg into two branches: the Spanish, of which Charles (and later Charles's son Philip) was the head, and the Austrian, soon to be aggrandized when Ferdinand's wife inherited Hungary and Bohemia.

In March 1521 Charles V offered Luther a formal hearing at the Diet (or Assembly) of Worms, a town on the Rhine. It led not to agreement but to the formalising of a position of opposition. 'Here I stand. I can do no other', Luther was reported to have said, while Charles, for his part, declared, 'My predecessors . . . left behind them the holy Catholic rites that I should live and die therein. . . . I have therefore resolved to stake upon this cause all my dominions, my friends, my body and my blood'.

Margaret of Austria had herself been one of the great ladies critical of the 'infinite abuses' in the Catholic Church and of the pope's attempts to exercise secular authority in her territories, had numbered humanists and moderate reformers among her friends, and had hosted Erasmus at her court. The Netherlands, the old Burgundy, had, after all, been the home of the *devotio moderna*, the more spiritual model of religion, particularly attractive to aristocratic ladies, to which Margaret's godmother, Margaret of York, had subscribed.

But after a papal legate arrived in Antwerp in the autumn of 1520, Margaret had to see men like Erasmus (and like some of her own aides) publicly attacked in sermons, to see books burned. The papal bull against Luther had been first published in the Netherlands. She issued the orders, which ended in 1523, with two reforming Augustine monks burned and their monastery razed to the ground: Martin Luther had been an Augustinian friar, and the monastery was believed to be a centre for the dissemination of his ideas.

'The heresies of Martin Luther', as Margaret wrote to the Prior of Brou, 'are a great scandal to our Holy Mother Church'. It seems likely that her first priority was and would remain to tamp down controversy insofar as was possible. But in a comparatively short space of time, it would be evident that Luther had opened Pandora's box, and he himself would be horrified at some of the beliefs and the new creeds flying out.

In France Marguerite of Navarre had long been interested in the reform, with a small *r*, of the Catholic Church. So, even, was her mother, Louise of Savoy, to a degree, as had been Anne of Brittany and her daughters, Queen Claude and Renée, while Marguerite's brother, François, was at this point interested in anything that kept him one step ahead of the papacy. (Pope Leo had already sided with Charles and would in 1522 be succeeded by Pope Adrian, a prelate who had actually been Charles V's tutor.) Lutheranism was never an option, but for a brief period early in the 1520s, Marguerite's way would be the goal of all the trinity: reforming the church from the inside, orienting it more toward the Bible, toward trained preachers, toward less emphasis on ritual, on worship by rote.

But as the 1520s got under way, Marguerite was coming up to a time of personal crisis. Her life since her brother's accession had seen her juggle the great ceremonies of court life with more personal and spiritual concerns.

A visit of the king and queen to her house in 1517 had been followed by a grant, the rich duchy of Berry, that not only made her financially independent of her husband but also (most unusually for a female, rather than a male, relative of the king) gave her the status of a *prince capetien* and the right to sit on her brother's councils. The wording of the lengthy grant explicitly spells out that this was to be territory under Marguerite's own governance, save only for a feudal allegiance to France, and there was no mention of her husband anywhere in the document.

The return visit for the betrothal of the baby Dauphin to Henry VIII's daughter Mary, at the end of 1518, saw Marguerite seated beside François in the courtyard of the Bastille, on a dais covered in cloth of gold, under a bower of flowers and greenery. A canopy of blue, spangled with stars and hung with gold balls, made the courtyard into a roofed room, while Louise of Savoy and Queen Claude sat in one of the galleries. While the king appeared with his man masquers in a white satin robe embroidered in gold, the ladies handed around sweetmeats. In the spring of 1519, Marguerite took a sponsor's role in the christening of what would prove an important boy, a second son for her brother, King François, named Henri. Holding him at the font with Marguerite, representing his master for whom the child was named, was England's new ambassador to France, Thomas Boleyn, whose daughter Anne would have been present (though unnoticed or at least unrecorded) at the engagement festivities.

But when Marguerite set about reforming the local convent of Almenesches, winning over the pope to her own choice of new abbess, she took care to have a small lodging built for herself within the convent grounds.

In the early years of her brother's reign, Marguerite visited Lyons with the royal party, and it is in the notably reformist Lyons, in the church of Saint-Jean, that she sites the story in novella seventy-two of her *Heptaméron*. In this story, the duchess of Alençon ('who later became queen of Navarre', as did Marguerite herself) overhears the sobs of another worshipper, a pregnant nun, who had been seduced by a monk. In the story, the duchess promises to take up the nun's cause and institute reforms, very much of the kind Marguerite was making in real life.

It is possible that in the autumn of 1519, Bonnivet launched another sexual assault upon Marguerite, though once again the suggestions are almost wholly literary. That autumn François, accompanied by his mother, sister, and a group of nobles, including both Marguerite's husband and Bonnivet, set off on a leisurely progress toward Cognac. They stopped at the king's new building project of Chambord, at Châtelherault, and, in January 1520, at Bonnivet's new Italian-style creation of Neuville-aux-Bois. The royal party left after just four days, leaving Bonnivet behind.

In novella four of the *Heptameron*, the heroine is in bed and presumably undressed when, 'without further ado, he jumped into bed beside her'. Her first thought is to denounce her attacker and demand that her brother order his head struck off. But the heroine's lady-in-waiting (whom the Seigneur Brantôme's writings identified as Madame de Chatillon, Marguerite's former governess) warns that everyone would say 'this poor gentleman . . . could not have attempted it without great encouragement. Everyone will say it hasn't been without fault on your side'. Madame warns the heroine to be more careful in the future, since 'many women who have led lives more austere than yours have been humiliated by men less worthy of love than he'.

It seems as if, around this point in her life, Marguerite of Navarre did suffer some sort of emotional trauma. In the early summer of 1521, Marguerite penned an extraordinary letter, the first of many, to Guillaume Briçonnet, the reforming Bishop of Meaux, a man at war with medieval superstition but at home with the mysticism to which Marguerite was drawn. (Meaux would become the centre for a group of progressive clergy, several of them connected with Marguerite and all eventually to come under attack by the Catholic Church, from which, however, none had at this stage any thought of splitting.) 'I must deal with countless matters that cause me to be afraid, and thus ask that you take up my cause and bring me spiritual succor', Marguerite wrote.

Some of the things she wrote were in tune with the new tenets of religion: 'Knowing that there is need of only one thing, I turn to you, entreating you to make yourself the means of reaching him [God] through prayer'. Some were more personal: in her second letter to Briçonnet, she wrote that she felt 'very much alone'. . . . 'Take pity on me. . . . I beg you at least to visit me in writing and stir up the love of God in my heart'. Her repeated insistence that she was 'unworthy', 'useless', 'worse than dead' must be seen in the context of reformist theology, which indeed believed humans were unworthy without God's grace. Nonetheless, it is hard not to read into her letters something more when Marguerite begs Briçonnet to help kindle her 'poor heart covered with ice and dead from cold', when Briçonnet a few years later congratulates her on having obeyed his rule 'of telling everything without fear'.

She wrote frequently of her 'sterility'—thirteen years of marriage, and, at thirty, she had not yet borne a child. In 1522 she believed she was pregnant but found herself mistaken. She was having also to nurse Louise of Savoy, who was suffering increasingly serious bouts of gout. Briçonnet, twenty years older than she, nonetheless offered himself as her adoptive son, and both took seriously the relationship (to sixteenth-century eyes a genuine one, made *par alliance*), Marguerite signing herself as 'your sterile mother'.

Briçonnet, however, had from the first other concerns: that Marguerite should recruit her mother and brother also to her spiritual quest, so that 'from you three will come forth as an example of life, a fire to burn and illumine the rest of the kingdom'. When she failed to do so fast enough, he reproached her: 'You have not taken your gloves off. I do not yet see any flames issuing from your hands'. In fact, by the end of 1522, the attempts made by Briçonnet's deputy Michel d'Arande to instruct Louise of Savoy were causing the king's confessor to complain to the theologians at the university, and this was the first red danger sign of troubles ahead.

ANNE DE BEAUJEU, THE LAST of her generation, died on 14 November 1522, just five weeks after François had settled the larger part of the disputed Bourbon lands on his mother, Louise. Anne's reaction was to bequeath her son-in-law, Charles, Duc de Bourbon, her own personal properties, in recompense for the 'good, great, praiseworthy and recommendable services and pleasures' he had given to her and her late daughter, Suzanne. Bourbon had now a daring, even treasonous, scheme: to marry Charles V's sister Eleanor and thus ally himself with François's enemy.

Such dissent in the French ranks was the more serious for the fact that in the summer of 1522, England had fulfilled the promise made earlier to Charles V—the fruit of all that eager diplomacy—and played their part in keeping the balance of power in Europe by declaring war on France. There had been a hint of the future storms back at the beginning of the year, when King François tackled Cardinal Wolsey on what might seem a trivial matter. The family of one of his wife's maids, young Anne Boleyn, had decided she should come home. What? Did they feel that France was no longer safe for Englishwomen?

Wolsey attempted to reassure the French king—it was no such matter, he said. Merely, a marriage had been arranged between Anne and her kinsman James Butler, the Irish Earl of Ormonde. But, of course, Anne Boleyn's future would not pan out that way.

PART III
1522–1536

Nor should you be melancholy or discomfited if you find yourself in some foreign or unpleasant alliance, but praise God and believe that He is always just and never does anything but what is reasonable. Therefore, my daughter, if it is so ordained and it happens that you have much to suffer, have complete patience, finding in whatever awaits you the will and pleasure of the Creator. . . . [I]f you want to live with peace of mind, protect yourself from stumbling into the snares of jealousy.

—ANNE OF FRANCE (ANNE DE BEAUJEU),
LESSONS FOR MY DAUGHTER (1517–1521)

15

'WILD FOR TO HOLD'

ENGLAND AND SCOTLAND, 1522–1524

✳

S pring 1522 in London, and at Cardinal Wolsey's palace of York Place, the pre-Lent festivities were celebrated with more than the usual splendour. The pageant might have come from the old Burgundian court: an assault on the *Château Vert*, the Green Castle or Castle of 'Vert'ue'. The castle was made of wood and green tinfoil, sturdy enough for its towers to support eight ladies dressed in white satin, each representing a virtue, and with her character or 'reason' picked out in yellow. The knights, led by King Henry VIII himself, and their spokesman, Ardent Desire, were dressed in cloth of gold and blue satin and were warded off, for a judicious interval, with a barrage of sweetmeats and rose water.

In the end, of course, the masculine attackers prevailed—the colder female virtues warmed by masculine ardour—and everyone danced, happily. But no one, for a few years yet, could guess how telling the pageant would prove to be. The lady representing Perseverance, newly come home from France, was Anne Boleyn.

The Anne Boleyn who appeared at the English court in 1522 would have been a very finished product—not beautiful, perhaps, but surely compelling: sophisticated, and with the all-important gloss of difference. Later reports show her as 'very eloquent and gracious, and reasonably good-looking'. Not one of the handsomest women in the world—as a Venetian diplomat would put it, when the time came that ambassadors took note of Anne Boleyn—'of middling stature, swarthy complexion, long neck, wide mouth, a bosom not much raised and eyes which are black and beautiful'.

But her years abroad had given her wide experience in the ways of a court. Indeed, if as seems likely, she had been called on to act as an Anglo-French interpreter, she may have gained not only experience of the queen's, the women's, rooms, but also an unusually direct appreciation of political dealings, the more so for the fact that her father had for a time also been attached to the French court.

Anne Boleyn's very Frenchness would have been a novelty to the English courtiers. It's hard now to realise, after centuries during which French has been the *lingua franca* of diplomatic and social circles, that it was not so in the early sixteenth century. Latin was the universal language, and when Wolsey went on a diplomatic mission to France, most of the nobles accompanying him did not speak the language. (He instructed them just to speak in English—very loudly, presumably, like a tourist on the Costa del Sol today.)

As writer, cleric, and diplomat Lancelot de Carles described Anne, 'No one would ever have taken her to be English, by her manners, but a native-born Frenchwoman'. By contrast, Katherine of Aragon was now thirty-six, not young by the standards of the day. Repeated pregnancies had taken their toll, and the ever-watchful ambassadors had for some time resorted to praising the beauty of her complexion rather than her figure. The five years' seniority to her husband was beginning to show.

As far back as 1514, there had been a rumour going the rounds of Europe that Henry VIII 'meant to repudiate his present wife . . . because he is unable to have children by her'—premature at the time, but seeming less so with every year that went by. It was probably in 1522 that Henry took as his mistress Mary Boleyn—Anne's sister—who all too appropriately represented Kindness in the York Place pageant. But whatever personal distress it may have caused Katherine of Aragon, assuming she knew, this was not a relationship to threaten her position as queen. Indeed, Henry was still at this point, publicly at least, very much the married man, moralising over the comportment of his sister Margaret Tudor in Scotland.

WE LAST ENCOUNTERED MARGARET ON her return to Scotland some five years before, complaining bitterly (in an anachronistic but very Tudor fashion) that her husband, Angus, no longer loved her. Henry VIII and his wife, Katherine, had been horrified, urging on Margaret the sanctity of marriage. But Scotland's affairs—which implicitly meant those of Margaret Tudor—had been a point at issue between Wolsey and Louise of Savoy at the discussions scheduled to follow the Field of Cloth of Gold.

The friar whom Henry and Katherine of Aragon had (again) sent north tactfully blamed certain of Margaret's councillors for having seduced her into seeking 'an unlawful divorce from lawful matrimony directly against the ordinance of God and utterly repugnant to man's law'. But Margaret was having none of it. 'I had no help of his Grace my brother, nor no love of my lord of Angus and he to take my living at his pleasure and despoil', she had written to Henry VIII's representative Lord Dacre. 'Methink my lord, ye should not think this reasonable, if ye be my friend'. Her allegiance had often wavered between her natal and her present country, had often been torn. But now: 'I must cause me to please this realm, when I have my life here'.

When the Duke of Albany returned from his visit to France in November 1521, Margaret Tudor welcomed him warmly. Though they had in the past been rivals for power in Scotland, she had perhaps learned that there were worse evils. When he reached Edinburgh, and the constable handed him the keys of the castle, Albany courteously handed them back to Margaret. It must have been balm to her wounded spirit. While Margaret and Albany set about joint rule, as Queen Mother and Regent, it was the turn of her estranged husband, Angus, to flee into French exile, and it was probably Angus's Douglas clan who first started the rumour that Margaret and Albany were having an affair.

Soon Henry VIII too was complaining of Albany's 'dishonourable and damnable abusing of our sister, inciting and stirring her to be divorced from her lawful husband for what corrupt intent God knoweth'. Margaret wrote to Wolsey complaining of false reports; Wolsey advised Henry that Margaret had clearly been suborned, but meanwhile, England's borders with Scotland were fortified.

ANGLO-SCOTTISH RELATIONS WERE THE WORSE for the fact that in one sense, Katherine of Aragon was now riding high. England's European interest at this point was no longer with France—Scotland and Albany's old ally—but with the Habsburgs. The end of May 1522 saw the arrival of Charles V in England for a six-week visit, celebrated with extraordinary splendour, to affirm his English alliance and, with his future marriage to his cousin Princess Mary, a permanent binding of England into the Habsburg hegemony. Charles and Mary's children would, if Henry himself had no sons, inherit an empire that stretched from England to the Mediterranean—to say nothing of Spain's colonies across the Atlantic—though this was for the moment secret, given that Mary was still officially betrothed to the French Dauphin.

At Greenwich Charles was greeted by Mary and her mother and asked for his aunt Katherine's blessing. Mary danced and played the virginals, and ambassadors reported that she was likely to become 'a handsome lady, although it is difficult to form an idea of her beauty as she is still so small'.

There were masques and masses, jousts and banquets, and one of the most successful entertainments was a reading of the list of grievances Henry VIII had sent to the French king. The treaty between the two allies declared that in 1523, Charles would invade France from Spain and Henry from Calais.

Much though she might have longed for it, Katherine of Aragon was not without concern about the alliance between her husband and her nephew. Though Henry might dream of claiming his 'antient right and title to the crown of France', Katherine had witnessed Henry's rage when, years earlier, her father, Ferdinand, had made an alliance only to let him down. Did she suspect that this time he would not forgive her the sins of her Habsburg connections so readily? In January 1523 she told Charles's ambassador 'vehemently' that Charles had to deliver all he had promised. 'It was much better to promise little and perform faithfully than to promise much and fail in part'.

Her anxieties were all too justified, for the Anglo-Habsburg 'Great Enterprise' of 1523 against France was a disaster. Margaret of Austria offered Habsburg troops to the English, but nowhere near the three thousand horse and five thousand foot the English demanded. And even those she offered, she could not find the money to pay. The English troops sent to capture Boulogne marched instead on Paris but were turned back by foul weather and lack of supplies. Charles (distracted by French successes on the Spanish frontier) failed to keep to his part of the plan, and the French general the Duc de Bourbon, now in open rebellion against the king, who had promised to join Charles and Henry, failed to turn up at all, fleeing instead to Italy.

Margaret had to stand the recriminations of Henry VIII and Wolsey, the latter declaring that they would not have expected a lady of her wisdom to have tried to excuse herself 'by inventions and compasses, by paraboles and assimulations'. By October Henry was secretly contemplating breaking his daughter's betrothal to her cousin Charles and instead allying her to her cousin on the other side, the young Scots king James V, Margaret Tudor's son.

This would certainly remove one thorn in England's side. The summer of 1522 had seen skirmishes between England and Scotland. Albany had led forces south, but the Scottish troops, remembering Flodden, refused to cross the border, and Henry was quick to cash in with the offer of a five-year peace. The following summer, Margaret Tudor caused to be read out in public a speech her young son had written in his own hand, urging that he should be allowed to make peace with his uncle of England. The Scottish authorities veered between waiting on Albany's guidance and clamouring for their young king to be set free from Albany's overclose tutelage;

Margaret's own popularity ebbed and flowed. As England burned the Scottish town of Jedburgh—as Margaret fed them information about Scotland's military dispositions—even her former supporters complained that she was 'right fickle'. In October 1523 Albany again tried to invade England with French and Scottish troops, only to be roundly defeated.

The Anglo-Habsburg alliance still, theoretically, stood; Margaret of Austria was certainly determined that it should. The English ambassador to the Low Countries reported her as saying she had always been 'utterly inclined' to Henry's good. But the following March, Katherine of Aragon would warn Charles's ambassador that Henry was 'very discontented', and it is notable that she had to send her confessor secretly to do so.

It would, the ambassador said, be 'regrettable' if the communication came to the ears of 'certain English': Wolsey was 'very restless' whenever he spoke to Katherine of Aragon and frequently interrupted his discourse with her.

Wolsey had been further alienated from the Habsburgs when, on the death of Pope Adrian, Charles V's old tutor, in September 1523 after less than two years in office, Charles and Margaret of Austria failed to win him the papacy. (It went instead to another Medici, Clement VII.) But however far the ever-more powerful Wolsey might be from falling in with Katherine's plans, he had time left to annoy another woman, too.

There is a widespread belief that enmity between Anne Boleyn and Cardinal Wolsey sprang up early in her English career, when he was personally responsible for putting an end to her love match with a young English nobleman, and that much of what followed in the next decade sprang from this injury. It may even be true—but the source that describes it, the book written by Wolsey's gentleman usher George Cavendish, was at once partisan and crafted some time after the event, as the few sources for this early stage of Anne's career tend to be.

Anne Boleyn's name was linked to three men before Henry VIII, but we have little certain knowledge of any of the relationships. She had been brought home from France to marry her kinsman James Butler, heir to the disputed Irish earldom of Ormonde, a match proposed by her powerful Howard relatives and one that might have sorted out several difficulties, since the Boleyns also claimed the earldom. It would, moreover—from the viewpoint of Wolsey and his king—bind the powerful Butlers more closely to English interests. But the marriage did not take place, and the question is why. There may have been some reluctance on the Butlers' part, but it is also possible that Anne herself had intervened.

As Cavendish tells it, while at court in attendance on Katherine of Aragon, Anne became acquainted with Henry Percy, heir to the great earldom of Northumberland and living in Wolsey's household. Accompanying Wolsey to court, Percy 'would fall in dalliance with the queen's maidens, being at the last more conversant with Mistress Anne Boleyn than with any other, so that there grew such a secret love between them that at length they were ensured together intending to marry'. But when Wolsey found out, he instantly upbraided Percy with his 'peevish folly'. Those of his rank were not supposed to marry for love. Wolsey had planned another, politically advantageous, marriage for him with a girl from the equally prominent Talbot family—and *if* Cavendish is to be believed, Henry had his eye on Anne already, though this last is perhaps unlikely.

Percy's father came roaring down to London, declaring his son was 'a proud, presumptuous, disdainful, and very unthrifty waster' (and though the words are from Cavendish, the earl did make an unscheduled visit to London in June 1523; the long-arranged Percy-Talbot match was for a time postponed). Percy was forbidden to see Anne Boleyn again and, browbeaten, complied. Anne, in Cavendish's tale, swore that 'if it lay ever in her power, she would work the cardinal as much displeasure'.

The third of these relationships was with poet and courtier Thomas Wyatt, whose family were neighbours of the Boleyns in Kent. No question of marriage here: Wyatt was already married, albeit very unhappily, but that only gave more impetus to his expression of the courtly love fantasy.

In the great game of courtly rivalry, one story has Wyatt (like Charles Brandon with Margaret of Austria) capturing a jewel from Anne and later flaunting it in front of Henry: the story itself is a useful pointer as to the competitive court context in which the king's interest was first aroused. (Another story—that Wyatt tried to warn the king that Anne had been unchaste with him, but was ignored—seems unlikely.)

It is impossible to be sure exactly how many of the poems Wyatt later wrote were written with Anne Boleyn in mind, though she is surely the 'Brunet' who 'set our country in a roar'. But one gives a striking testimony to Anne's allure:

> *Whoso list to hunt: I know where is a hind.*
> *But for me, alas I may no more;*
> *The vain travail hath wearied me so sore,*
> *I am of them that farthest cometh behind.*

> *... graven with diamonds in letters plain*
> *There is written her fair neck round about:*
> *'Noli me tangere, for Caesar's I am,*
> *And wild for to hold, though I seem tame'.*

It paints Wyatt himself as the unsuccessful suitor and Anne, the hind, as evasive, chaste. But it also breathes the kind of edgy romantic glamour guaranteed to make Anne a star and a quarry to the young men of the court and to the not-quite-so-young man who led them. Even if—or, perhaps, especially because—that man was already married to the now less than glamorous Katherine of Aragon.

It was probably in 1524 that Katherine of Aragon's sexual relations with Henry came to an end. She was thirty-eight, and Henry, himself five years younger, can no longer have felt that there was any point in trying to get another child from her. The queen's own energies would from now on be devoted to raising her only child, Princess Mary. 'Daughters', Anne de Beaujeu had written, 'are a heavy responsibility—when they are young, you must watch over them carefully'.

The well-educated Katherine herself helped teach her daughter Latin, French, and some Spanish. A fine musician and dancer, Mary was educated in penmanship as well as needlework. Katherine also obtained the advice of the Spanish-born scholar Juan Luis Vives, whom in 1523 she commissioned to write *The Education of a Christian Woman* and who, while advocating a certain amount of classical reading, nonetheless believed a woman should know only 'what pertains to the fear of God'.

To Vives, the question was not of women's mental inferiority or otherwise; it was in the physical that their vulnerability lay. 'In the education of a woman the principal and, I might say, the only concern should be the preservation of chastity'. A better education might indeed lead to more strength in virtue, but it is hard to feel that Mary was encouraged to let her mind run as free around the new humanist learning as, a decade or two later, her half sister would be.

IN SCOTLAND, MEANWHILE, KATHERINE OF Aragon's sister-in-law Margaret Tudor was also contemplating her offspring's maturity. Her ally or lover Albany had never succeeded in establishing undisputed control of the turbulent country, and in May 1524 he retired to France (where Margaret's estranged husband, Angus, was now also living and stirring up trouble for his rivals in Scotland wherever he could).

Margaret Tudor now seized power, with the support of certain power-ful allies within the nobility. It was in everyone's interest (whatever terms Albany and Margaret had or had not been on) to end the absent Albany's regency: he himself had insisted, before leaving Scotland, that 'the Queen should be obeyed in all her rights'. Margaret's solution was to declare her twelve-year-old son, James, of age and able to rule his own territory, with the help of his mother, naturally.

In England, Henry VIII was anxious to distance Scotland from the French connection that Albany's 'usurped' powers represented, and it was at this all too opportune moment that Angus managed to make his way back across the Channel to the English court. Henry and Wolsey were happy to back a plan by which Angus should assume an Anglophile rule of Scotland, with young James V a nominal ruler and his mother likewise exercising a largely ceremonial function. But endless letters from Margaret declared that rather than this, she would turn to France for help and that Angus would create 'great jealousies'.

On 26 July James was brought from Edinburgh to Stirling and—despite the fact that Scottish sovereigns were not supposed to assume rule until the age of fourteen—formally invested with the crown. Henry sent his nephew a jewelled sword, made him a member of the Order of the Garter, and sug-gested that he might marry his cousin Princess Mary, a plan with which Margaret Tudor was delighted to concur.

But Henry also sent James's stepfather, Angus, north toward Scotland with a force. 'It is right to use the Queen of Scots as an instrument in this matter, but not so as all shall depend on her', Wolsey wrote. 'A good archer should have two strings to his bow, especially when one is made of threads wrought by woman's fingers'.

A reconciliation between Margaret Tudor and her husband, Angus, seemed the obvious next step—obvious to everyone except Margaret. Angus was instructed 'to endeavour to recover the Queen's favour'; Marga-ret was urged that this reconciliation would be for the good of the country, that her personal feelings were not the point.

Despite Margaret's furious protest, Angus crossed the border into Scotland. As Parliament sat in Edinburgh, Margaret closed the city gates. Angus and his supporters scaled the walls of the city, declaring in time-honoured fashion that they were the young king's loyal subjects, seeking only to sit in Parliament as their ancestors had done. Down the Royal Mile at Holyrood with her son, Margaret hastily assembled a matching force and, to the English ambassador's dismal bleating about her 'willfulness', ordered the cannons to be trained on her husband. At the young king's command, Angus and his allies retreated. Margaret and her son processed by torchlight up the hill into the greater security of Edinburgh Castle, whence Margaret sent a firmly worded request that her brother in England should not interfere in Scottish affairs.

Parliament confirmed her regency, but if Margaret Tudor had already demonstrated an unfeminine defiance, worse was to follow. The early months of 1525 saw Margaret ever more determinedly seeking a divorce from Angus. She ignored all her brother's protests that marriage was 'divinely ordained', the more so since she was by now in love with one Henry Stewart, a young man of the royal household, eleven years younger than she but now promoted from the king's carver to captain of the guard. A letter from her brother Henry VIII provoked an hour-long storm of tears and a protest that such 'had never been written to a noble woman'. That summer, she accepted for form's sake the appearance of a reconciliation with Angus, but as Parliament was reopened—the king and his mother heading the procession, Angus carrying the crown—some two thousand of Angus's clansmen outside Edinburgh's walls faced Margaret's guns within.

A deal was struck whereby four parties—Angus and three other nobles—would each in turn have custody of the young king. But at the end of 1525, after his three-month stint, Angus refused to give the boy up. James was forced to write an official letter saying he wished to remain in his stepfather's care, but he sent another in secret, begging his mother to rescue him. She gathered an army and rode to Edinburgh, but when Angus brought James out of the city beside him, her men dared not fire on 'the person of their Prince'.

James V would spend the next two and a half years in what, by his mother's report, amounted to polite captivity, while attempt after attempt at rescue failed. Is it unfair to say that in Scotland the game was in men's hands? Margaret had been born royal, had tried to claim every power of queenship, had fought her way back from overthrow after overthrow. She had faced an impossibly difficult situation in Scotland, but her own choices had also contributed to her problems. She had proved herself something of a wild card (just as, at the English court, Anne Boleyn was beginning to do). Perhaps the game of queens was not one she was ultimately fitted to play.

16

PAVIA

Italy, France, the Netherlands, and Spain, 1525

In France another woman was about to come into her own—two other women, maybe. Louise of Savoy had fantasised (with fear and perhaps also with hope?) that the future of her whole house would come to rest on her shoulders. She was about to find that dream come true. By contrast, Louise's daughter, Marguerite, had known all her life that she was, in her own words, the least useful of their family trinity. But that was about to change.

The trigger was, as so often, a twist of the endless wars between France and the empire. The 1523 Anglo-Habsburg invasion might have fizzled out, but that was far from the end of the story. The revolt of the disaffected Duc de Bourbon and the consequent trial of his allies had left a bad taste: he had roused much sympathy in a populace angry about the money mulcted from them to pay for François's Italian Wars. The French army trying (under Bonnivet's command) to capture Naples in the spring of 1524 was soundly defeated. But that summer François decided once more to venture his hand in Italy, determined, he said, to win 'nothing less than the entire state of Milan and the kingdom of Naples'.

In that summer, Queen Claude was clearly seriously ill. François declared that 'never could I have believed that the bond of marriage enjoined by God would be so firm and difficult to break'. He nonetheless set off for the south, accompanied by his wife and sister.

But Louise of Savoy, who in the past year had suffered two bad bouts of pleurisy, was soon in a state of collapse, as her daughter, Marguerite, reported: 'What with the fatigue of the roads and the extremity of worry which she has to bear, [she] has had a flux of bleeding from all parts, just as in her bad fever'.

That autumn Queen Claude died, followed weeks afterward by her daughter Charlotte. It was Marguerite who nursed the little girl and tried to keep the news of her granddaughter's death from Louise of Savoy, already distraught at the thought of her son's departure. But in October, François appointed his mother as regent once more and led his army over the Alps, despite all Louise could say.

To maintain a campaign through the winter season was a challenge, but François insisted on camping out beside the city of Pavia, some twenty miles from Milan. In the last week of February 1525, matters came to a head. When on 24 February a Spanish imperial army attacked and succeeded in dividing the French army, the four-hour battle saw the French suffer the greatest loss of noblemen since Agincourt, with Bonnivet among the fallen (having, it was said, ridden out to seek his own death after urging François to fight that day). In the catastrophic French defeat, one of the few to evade either death or capture was Marguerite's husband, Alençon—but François I himself was taken into imperial captivity.

Nothing was left to François 'but my honour and my life'. He wrote to his mother immediately, begging her not to lose heart, 'but to exercise your accustomed prudence'. Louise of Savoy forced herself to write reassuringly back, while her daughter, Marguerite, wrote to one of his companion noblemen, Montmorency, a marshal of France: 'All my life I will envy you because I cannot perform for him the duties you are now performing; for although my will to do so is greater than yours, it is impossible, since fate has wronged me by making me a woman'. Montmorency, in return, asked Marguerite to write often, since news of herself and her mother was 'the only thing which gives [the king] the utmost pleasure'.

François was never going to be treated other than honourably. Soon one of the noblemen who shared his captivity wrote to Louise that he required not only money but also silver plate. There was, however, concern about François's desire to fast several days a week, and soon his sister was writing that if he would not eat meat and eggs in Lent, he should remember fish did not agree with him. (In the end, he observed the meat-free season by eating tortoises.)

Some three months after his capture, François was taken to Spain, finally reaching Madrid at the beginning of August but royally entertained the whole way. Meanwhile, his mother was left to deal with the effects of his captivity. 'Being so unfortunate', François wrote to his subjects, 'I have had no greater satisfaction than to know of the obedience which you have shown to Madame, as loyal subjects and as good Frenchmen. I recommend her to you'.

'Come soon, for never had I such longing to see you', François had written to his mother. But this was impossible. Louise of Savoy had too many other problems to manage—first to ensure that Charles V (or his ally Henry VIII) did not follow up the French defeat by invading France itself. Burgundy, now French but the ancestral home of Margaret of Austria's family, was a particular concern, since Charles had a special interest in recapturing this part of his heritage. More ships were commissioned and the returning remnants of François's army paid and heartened.

Louise of Savoy had, moreover, to defend the crown itself against any incursions, under these circumstances, on royal authority. Murmurings that the regent should be not the king's mother but his nearest male kinsman quickly died when the said nobleman instead accepted a place on her council, but the Paris Parlement had still to be won around and Louise had to use all her tact.

One particular cause of complaint was that the royal family had been too lax on religious unorthodoxy, had expanded their privileges at the expense of the church's authority. Here Louise—naturally more conservative than either of her children, or perhaps simply more fearful—did make some concessions. After all, she needed the new pope's support more than ever against Spain.

Across Europe, 1525 was something of a turning point in religious affairs. In Spain the Inquisition clamped down on the mystically oriented 'Illuminati' within its ranks; in Germany Luther's divergence from the main humanist reform movement became apparent. In this year the first of a growing number of German princely rulers followed where the cities were already leading and joined hands with the Lutherans. Conversely, when peasant revolt broke out across Habsburg lands, it was linked, not altogether to Luther's pleasure, to the religious Reformation. It was also the year in which the more radical Swiss reformer Ulrich Zwingli both introduced a new liturgy to replace the Mass and dedicated his *Commentary on the True and False Religion* to the king of France.

An important tenet of the new faith was that ordinary people should be able to read the Bible in their own language rather than having it confined to priestly Latin. But in this new climate, the publication of Bibles in the vernacular French was banned. Marguerite's mentor, Briçonnet, would escape heresy charges only because of his court connections. Nonetheless, wrote the chancellor Duprat to King François, Marguerite's mother 'manages so well that she has completely rehabilitated the realm'.

Louise of Savoy had real success with her foreign policy. On 30 August the peace of the More (with Cardinal Wolsey as one of the prime negotiators and Thomas Boleyn one of the signatories) restored harmony with

England. She also sent envoys to the Ottoman sultan in Constantinople, Suleiman the Magnificent, warning that if he did not come to France's assistance, Charles V would soon become 'the master of the world'. But one of her overtures brought trouble for another lady.

MARGARET OF AUSTRIA HAD GREETED the news of Pavia with a public display of rejoicing: fireworks, processions, and prayers. She was, however, concerned that the vulnerably placed Netherlands might be threatened by an alliance between France and England. And she was receptive when Louise of Savoy sent her secretary to the Netherlands to arrange a six-month truce. But Charles was furious when he heard that Margaret had arranged an armistice for those territories under her authority without waiting to hear his overall plan.

'I cannot conceal from you, madame, that I have found it very strange, and very far from satisfactory, that this should have been done without knowing my intentions, and without receiving instructions on this behalf, and powers from me', he wrote on 15 August. His own treaty concerning the cessation of hostilities was to be published immediately, and her own should be regarded as 'null and void . . . for it is my express intention that it should not be held of the smallest force or value'. She was still his 'good mother and aunt', but all the same . . .

Wolsey was likewise annoyed that Margaret of Austria had concluded peace with France without consulting him: 'I should never have thought that, after so many stipulations, promises, and declarations made by madame, she would have been the first to break through them', he told the imperial envoys. 'The perplexity and doubt by which madame is said to be assailed, and which have induced her to take this step, are no excuse'.

BY CONTRAST, THE IMPRISONED FRANÇOIS greeted the letters brought to him by Margaret of Austria's envoy with compliments and gratitude. He referred all questions to his sister, Marguerite of Navarre, travelling to Madrid to negotiate the peace and François's freedom.

François had refused to negotiate with his captors while a prisoner, insisting everything should wait on his sister's arrival. This was Marguerite's chance, and she would, she said, 'throw the cinders of her bones to the winds' to do her brother service.

She was, after all, by now free of other ties. Her husband, Alençon, almost the only noble to escape from Pavia, had been jeered at by crowds as he made his way back to France, variously blamed for having ordered a retreat when none was needed and for having fled the field. Marguerite wrote that he, 'the prisoner of his freedom', now found his life 'a living death'. Whether she blamed him (as it seems her mother did) or not, she nursed him in the fatal illness that followed and on his death wrote to François that her grief 'made her forget all reason'. Three days later, however, she was carefully composing her face so as not to upset Louise: 'I would feel miserable, seeing I am of no use to you', she told François, 'if I were to disturb the person who is doing so much for you and for what is yours'.

In July, she received her safe conduct to travel through the emperor's lands and wrote again to François (the trinity kept up a speedy interchange of letters and poems) that 'fear of death, prison, or any other ill have now become so familiar that to me they are liberty, life, health, glory and honour, since I believe that through them I could share your fortune, which if I could I'd bear alone'.

But by the time she could set sail at the end of August, the Mediterranean waves were so bad, her whole retinue was seasick. When she landed, riding across Spain with an honour guard sent by the emperor behind her, she heard that François was gravely ill, news that made her pick up the pace still further, travelling ten or twelve leagues a day until most of her servants were left behind. 'I cannot get over my fear of being inadequate', she wrote.

As she drew near Madrid, she sent off another note to François's companion Montmorency that 'never did I know what a brother is until now; and never would I have thought I could love him so much!' But on arrival on 19 September, she found the doctors had given François up for lost. Not so Marguerite. One of Louise of Savoy's envoys in Madrid described how she 'asked all the gentlemen of the king's household and her own, as well as the ladies, to pray to God. They all took communion and afterwards mass was said in the king's chamber. . . . After the mass, my lady the duchess had the Blessed Sacrament presented to the king so that he might adore it'. François managed to swallow a piece of the sacred wafer, and Marguerite took the rest.

From that time, François's fever abated. (It seems likely the abscess in his head had burst.) Marguerite despatched a messenger—with orders to press his horse until it foundered under him—to their mother, from whom the news of François's illness had hitherto been kept. Louise wrote back to Marguerite of her 'resurrection', as the idea of François's danger had thrown her into 'passion and death'.

Marguerite's nursing, or her prayers, may have saved François, but as she began peace talks with the emperor at Toledo, her diplomacy was less successful. Charles V had been warned against himself receiving Marguerite: 'Being young and a widow she comes . . . to see and be seen'. Now Charles ordained that the two should meet 'alone in a chamber with one of my ladies to guard the door'. But Marguerite found him 'quite cold', putting her off by saying he had to consult with his council.

She got on better with his sister Eleanor, one of the children Margaret of Austria had raised, the now-widowed queen of Portugal who had returned to live at her brother's court. The two women spoke late into the night, but when in subsequent days Marguerite tried to use Eleanor as a conduit, she found her unresponsive: 'They keep her on a tight rein'.

None of the proposals Marguerite was able to put to Charles V was acceptable. The talks were suspended, and Marguerite took to spending her days visiting convents, for prayer and consolation. Another attempt, almost a month later, again failed. The stumbling block was always France's reluctance to return Burgundy, while Charles made it clear he had no intention of ransoming François simply for cash. At the beginning of December, with the truce almost expired, Marguerite was forced to leave for France again, without promise of her brother's release, sending with almost hysterical frequency as many as several letters as day to be sure her brother did not want her to return.

She was greatly distressed at having failed in this, the most important mission of her life, writing to Montmorency that 'the farther I go, the unhappier I am to know that I am not worthy to serve the one who so deserves it'. The journey itself was exhausting, the stringent terms of her safe conduct meaning that 'every day for a month I was on horseback at six o'clock in the morning and did not arrive at my destination until night'.

It was Louise of Savoy who decided that even Burgundy (along with François's Italian claims and other border territories) was a price worth paying to free François from what was beginning to look like perpetual captivity. Earlier the imperial ambassador had written that she was the one who might be in any degree flexible in this, though in fact Marguerite, on her journey north, was likewise urging François, 'Do not be held back by lands or children, for your kingdom needs you'. The Treaty of Madrid, signed in the first weeks of 1526, ordained that the French king should immediately be set free and that he should marry the emperor's sister Eleanor but that his two eldest sons, aged six and eight, should be sent to Charles V as hostages.

Meeting Eleanor, his future bride, François's deportment was everything courtly. But he had already made a secret declaration disavowing any promises made under duress. He had no intention of fulfilling the terms of the treaty. Nonetheless on 17 March, by careful negotiation, two boats rowed toward each other across the border river of Bidassoa. On a bark moored in the middle, they exchanged passengers: François travelling on to Bayonne where his mother, sister, and ministers were waiting and his two small sons going into Spain to take their father's place in captivity.

17

'A TRUE, LOYAL MISTRESS
AND FRIEND'
ENGLAND, 1525–1527

❊

Events in Europe, inevitably, also had their effect in England—and on two women close to Henry VIII. The first to feel them was Katherine of Aragon. Henry's first reaction to the news from Pavia early in 1525 had, of course, been delight. His ally's victory was, Henry assumed, a fulfilment of the long-held dream: the rebirth of English power in France. An equally delighted Katherine of Aragon wrote to her nephew of her 'great pleasure and content', reminding Charles V that her husband had been, she said, his 'constant and faithful ally' and urging that 'from the continuance of such friendship and alliance the best result may be anticipated'. But the rejoicing proved premature.

Instead, as quickly transpired, the new adjustment of power in Europe, with Habsburg Charles so clearly in the ascendant over a humiliated France, meant that Henry had lost his precious, precarious position as the keeper of the balance. Charles no longer needed him (and was aware, moreover, that Henry had contributed neither men nor money to the victory from which he hoped such gains). That summer Charles demanded either that Henry's nine-year-old daughter, Mary, should be sent to Spain, to be educated in the ways of the country in preparation for her marriage, or that he should be released from the contract.

Mary's age was part of the problem, as Charles was careful to explain. Not only was he, at twenty-five, eager to get on with fathering a family, but an adult bride was (given the Habsburg proclivity for female regents) the best answer to his immediate problem: Who should be his regent to govern Spain while he himself was absent in Italy?

Charles V now sought to marry his cousin, the well-dowered twenty-one-year-old Isabella of Portugal: 'Were this marriage to take place, I could leave the Government here in the hands of the said Princess', he wrote to his brother, Ferdinand. To Henry, he explained, 'My subjects are pressingly requesting me to marry a princess who may fill my place, and govern during my absence'. His marriage to Isabella took place the following year, in March 1526.

But Henry VIII, of course, was never going to see the force of these arguments. His disenchantment with the Habsburg alliance, which Katherine represented, may explain what came next. If Mary was no longer to marry Charles, then the future of England could no longer be left in a son-in-law's hands. In June Henry made his illegitimate son (by Elizabeth Blount) Duke of Richmond (Richmond being a title with particular importance to the Tudor dynasty, since the young Henry VII had borne it). Now also, nominally, Lieutenant-General of the North, the boy was to be addressed henceforth in official documents as 'the right high and noble prince Henry'.

Katherine of Aragon made her views clear, encouraged, so the Venetian ambassador reported, by three of her Spanish ladies. All she achieved was to provoke the king, who dismissed the ladies—'a strong measure', the Venetian admitted, 'but the queen was obliged to submit and to have patience'. Inevitably, there was speculation that Henry was planning to make the boy his heir.

But his intentions were far from clear. Just weeks later Princess Mary was sent to Ludlow as nominal governor of Wales, with a household even grander than Richmond's, kitted out in her livery colours of blue and green and with instructions from her father that she should be treated as to 'so great a princess doth appertain'.

Ruling a miniature court as a small queen, she would be educated in Latin and French 'without fatigacion [sic] or weariness', to enjoy a diet 'pure, well-prepared, dressed and served, with comfortable, joyous and merry communication'. It must have been a grief to Katherine in one sense, being deprived of her daughter's company—'the long absence of the King and you troubleth me', Katherine wrote to her daughter—but also an honour, surely.*

---

* Mary was not formally created Princess of Wales, but that was not a mark of personal disfavour. As a female, she could only ever be heir presumptive, not heir apparent, since her father, if not by Katherine then by some future wife, might still father a legitimate boy. The same issue was debated in the 1940s, when it was asked whether the future Elizabeth II could be invested as Princess of Wales, and decided, regretfully, that she could not. This situation changed only with the revision to the laws of succession in the twenty-first century.

It is uncertain whether, with Katherine of Aragon's childbearing clearly at an end, Henry already contemplated setting her aside. But there was in either case no thought of the shocking and controversial turn the king's marital career would next take. In the course of the summer peregrinations of 1525, however, Henry's interest in Anne Boleyn may have begun.

IN THE SUMMER OF 1525, Anne's sister, Mary Boleyn, fell pregnant, whether by her husband, William Carey, or by Henry VIII it is impossible, now, to say. Either way, her pregnancy would have made Mary less attractive to Henry. One school of thought holds that her family effectively put Anne forward as an alternative, another female pawn who could be brought into play to ensure that the king's face was still turned the Howard-Boleyn way.

The exact nature of the mating dance that would soon be performed between several forces—dynastic necessity, Henry VIII's affections, Anne Boleyn's own will, and the impact of the new religion—remains one of the most debatable topics in history. Exact facts and precise chronology often cannot be found. But two things should perhaps be said.

First, the pattern of European events—Henry's turning away from things Spanish and toward things French—provided a context. There was widespread concern at Charles V's dominance and especially his preeminence in Italy, where, in May 1526, an alarmed Pope Clement joined in a 'Holy League' with France, Venice, Florence, and Milan (a league that had England's tacit support) against the Holy Roman Emperor.

Second, on a personal level too, Henry's initial pursuit of Anne—his attempt to make her (in several different senses) his mistress—can be set within what one might call another European context: the long fantasy of courtly love.* This was what was enacted in the masques and tournaments; this was the game played out in poems and pageants: the cruel superior mistress and the yearning lover who must always obey. Born in the courts of Provence and finding its English apogee in the days of Eleanor of Aquitaine, it had enjoyed a late rebirth in the fifteenth century under Burgundian aegis. Modelled at once on the devotion man owes to God and the service a feudal vassal owed his lord, courtly love might yet allow a measure of masculine violence—at this later, more cynical, stage of its development, anyway. That is what lay behind Margaret of Austria's poetry—and behind the warnings Anne de Beaujeu had issued so clearly. But for better or for

---

* A centuries-long movement 'compared to which the Renaissance is a mere ripple on the surface of literature', so C. S. Lewis wrote.

worse, this was the game that, significantly, those of Margaret of Austria's court loved to play. And Henry VIII too was besotted with all the games of chivalry.

It is possible that Henry Tudor's initial pursuit of Anne Boleyn had an element of competitiveness in it. Anne, fresh from the continent, would provide an arena in which to compete not only against his own courtiers but also against the French king—a field of cloth of gold in her own person, you might say. (The trouble, in years ahead, would perhaps be that she tried to keep up that spirit of rivalry.) Just so did François, too, compete with cronies like Bonnivet.

Early in 1526 Henry began to sound out opinion on his marriage, but there is no reason to suppose this was directly connected to any approaches he may already have made to Anne Boleyn. At the Shrovetide jousts in February 1526, Henry rode under the device 'Declare I dare not', which has often been seen as an approach to Anne. But at the banquet that followed, in his role of gallant, he waited on Katherine, and many a queen (Katherine's own mother among them) might be expected to tolerate her husband's infidelities, so long as he paid tribute to her position in public. 'You owe [your husband] nothing less than compliance and obedience so that you do not provoke his folly; God and the world expects nothing less of you', Anne de Beaujeu had written.

Henry VIII's letters to Anne probably started slightly later that year.* In the first of them, he describes himself three times as Anne's true servant, while she is the 'mistress', in the controlling rather than the carnal sense, a distant, unattainable star whose resistance only increased her desirability.

Henry's next letter repeats the theme: clearly, Anne had protested her duty of service to the king. 'Although it doth not appertain to a gentleman to take his lady in place of a servant, nevertheless, in compliance with your desires, I willingly grant it to you'. Another is more revealing. Its lengthy and closely reasoned argument is the more striking for the fact that Henry was notoriously reluctant, under normal circumstances, ever to write: 'Debating with myself the contents of your letter, I have put myself in great distress, not knowing how to interpret them . . . praying you with all my heart that you will expressly certify me of your whole mind concerning the

---

* None of Henry VIII's letters to Anne Boleyn are dated, nor is there any agreement among historians as to their chronology. None of Anne's letters to him survive. We can only deduce their contents from the seventeen we have of Henry's. But the tone of this one at least must have echoed that which can be seen in the extant letters François's mistress Françoise de Foix wrote to him.

love between us two'. He has been now 'above one whole year struck with
the dart of love, not being assured either of failure or of finding place in your
heart and grounded affection'.

It is the last point, he says, that prevents him 'from calling you my mistress, since if you do not love me in a way which is beyond common affection that name in no wise belongs to you, for it denotes a singular love, far
removed from the common'. Henry had obviously started out by trying to
have Anne Boleyn as his partner in just another affair, the kind of mistress
Katherine of Aragon would have accepted and the kind Mary Boleyn had
been. But now he seems to be adjusting his offer. 'If it shall please you to
do me the office of a true, loyal mistress and friend and to give yourself up,
body and soul, to me . . . I promise you that not only shall the name be
given you, but that also I will take you for my only mistress, rejecting from
thought and affection all others save yourself, to serve only you'.

Though the double sense of mistress is, of course, confusing, Henry
seems to be making the subtle to modern eyes but important difference of
offering Anne the position of *maitresse en titre*.* Perhaps the offer was a tribute to Anne Boleyn's French years; the question was why she did not accept.
But the experience of Marguerite of Navarre, and of Margaret of Austria
before her, taught that a woman was not necessarily a winner if at one time
she had engaged in the *guerre d'amour*; nor had Anne's sister, Mary, walked
away with any great gains from the king's favour.

We can in the nature of things have no sure information as to the point
at which the relationship became sexual. The picture may be one of seven
long years' frustration, traditionally seen as being imposed by Anne, but it
has to be admitted as a possibility that they did have sex at the start of the
relationship, before marriage and legitimate children became the ultimate
goal, and then later refrained, a restraint in this case at least as likely to
be imposed by Henry. The answer to the perennial question—how they
managed it—may, however, lie in the question of what we mean by sex. Or
rather, what was considered sex in the realm of courtly love.

Courtly love permitted an extended experience of what we would call
foreplay but could instead be accepted as an alternative to full intercourse.
A manual written by a monk for one of Eleanor of Aquitaine's daughters
had instructed that a lover might enjoy the embraces of his lady naked in a

---

* Though the phrase developed only slightly later, the reality could already be seen in France.
François was far from being a fool for love, but Anne d'Heilly, the mistress for whom he abandoned Françoise de Foix after his return from Pavia, could be seen openly at his side on state
occasions.

bed as long as 'the final solace' was denied to them. Indeed, given the patterns of late marriage (and only the most limited contraception) prevalent in sixteenth-century England, this seems to have been the practice well beyond courtly circles.

But courtly love, in essence adulterous, was never meant to end in marriage; it produced ecstasies but no heirs. This, ultimately, would be why the game had to end—it could not give Henry all he wanted. Again, we cannot know exactly when Henry's interest in Anne changed its focus, when the idea of marriage was first mooted between them. But in the course of 1526, things took a serious turn.

By December of that year, Katherine of Aragon was isolated at court. When Charles V's new ambassador, Inigo de Mendoza, arrived, he found it impossible to see Katherine, finally hearing from her that any interview would have to be arranged through Wolsey, conducted in his presence, and that the utmost discretion would have to be preserved. After their first meeting in the spring, Mendoza concluded that to seek another would merely 'add further damage to what might be said' about the Spanish queen.

It was probably to celebrate the new year of 1527 that Anne Boleyn sent Henry VIII a gift he received with delight. The 'fine poesies' of the letter that came with it—the 'too humble submission', as the lovesick king protested—have long since been lost, but the message is still plain to see. The gift is a jewel, once hung with a diamond, representing a ship on which a damsel is borne above a stormy sea. The diamond is the heart—hard, but steadfast, as the myths of courtly love had it—and the damsel was Anne, the giver, surely. Was Henry now to be her refuge from the storms of life? Even if it meant another woman, the king's loyal wife, would be cast adrift on the sea?

At some point, Anne seems to have withdrawn herself to Hever. One of Henry's letters to her laments that she 'will not come to court, neither with my lady your mother, and if you could, nor yet by any other way'. It may have been tactics—a strategic withdrawal on Anne's part—since Henry protests in wounded tone that he marvels at her decision, since he is sure he has committed no fault. (This may be a more complex statement than it seems: in courtly parlance, the sinful lover was supposed to derive vicarious moral benefit from his mistress's virtue.) It was around Easter 1527 that the king informed Wolsey he had serious 'scruples' about his marriage.

Conversely, however, Princess Mary was brought back from Ludlow, to be displayed as a suitable bride for one of King François's sons. (The match would be the less welcome to Katherine of Aragon, it was reported, for the

fact the French king's mother was 'a terrible woman'.) Curiously, Anne Boleyn played a part in entertaining the French envoys, dancing with the king
while the French ambassador danced with Mary. If it was a snub to Katherine of Aragon's Spanish affections, then it was also a sign Mary was still
publicly seen as England's princess. But the end of April saw the Treaty of
Westminster, an alliance made between England and France against Katherine's nephew.

In May 1527 Wolsey, surely by arrangement with his king, summoned
Henry VIII to appear before an ecclesiastical court, to discuss matters af-
fecting the 'tranquillity of consciences'. The court was held in the greatest
secrecy at Wolsey's residence. But Katherine was not wholly in ignorance:
'Spanish ladies spy well', as Francis Bryan, a kinsman of Anne Boleyn's,
once said. The day after the first meeting of Wolsey's inquiry, Charles V's
ambassador de Mendoza was able to report on it, adding that 'though the
queen herself has not ventured, and does not venture, to speak to me on the
subject, that all her hope rests, after God, on your imperial highness'. She
was communicating with Mendoza through a third party 'who pretended
not to come from her, though I suspect he came with her consent'.

Two different strands of debate were raised about the validity of the
king's original marriage contract: the theological interpretation of the Bible
and the validity of the dispensation granted for Henry to marry Katherine
at the beginning of the century, a dispensation so hedged around by the parents, Ferdinand and Isabella and Henry VII, as to leave several anomalies.

In the book of Leviticus, the Bible says, 'If a man shall take his brother's
wife, it is an unclean thing: he has uncovered his brother's nakedness. They
shall be childless', which, Henry was easily persuaded to believe, meant
without male child. Although the book of Deuteronomy urged on the contrary that a man had a positive duty to marry his deceased brother's widow
('and raise up seed for his brother'), much of the debate would in the end
centre on the question of to what degree Katherine had really been Henry's
brother's wife, whether she and Arthur had consummated their relationship. But Katherine was in any case unlikely to be impressed by Henry's
suggestion that their marriage was incestuous and therefore cursed. Two
of her sisters had been married in turn to King Manuel I of Portugal, who
had subsequently made a third marriage with their and Katherine's niece
Eleanor, while just recently, in 1525, Eleanor's youngest sister, Catalina, had
married Manuel's son.

Henry, and Wolsey, must have had real hopes of papal sanction for ending his marriage. It had, after all, been only earlier in the spring of 1527 that

Clement had finally given Margaret Tudor an annulment, while her sister Mary's husband, Charles Brandon, had received two such. Events, however, were to overtake them, and in the most dramatic way. The proceedings of the enquiry were abruptly broken off when news filtered through of what was happening in that European bear pit, Italy.

In the pursuance of Charles V's Italian Wars, the peninsula was now overrun not only by Spanish troops but also by the emperor's unpaid German mercenaries and by the French traitor Bourbon's men. Advancing southward into the Papal States, on 6 May the famished, furious soldiers surged into Rome itself, forcing the pope to flee and committing, in the words of Spain's own diplomat, 'unparalleled atrocities'. The slaughter raged for more than ten days, and it has been estimated that as many as twenty thousand died, eight thousand on the first day alone—nuns raped, St Peter's sacked, and unburied corpses piling high in the streets.

Katherine of Aragon had been prophetically accurate to say that 'all her hope' rested on her nephew Charles V. After the sack of Rome, the emperor held the pope's fate in his hands, and how likely was the pope to give a judgment against Katherine, the emperor's aunt?

Forced to act on his own initiative, Henry VIII on 22 June at last confronted Katherine and told her he wanted a formal separation. Katherine's reaction was an outburst of tears, followed by the steadfast denial that her marriage with Arthur had been consummated: this, the physical rather than the legal, would remain the bedrock of her case. If Anne Boleyn's story was now openly political, Katherine's body was a battleground. Wolsey sent instructions that his representative should tell the pope of 'certain diseases in the queen defying all remedy, for which, as well as for other causes, the king will never again live with her as a wife'.

That summer of 1527, Henry VIII and Anne Boleyn agreed to marry, as evinced by the terms in which, in September, a dispensation was requested from Rome. Henry sought permission 'to marry a woman with whose sister he had already had sexual intercourse' (presumably Anne's sister, Mary) or 'one with whom he had himself had sexual intercourse'. This second proviso begs the question of whether Anne had indeed preserved her chastity as rigorously as is usually supposed or whether she and Henry had in the early days consummated their relationship, only to pull back when the question of marriage arose and with it the legitimacy of any child Anne might bear.

In September Wolsey, returning from a mission abroad, found himself effectively summonsed by Anne into the king's presence—a sign of how power was shifting. In October Henry asked Thomas More—rising rapidly as a politician and administrator and respected for his ethical principles as well as his sharp legal brain—his opinion on the passage in Leviticus. In November he invited a number of scholars to Hampton Court.

Wolsey had been putting pressure on the pope to help Henry, and Clement had indeed been persuaded to issue a somewhat anomalous document: permission for Henry to marry Anne if his marriage to Katherine were once dissolved, without saying how that goal might be attained. In February 1528 new envoys were sent toward Rome, with instruction to call, on their way, on Anne, who had now withdrawn herself to Hever.

The last two years had seen dramatic changes in the positions of Katherine of Aragon and Anne Boleyn. Anne now had to be regarded as the king's future bride. But there was a danger here.

The rules of the new chess declared that a lowly pawn, winning through to the enemy's back row, might itself become a queen, with all the powers that implied. But a half century before, a Catalan poem called 'Scachs d'Amor, Chess Game of Love', had made a stipulation: no pawn could be 'queened' until the queen of its colour had been taken—there could not be two white, or two black, queens at one time.*

---

* The poem had possibly been influenced by the struggles of Isabella of Castile with La Beltraneja, her rival for the Castilian throne. But it still had resonance in Isabella's daughter's day.

18
NEW PIECES ON THE BOARD
Scotland, the Netherlands, Hungary, Italy, and France, 1526–1528

In England a new phase of the story had begun, but the last years of the 1520s were something of a turning point all around. Some actors would leave the stage, while others waited in the wings before another act of the play.

In Scotland two rescue attempts in 1526 failed to get the young James V out of his stepfather Angus's hold, but in June 1528 James would escape. Colourful stories made a legend out of it—the boy king getting his custodian drunk, dressing as a groom, and galloping away to Stirling, where his mother was waiting to raise the drawbridge once he was safe inside. With Angus and his cohorts forbidden to come near his person, he would at sixteen begin ruling in reality.

He was younger than François I had been when he inherited France, but Margaret Tudor was no Louise of Savoy. On 3 March that year Margaret had married her young lover, Henry Stewart, whom James created Lord Methven, 'for the great love that he bore to his dearest mother'. (Margaret's brother Henry VIII, by contrast, would continue—with sublime disregard for the proverb about pots and kettles—to call Margaret 'a shame and disgrace to all her family'.)

James V gave his mother his blessing; what he withheld was power. While Margaret's third marriage came to prove her unhappiest yet, she would have comparatively little political influence in the years immediately ahead. From the end of the 1520s, Margaret Tudor's would be largely a personal, rather than a political, story.

New pieces, however, were appearing on the board, in each of the great European dynasties. In 1526 Charles V had married his cousin Isabella of Portugal, and in the same year his widowed sister Eleanor, another of Margaret of Austria's nieces, had, of course, become engaged to François during his captivity, though the marriage would not immediately take place. The year 1526 also brought momentous change for yet another of Charles V's siblings, and evidence that the pattern of European power would soon be changing, under the pressure of a new threat.

MARY 'OF HUNGARY', AS SHE would come to be known, the fifth child of Philip of Burgundy and his Spanish wife, Juana, had been betrothed in her cradle to Louis Jagiellon, the eldest son of the Hungarian king. Initially raised at Margaret of Austria's Mechelen court, Mary was sent to the court of her grandfather Maximilian in Vienna before she was ten. There she was raised in company with the Hungarian king's daughter, who was herself to be married to Mary's brother Ferdinand. The double alliance was intended to secure Habsburg interest in the extensive kingdoms of Hungary and Bohemia and was especially important as representing Europe's frontier with the Turks.

In 1521 Mary had gone to Hungary as its queen, and within three years the teenager had won considerable influence, placing herself at the head of one of the great political factions. This was, however, a turbulent kingdom, with the Hungarian nobility in a perpetual state of warfare with each other, with their own peasantry, and with the Ottoman Turks under the great Suleiman. In 1526 Suleiman broke through the Hungarian frontier, and at the battle of Mohacs at the end of August the Hungarian army was devastated and Mary's husband killed.

Mary sent urgently for her brother Ferdinand (who claimed Hungary through his wife), but instead Ferdinand appointed her as his regent in Hungary.[*] It was Mary who kept the throne for Ferdinand, engineering his election as king of Hungary in the teeth of any rival. By the time he arrived a year later, she had, however, already asked for, and been refused, leave to resign her regency, and this lack of appetite for power was to be a characteristic of her next decades, which were likewise permeated by an ever-growing Ottoman threat.

Another of Margaret of Austria's nieces, Isabella, had also been unlucky in her spouse. Married off to Christian of Denmark, Isabella had arrived in

---

[*] Or rather, in that westernmost section of Hungary that remained under Habsburg rule, since part was now put under Ottoman control and yet a further part became the separate principality of Transylvania, itself to enjoy a notable female ruler in the shape of Isabella Jagiellon, a great-niece of Caterina Sforza. Isabella Jagiellon would become the first ruler to issue an edict of universal religious toleration.

that country to find any place she might have hoped to occupy was already taken by her husband's Dutch-born mistress and her mother. Moreover, Christian ('Christian the Tyrant' as he was known in Sweden, over which he also briefly reigned) was no man to make the friends needed for success in the elective monarchy of Denmark and Norway. In January 1523 he was deposed by his uncle Frederick. In 1531 he would attempt to regain his throne, be captured, and end his life a prisoner, but meanwhile, Isabella and the children she had borne him had been taken back into the care of her family.

This Isabella herself had died in 1526, and Margaret of Austria was determined to rear Isabella's daughters, her own great-nieces, Dorothea and Christina. Margaret also took a firm line with Isabella's errant spouse, refusing even to transmit letters between Christian and Charles, from whom he hoped to get troops to regain his kingdoms.

The year 1526 saw also the start of marriage negotiations for yet another child being raised in Margaret of Austria's care, whose future would be intertwined with the Netherlands. The illegitimate issue of Charles V's youthful fling with a Flemish servant, Margaret 'of Parma' was acknowledged by her father and in 1527 betrothed to the pope's nephew (or more probably illegitimate son) Alessandro de Medici, or de Medici.

THE RISE OF THE FLORENTINE banking family of Medici had begun during the late fourteenth century, gathering pace under Cosimo de Medici in the fifteenth. The artistic patronage they extended had led to the great flowering of the Florentine Renaissance, but their assumption of dynastic power angered the old noble families. The beginning of the sixteenth century had seen them cast into exile, but in 1512 they had once again seized power, while the election of a Medici to the papacy as Leo X in the following year gave them even greater prominence. Now another Medici sat on the papal throne as Clement VII.

But when in the spring of 1527 imperial troops had sacked Rome and taken Pope Clement himself prisoner, the hostilities had of necessity involved the pope's whole Medici family. In a riot of violence—a chair thrown from a palace window even smashed the arm of Michelangelo's *David*, recently installed outside the Palazzo Vecchio—the republic of Florence threw off the Medici yoke. One representative, however, remained inside the city, the eight-year-old Catherine de Medici.

Her father had been Lorenzo de Medici, Duke of Urbino, the pope's nephew, but he had died weeks after Catherine's birth; her French-born mother had already died of puerperal fever. During the short time remaining to them, her parents, according to one contemporary, had been 'as pleased as if she had been a boy'; nonetheless, hers would be a difficult start even by the standards of the day. But now Catherine was being raised under the auspices of a formidable aunt, Clarice Strozzi, of whom Pope Leo X said that it would have been 'well for the family if Clarice had been the man'.

When in May 1527 Florence turned against the Medicis, most of Catherine's male relatives fled, but the child was left behind, to become a hostage for her family. She was placed in the Santa Lucia convent for her own security, but it was an establishment at odds with the Medici family. At the end of that year, amid a visitation of the plague, she would be moved (veiled, and at dead of night, to avoid aggression from the Florentine people) to the more sympathetic Murate convent, but the European politics that made Italy a battleground still made Florence dangerous territory for her.

In France, too—the country with which Catherine de Medici would be so much associated—there was also a new generation on the way. Late in 1526 François I asked his sister, Marguerite, to help him by marrying Henri d'Albret, the king of Navarre, a small but strategically important neighbouring kingdom of which the larger part, however, had been annexed by Spain in 1512.* The provisions made for her security were exceptional, the marriage contract stipulating that she would have joint control with her husband of any territories François might give him, that she would retain control of any territories she already possessed or that Henri might give her, and, in the event of his death, that she would retain control of any children, without the male guardian that had so troubled Louise of Savoy.

Marguerite accepted the not disagreeable young man, nine years her junior, and the match proved a happy one. In autumn 1527 they set off south on a visit to his kingdom, and though Marguerite came to feel isolated so distant from the French court, she wrote with a typically cautious optimism that her marriage was going so well 'up to this point . . . that I congratulate myself upon it'.

Perhaps she was better off at one remove from Paris. She had been in the highest favour after François's release from Habsburg captivity, his ally in the continued international negotiations through which he sought to talk his way out of the treaty with Charles that he had signed. But the months

* Henri had also inherited the large nearby territory of Béarn, and though it was Navarre that would give Marguerite, and in time her daughter, the title of queen, Béarn was the richer property.

during which François was in Spain had seen the conservatives harden their grip on religious affairs. On his return, François, it is true, had moved to protect the reformers once again—and Marguerite wrote promising to maintain their cause—but the conservatives did not give up easily.

An example of the difficulties was the plight of Louis de Berquin, the scholar Marguerite of Navarre esteemed 'as much as if he had been my-self'. During François's captivity, Berquin had been arrested and accused of having committed heresy for a second time, a lapse that carried the death penalty. On the king's return, he was reprieved only through Marguerite's intervention; she was, after all, still actively encouraging the production of works—the translation of the scriptures into the vernacular—that the reli-gious authorities condemned.

In the spring and summer of 1528, she was back at court, and pregnant, after the 'sterile' years of her first marriage. She wrote to François that she had felt the baby stir for the first time while reading a letter from him, and 'now I sleep contented, and wake up feeling so well that with my whole heart I praise the one who has not forgotten us'. As the birth came closer, how-ever, she wrote frankly to her brother also about her qualms—'the suffering that I fear to undergo, as much as I desire it'. She longed for his presence at the birth.

When labour began it was indeed long and difficult, but on 16 Novem-ber she was delivered of (as she herself had always expected) a daughter. This baby, Jeanne d'Albret, was her father's heir presumptive since Navarre, unlike France, was not governed by the Salic Law. (Indeed, Jeanne's father had himself inherited Navarre from his mother, Catherine de Foix, albeit that her accession in 1483 had been challenged by her uncle, claiming that the Salic Law should apply here as in France, and followed by a long period of civil war.)

'Finally, my daughter', Anne de Beaujeu had written, 'as good counsel and as a general rule, make sure that all your desires, works, wants, and wishes are in God and to His credit, meanwhile awaiting His grace and just dispositions in great humility of heart'. But she wrote at a time when God's own wishes had not seemed a matter of such uncertainty as faced her read-ers a few decades into the sixteenth century.

Religious dissent was growing more acute. In France, on 1 June 1528, while Marguerite was occupied with her pregnancy, extremists on the re-form side had defaced a public statue of Virgin and Child, an act of vandal-ism that caused a widespread and violent outrage.

When, in this climate, the trial of Louis de Berquin was resumed a few months later, Marguerite wrote to her brother on behalf of 'poor Berquin', who was, however, sentenced to life imprisonment and to having his tongue pierced. Berquin made the mistake of appealing to the Paris Parlement, which ordered that he should be executed. Since François was at the time away, Marguerite's hands were tied, and Berquin was burned alive, along with his books.

Marguerite would remain a good Catholic, albeit of the reforming variety. (Though some of the Meaux circle of reforming Catholics she supported would join the new faith, others had denounced Luther as early as the start of the decade.) That position, however, was becoming harder to maintain.

In the Netherlands Margaret of Austria, too, was having to clamp down on Lutheranism, forbidding the meeting of groups to study the Bible, which she believed distanced the people from 'the reverence due to the sacraments, the honour due to the Mother of God and the saints'. At the beginning of the decade, she had been able to see off a chief inquisitor of the Low Countries she regarded as too cruel and autocratic, but in 1525 new inquisitors were appointed, and with greater powers. The next year, 1526, her ambassador was instructed to tell Charles that his aunt 'had the greatest pleasure' in trying to extirpate the Lutherans.

Religious dissent within Christendom perhaps gave the rulers of Europe a reason to break off their great game of internecine warfare, which had exhausted everyone's country—and everyone's treasury. So too, more forcibly, did the ever-mounting threat from without, the Islamic Ottoman Empire, on Europe's eastern frontier.

Early in 1528, Wolsey urged Margaret of Austria to use her influence for a general peace. Yet the initial moves may have come from elsewhere. In October Margaret's state secretary, while in Paris, was summoned to see Louise of Savoy, who told him of her great desire to peace, a desire he was to communicate to Margaret. Louise also sent her own secretary Bayart to Mechelen.

Margaret of Austria played hard to get, perhaps from a genuine lack of interest (her nephew Charles V was doing better in the wars than Louise of Savoy's son) or perhaps simply because she was the better tactician, manoeuvring Louise into the position of supplicant. In dubious tones, she was telling the English envoy to her court that 'considering the odious writing of the Princes to each other, she thought the matter was not so soon to be pacified'.

Two days later, when the French emissary saw her again, she would allow only that if by any chance she should change her mind, she would need Louise to provide very good reasons the emperor should listen to her. Five weeks later, Bayart was back in Mechelen with definite proposals from Louise and her suggestion that she and Margaret should meet.

The negotiations went backward and forward. Louise of Savoy's first (and second) proposals for the peace terms they would discuss were described as 'captious and ambiguous' by Margaret of Austria's council; Louise's changes to the amended version were vehemently rejected by the Netherlands envoys.

Even when a compromise had been reached between the two women or their negotiators, Louise had moreover to try to explain the Netherlanders' presence in Paris to her son, whom she had not yet consulted, and the envoys, with difficulty making their way on to Spain, had still to persuade Charles.

But Charles, perhaps unexpectedly, gave his aunt all authority. Peace—at least a ladies' peace—was clearly an idea whose time had come.

19

'LADIES MIGHT WELL COME FORWARD'

The Netherlands and England, January–June 1529

Throughout the crucial year of 1529, in the small arena comprising two sides of the English Channel, two dramas were running in tandem. Both were focused upon women, extraordinarily. In continental Europe, two women were coming together in search of peace. And in England, two others were locked into their own personal war.

On 3 January 1529 Margaret of Austria wrote a letter to her chief steward, expounding specifically the idea that peace between her nephew the emperor and France would stand a better chance if discussed by ladies. Neither of the two sovereigns, Charles V or François I, she wrote, could compromise his dignity by being the first to talk of reconciliation—'On the other hand, how easy for ladies . . . to concur in some endeavours for warding off the general ruin of Christendom, and to make the first advance in such an undertaking!' No less an authority than Christine de Pizan had declared that peace was women's special province.

The male rulers might fear loss of honour if they showed themselves too ready to forget the causes of the war, Margaret said, 'but ladies might well come forward in a measure for submitting the gratification of private hatred and revenge to the far nobler principle of the welfare of nations'. The king of France and the emperor, moreover, would have to answer to their friends and allies (notably England) for anything to which they might agree, but allowing their womenfolk to do it for them would 'take away all responsibility'.

That phrase of Margaret of Austria's about the 'general ruin of Christendom' is perhaps key: the Ottoman threat was looming large in everyone's mind. (Indeed, when the fighting season began again later that spring, the

Turkish advance on Europe would lend the whole matter more urgency.) That spring, Margaret was busy trying to draw everybody in. On 15 May she was telling a potentially suspicious Henry VIII that it was Louise of Savoy who had often urged her to talk of peace, and she had come to feel she had no choice but to listen. She had 'no doubt' that King Henry would be pleased to hear the news. On the twenty-sixth she wrote in cipher, telling her nephew a meeting with Louise of France had been agreed, but that it was important to keep England happy.

In a postscript the next day, she added that a messenger had just arrived from Katherine of Aragon, saying that Henry was pushing ahead with the judicial proceedings to try his marriage and that Katherine urgently needed Margaret to send her lawyers. Any overt partisanship for Katherine at this point might well have embarrassed Margaret's diplomacy; nonetheless, she did look for advice on Katherine's behalf. On 26 May she wrote to Charles V that she was 'sending to Malines [Mechelen] to obtain the opinion of experienced lawyers in that place. . . . [T]he poor Queen is very perplexed, and there is no one in England who dares take up her defence against the King's will'.

The story of the Ladies' Peace was intercut with, in England, two other women's stories.

IN ENGLAND, IN 1528, THE dreaded sweating sickness had almost brought an end to the vexed question of Henry VIII's love life. In the middle of June, one of Anne Boleyn's ladies fell sick, and Henry, always terrified of disease, sent Anne hotfoot down to Hever, writing to her that his doubts about her health 'disturbed and alarmed me exceedingly'. (He ended by saying that 'I wish you in my arms, that I might a little dispel your unreasonable thought', an illuminating glimpse of their relationship.) A couple of days later, Henry heard that Anne had indeed fallen ill; 'the most afflicting news that could have arrived' was how he described it, adding with equally illuminating precision that he would gladly bear 'half' her illness to make her well.

But in July a recovered Anne was back at court, and the question of Henry's plans for her was still on the pope's plate. While a French success in Italy might have relieved the necessity for the pope to appease the emperor, in June 1528 Charles had started winning, and from now on the pope's fear of Charles's armies in Italy would be a dominant feature of the case. Nonetheless, the pope did appoint a representative to look into the validity of Henry's marriage, Cardinal Campeggio, who arrived in England in October 1528.

Campeggio went to Katherine of Aragon, suggesting she retire to a nunnery, relying on her 'prudence' and 'example of a queen in France who did the same and is still honoured by God and that kingdom', Louis's first wife, Jeanne. This would—with a little fudging—have allowed Henry to marry again, since Katherine could be seen as dead to the world, and it would have no implications for their daughter's legitimacy.* But Katherine was having none of it.

She saw Henry the next day and demanded, as she had before, some 'indifferent' (that is, impartial, not English) counsel, and the next day she was with Campeggio again. Obsessively running over past events, she declared 'on her conscience' that her marriage to Henry's elder brother, Prince Arthur, had left her as 'intact and uncorrupted as the day she left her mother's womb' and that they could tear her 'limb from limb' before she altered her intention 'to live and die in the estate of matrimony'. Campeggio, at the end of it all, could only report feebly that 'nothing more occurred to me' to say.

And Katherine of Aragon now had a trick up her sleeve. Among the papers of the late Spanish ambassador de Puebla had been found a copy of the document the pope had sent to Katherine's mother, Isabella, on her deathbed, meaning that Katherine was free to marry Henry whether she had slept with Arthur or not. In it, declared Charles V's current ambassador Mendoza, 'consists the whole of the queen's right'.

At the Christmas celebrations Henry and Katherine displayed a public front of unity, but Anne Boleyn was in a lodging nearby. As Campeggio put it, 'The king persists more than ever in his desire to marry this lady [Anne], kissing her and treating her in public as though she were his wife'.

Matters were reaching a crucial point. At the end of April 1529, Charles's envoys in Rome had presented the pope with a formal petition that the case should be tried in Rome since Katherine of Aragon 'would never obtain justice' in England. But on 31 May Campeggio's summons to appear at a hearing at Blackfriars went out to king and queen.

On 14 June Henry and Katherine moved to Greenwich, a few miles downriver, in readiness. But Katherine two days later made what was in effect a preemptive protest, recording (in her own lodgings but in the presence of two notaries) her appeal to Rome. She knew, Mendoza reported, 'that instead of calming her husband's irritation against her, she has increased it by her act'. But she felt she had now no choice.

---

* Legitimacy was in any case something the pope had the power to bestow. A child might be considered legitimate—as was Margaret Tudor's daughter, Margaret Douglas—even after divorce or annulment, if his or her parents had married in good faith.

The royal couple were summoned to make a first formal appearance at the legatine court at Blackfriars, in person or by proxy, on Friday, 18 June. Henry VIII sent proxies, but Katherine took everyone by surprise when she herself made an entrance, surrounded by advisers, four bishops, and a swarm of her ladies. Then, 'sadly and with great gravity', she read the appeal to Rome she had recorded two days before. She was told that her appeal against the jurisdiction of this English court would be answered on Monday, 21 June.

Katherine of Aragon had not always been a dramatic figure, but when Monday came, this was one scene she knew how to play. Henry himself spoke briefly; then Wolsey, to declare that he and Campeggio would judge the case on its merits, despite all the favours he had received from the king; then Campeggio, formally rejecting the protest Katherine had lodged; and then the crier: 'Katherine, Queen of England, come into the court!'

Later writers (during the reign of Katherine's daughter, Mary) would be fond of figuring Queen Katherine as a Patient Griselda, an endlessly suffering kind of *mater dolorosa*. But there was method in her display of marital meekness. Setting aside the chill formality of the legal process, rising from her seat, she crossed the floor and knelt at her husband's feet. 'Sir, I beseech you for all the love that hath been between us, and for the love of God, let me have justice'.

Observers noted that after all her years in the country, she still, at least under this stress, spoke in broken English, but what she said, as Wolsey's former gentleman and biographer George Cavendish recalled it, was eloquent enough. 'Take of me some pity and compassion, for I am a poor woman and a stranger born out of your dominion. I have here no assured friends, and much less impartial counsel.

'Alas! Sir, wherein have I offended you, or what occasion of displeasure have I deserved? I have been to you a true, humble and obedient wife, ever conformable to your will and pleasure. . . . I never grudged in word or countenance, or showed a visage or spark of discontent'. She had borne the king 'divers children, although it hath pleased God to call them out of this world'. Then came the crunch. 'When ye had me at the first, I take God to be my judge, I was a true maid without touch of man. And whether it be true or no, I put it to your conscience.

'If there be any just cause by the law that ye can allege against me, either of dishonesty or any other impediment to banish and put me from you, I am well content to depart to my great shame and dishonour. And if there be none, then here, I most lowly beseech you, let me remain in my former estate'. She invoked the memory of the old kings—Henry's father and her own—who had made the match; she spoke bitterly of the 'new inventions' of this new court. She asked Henry's permission to write to Rome, and he, taken by surprise, could do nothing but agree. She rose to her feet—off the knees from which Henry had twice tried to raise her—made a low curtsy, and, instead of returning to her seat, marched toward the door.

Once again the crier called to her: 'Katherine, Queen of England, come into the court', but she did not pause: 'It is no indifferent court for me, therefore I will not tarry'. Though the trial dragged on, with elderly witnesses describing what (they thought) had or had not happened in Katherine and Arthur's wedding bed all those years before, the process never recovered.

The common people of England were with Katherine—the women especially. Outside the court, the French ambassador noted, 'If the matter were to be decided by the women, the king would lose the battle, for they did not fail to encourage the queen at her entrance and departure by their cries'. But Katherine of Aragon was looking elsewhere.

Her appeal that the case should be heard in Rome and the supporting documents were rushed over to Brussels, where Mendoza sent them on to the Vatican by express messenger. When agreement to Katherine's request was wrung from a reluctant and distraught pope, copies of the papal decision were sent back to Flanders, some for posting there and others for Margaret of Austria to send on to Katherine.

In one meeting with Wolsey and Campeggio, Katherine warned that the king and his ministers should consider the reputation 'of her nation and her relatives'. It was a declaration of the importance of Katherine of Aragon's own blood legacy, and indeed her fortitude was perhaps inherited from her mother, Isabella.

'Remember that whatever great alliance you achieve, you must never out of some foolish pride fail to value highly your own ancestors, those from whom you are descended—to fail in that would be against right and reason', Anne de Beaujeu had said. And this summer of 1529 was the one in which women were inclined to stake their claim most assertively.

On 5 June, as Katherine of Aragon was readying her case, Margaret of Austria's envoy to England reported that Wolsey had asked him 'to declare on his word of honour whether he really thought the two Duchesses were in earnest' in their plans for peace. The envoy declared 'that he could answer for one of them; as to the other, time would tell'.

Margaret of Austria's meeting with Louise of Savoy was set for July, in the border town of Cambrai, and all Europe was watching. Mendoza wrote to Charles V, 'Some think that the meeting of the two ladies will come to nothing', but in his humble opinion, 'it cannot do harm, even if things do not immediately turn to good'.

As the meeting at Cambrai neared, the flurry of messages as to the precise stages of both ladies' journey resembled the behind-the-scenes work on a modern summit. Louise of Savoy declared her intention of bringing her chancellor and the women of her chamber, but none of the French nobility. As she said to Margaret of Austria's envoy, 'You may tell my sister [Margaret] what my plans are, and that I hope we may hear of each other daily. Write also to her boldly that we must necessarily contend and argue, but that I sincerely hope it will be without anger or ill-will'.

Margaret of Austria had been warned not to go to Cambrai, for fear King François would take her prisoner, but she said that 'if any of her councillors or courtiers were afraid, they might go home'. Told that she should at least take a strong escort, she replied that 'if she brought one single armed man in her suite, people might imagine she was going on a warlike enterprise, and not on a work of peace'.

Machiavelli had advised that war was of supreme importance for a ruler, but this was, of course, irrelevant or even damaging advice for women leaders who could not lead their own armies into battle. But he also stressed the importance of presentation, and there they were surely even ahead of him.

20

THE LADIES' PEACE
Cambrai and England, July–December 1529

✸

Women—Castiglione had written in *The Book of the Courtier*—'have often corrected many of men's errors'. This was the unspoken thought behind the interchange of letters between Margaret of Austria and Louise of Savoy, and this was the spirit in which they set out toward Cambrai. On Monday, 5 July, Margaret of Austria was the first to arrive, in a magnificent litter, surrounded by twenty-four black-clad mounted archers, to take up her residence in St Aubert's Abbey.

Two hours later Louise of Savoy arrived, accompanied by her daughter, Marguerite. A Venetian envoy sent back a report: Louise arrived 'in great state being clad in black velvet, with four ladies' litters, and with her daughter the Queen of Navarre, and ladies on horseback. The Lord Chancellor preceded her and ambassadors followed'.

Louise of Savoy had, in the event, brought across France leading members of her son's council and indeed her son the king, though he stayed some little distance away and spent the days hunting. Perhaps she didn't feel quite as confident in her own experience of diplomacy as did Margaret of Austria (whose nephew Charles was many miles away).

Louise had also her priests and her painter, her choristers and the keepers of her furs and her silver. A chronicle describes the 'triumphant' sight of the train of clergymen and ladies: 'It stretched from our House for half the road to St Pol and after them came hackneys and mules, very well appointed'. The town—struggling to feed and lodge all these people—had laid down rules for these huge and splendid retinues: no carrying of arms, serving men to observe a curfew.

Louise and Marguerite were taken immediately to Margaret of Austria, with whom they spent two hours, before taking up residence in the Hotel St Pol opposite. It must have been an emotional moment for Margaret and for Louise, meeting after so many years. Marguerite of Navarre's official role was to act as hostage for the imperial side, to guarantee the safety of Margaret of Austria. It is unclear whether she played any more active part. By now her interests were no longer necessarily identical with those of her brother and mother's France. She had also responsibilities to her husband, whose prime goal was the restitution of that part of Navarre that Spain had snatched.

The discussions took three weeks and took a toll on both sides. Louise of Savoy was seemingly the fragile one, retiring each night in pain from the gout that had long plagued her, but when the Venetian envoy went to visit Margaret of Austria, he found her, too, 'in bed, dressed, having a slight pain in her leg'. Margaret began by making a lot of demands—she was, after all, operating from a position of strength, given her nephew's recent victories.

All Europe was watching, nervously. England, Venice, and Florence were all afraid France would make a peace with Charles that would leave them out in the cold. King François too was edgy, on 17 July writing to his mother that since the emperor valued his friendship so low, Louise should remind him that he could be just as strong an enemy. He was desperate to get away to where his soldiers were assembled for the war he still believed was coming, but he dared not leave without Louise's assent.

On 24 July peace was declared—prematurely. Margaret of Austria caused a hitch with a last-minute demand for certain border towns; Louise of Savoy and her daughter ordered their bags packed, and the papal nuncio had to intervene. Margaret now offered concessions, relinquished some of her demands, and engaged personally to arrange the return of François's sons, the French princes, still held hostage in Spain. In the closing days of July, a treaty was ratified at last.

On 1 August the three ladies—Margaret of Austria, Louise of Savoy, and Marguerite of Navarre—went to vespers in the abbey, receiving the congratulations of the men on both sides and, as the contemporary chronicle records, 'taking each other's hands, a beautiful thing to see'. On the fifth the peace was celebrated with a huge public mass in Cambrai cathedral and a sermon on the text of 'Blessed are the peacemakers'. The Treaty of Cambrai would be better known as the *Paix des Dames*, the Ladies' Peace.

The terms were definitely favourable to the emperor's party—'so advantageous to the Emperor', reported an ambassador gleefully, 'that some deception is suspected'. So advantageous, indeed, that François was reported less than happy with what his mother had done; though in the last resort, as always, he had vouchsafed to 'place myself in your hands, to do what you think best'.

Charles V agreed not to press his claims to Burgundy, accepting a hefty ransom in its place, while François's sons, still hostage, should be released from their Spanish captivity on the payment of a further sum. François gave up his suzerainty over Flanders and Artois as well as his Italian claims. To cement the deal, it was agreed that the marriage of François to Charles's sister Eleanor, promised after Pavia, should soon be solemnized. The role of England as the emperor's long-term ally had not featured in the negotiations—Wolsey, who had been invited to attend and longed to go, had been kept in England by a Henry VIII intent on the Blackfriars hearing—but at the last minute they were included in the deal.

The choir sang a *Te Deum*, alms were thrown to the crowd, and wine flowed from the conduits. On 9 August King François came to join the party, and the emperor Charles sent Margaret of Austria his congratulations, as well he might.

MEANWHILE, IN ENGLAND, ON 23 July Cardinals Campeggio and Wolsey were to have given their verdict. But instead, Campeggio formally referred the case to Rome. It was a triumph for Katherine, of a sort, but it proved to be a very hollow victory.

On 11 September both cardinals formally relinquished their authority in the case. A month later came something that would have seemed unthinkable, once, in Wolsey's recent heyday. The great minister was arrested, the Venetians reporting that 'he has at length found fortune irate and hostile beyond measure . . . ruin, which may be said to exceed his late fame and elevation'.

There is no doubt who Wolsey himself saw as responsible for his downfall, speaking of 'a continual serpentine enemy about the king'. Later he urged his supporters that everything should be tried in order that 'the displeasure of my Lady Anne be somewhat assuaged. . . . [T]his is the only help and remedy. All possible means must be used for attaining of her favour'.

On 3 November Henry opened what would come to be known as the Reformation Parliament. A month later Thomas Boleyn was made Earl of Wiltshire, and at the banquet that followed the ceremony, Anne was given precedence over all other ladies (even the king's sister Mary).

Katherine of Aragon, though still queen of England, cannot have looked back with any satisfaction as this momentous year came to an end.

But neither, altogether, can Anne Boleyn. When, at the end of November, Henry and Katherine had an open confrontation about Anne, Anne's furious response made her insecurity clear. 'Did I not tell you that whenever you disputed with the queen she was sure to have the upper hand? I see that some fine morning you will succumb to her reasoning and that you will cast me off . . . alas! Farewell to my time and youth spent to no purpose at all'. It was a stalemate, basically.

21

EXITS AND ENTRANCES

The Netherlands, France, and Italy, 1530–1531

In continental Europe, neither of the protagonists of the 'Ladies' Peace' lived long to enjoy their triumph of diplomacy.

In February 1530, after a triumphal progress through Italy, Margaret of Austria's nephew Charles V was formally crowned at the pope's hands as Holy Roman Emperor. It was Margaret's triumph. The children she had nurtured, her brother Philip's progeny and their offspring too, now held the reins of power across Europe, from Valencia to Vienna, Lisbon to Louvain.

A letter she wrote to Charles in the months after Cambrai, concerning the state of the Habsburg empire and her advice for his dealings with it, shows she was still active. But Margaret was nearing fifty. She had already thought of relinquishing her responsibilities and retiring to a convent outside Bruges. She wrote to the mother superior, putting in place her financial provisions for the convent and adding that 'the time approaches, since the emperor is coming, to whom with God's help, I will render a good account of the charge and government which he has pleased to give me'. But she was not to have the opportunity.

According to the account of one Augustinian monk, in November 1530 a maid dropped a glass goblet near her bed, and Margaret got a splinter in her foot. The tiny wound became infected and then gangrenous, and an amputation was decided on. Agreeing to it, she shut herself up for four days in prayer and preparation, receiving the sacrament and revising her will. But the dose of opium given to her was so strong that, on 1 December 1530, she died before facing the operation.

Her work on behalf of her nephew Charles—she wrote to him proudly in a last letter—had been such that she might hope for 'divine remuneration, contentment from you, monseigneur, and the goodwill of your subjects'. Her last wish was that Charles should keep peace with France and

England. Her heart was briefly placed in the tomb of her mother, Mary of Burgundy, before being taken south to join that of her last husband, Philibert, at Brou in the mausoleum she had so carefully rebuilt.

FOR LOUISE OF SAVOY, MEANWHILE, the Ladies' Peace meant the return from their long captivity in Spain of her grandsons, the French princes. During the course of their four-year captivity, the conditions in which they were kept had become more and more miserable, held in a poorly furnished cell without entertainment or French-speaking company. Margaret of Austria, as well as the French royal women, had become concerned about it, had written to her nephew to expostulate. But at the start of the 1530s, Louise's trinity set out toward Bayonne, where the boys were to be handed over to François along with the emperor's sister Eleanor, now François's bride by the terms of the Ladies' Peace.

But Marguerite of Navarre, pregnant once again, had to be left behind at Blois—'banished', as she put it, because of her 'massive and too heavy belly'—while the other two who made up the 'perfect triangle' went on without her. This time she was convinced that the child would be a boy, but the thought did not seem to bring her joy, as witness some of the poetry she addressed to her absent brother:

> You tell me to take comfort
> in my child, but I cannot. . . . [I]t is he who keeps me from doing my duty
> to those I love a thousand times more than him.

Another poem, to her mother, resentfully recalled how much she, Marguerite, had done to bring about the release first of François and then of her nephews, and now she could not be present at the consummation.

> How vexing it surely is, for a brave heart
> that is unvanquished,
> to be brought low by a mere baby.

Perhaps as so often, guilt played a part in her complex tangle of emotions, guilt at what the boys had suffered, or possibly about the way she was now divided from her brother by the interests of her husband, Henri of Navarre, whose infidelities added to her distress. On 15 July she would indeed give birth to a boy, Jean, who, however, would die on Christmas Day. Marguerite wrote of the will of God, but from that time she wore only black.

Early in 1531 she was (most unusually for a woman and a royal woman) preparing the text of one long poem she had written for publication, and publication by an evangelical publisher, Simon du Bois. Marguerite's lengthy religious *Miroir de l'âme pécheresse* (*The Mirror of Glass of a Sinful Soul*) was later translated by Elizabeth Tudor as a gift for her reforming stepmother, Katherine Parr.

In it, as Elizabeth paraphrased, Marguerite 'doth perceive how of herself and of her own strength she can do nothing that good is or prevaileth for her salvation, unless it be through the grace of God'. Its description of the sinful soul redeemed by grace may have spoken to something in Marguerite's own nature, but salvation by grace alone (rather than devotional rituals or even good works) would also, of course, be a central piece of Protestant doctrine. This was dangerous territory: in 1530 the Diet of Augsburg had tried and failed to settle the divisions within the church. The year 1531 saw the formation of the Schmalkaldic League, an alliance of the Lutheran princes within the Holy Roman Empire.

Marguerite's health continued to give cause for concern. Pregnant again, she miscarried the baby, and her failure to provide more male babies to serve her brother seems to have been yet another arrow in the quiverful of guilt she carried. March 1531 saw the French royal family celebrate the coronation of François's new queen, Eleanor. But Louise of Savoy's health was failing fast.

Louise had long been suffering from painful and debilitating bouts of gout and 'the gravel'—kidney stones. Marguerite had been her nurse as much as her adviser at Cambrai. By the end of the summer, it was obvious Louise's condition was serious. Marguerite wrote frantically to her brother, François, begging he should come ('because she is not content with me'), but to her distress, and that of Louise, he stayed away. Only Marguerite was present in the château where on 22 September Louise died at the age of fifty-five. And saying—or so Marguerite later wrote in *Les Prisons*—that the sight of Marguerite caused her to feel pleasure and attachment to this world, when she needed to think only of God and the next, Louise sent Marguerite out of her presence at the last.

MEANWHILE, THREE HUNDRED MILES AWAY in Florence, a convent had not long disgorged a frightened young girl. For Catherine de Medici, the repercussions of the Ladies' Peace had not been happy.

Charles V, eager to confirm his position as dominant influence in the Italian peninsula, had entered into negotiations with the pope, whose preoccupation was to restore his Medici family's influence in Florence. The results would be terrifying for the eleven-year-old Catherine de Medici.

Catherine had spent the last three years tranquilly and happily in the Murate convent, where the aristocratic nuns treated her with every show of affection. The Florentine authorities 'would gladly see her in Kingdom Come', noted the French ambassador, who (Catherine's mother having been a Frenchwoman) kept a protective eye on her. He added—interestingly, in terms of Catherine's future—'I have never seen anyone of her age so quick to feel the good and ill that are done to her'. And on 20 July 1530, great ill seemed to have come.

Charles V had placed at the pope's disposal an army that in October 1529 began what would prove a ten-month siege of the city, with the aim of restoring Medici rule. Catherine's male relations had fled when the city established a republic two years before. Now came that threat of which the French ambassador had warned, a hammering in the middle of the night, on the doors of the Murate. The child inside the thick walls, however, had herself already decided how to combat this new danger.

While the mother superior persuaded the men to come back in the morning, Catherine—convinced the summons could only be to her execution—cut off her hair and donned a nun's habit, shouting that no one dared take a bride of Christ from her monastery.

She was wrong; as one of the nuns put it, such force was used 'that we had to give her up'. But in the event, the city authorities did nothing worse than to set her astride a donkey and escort her through the baying crowds back to the very convent where she had first been placed three years before. There had, however, been calls for the child to be stripped naked and suspended from the walls or else placed in a military brothel for the amusement of the soldiery. Even after the city surrendered a few weeks later, contemporaries noted that she never forgot—could not stop talking about—her ordeal. It is something to remember when, in Paris four decades later, Catherine de Medici would once again be faced with the fear of violence ripping through her city.

When peace, and the Medici family, was restored to Florence, Catherine went back to visit the nuns of the Murate and celebrate with them. She would send them money and letters for the rest of her life. But her uncle the pope now had plans for her beyond convent walls. Moving her to Rome, and placing her in the house of a relative instructed to give her a cosmopolitan gloss, he managed (with the promise of a half-dozen Italian cities, Pisa among them, as her dowry) to betroth her to the French king's second son, Henri, to cement the mood of all-around accord.

The 'greatest match in the world', the pope called it—and he was something of a connoisseur, having also betrothed the new young Duke of Florence (his nephew or illegitimate son) to Charles V's illegitimate daughter, Margaret 'of Parma'. In the spring of 1533, the fourteen-year-old Catherine de Medici would have the duty of welcoming the ten-year-old Margaret of Parma into Florence.

CATHERINE DE MEDICI AND MARGARET of Parma were perhaps the first representatives of another generation of women—one that would be associated with the latter half of the sixteenth century. But of course, the generations did not divide so neatly. In the Netherlands, in 1531, Margaret of Austria was succeeded by another female regent—her twenty-five-year-old widowed niece, Mary 'of Hungary'.

After successfully holding Hungary for her brother Ferdinand, the king of Hungary, Mary had refused his offer of a second regency in 1528; such affairs 'need a person older and wiser', Mary said. Her reluctance was understandable: it had been the turbulence in Hungary that encouraged the Ottoman Empire to launch the campaign that culminated, just weeks after the Ladies' Peace, in the Siege of Vienna. That campaign almost cost Ferdinand all he had won and struck a terrifying blow deep into the Habsburg heartland.

But Mary was undoubtedly able. A Hungarian correspondent had written to Erasmus, 'I wish that . . . the queen would become the king: the fate of the homeland would then be better'. And the Habsburg empire was ever greedy for loyal lieutenants. 'I am only one and I can't be everywhere', Charles V would later complain to Mary. As Ferdinand said, telling Mary of their aunt Margaret's death in December 1530, her life might now 'take a different course', and the next month Charles did indeed ask Mary to assume the regency of the Netherlands.

Family duty impelled agreement. Mary was now 'Mary, by the Grace of God, Queen of Hungary, of Bohemia, etc., governor of the Netherlands for His Imperial and Catholic Majesty, and his lieutenant'. Like Margaret of Austria before her, she was determined not to allow her family to marry her off again. But neither did she wish to remain as a queen without kingdom, income, role, or offspring. (Margaret of Austria herself had once, before she found her role as regent, lamented that she might 'be left to wander about the world like a person lost and forgotten'—or so her father recalled.)

Mary of Hungary continued, however, to display a more ambivalent attitude toward responsibility than her aunt Margaret had done, complaining a few months into the Netherlands job that it felt like having a rope around her neck. She did not, she said, perhaps pointedly, wish to act 'like those women who interfere in many things which are not demanded of them'. Conversely, it was said of her that she ruled by rigour, whereas Margaret had done it by charm.

The Venetian ambassador to the Hungarian court had written that 'by reason of her natural volatility and from too much exercise'—Mary was notoriously obsessed with hunting and falconry—it was generally assumed she would never have children. He added a description, that she was 'of diminutive stature, long and narrow face, rather comely, very spare . . . lively, never quiet either at home or abroad'. The late sixteenth-century writer Brantôme described her as *un peu homasse*, a little mannish, adding that 'she made war well, sometimes through her lieutenants, sometimes in person, always on horseback, like an Amazon'.

Her brother Charles V told her on another occasion that she did 'not react in such a feminine manner as others of your sex, who are of a more delicate disposition'. Later, in 1537, when the French were attacking the Netherlands, she would appear in a black leather jerkin fitted with the eyelets that would hold a cuirass, swearing she would show François I 'to what purpose God can give a woman strength'. She had strength, and she would stand in need of it—as, in their different way, Louise of Savoy and Margaret of Austria had done, as Catherine de Medici would continue to do.

22

'THUS IT WILL BE'

ENGLAND, 1530–1531

✴

In England, Anne Boleyn launched into her own battle, metaphorically picking up the weapons herself once it had become all too apparent that Henry VIII's divorce would not be obtained the old clerical way. As she did so she had two great allies: the new reformed faith and the French upbringing that had given that country a stake in her success.

Generations of historians have chosen to see Marguerite of Navarre as a mentor—a mother figure, if you like—to Anne Boleyn. There is no evidence to support the suggestion (made by some near contemporaries as well as subsequently) that Anne had actually been in Marguerite's service during her time in France. But there would shortly be evidence that Marguerite was a role model for Anne, and in this their common interest in religious reform was key.

One of the many debates about Anne Boleyn remains the precise nature of her religious stance. Later, in the reign of Anne's Protestant daughter, Elizabeth, the Protestant martyrologist John Foxe would declare of her: 'What a zealous defender she was of Christ's gospel all the world doth know'. Scots reformer Alexander Ales told Elizabeth that 'true religion in England had its commencement and its end with your mother'.

Certainly, Anne was in the habit of both studying and speaking about the Bible. She even supported the illegal trade in vernacular Bibles. But then so too had Marguerite of Navarre, and Marguerite managed to remain a Catholic. The books Anne owned included several by those close to Marguerite and indicate a strong interest in the new learning: a French Psalter with a translation credited to the unfortunate Louis de Berquin and a French Bible translated by another of the Meaux circle, Jacques Lefèvre d'Etaples. When poet Nicolas Bourbon, whom Marguerite had made her daughter's tutor, found France too hot to hold him, he fled to England and Anne's protection.

In the years ahead, Anne Boleyn would undoubtedly be active in seeking out abuses in the Catholic Church—but then so was Marguerite of Navarre. (It was, for example, Anne's emissaries who revealed that the blood held up for veneration at Hailes Abbey—supposedly holy blood—was in fact that of a duck.) Anne would be sufficiently active in promoting the appointment of reformers in the church to be able to speak of 'my bishops'. But though some of the clergy she supported would continue to move further toward a new faith, it was not true of all. There is no reason to doubt the sincerity of Anne's beliefs, but the question is how far her enthusiasm for purity in religion might take her.

A sermon later preached by her almoner John Skip would describe the 'little ceremonies of the church', anathema to any radical reformer, as 'very good and commodious', as long as properly used. Nor were her own religious practices stripped of all the old ways. She would plan a pilgrimage, put faith in a prophecy—say, near her death, that she would go to heaven because she had done good deeds—and spend her last night, even, praying before the consecrated bread and wine. All these things belonged to the old brand of faith, not the new. But perhaps (only fifteen years after Luther's voice first made itself heard on the European stage) we should not be surprised that Anne, like many of her contemporaries, could not easily set aside all the traditions in which she had been raised. Heaven knows, Henry's beliefs and practices would be even more complex, or contradictory.

Even before the Blackfriars showdown, Anne Boleyn had shown Henry VIII passages in an illicit book, *The Obedience of the Christian Man and How Christian Rulers Ought to Govern*, published by the exiled William Tyndale. (Famous for his translation of the New Testament with Lutheran prologues, Tyndale had taken refuge in the Netherlands, where the regents were, for as long as possible, turning a blind eye to this cuckoo in their midst.) The book was a defiance of papal authority, declaring that the subject is accountable to the ruler and the ruler to God alone. It was the idea Henry had been looking for: 'This book is for me and all kings to read'.

If the traditional function of a woman behind a powerful man was to be advisory—intercessory, the conduit through which ideas as well as clemency could flow—then Anne fulfilled it very successfully, in that her ideas would win through. But these ideas were coming to give a more overtly religious framework to the question of King Henry's marriage.

A timely new introduction at court, in the months after the hearing at Blackfriars, was Cambridge scholar Thomas Cranmer. He suggested that Henry's was not a case of canon law but a theological problem of the pope's right to dictate to princes and that theologians (at the universities of Europe as well as England) should thus be canvassed. He was sent away to formulate his ideas in the care of the Boleyn family.

Through the following spring, one theological authority after another was persuaded to give Henry VIII the answer he wanted until at last (once King François's sons were safe back in their own country), even the University of Paris gave way. In June 1530 Henry was handed the *Collectanea satis copiosa*, a data bank of biblical and historical material suggesting the pope was not necessarily supreme. In August he summoned his council to another conference at Hampton Court. In September, warned by a newly arrived papal nuncio that the Vatican trial of the marriage Katherine of Aragon had requested would have to begin soon, Henry issued a proclamation forbidding any suit to Rome.

Charles V's horrified ambassador Eustace Chapuys warned that if 'the Earl and his daughter' (Anne Boleyn and her father) remained in power, they would 'entirely alienate this kingdom from its allegiance to the Pope'. In October Henry suggested to his gathering of clerics and lawyers that his own Archbishop of Canterbury should be empowered to decide the divorce suit, though the idea did not immediately bear fruit.

It was now a propaganda war, and some of the weapons were women's. Anne Boleyn had been angered to learn that Katherine of Aragon was still stitching Henry's shirts (as her mother, Isabella, had once embroidered Ferdinand's) and insisted she should—briefly, as it proved—take over the task. She would have learned the traditional female arts back at Mechelen, where Margaret of Austria's personal possessions included a distaff and spindle with which to spin. (Margaret once sent her father, Maximilian, some shirts she had helped to make. 'Our skin will be comforted with meeting the fineness and softness of such beautiful linen, such as the angels in Paradise use for their clothing', Maximilian wrote in the chatty letters they exchanged.)

Before Christmas 1530 Anne ordered a new livery for her servants, which would bear her recently adopted motto: 'Thus it will be, Grumble who will'. It had been the motto of Margaret of Austria's court. Chapuys reported Anne on New Year's Day 1531 declared 'that she wished all Spaniards were at the bottom of the sea . . . that she cared not for the queen or any of her family, and that she would rather see her hanged than have to confess that she was her queen and mistress'.

In February Henry VIII demanded that the church authorities recognise him as 'sole protector and supreme head of the English church and clergy'. Anne Boleyn, Chapuys reported, made 'such demonstrations of joy as if she had actually gained Paradise'. In fact, her marriage to Henry was far from a done deal; many even of those who had backed Anne as a political counter to Cardinal Wolsey still baulked at the prospect of Anne as queen. But the situation was worsening dramatically for Katherine of Aragon.

At the end of May, Henry's emissaries had a final attempt at persuading Katherine to see reason. She refused with a fortitude that belied her description of herself as 'a poor woman without friends or counsel'. Anger at her recalcitrance brought, at last, an end to these strange last two years in which Katherine had retained her place as queen, moving around the country at the king's side, even though Anne might also be one of the party. Early in July they were all three at Windsor; on the fourteenth Henry and Anne rode away to hunt at Chertsey Abbey, ordering Katherine to remain behind. Some days later, Henry's council rejected her message, asking if she might bid her husband farewell, in the first letter not to address her as queen.

Her husband was not the only member of the family from whom Katherine of Aragon was to be separated. Her daughter, Mary, had been with her at Windsor. When Katherine was sent away to one property, Mary was sent to another some miles away. There are some indications that Henry may have been forced by pressure of public opinion to allow a brief visit in 1532, but what is certain is that mother and daughter would never be allowed to live together again.

For the moment at least, Katherine of Aragon still kept her state—a Venetian visitor reported that she still had thirty maids of honour around her as she ate and a court of two hundred—but she regarded herself as a virtual prisoner, telling the imperial ambassador Chapuys she would rather be in the Tower and overtly locked up. The Venetian also gave it as his opinion that the people would accept no other queen.

Keeping Katherine and her daughter apart was a punitive measure. But there was, too, a genuine fear that Katherine—'a proud, stubborn woman of very high courage', wrote Henry—might, in her defence of Mary's interest, 'quite easily take the field, muster a great array, and wage against me a war as fierce as any her mother Isabella ever waged in Spain'. (In fact, had the authorities but known it, Katherine wrote that war 'is a thing I would rather die than provoke'.) Told, she said, that 'the next parliament is to decide whether I am to suffer martyrdom', Chapuys wrote to Charles V that the queen was 'so overscrupulous' that she preferred to suffer.

In the event, the very separation became a perverse reinforcement of the bond between mother and daughter, a hatred of the forces that had kept them apart, a harsh and unyielding commitment to her rights and her religion, which would be Mary's hallmark. The Game of Queens was an unforgiving one.

23

'A NATIVE-BORN FRENCHWOMAN'

ENGLAND, 1532–1535

❋

In 1532 Anne Boleyn had the chance to deploy another weapon in her armoury. Politically as well as in her religious tendencies, she had long made a point of playing up her French connections, the fact that she seemed, as French diplomat Lancelot de Carles had put it, 'a native-born Frenchwoman'. Indeed, in 1530 imperial ambassador Chapuys had written that it was her alliance with Henry VIII 'on which alone depend the credit and favour the French now enjoy at this court'.

By 1532 a French alliance had become a more general goal. It was, after all, the French who were likeliest to assist Henry in putting pressure on the pope to grant his divorce. Practical control of the king's 'Great Matter' was now largely in the hands of that new man on the scene, Thomas Cromwell. Rising from the ashes of his erstwhile master, Wolsey, Cromwell had been a member of the Privy Council since the end of 1530. Now he would mastermind the process by which, this spring, first Parliament and then the clergy were persuaded to ratify Henry as sole head of the church.

But in the latest negotiations, Anne Boleyn too was still key. As French ambassador De La Pommeraye accompanied the English court on the summer hunting trip cum progress, King Henry discussed his private affairs with the envoy and took 'as much trouble to give me good sport as though I were some great personage', De La Pommeraye reported proudly. He was often stationed 'quite alone' with Anne, who had given him a new set of hunting gear, complete with hound, for the occasion.

Henry VIII had determined to further his goal of an Anglo-French alliance by meeting his brother king face-to-face in Calais, come the autumn. Anne took the plan further. She was herself an ardent friend to France, she told De La Pommeraye, but many of Henry's advisers felt differently. Would it not be best if she too were present at the meeting? De La Pommeraye was persuaded, writing home that François I 'should request King Henry to bring Lady Anne with him to Calais', adding, 'but then the King [François] must bring the queen of Navarre with him to Boulogne'.

The French ambassador told Chapuys that Anne Boleyn's services to France were more than could ever be repaid. But the debt did not go only one way. French backing gave Anne, the commoner, a measure of credibility. There was even a notion that she and Henry might marry during this summit, in Calais, with King François present at the ceremony. Katherine of Aragon was, Chapuys said, very much afraid of it, though Anne had told a confidant she, instead, wished the ceremony to be 'in the place where queens are wont to be married and crowned'. Nonetheless, the idea was a persistent one. Well after the French trip had gotten under way, Venetian reports could still declare with confidence that the marriage would take place the following Sunday.

In September Henry declared that Katherine of Aragon should hand over her jewels—even those she had brought from Spain—to deck Anne for the forthcoming encounter. Katherine retorted that it was 'against her conscience to give her jewels to adorn a person who is the scandal of Christendom', but that if Henry sent a direct command, she would comply. Anne got her jewellery, and Chapuys reported that 'the Lady', as he called her, was also busy buying costly dresses. On 1 September, Henry created Anne Lady Marquess of Pembroke, to raise her status for the encounter ahead. Immediately afterward—no coincidence—came ratification of England's treaty of mutual aid with France, in the event of any Habsburg aggression.

But these plans meant that Marguerite of Navarre had now to make a difficult diplomatic decision. French queen Eleanor, as Katherine of Aragon's niece, was never wished or expected to attend. But at the last minute, Marguerite too withdrew. She may have been ill—the diplomatic excuse—or she may, as one report said, have come to see Anne not as a fellow reformer but as a figure of scandal. But the decision may not have been wholly her own: though French reforming thinkers believed their country should stand with Henry and Anne, there was a strong and divisive counteropinion.

Chapuys reported to Charles V that Henry VIII was 'vexed that Madame d'Alençon will not come' and that François instead suggested bringing another lady, who might be accompanied by some of the more disreputable elements of the French court. 'These people [Anne and Henry] cannot see

The game of chess, with its all-important queen, was both popular and an acknowledged metaphor of rule in the fifteenth and sixteenth centuries. Sofonisba Anguissola painted her sisters playing chess (above). Both Isabella of Castile, pictured with her husband Ferdinand (below left), and Anne de Beaujeu (below right) were notable players.

The young Margaret of Austria (far left) could not have known that she would one day be seated across the conference table opposite her erstwhile playmate Louise of Savoy (left). Louise's daughter, Marguerite of Navarre (right) was also an important player in the great game of international diplomacy, as seen at the spectacular festivities of *The Field of the Cloth of Gold* (above).

The Tudor dynasty was split by the contest between Katherine of Aragon (below) and Anne Boleyn (above right)—the first and second wives of Henry VIII. Henry's sister Margaret Tudor (above left), married to the King of Scots, also got drawn into the debate.

The personal and religious conflict between Anne Boleyn and Katherine of Aragon would be inherited by their daughters Mary (above right) and Elizabeth (above left). *The Allegory of Succession* (below)—adapted in Elizabeth's reign from an earlier painting—shows the Protestant Elizabeth I attended by the goddesses of peace and plenty, and the Catholic Mary by the god of war.

While Marie de Guise (above left) fought to maintain Catholicism in Scotland, religious divisions were also clear on the continent. As Regents of the Netherlands both Mary of Hungary (above right) and Margaret of Parma (below) were compelled to crack down on Lutheranism. Margaret is pictured fishing for goods in a river of blood as Protestant rebels are condemned to death.

In France, Jeanne d'Albret (above left) became the heroine of the Huguenots, while Catherine de Medici (above right) was widely blamed for the Massacre of St Bartholomew's Day (below).

Two queens in one isle ... Elizabeth I and Mary, Queen of Scots, were divided not only by personal rivalry but by the warring religions that made Mary a contender for Elizabeth's throne. Mary's execution at Elizabeth's hands was a final move in the sixteenth century's Game of Queens.

·MARIE·STVART·REYNE·DESCOSSE·
VEVFE·DE·FRANCOIS·SECOND
·ROY·DE·FRANCE·

the mountains in their own eyes and wish to take the straw from the eyes of others', added Chapuys acidly.*

Perhaps in the last resort Marguerite of Navarre was more of a royal than a reformer. It was a pity, Anne recalled looking back two years later: 'There was no one thing which her grace so much desired . . . as the want of the said queen of Navarre's company, with whom to have conference, for more causes than were meet to be expressed, her grace is most desirous'. As queen, Anne would not forget her goal of contact with Marguerite of Navarre, would send word to Marguerite herself that 'her greatest wish, next to having a son, was to see you again'.

Still, when October came Anne Boleyn was greeted in Calais with every sign of pleasure (and a very valuable diamond) when François and the men of the French court came over from Boulogne, where the bulk of the encounters between the two kings had taken place. She would, after all, have known these men a decade before. And it was almost certainly either at that meeting in Calais or on the way home—forced to dawdle by a massive storm for days after the formalities had ended—that Anne and Henry VIII started sleeping together. It was perhaps Anne's throw of the dice: a pregnancy would force an end to all delays.

Anne was indeed pregnant by the time she and Henry married, at the end of January 1533, in a secret ceremony. In February Anne, surely intentionally, let the cat out of the bag with a public joke about her great longing to eat apples. A fancy for a particular food was known as a sign of impending maternity.

By the end of the month, Chapuys was spreading the news. Katherine of Aragon was informed that she was no longer to be addressed as queen and her state and income greatly reduced. That Easter Anne was prayed for as queen. In the Netherlands there was a rumour that the emperor, with certain English nobles, would go to war for Katherine, would 'assist her from field to field . . . with her crown upon her head'. But short of actually that, there was nothing anyone could do.

The old Archbishop of Canterbury had died the year before, and on 30 March Thomas Cranmer was consecrated in his place. In April the Act in

---

* Mary Tudor, Anne Boleyn's former mistress, was also absent. Her health really was poor; she would die within the year, amid rumours she was killed by the 'sorrow' of seeing her brother Henry abandon his wife. But her hostility was in contrast to the attitude of Henry's other sister, Margaret Tudor in Scotland, who would write to Anne, once queen, as 'our dearest sister' and who was happy to see her daughter, Margaret Douglas, welcomed to Anne's court.

Restraint of Appeals forbade appeals to Rome on any matter, which meant Katherine's fate was now entirely in Henry's hands. On 23 May Cranmer used his new power to declare Henry's marriage to Katherine of Aragon void, and, five days later, to validate that of Henry and Anne Boleyn.

On 1 June Cranmer was able to crown Anne in a deliberately resplendent public ceremony. The official entry of a queen into her city was supposed to reflect the assumption of the Virgin Mary into heaven, and this one did. The new emphasis on classical as well as biblical mythology, however, may have been something Anne had gleaned from the French court. Anne dressed in the French fashion, and in white, for the procession to Westminster Abbey, a procession headed by the French ambassador's servants, in blue velvet and white plumes. The report Chapuys sent to the Netherlands declared that the crowd had withheld any sign of pleasure, but the crown of Saint Edward, hitherto used only for monarchs, was placed on her head.

'Queen Anne, when thou shalt bear a new son of the King's blood; there shall be a golden world unto thy people!', the pageants at the coronation declared, and both parents seemed confident in the prophecy. But when Anne's child was born on 7 September, at three o'clock in the afternoon, it was, disappointingly, a daughter, who was nevertheless named Elizabeth after the king's mother (and Anne's).

The official line was that the birth of a healthy daughter was surely a pledge that a healthy son would follow. Though the tournament planned for the arrival of a prince was cancelled, the prewritten letters of announcement were sent out with 'prince' altered to 'princes[s]', and the French ambassador was once again guest of honour at the splendid christening. But the fact remains that if Anne Boleyn's baby had been a boy, her position would have been unassailable—she would have won. With only a daughter in the cradle, everything was still to play for.

A daughter was certainly enough to ensure Anne's unremitting hostility to that other mother and daughter who might stand in hers and Elizabeth's way. She sent orders not only that Katherine of Aragon's daughter, Mary, should come to attend on her daughter, Elizabeth, when the baby heiress was given her own household, but also that if Mary should insist on being called princess, Elizabeth's attendants were to box her ears 'as the cursed bastard that she was'.

In part, no doubt, her aggression sprang from fear. 'She is my death, and I am hers', Anne is reported to have said. On several occasions Anne would in fact make conciliatory gestures toward Mary, which would always be rejected, an attitude very actively endorsed by Katherine of Aragon. Perhaps

Henry and Anne were right when they were both, separately, credited with attributing Mary's obstinacy to her 'unbridled Spanish blood'.

On 23 March 1534—the very day, ironically, that the pope tardily declared in Katherine's favour—Parliament passed the first Act of Succession, declaring Anne Boleyn Henry's lawful wife and their children the heirs to the throne. Everyone of consequence would be asked to swear to it. Princess Mary had been bastardised, and mother and daughter knew that Mary would be asked to renounce her title. 'Daughter, I heard such tidings today that I do perceive, if it be true, the time is come that Almighty God will prove you; and I am very glad of it', Katherine of Aragon wrote, in terms that reflect her belief that their very lives might be in jeopardy. 'If any pangs come to you, shrive yourself; first make you clean; take heed of His commandments, and keep them as near as He will give you grace to do, for then you are sure armed. . . . [W]e never come unto the kingdom of Heaven but by troubles'.

That November the Act Respecting the Oath to the Succession required swearers 'to be true to Queen Anne, and to believe and take her for the lawful wife of the King and rightful Queen of England, and utterly to think the Lady Mary daughter to the King by Queen Katherine a bastard, and thus to do without any scrupulosity of conscience'. It also required that they abjure any 'foreign authority or potentate'.

At the end of the year, Henry opened Parliament to pass the Act of Supremacy, declaring that Henry VIII was and always had been 'the only supreme head on earth of the church of England'. It was Henry's, and Cromwell's, determination to crush any opposition, but Anne has certainly gotten much of the blame.

For a woman to act as scapegoat was perhaps the reverse side of a queen's traditional intercessory function, the same distancing of responsibility from the monarch himself that had allowed Margaret of Austria and Louise of Savoy to make peace more easily than their men. But in June 1534 Chapuys had reported fear that if Henry went abroad, Anne swore that when she was left in authority during his absence, she would have Mary's life.

The interesting thing is that Anne Boleyn assumed she would be given these regent's powers, would follow in the footsteps not only of Katherine of Aragon but also of the great and potent European women she had known.

24

'INCLINED TOWARDS
THE GOSPEL'

France and the Netherlands, 1533–1536

❊

Across the Channel as in England, religious divisions had hardened in the year or so that followed the deaths of Margaret of Austria and Louise of Savoy. In France, when Gerard Roussel, chaplain to the king's sister, Marguerite of Navarre, preached a Lenten sermon at the Louvre, he became an overnight star, to the fury of the Catholic conservatives. But Roussel (as French-born reformer John Calvin angrily wrote to him) was, like his patroness, treading an impossibly fine line between evangelical ideas and continued loyalty to the Catholic Church.

As both sides carried placards through the street, moderates blamed the University of Paris for the hysteria of their response, while conservatives spoke of Lutheranism and accused Marguerite and her husband, Henri of Navarre, along with Roussel. King François intervened, but Roussel was arrested and Marguerite had to rush to his defence, eventually finding him a bishopric safely within her husband's own territories. Nothing Roussel had said was heresy, she protested—how could it be? He was in her service, and she would never have listened to 'such poison'.

When Marguerite of Navarre was viciously mocked in a farce at the university, François took the insult on himself. When in February 1534 an orator accused her of being the spokeswoman for the reformers, François demanded the speaker's imprisonment. Marguerite's own first instinct was not to sound the retreat; instead, she was pressing for a political alliance against the emperor with the German princes, Protestant as well as Catholic, and attempting to bring to France scholar Philip Melanchthon, Luther's close associate. But the French court was coming to be split along religious lines.

One unlikely recruit to the reformist faction was newly arrived in France, the pope's young niece Catherine de Medici. In the autumn of 1533, escorted by the Duke of Albany (who was married to her mother's sister), Catherine arrived in Marseille to marry François I's second son, Henri.

An entire district of the city had been blown up to make way for the accommodation of her retinue and that of the pope, her uncle. Catherine brought with her a staggering wardrobe and an unparalleled array of jewels (as well as Marie the Moor and Agnes and Margaret the Turks, captured 'in expeditions against the Barbary'). She wore gold brocade and violet velvet for the marriage ceremony, trimmed with ermine and thick with gems, a handsome-enough figure despite her strong features and protruding eyes. 'She is a beautiful woman when her face is veiled', said a courtier later, ungallantly.

The holiday atmosphere of this seaside wedding reputedly had a loosening effect on the already lax morals of the French court, but Catherine de Medici and her spouse, Henri, must have found the wedding night an ordeal. François insisted on remaining in the nuptial room and afterward (Brantôme writes) declared that both the fourteen-year-olds had performed well in 'the joust'.

Catherine received a more understanding welcome from Marguerite of Navarre, but her early years at the French court were difficult ones. When in September 1534 her uncle the pope died, the value of the Medici alliance plummeted, causing François to complain in horror (when the new pope refused to pass on Catherine's promised dowry) that his son's bride had come *toute nue*, stark naked. All too obviously uninteresting to her youthful husband, she was sneered at by the French courtiers as a merchants' descendant.

Marguerite of Navarre's position, too, was becoming ever more challenging. October 1534 saw the 'Placard Affair', when the inhabitants of Paris and a handful of other cities woke up to find placards nailed up in the streets attacking 'the horrible, great, and insufferable abuse of the papal Mass'. Legend says there was even one affixed to the king's bedroom door. When the reformers (or, as Marguerite later swore, conservatives trying to discredit them) began insulting even the sacraments, it was war. Amid widespread panic, a special commission was set up to try suspects, and when in January 1535 the protesters managed the dissemination of a radical tract, the authorities clamped down yet further. Marguerite, perhaps wisely, had by this time withdrawn to her husband's estates in Béarn, and though she clearly distanced herself from those behind those *vilains placards*, her closeness to her brother seems in the years ahead to go into slight eclipse.

The publication of 'Lutheran' texts was banned (though many of the dissidents now followed not Luther's teaching but those of the far more radical Swiss Ulrich Zwingli).* Many of Marguerite of Navarre's former associates found it prudent to flee abroad. Those who harboured heretics were to be punished as severely as they, and one who suffered the ultimate penalty, being burned at the stake, was the man who had published the second edition of Marguerite's *Miroir*. The book had itself come to attract hostility from theologians at the University of Paris, though when it was briefly placed on the list of banned books, François once again intervened.

In July 1535 François ordered an end to the persecution and the release of all religious prisoners (who had, however, only six months' grace in which to renounce their views). He and his sister were shortly back together again and united in trying for Marguerite's old dream, an alliance with the German princes against the emperor. At the start of 1536, when the pope (still in pursuit of that Christian alliance against the Turks) organised peace talks between François and Charles V, Marguerite attended as France's representative, though the peace talks failed.†

In the years ahead, Marguerite of Navarre would spend increasing amounts of time in the South and writing. Even Marguerite's husband, if the recollections attributed to her daughter are accurate, seems angrily to have warned her off her dangerous experiments of faith. Her prodigious output saw her turn increasingly to secular texts, albeit with often a moral or even a religious message under the surface. Crucially, almost none would be published within her lifetime.

IN THE NETHERLANDS, MARY OF Hungary had likewise, in her earlier years, been accused of too much sympathy with Protestants, and was rumoured to be *bonne luteriene*, a good Lutheran. She had greatly admired the humanism of Erasmus, who wrote admiringly of her, and she had also spent formative years around the Germanic circles where Luther's teachings were

---

* Though both Zwingli and, by now, Luther rejected the idea that the bread and wine consecrated by the priest during the Mass became literally the flesh and blood of Christ, Luther still held by Christ's 'real presence' at the ceremony, which was denied by Zwingli and his 'sacramentarians'.

† In the war that followed, Marguerite—inspecting troops and reporting their condition, taking part in the interrogation of a spy—regretted that she could not do more, since the emperor's iniquities were enough 'to make all women want to be men'. 'Since I cannot give you the help I would like to, being a woman, I will not stop assembling a battlefield of praying supplicants', she wrote, in words that would be echoed in Saint Teresa of Avila's plan to restore the church with a praying army.

most in currency. When she became queen of Hungary, she aroused controversy there by appointing as her preacher Lutheran Conrad Cordatus, who then launched an attack on the papacy in front of the whole court.

In 1526 Luther had dedicated four psalms to Mary, having heard that she was, as he wrote, 'inclined towards the Gospel', despite anything the 'godless bishops' of Hungary could do to dissuade her. Her brother Ferdinand wrote reprimanding her, but Mary wrote back that she couldn't control what Luther had to say . . . without, however, dissociating herself from the connection.

Yet when the question of the Netherlands regency first came up, Mary had been anxious—for all her loudly professed aversion to the post—to reassure her other brother, Charles V, that she still held firmly by the family faith and would prove it by dismissing any possible Lutherans in her train. Charles, for his part, had warned that he would send even his closest relative—parent, child, or sibling—to the stake rather than condone heresy. But perhaps in the end their attitude was not so dissimilar; for Charles, certainly, this was less a matter of conscience than of civic order. 'By turning away from the Catholic faith, people will at the same time turn away from loyalty and obedience to their ruler', he said.

Once in place in the Netherlands, Mary of Hungary had proved a reasonably successful governor, making her court a centre of luxury and culture, eventually building a wonderful Renaissance palace at Binche for her home. Just as Mary and her sisters had themselves been raised by Margaret of Austria, so Mary continued the work, raising those of her nieces who had already come into Margaret's care. When Christina of Denmark in 1533 was, at the age of eleven, married to the Duke of Milan, her uncle Charles agreed she should immediately assume her wifely duties. But Mary—like Margaret before her—first protested and then stalled: 'You may endanger her life, should she become pregnant before she is altogether a woman', Mary wrote. She begged her brother to forgive her for speaking out, but 'my conscience and the love I bear the child compel me'. Forced to send Christina to Milan immediately after her twelfth birthday, Mary fell ill and asked to resign her post.

Like other women in power here, she found that stress took a physical toll, and the times remained taxing ones. In 1534 religion was once again the problem. In the neighbouring German duchy of Westphalia, Anabaptists seized the town hall of Münster and declared the new Jerusalem, founded on common ownership and the equality of man. When they called on the faithful to join them, many in the Netherlands heeded the call and set out up the Rhine.

Besieged by its expelled bishop, Münster fell only in June 1535, so it was against this background, and heightened Franco-imperial tension, that Charles V finally agreed to something for which his sister Eleanor, now queen of France, had long been pleading: that, after many years apart, she and her sister Mary of Hungary might meet.

In the summer of 1535, the two sisters did indeed meet, and at Cambrai, where Margaret of Austria and Louise of Savoy had faced each other just six years before. But this time Charles had decreed that no politics were to be discussed, and though Eleanor came with a great retinue, at least some of whom surely hoped for diplomatic discussion, Mary unyieldingly followed her brother's script.

A sign of the changing times, perhaps, or just of very different personalities. Certainly, no great results were achieved by *this* meeting at Cambrai.

25

'TO DOUBT THE END'

ENGLAND, 1536

✳

'Take great care to live well so that you have no reason to doubt the end, and so that you have the grace of God in this world and in the next', Anne de Beaujeu had warned. The Game of Queens was played for high stakes and could carry a deadly penalty. The first half of 1536 would see the death of not one but two English queens. Before the corn was ripe in the fields, Katherine of Aragon's painful battle would be ended and her rival, Anne Boleyn, would have knelt in the straw of the scaffold to await the executioner's sword.

Like Katherine, Anne Boleyn had failed to produce another child; she probably miscarried in the summer of 1534 and possibly again in 1535. But Henry VIII's concern over what was perceived to be her lack of fertility would pick up shocking speed in 1536.

Katherine of Aragon died on 7 January, probably of cancer of the heart. She had been transferred sixty miles north to Kimbolton in Huntingdonshire, where she continued the dismal practices she had followed in her last place of imprisonment: having her meals prepared by the few old servants she trusted, for fear of poison, and refusing to leave her own room. She eschewed the new servants Henry had put in place, whom she regarded as 'guards and spies'. In the hours before she died, she wrote a last letter to Henry—'My most dear lord, king and husband'—urging him to prefer the 'health and safeguard of your soul' to worldly matters and to 'the care and pampering of your body'.

She said she pardoned him everything and prayed that God would do the same. 'Lastly, I make this vow, that mine eyes desire you above all things'. The defiant signature was that of 'Katherine the Queen'. Henry VIII and Anne Boleyn celebrated the news of Katherine's death with a party, but

Anne was acute enough quickly to realise that for her at least, the celebrations may have been premature.

The evidence is contradictory as to whether Henry and Anne's marriage was already in trouble or whether the events of 1536 came out of a clear blue sky. Was the marriage on the rocks? Imperial ambassador Chapuys reported so, but then he had, in a hopeful spirit, been saying so for years. There had continued to be regular reports of the couple as 'merry', and if there were also stories of squalls, then that had, certainly in the early days, been the nature of their relationship. Even Chapuys admitted that some of their broils may have been mere 'lovers' quarrels'.

But it is possible that what had attracted Henry in the mistress came to repel him in the wife. And if the king's attraction faltered, Anne Boleyn, unlike Katherine of Aragon, had no ruling European family behind her. Anne de Beaujeu had written wisely: 'Nor should you talk too much or too sharply, like many foolish and conceited women who want to attract attention and, to be more admired, speak boldly and in a flighty way'.

Shortly before Katherine's end, Henry had said to Chapuys that if she died, then Charles V would have no cause to trouble himself about English affairs. Crudely and callously put, perhaps, but it was true that Henry could now renew his relations with Charles without having to take Katherine back as part of the price. On the contrary, it was now the Francophile, the intrusive Anne herself, rather than the wounded figure of Katherine, who stood in the way of a new imperial alliance.

Anne Boleyn had been identified with the French interest almost as though she were indeed a Frenchwoman. (After Anne's death, Mary of Hungary, despite their childhood acquaintance at Mechelen, would remark that she had been a Frenchwoman and thus the Habsburgs' enemy.) And almost as though she had been a French princess married off and then abandoned, almost like others in this story, she found herself caught between both sides.

France had long been ambivalent about the new situation in England. Henry VIII had certainly believed François supported his search for an annulment, but France had proved unwilling to confront the pope to secure it. In 1535 Anne Boleyn had been shocked when France suggested a match between the officially illegitimate Mary and their Dauphin, more so when they proved lukewarm about the marriage of the baby Elizabeth even to one of François's younger sons. France's mounting persecution of reformers, moreover, alienated Anne's reforming friends.

Anne thought she had a trump card to play: she was once again pregnant. But on 29 January 1536—the day of Katherine of Aragon's funeral—Anne

Boleyn miscarried again, disastrously. She blamed it on the shock, five days before, of hearing that Henry had been injured in a joust. She had, as Chapuys reported, 'miscarried of her saviour'. 'I see that God will not give me male children', Henry told her ominously, later adding to a male courtier that he had been 'seduced by sortileges [enchantments]' into the marriage.*

No wonder Chapuys wrote to the emperor that Anne's reaction to Katherine's death had not been unmixed joy. She had, when she paused to think, begun to fear she would meet the 'same end'. In mid-January she had changed tack or at least tactics in regard to Katherine's daughter, writing to those in Hatfield—where Mary had been transferred, to join the baby Elizabeth's household—that Mary should no longer be pressured to acknowledge Elizabeth as her superior in rank. She must have been aware that Henry was now attracted to Jane Seymour, one of her own ladies-in-waiting: pale, passive, wholly English—a much more traditionally submissive model of femininity.

But the signs were contradictory. Anne Boleyn herself must have found them so. On 18 April Chapuys was persuaded or manoeuvred into doing what he had for so long avoided and acknowledged Anne, in her capacity as queen, as she passed through chapel—exchanging the 'mutual reverences required by politeness', as he put it—making Katherine's daughter, Mary, 'somewhat jealous' when she heard. That King Henry should insist the ambassador of the emperor, Queen Katherine's nephew, should acknowledge Katherine's supplanter, Anne, as England's queen surely suggests that Henry was not at this moment actually intending to put Anne away, though, conversely, having won this point may have meant that his ego was no longer so closely tied to having Anne accepted.

Henry VIII had come to doubt whether Anne Boleyn would give him a male heir; he wanted Jane Seymour. But there was another chain of dissent here. On 2 April 1536 Anne's almoner Skip had preached a sermon in front of the king's councillors, describing how King Ahasuerus was almost persuaded to the massacre of the Jews by his evil counsellor, Haman, and saved only by his wife, Esther. At her coronation, Anne (like, ironically, Katherine) had been compared to Esther, and Haman could easily be identified as Thomas Cromwell.

---

* The question has often been raised of whether the foetus was deformed—a 'shapeless mass of flesh' in one later report—raising the question, to the sixteenth-century mind, of witchcraft or satanic practices. See the Notes and Further Reading. But though the accusation of witchcraft had been levelled against several great ladies in the fifteenth century, notable Henry IV's widow, Joan of Navarre, and Elizabeth Woodville's mother, Jacquetta, it was not an issue raised in Anne's own day, nor did witchcraft feature in the formal accusations made against her.

Chapuys would write at the very end of Anne's life about 'the heretical doctrines and practices of the concubine—the principal cause of the spread of Lutheranism in this country'. But it is possible reform was proceeding along lines she had not envisaged. Already, in 1535, there had been a general inspection ('visitation') of the monasteries under Cromwell's aegis and some smaller institutions scheduled for suppression. But it was obvious the process would pick up speed. And Anne may have clashed with Cromwell over just where the proceeds of the Dissolution of the Monasteries should go, into education and social reform, as Anne wanted, or into the king's coffers.

The accusations made against Anne in the spring of 1536, however, were framed in terms of sexual misbehaviour. After Anne Boleyn's death, Lancelot de Carles, secretary to the French ambassador, said that Lady Worcester, a member of Anne's household, herself accused of lax morality, had exclaimed in her defence that her own faults were nothing compared to those of the queen. That the queen had had carnal knowledge of her musician Mark Smeaton; of one of the king's favourite gentlemen, Henry Norris; and of her own brother, George.

On 30 April Mark Smeaton was taken to Cromwell's house for questioning and—possibly under torture or the threat of it—confessed to having three times had sex with the queen. Anne herself described a recent exchange of words that seemed to show him languishing after her, languishing, perhaps, in the tradition of the game of courtly love that, however, his lowly rank did not allow him appropriately to play. Other remarks she made to other men, too, might seem to suggest the game of courtly love gone sour, but the point is that Smeaton's confession, true or false, put a whole new complexion onto all subsequent enquiries, which would now be operating from a presumption of Anne's adultery.

Henry was surely told of this. Scottish reformer Alexander Ales later told Anne's daughter, Elizabeth, that he remembered, after Smeaton's confession, 'your most religious mother carrying you, still a little baby, in her arms and entreating the most serene King, your father, from the open window. . . . [T]he faces and gestures of the speakers plainly showed that the King was angry'. The scene shows both Anne and Henry in distress, but surely still also in uncertainty. Henry decided to postpone for a week his planned and imminent trip with Anne to Calais, but the jousts to celebrate May Day the next day were still to go ahead.

Anne Boleyn must have sensed where she was vulnerable. Also on 30 April she had begged Norris to swear before her chaplain that she 'was a good woman', a reaction to another incident capable of a deadly interpretation.

Asking Norris, who was betrothed to marry one of her ladies, why he had not yet gone ahead with the match, Anne had suggested a scandalous reason: that Norris hoped to marry Anne herself: 'You look for dead men's shoes; for if ought came to the king but good, you would look to have me'. Under the Treason Act of 1534, words that intended harm to the king were treasonable.

As Henry VIII and Anne Boleyn attended the May Day jousts at Greenwich, Henry still showed Norris every sign of favour. But when the king abruptly left the festivities—something at which 'many men mused but most chiefly the queen'—the king began questioning Norris, promising him pardon if he would but speak the truth. Norris stoutly maintained his innocence, but, the next day, he was taken to the Tower, where Smeaton was already held, along with Anne's brother, George.

Four others were also arrested, accused of adulterous relations with Anne, including her old admirer the poet Thomas Wyatt and Sir Francis Weston, a gentleman of the king's privy chamber. Weston had been flirting with a lady of Anne's chamber but said that he loved another in Anne's chamber better and, when she pressed him as to whom, said 'it is yourself'.

'Thus, my daughter, whatever your age, guard against being deceived and remember what I told you before because you can be blamed even for something very slight', Anne de Beaujeu had warned.

All of this must have been running through Anne Boleyn's head. She surely had some inkling of trouble ahead: in the last week of April she had asked Matthew Parker, her chaplain, to have a special care of her daughter.[*] But it was a stunning blow when on 2 May she was arrested, accused of having had sexual relations with Norris, Smeaton, and one other. She said that 'to be a Queen, and cruelly handled was never seen', hoping that the king was doing it only to 'prove' her, a regular trope of courtly love.

Taken to the Tower, Anne asked if she would be placed in a dungeon. She was told that she would be housed in the royal lodgings she had used before her coronation. But she fell to her knees: 'Jesu have mercy on me'. The indictment drawn up preparatory to the trials said that she 'following daily her frail and carnal lust, did falsely and traitorously procure by base conversations and kisses, touchings, gifts, and other infamous incitations, divers of the King's daily and familiar servants to be her adulterers and concubines'.

More explicitly yet, she 'procured her own natural brother to violate her, alluring him with her tongue in his mouth, and his tongue in hers,

---

* Parker would become Elizabeth I's Archbishop of Canterbury.

against the commands of Almighty God and all laws human and divine'. This was the way in which a queen could be brought low and, as Anne herself protested in a memorable image, accusations she could deny only 'without I should open my body'.

On 12 May the four commoners actually to be charged were tried (Wyatt and another having been suspected but released). Smeaton again confessed his guilt, and the others pleaded not guilty. They were inevitably all four sentenced to a traitor's death. Three days later, on the fifteenth, Anne Boleyn and her brother, George, were each tried separately before a jury of their peers.

She entered the Great Hall of the Tower of London 'as though she were going to a great triumph', an eyewitness wrote. In front of some two thousand spectators, she answered firmly 'Not guilty' to each charge. 'She made so wise and discreet answers to all things laid against her, excusing herself with her words so clearly as though she had never been faulty to the same', recorded the Windsor herald Charles Wriothesley.

When George Boleyn's turn came, he both confused the issue and upped the stakes by reading aloud the accusation that had been written down for him: that he and Anne had laughed together over the king's lack of virility. But inevitably, again, all twenty-six peers found them guilty, and Anne's uncle the Duke of Norfolk pronounced the sentence: that she should be burned or beheaded, at the king's pleasure. Two days later, the five men were executed, and on the same day Anne's marriage was annulled.

On the nineteenth Anne Boleyn herself came to the block. In those agonising days in the Tower, she had cried out that her fate would be the death of her mother—that blood mother who figures so little in the stories of Anne. But otherwise, she seemed, so the Lieutenant of the Tower reported, to have 'much joy' in death.

WHY DID ANNE BOLEYN HAVE to fall? At the time, the obvious assumption was that she was guilty of the crimes with which she was charged. As one John Hussey wrote: 'If all the books and chronicles . . . which against women hath been penned . . . since Adam and Eve, those same were, I think, verily nothing in comparison of that which hath been done and committed by Anne the Queen'. But Archbishop Cranmer, as Scottish reformer Ales reported him walking in the gardens of Lambeth Palace in the early hours before Anne's execution, protested that 'she who has been the Queen of England upon earth will today become a Queen in Heaven'.

One theory, of course, continues today to hold that Anne was guilty of adultery, if not quite as charged. But it has few subscribers, the more so for the demonstrable inaccuracy of much of the detail of the accusations—the fact that she and her supposed lovers were often not even in the same place on the alleged date. (Also perhaps for the fact that Anne repeatedly swore to her innocence in the face of her death—'on peril of her soul's damnation'.)

But Anne Boleyn herself said that she 'believed there were some other reason for which she was condemned than the cause alleged'. Another and far more palatable theory sees her erstwhile ally Thomas Cromwell as the agent of her destruction. It is wholly credible that once Cromwell and Anne had fallen out, he feared for his own safety if she remained in place, the more so if he, like so many, saw her as having engineered the fall of Wolsey.

Yet another theory sees Cromwell as merely the tool of his royal master, Henry VIII, who—either genuinely convinced of Anne's guilt or cynically cruel enough merely to be seeking an excuse to be rid of her—ordered Cromwell to substantiate a case. Henry announced his betrothal to Jane Seymour the day after Anne's death and married her with indecent haste: even Chapuys on 18 May noted public anger that the king was so happy 'since the arrest of the whore'. Here essentially is the great problem for historians of these years: that Henry appears as either mutt or monster.

But perhaps there is a fourth, a compromise, position that allows for at least an element of confusion—of self-deception rather than deception by any third party—in the English king's reaction. Perhaps Anne died for an idea, and not any idea of the reformed religion but the old ideal of courtly love. The game she had learned in the European courts, the game that permitted—demanded—a measure of freedom with the men around her. The game with which she had at first enchanted Henry; the game she had never learned when *not* to play.

Early in her queenship Anne's chamberlain had written, 'As for pastime in the queen's chamber, [there] was never more. If any of you that be now departed have any ladies that ye thought favoured you and somewhat would mourn at parting of their servants, I can no wit perceive the same by their dancing'. *Servants* is the term from courtly love, but perhaps by this late stage in the long courtly tradition, the term could only be used cynically.

Anne Boleyn was, after all, not born to be a major player in that other game, the Game of Queens. She was a pawn 'queened', who had won for herself the right to move with a queen's freedom. And if she had found that that freedom had definite limits, well, so had others, better born than she.

Katherine of Aragon had been born into queenly rank, daughter of the woman whose authority had seemed to offer a lesson for the century. Yet she too had wound up in actual fear for her life and dying in a state that would have seemed absurd in her heyday.

If Anne had been in so many ways a transgressive figure, then Katherine had played by the rules throughout her marriage, transgressing only in her refusal to end it quietly. Yet her fate, like Anne's, served to show how conditional was a woman's power, a woman's privilege, in the first half of the sixteenth century. Conditional on a man's will; conditional on not being betrayed, in any one of a number of senses, by the vulnerability of their body, whether exposed in terms of their chastity or of their fertility.

Anne Boleyn's rise to queenship had revealed the powers of the role, but also its ultimate vulnerability. On the chess board the queen had assumed new powers, yet the safety or otherwise of the king is still all that mattered, ultimately. In the years ahead, Saint Teresa of Avila, in *The Way of Perfection*, would use the chess queen as her model for humility, because of her commitment to her lord.

These decades had seen a number of women exercise great authority. But with the sole exception of Isabella of Castile, all had exercised it conditionally, in the temporary absence or incapacity of a son, nephew, husband, brother. This made palatable a woman's exercise of power. In the latter half of the century, a new set of female monarchs—queens regnant, not regent—would present a new set of challenges, different not just quantitatively but qualitatively.

IN ENGLAND, SO THE NEW Second Act of Succession declared, both Henry VIII's daughters had now been declared bastards, bastards like Bessie Blount's son Richmond. And, as Chapuys reported, it might well have been decided that a male bastard trumped a female one. But on 23 July Richmond died.*

Illegitimated though they might now have been, time would not leave the Tudor sisters, Mary and Elizabeth, in obscurity. They would carry their mothers' rivalry—and, as religious divides continued to harden, their mothers' religious legacies—into the second half of the sixteenth century.

France too, in the summer months of 1536, saw the unexpected death of the Dauphin, its heir. (Contemporaries suspected, surely wrongly, that the

---

* Richmond's death was the more distressing for the fact that the king's niece Margaret Douglas—Margaret Tudor's daughter and another heir to the throne—had weeks earlier been caught out in a secret betrothal to Thomas Howard and sent to the Tower.

emperor had had him poisoned; other suspicions lighted on Catherine de Medici, the more so since the servant suspected of doing the deed was an Italian who had come to France in her retinue.) This left François's second son, Henri, as the new heir and meant that Catherine de Medici, formerly the disregarded wife of a mere younger son, was now the future queen of France. Truly, a new generation was on the way.

PART IV
1537–1553

My lord Gaspar shall not find me an admirable man, but I will find you a wife or daughter or sister of equal and sometimes greater merit.

—Baldassare Castiglione,
The Book of the Courtier (1528)

26

DAUGHTERS IN JEOPARDY

England and Scotland, 1537–1543

The middle years of the sixteenth century represent something of a hiatus in the story of powerful queens or regents. Across France and Spain, as well as in England, women resumed their traditional place: behind a powerful man. There were, however, two notable exceptions: Scotland and the Netherlands. Coincidentally or otherwise, these were among the lands where the Reformation battle was being fought most fervently.

In England these years represent the gap between the deaths of Katherine of Aragon and Anne Boleyn and the accession of Katherine's daughter, Mary. Henry VIII's marital adventures continued with the birth of his son Edward and the death of Jane Seymour in October 1537, his marriage to and divorce from Anne of Cleves in 1540, followed hard by his marriage to Katherine Howard (Anne Boleyn's kinswoman) and Katherine's downfall and execution in 1542.

The tales of all of Henry's wives are, of course, among British history's most dramatic personal stories. But if they point out a lesson in this context, it is if anything how disposable royal women could be. Henry's third, fourth, and fifth wives showed no sign of being active players in the political story.

What of his daughters? Elizabeth was a toddler—not yet three—when in 1536 her mother died. For all her noted precocity, she was a child throughout her father's remaining lifetime and not required to make any particular accommodation with his policies. But for Mary Tudor—already turning twenty when her mother died—it would be a different story.

The Act of Succession passed in the summer of 1536 decreed that the throne should go only to Henry VIII's children by Jane Seymour or by any subsequent wife. Elizabeth Tudor, like Mary, was 'illegitimate . . . and utterly foreclosed, excluded and banned to claim, challenge or demand any inheritance as lawful heir'.

But if they were bastards, they were still royal bastards: Mary stood as godmother at the new Prince Edward's christening, while Elizabeth (herself still so small she had to be carried) held up the end of his christening gown. And when the baby Edward in his turn was sent away from the court for his own health and safety, it was to join his sisters in Hertfordshire, with Mary as the pseudoparent in a kind of communal royal nursery.

At Hatfield, Hunsdon, Ashridge, and Hertford Castle, Elizabeth began to be educated in French, Italian, Spanish, and even Flemish as well as Latin; history and geography, astronomy and mathematics, as well as dancing and riding, music and embroidery—a fine humanist education of the sort that might be given to a boy. Elizabeth was not given any specific training for the throne, of the sort that had briefly been given to Mary at Ludlow, but then, as a female bastard, why should she be?

The problem was to know just what future could be planned for Henry's discredited daughters. Even Henry's own council noted that the girls were unlikely to be marriageable abroad unless they were made 'of some estimation' at home. But first, in Mary's case, came the question of submission to her father's authority.

Hard on the heels of Katherine of Aragon's death, Henry's men came to Mary, demanding that she sign a document declaring her acceptance that her parents' marriage had never been valid, that it 'was by God's law and Man's law incestuous and unlawful'. They had often before tried to wring such an acceptance from both mother and daughter, but now the mother was gone.

Mary at first refused, but still the pressure mounted. She wrote to her father, begging him to consider 'that I am but a woman and your child'. Finally, terrified for the lives of her friends and indeed for her own life, Mary capitulated and signed. The same document forced her to declare that she did 'recognise, accept, take, repute and [ac]knowledge' her father as head of the church in England and refute 'the Bishop of Rome's pretended authority'.

Her capitulation was as she saw it a weakness, and Mary Tudor probably never forgave herself for an action that helped to shape her as much as her mother's firmness. It did, however, signal the start of a new rapprochement with Henry.

On 6 July 1536 Henry's 'dear and well-beloved daughter Mary' rode secretly to join the father who had not spoken with her in five years. She received gifts, moneys, precedence over all but Queen Jane. Her position was a curious double-edged one. On the one hand, she was favoured; on the other, she was watched, and closely.

Some around her suffered after the uprisings of 1536 and 1537 against Henry's religious changes. The Catholic rebels of the 'Pilgrimage of Grace' demanded she be reinstated as her father's heir. But if Mary lamented their failure, and the savage penalties the rebel leaders suffered, she did so silently. In 1538 she was warned by Cromwell about the 'lodging of strangers' at Hunsdon. In 1539 the discovery of a supposed Yorkist plot against King Henry resulted in the execution of the sixty-eight-year-old Margaret Pole, the kinswoman and former governess whom Mary had called her 'second mother', among others. As Chapuys commented bitterly, 'It would seem that they want to leave her as few friends as possible'.

Mary made the best of what personal relationships were left to her. Late in 1536 she wrote to her father that Elizabeth was such a child 'as I doubt not but your Highness shall have cause to rejoice of in time coming'. She got on well with her father's fourth wife, Anne of Cleves (despite the fact that the latter had been married to cement a Protestant alliance), but badly with the flighty Katherine Howard, not only Anne Boleyn's cousin but nineteen to Mary's twenty-three. As 1543 dawned, she must have been relieved when news came of the king's impending and, as it turned out, final nuptials, to a cultivated and self-controlled widow of thirty.

Indeed, Katherine Parr was a member of Mary's household while Henry was courting her, and her mother had served Katherine of Aragon. Katherine of Aragon may even have stood godmother to her namesake and eventual successor. Now, ironically, Katherine Parr, like Katherine of Aragon before her, would come to represent the English side in the long story of the Scottish wars.

IN SCOTLAND MARGARET TUDOR was now completely estranged from power under her son James V's rule. Her dream of an English alliance had never gone away; in the early months of 1536, she had been preparing for what in fact would never happen, a meeting between her son and her brother. But she could only watch as her third husband, Henry Stewart, cuckolded her and squandered her money. She even tried to escape across the border into England, only to be brought north again. Something between an irrelevance and an embarrassment to both countries, Margaret Tudor could be found grumbling to the English envoy Sir Ralph Sadler that she had no letter from Henry: 'Though I be forgot in England, shall I never forget England. It had been but a small matter . . . to have spent a little paper and ink upon me'.

But Margaret's relationship to James would grow a little easier with her new role of grandmother (to two short-lived boys, not to her famous grand-daughter Mary).

In 1537, to reseal the 'Auld Alliance' with France, James V married King François's daughter Madeleine. He went to France to woo and wed her himself—as royal marriages go, it was a romantic story. But Madeleine (already ill with tuberculosis) died seven weeks after her arrival in Scotland. James still needed a bride, but King François was reluctant to commit his younger daughter to the Scottish clime. Luckily, there was an alternative, a young widow from an already prominent French family.

Marie de Guise (Mary of Lorraine) had been born, on 20 November 1515, into a clan rising fast through the French territories. Her father, Claude, Duc de Guise, was from the start of the reign a contemporary and crony of François. Claude's father owned the huge independent duchy of Lorraine, as well as large estates within France itself, and laid claim to the kingdoms of Naples and Jerusalem. (He was thus descended from the family that had produced Margaret of Anjou, wife of England's Henry VI and the woman who had played so controversial a part in the Wars of the Roses.)

Claude's mother, a cousin of François's mother, Louise of Savoy, was herself a famous figure. Philippa of Gueldres was a noted beauty in her youth, who ignored the pleas of her family in order to retire into the austere embrace of the Poor Clares when the youngest of her thirteen children was still only twelve. Not only Claude and his elder brother, Anthony, but King François himself would brave the convent walls to consult her.

Claude became a hero of François's first Italian campaign, wounded almost to death at the battle of Marignano but sufficiently recovered to ride at François's side as the king entered Milan in triumph. From that time, the Guise star was set in the ascendancy. When François's wars took him back to Italy in 1525, he left Claude as principal adviser to Louise of Savoy.

When German reformers took advantage of François's preoccupation to invade Lorraine, Claude was advised by his mother, Philippa, that while some illnesses could be cured by gentle care, heresy was a gangrene that had to be cauterised by fire or sword. From now on, Claude (created duke on François's return) would be seen as a Catholic hero.

One of the biggest influences on Claude's daughter, the young Marie de Guise, was probably her own mother, the forceful and devout Antoinette de Bourbon (though the Guise and Bourbon clans would be dramatically at odds later in the century). Antoinette was left to run the family estates in her husband Claude's frequent absences. Their eldest daughter, Marie, may have been intended for the church, since as she entered her teens she was sent to join her grandmother Philippa in the convent of the Poor Clares. But it seems to have been her own budding charms that, after two or three years, instead made her uncle Anthony decide she could be better deployed for the advantage of her family.

Marie's court debut in 1531 soon saw her treated by the king almost as one of his own daughters. There may have been some thought (in her family's mind at least) that she might marry one of François's sons, but a few weeks after Henri was betrothed to Catherine de Medici, Marie was instead betrothed to the Duc de Longueville, one of France's premier peers. The marriage was happy, and Marie soon gave birth to a son. She was back at court in time to be one of the principal guests when her friend Madeleine married the Scottish king.

Just four weeks before Madeleine's death, Marie de Guise's husband, Longueville, also died, and a month later she gave birth to their second son. The French king offered Marie to James V before her husband was two months buried.

Marie was appalled and the match beset with difficulty, not least as to how much of her dowry should come out of the Longueville estates, to the disadvantage of her sons. Rumour was saying François's son Henri wanted to put Catherine de Medici aside in Marie's favour, and soon another suitor entered the lists, in the increasingly portly shape of Henry VIII of England. Henry was attracted by everything he had heard of Marie, not least her large physique. 'I may be big in person', she famously retorted, 'but I have a little neck'.

At this already stressful moment, Marie's second son died, just four months old. Letters between Marie and her father, Claude, and mother, Antoinette, agreed that nothing should be done without Marie's consent; Marguerite of Navarre offered to mediate with her brother, King François, but Marie (once an advantageous contract had been drawn up) took the sensible course. She set sail for Scotland in June 1538, leaving her surviving son, and the Longueville estates, in the care of her mother, Antoinette.

Arriving in Scotland, Marie de Guise did everything right, encouraged by an exchange of lovely letters with her mother, saying politely that James V's new castles were the equal of anything on the Loire, befriending his illegitimate children, and making a friend of Margaret Tudor, her new mother-in-law. The extent of Marie's influence is unclear, unless we take anything from the fact that James resisted his uncle Henry's efforts to urge him toward making his own break with Rome, but the marriage could be accounted, broadly speaking, successful. There were, however, hints of personal dissent. In May 1540 Marie gave her husband a son, with another born just eleven months later. Within weeks, however, both babies were dead, to the great distress of both parents and of their grandmother Margaret Tudor (who would die of a stroke that November).

Soon there was another problem on the horizon—a renewed threat from England. Henry VIII's attempt to assert a historic overlordship of Scotland failed, but when James V tried to ward off a military assault by himself invading England, he found that too many of his nobles had been bought off by English gold. He pressed ahead nonetheless, and while he was not himself present at the disastrous battle of Solway Moss, in November 1542, some stories say news of the defeat overset his already fragile reason. Nor was Marie in any position to help him, being by now in the last stages of another pregnancy.

On 6 December 1542 James V took to his bed; on 8 December Marie de Guise was delivered of a daughter. Legend has it that James, hearing the news, murmured that 'it cam w' lass and it will gang wi' a lass'. (The Stewart family had inherited the crown through Robert the Bruce's daughter, Marjorie.) On 14 December he died, leaving the throne to be inherited by his six-day-old daughter, Mary Stuart.

Marie de Guise was not left in the officially sanctioned position in which Margaret Tudor had been. Her husband had left no will naming her as protector, and insofar as Margaret Tudor might be regarded as a precedent, it was not an encouraging one. Protocol, moreover, required Marie to remain in her apartments, in her capacity both as a mourning royal widow and as a newly delivered royal mother. Meanwhile, dominant position on the regency council was a bone to be fought over between the Earl of Arran (who if the baby died would inherit the throne himself) and the Archbishop of St Andrews, Cardinal Beaton.

Marie let it be known she sided with Beaton. Not only were his anti-English policies closer allied to her own French interests, but she probably had qualms about allowing Arran—so tantalisingly close to the throne himself—sole control of her vulnerable infant. Within a month of James V's death, Arran was indeed proclaimed Lord Governor of Scotland, but Beaton was to be Lord Chancellor.

Between them all, they had to find a way of confronting the ever-present English threat and of holding the throne for the infant Mary, Queen of Scots. Henry VIII proposed his own solution: to marry the infant Queen of Scots to his son Edward and have her raised at his own court, thereby securing control of her country. There was a real fear that if his proposal was refused outright, he would launch an invasion, and Marie de Guise could only play for time.

The first thing Marie did—amid fears that either England or Arran (vacillatingly in support of the English match) would kidnap the baby queen—was to get herself and Mary out of what was effectively Arran's custody and into the greater security of Stirling Castle. Soon, Marie was proudly showing off her infant to Henry VIII's envoy Ralph Sadler with every sign of pleasure in the forthcoming alliance. On 1 July the Treaties of Greenwich agreed to peace between Scotland and England during the lifetimes of Henry VIII and Mary Stuart, to a marriage between Mary and Henry's son Edward to be concluded when she was eleven, and to Arran meanwhile remaining as Scotland's governor.

But Marie had no intention of ever seeing these plans fulfilled, and she derived considerable support from their extreme unpopularity with the majority of Scots. A deal was struck that saw the infant Mary placed in the custody of four lords—rather than of Arran—and Antoinette in France wrote to congratulate her daughter on her escape from 'such a great and long captivity'. The baby Mary, Queen of Scots, was crowned at Stirling on 9 September 1543.

It was the French ambassador La Brosse who helped Marie de Guise and Cardinal Beaton find an excuse—Henry VIII's seizure of some Scottish ships, a breach of the peace—to declare void the Treaties of Greenwich made only months before and formally to renew the alliance with France. The summer of 1544 saw the start of the so-called Rough Wooing, a years-long and punitive campaign launched by an infuriated Henry to pay back the Scots for what he called 'their falsehood and disobedience . . . putting man, woman and child to fire and sword'.

The ensuing devastation was no advert for Arran's leadership of the country, and Marie de Guise decided to launch her own bid for the regency. Though the council agreed, the bid failed in view of the greater military power Arran could wield, but Marie won a role as leader of the special council that would now advise the Lord Governor.

Anne de Beaujeu's advice—that widows should strive to keep power in their own hands—might have been ringing in her ears. Marie de Guise had preserved her daughter's throne. But in England it remained unclear whether Henry VIII's daughters could find such a female protector, or role model—whether they would be so lucky.

27

PAWNS AND PRINCESSES
The Netherlands and France, 1537–1543

✤

As the infant Mary, Queen of Scots, assumed a throne she was too young to recognise—as Henry VIII's daughters faced an uncertain future—in France and the Netherlands, other princesses' lives seemed set on the traditional path: moved like pawns for the advantage of their families.

In the Netherlands, Mary of Hungary had scored one small but telling victory on behalf of one of her quasi daughters when, in 1538, she supported her niece Christina of Denmark—at sixteen already a widow—in her urgent desire not to make a second marriage with Henry VIII. The Holbein portrait painted in the course of the courtship gives little hint of the strong character behind Christina's reputed declaration that if she had two heads, one of them would be at the king of England's disposal.

Perhaps she got her trenchant tongue from Mary of Hungary herself, for when Mary heard that Henry had married again after Anne Boleyn's execution, she wrote to her brother Ferdinand: 'It is to be hoped, if one can hope anything from such a man, that if this one bores him he will find a better way of getting rid of her. I believe that most women would not appreciate it very much if this kind of habit becomes general, and with reason. And although I have no inclination to expose myself to dangers of this kind, I do after all belong to the female sex, so I shall also pray God that he may protect us from such perils'.

Mary's work in centralising the government of the various Netherlands provinces was too often hampered by the financial and military demands made by her brother Charles V. To pay for his Italian Wars, taxes were raised across the empire, and in 1539 the citizens of Ghent rebelled, their violent uprising put down only when Charles himself arrived with an army. (He paraded the rebellious burghers with halters around their necks, only to pardon them at Mary's public request: an exercise of a queen's traditional intercessory function equivalent to the one in England two decades before, when three queens had pleaded for the apprentices' lives.) After the revolt was quelled, Mary of Hungary begged her brother to relieve her of her post, but instead her appointment was renewed.

IN FRANCE, MEANWHILE, FRANÇOIS HAD from the first largely ignored his new queen, Charles V and Mary of Hungary's sister Eleanor. Yet the ghost of the Ladies' Peace never quite went away. Eleanor was present at the peace negotiations between Charles and François in 1538 and would be asked to take a more active role in 1544, when she met with Charles as well as Mary.

Eleanor's marriage to François remained childless. So, more seriously, did that of the heir to the French throne, Henri, to Catherine de Medici. Marguerite of Navarre had comforted Catherine: 'God will give you a royal line when you have reached the age at which women of the House of Medici are wont to have children. The King and I will rejoice with you then, in spite of these wretched backbiters'.

Catherine had won for herself the support of the older generation; King François himself was always fascinated by anything from Italy, the cradle of the Renaissance, and pleased by Catherine's membership of the *Petite Bande*, the gang of hard-riding, hard-living young ladies with whom he surrounded himself. When in 1538 there were even suggestions that the marriage might be set aside, Catherine spoke to her father-in-law, who assured her of his continued protection. The Venetian ambassador reported that she offered to go into a nunnery or to serve the lady who became her husband's next wife, behaviour diametrically opposite to that of Katherine of Aragon.

But Catherine's husband, Henri himself, had never warmed to his bride. He was falling increasingly under the influence of Diane de Poitiers, the legendary court beauty who now, despite the twenty-year age gap between them, became Henri's mistress.* Catherine de Medici—so the story goes—had holes sawed in the floorboards so she could watch, and learn from, what her husband and his mistress did in bed. (Ironically, Diane would over the next decade be one of Catherine's strongest supporters, believing the disregarded Italian wife to be less of a threat to her own position than another, better loved, consort might be.) More certainly, a royal doctor was called in to examine both Catherine and Henri and found slight abnormalities in both.

---

* Diane had a long court career behind her. Another woman raised in part under Anne de Beaujeu, she had served both King François's wives as well as his mother, Louise of Savoy. She was indeed related to Catherine, through their shared descent from the La Tour d'Auvergne family.

His advice—sadly unrecorded—seems to have been some slight change of practice or position. It was successful: in the summer of 1543 Catherine de Medici at last fell pregnant. The baby was born in January 1544 and named for his grandfather François, thus beginning another, and better-known, stage in Catherine's journey. (King François—present at the event itself—took such an urgent interest in proceedings that he demanded even to view the afterbirth.) Marguerite of Navarre wrote to her brother that this was 'the most beautiful, the most longed for, and the most needed day that you and your kingdom have ever seen'.

Marguerite had continued to be a force in French affairs and an ardent ally of her brother, attempting even, in 1540 and subsequently, to mediate an Anglo-French peace, with or without François's knowledge. But she would find herself increasingly torn by the differences between her brother and her husband. By 1537 the Navarrese couple, attempting to regain that part of Navarre annexed by Spain, had entered into their own secret negotiations with the emperor Charles V, whose son Philip, they suggested, might marry their daughter, Jeanne d'Albret. Every letter to Marguerite's brother breathes, in its exaggerated protestations of love and loyalty, her anxiety about acting against his interests in this way (and perhaps her desire to reassure him). The battlefields of Marguerite's ever-troubled loyalties were about to see their most bitter conflict.

IT IS POSSIBLE THAT MARGUERITE of Navarre's relationship with her daughter had indeed been affected by the difficult relationship she had had with her own mother, Louise of Savoy. Jeanne was at first raised largely in Normandy, where her foster mother, Aymee de Lafayette, lived. Jeanne's father, Henri d'Albret, was occupied either at court or in his own southwestern territories, while Marguerite had always been preoccupied by her role as supervisor of her brother's royal nursery.

Mentions of Jeanne in Marguerite's letters are scarce—only two during the first seven years of her life, and in one of those Marguerite was writing that she needs to rest 'away from my daughter, who is too noisy and boisterous'. By contrast, there was mention of Jeanne's always frail health when Marguerite was planning to take her away for a change of air in 1533.

In 1537, before she was ten, the question arose of Jeanne's best deployment as a marriageable pawn. Her father hoped she could be used to win the reunification of Navarre; her mother, deeply conflicted, wavered between supporting him or her brother, who had no wish to see the vital frontier state of Navarre thus allied to the Habsburg empire.

That summer François sent for his niece, but the child was seriously ill with, as Marguerite of Navarre wrote, 'fever and looseness of bowels with blood, which was so fast and furious that if God had not brought down her fever after twenty-four hours her little body would have had more than it could stand'. But Marguerite added, 'I hope that He who put her in this world to be of service to you will give her grace to fulfill the desire of mother, father, and herself, which is rather to see her dead than [commit] any deed against your intention. . . . On this I base my hope of her recovery'.

The hope was not misplaced: Jeanne recovered and (with her parrot and her pet squirrel) was taken away by her mother to recuperate. From her tenth to her twentieth years, Jeanne resided chiefly in Plessis-les-Tours, largely without either of her parents, but on the orders of an uncle, François, determined they should not dispose of her to their own advantage rather than to his.

While Jeanne d'Albret's parents were angling for the Spanish match that might reunite the kingdom of Navarre, François had very different plans. In January 1540 he received an offer for Jeanne's hand from the Duke of Cleves, a duchy in the Rhine. François was always keen to break the empire's hold on the German states, a hope the more realistic for the fact that some of them were tending toward the reformed religion. The marriage contract was drawn up in July that year, and Jeanne, informed of her uncle's plans in her mother's presence, declared herself 'content'.

It was understandable that her mother should delay as much as possible— Jeanne, after all, was only twelve when, the following spring, Marguerite of Navarre wrote tearfully to the prospective bridegroom that the marriage was 'not yet ripe according to God and nature'. François, however, was pressing for an early conclusion to the alliance and ordered her parents to bring Jeanne to court, where her Cleves bridegroom had now arrived. Marguerite had only succeeded in winning the hostility of both her husband (angered she had bowed to François's wishes) and her brother (irritated she had not done so more swiftly).

What happened next is a matter of some conjecture, the more so since only one report, from Spanish spy Juan Martinez Descurra, survives. According to Descurra, Marguerite of Navarre now suggested that her daughter should make a formal protest against the marriage before witnesses. With that protest in their pocket, Jeanne's parents could safely allow the betrothal to go ahead, insisting on keeping Jeanne with them until she was a few years older, and trusting that time would make an alliance between France and Cleves less pressing. Henri of Navarre agreed, warning his wife, however, that if she blabbed and word of the plan got out to her brother, François, he would see that she had 'as bad an old age as any wife or woman ever had'.

The formal protest was safely stowed away, but with François himself now bringing the duke to meet his bride, it was up to Jeanne d'Albret to tell her formidable uncle that she had changed her mind. François asked who had coached her, and the angry conversation (which Descurra reports in extended dialogue form) saw Jeanne sobbing and shouting that she would rather throw herself down a well than marry the Duke of Cleves. François told her and those around her, ominously, that 'heads will fall for this'.

As Jeanne reiterated her threat of suicide, her parents received a letter indicating that the emperor had no immediate intention of offering his son as an alternative husband. Marguerite and her husband had little choice but to let the Cleves marriage go ahead (at least in its initial stage).

What happened next is a confusing and worrying story. Marguerite of Navarre wrote to her brother, King François, that she had learned only with horror of her daughter's defiance, that 'my daughter, appreciating neither the great honour you conferred upon her by condescending to visit her nor realising that a good daughter has no right to have a will of her own, has been so foolish as to beg you not to marry her to the Duke of Cleves'. She, Marguerite, would be only too happy to punish anyone who had put such 'insolence' into her head.

By the end of May, François was preparing resplendent wedding festivities. On 13 June 1541, at the chateau of Châtelherault near Poitiers, the betrothal was celebrated, the king himself escorting the twelve-year-old Jeanne.

Both parties were asked for, and gave, their assent, though later in life Jeanne d'Albret would tell her own historian, Nicolas de Bordenave, that when asked for the third time whether she would marry the duke, she said only 'Don't press me'. She had, however, made another lengthy declaration, 'that the marriage proposed between me and the Duke of Cleves is against my will, that I never have consented to it, and that I never will'. Anything she might say to the contrary—the document continues—will have been spoken out of fear. Fear of her uncle, of her father, 'and of my mother the Queen, who had me threatened and beaten by the Baillive de Caen, my governess. [She] has several times brought pressure on me at the command of the Queen my mother, threatening that if I did not do everything the King wished . . . I would be so beaten and maltreated that I would die, and that I would be the cause of the ruin and destruction of my mother and father and

of their house. . . . I do not know to whom to appeal except to God, when I
see that my mother and father have abandoned me'.

As the marriage was celebrated with great solemnity, Jeanne—dressed
in crimson satin trimmed with ermine, a golden crown, and a gold and silver skirt trimmed with precious stones—was observed not to take a step
toward the altar, whether, says Brantôme, 'because she could not move
under the weight of her costume, or whether she wished to protest to the
last minute'.

François ordered the Constable of France, Montmorency, to take her
by the collar and carry her there. The nuptial Mass was followed by dinner
and by masquerades, but the putting of the couple to bed was a purely no-
tional ceremony, the bridegroom putting only a single ritual foot between
the sheets. A week later the duke set out for Cleves, and Jeanne—seriously
ill—was taken back to Plessis by her mother.

What had really been going on here? Various historians, through the
centuries, have put forward various explanations, but there is a problem
with each one. If we follow the spy Descurra's saga, then we see a Marguerite of Navarre who first set up the pretence of Jeanne's refusal and then
backtracked to protect her own position, leaving the child to bear the king's
anger alone. If we give credence instead first to Marguerite's own letter to
François, then we see perhaps the most extreme example of her prioritis-
ing her brother's needs over those of husband or child. If we believe Jeanne
d'Albret's declaration, of course, then Marguerite had gone further than
that, threatening to have her daughter beaten within an inch of her life . . .
and this the woman whose lifelong writings proclaim the female cause!
The kindest explanation is that it was all to some degree a put-up job, with
Jeanne complicit in her parents' pretence, though this scenario would surely
have required a good deal of the twelve-year-old's acting ability.

Jeanne herself gave a measure of explanation later in life, though it still
leaves much unclear. 'The marriage was performed . . . against the will of the
bride and of her father, who endured it rather than consented, in order not
to anger the King. The daughter did not dare to oppose [it] openly, as much
out of fear and respect for her uncle and for her mother (whom her brother
had won over) as because of the embarrassment and simplicity of her age
and sex'.

The narrative Jeanne commissioned relates how she secretly drew up
a protest, 'whether she was advised to do so or whether she did it on her
own initiative'. It is hard to imagine an unadvised twelve-year-old coming up
with such a ploy. But it is easy—the more you read Jeanne's own declaration,

with its dramatic tale of threatened beatings—to suspect you are witnessing Marguerite of Navarre's ability with fiction. Perhaps what we are seeing here is a teenager set in motion by her parents but then unable to retreat from the stand she had taken, as a more experienced politician might do. In all events, this was a wound that would fester, and this was not (with Jeanne technically now Cleves's wife) ever going to be the end of the story.

Small wonder that a letter from Marguerite to her son-in-law that winter describes Jeanne as still thin and poorly: 'We are doing everything to fatten her up, but she does not gain weight.'* Jeanne herself wrote to her new husband, 'There is no medicine in the world which could do so much for my health as knowing that yours is good'. Perhaps she had learned how to dissimulate in a good, or a politic, cause. Or perhaps the coaching went on.

France and Charles V were once again at war when, early in 1543, Jeanne d'Albret was despatched to join her new husband, who was proving himself a valuable French ally. But she was still on French soil when word came that the Duke of Cleves had instead been forced to switch sides and renew his country's old allegiance to the emperor. François immediately demanded an annulment of the marriage and instructed Marguerite and her husband to provide the evidence.

It was now that Marguerite of Navarre produced the signed protest from Jeanne, declaring she had married under duress. Marguerite and her husband would never have dared speak out, she claimed: 'If Cleves had behaved to you as he should have and as I hoped, we would never have entertained such a thought, and would have preferred to see our daughter die, as she said she would, rather than lift a finger to prevent her going to any place . . . where . . . she could serve you. Since he is so infamous we no longer fear to speak the truth'. Jeanne was forced to sign yet another witnessed declaration, this time with her uncle François's full approval, and even then there was yet another coda to this story.

Though Cleves himself had decided instead to seek an alliance with one of the emperor's nieces, before the fraught annulment could finally go through the pope had to be convinced by letters from Marguerite of Navarre in the spring of 1545, declaring she had 'forsaken all maternal tenderness' to force her daughter into the alliance, and from Jeanne, declaring that 'my mother, the Queen, preferred obedience to the king to her own life, and to mine'.

---

* Marguerite also instructed the French ambassador in England Marillac to intercede on behalf of Anne of Cleves, now in some sort her in-law.

The marriage was finally annulled that November. Whatever the truth of the affair, it is once again unlikely the fourteen-year-old Jeanne understood or forgave it completely, and the bitterness she felt may have been a lasting legacy.

BY CONTRAST, MARGUERITE OF NAVARRE and her brother, François, seemed back on their usual terms, apart from the ever-present religious question. A conference in 1541 attempted to find some common ground between Protestant and Catholic, but its failure would see increased persecution of Protestants (as they would come to be called) both in the Low Countries and in France.

The mood of the times was growing ever harder. When in 1542 François resumed his war with the emperor Charles V, he dared not leave behind him a country split by any challenges to state or church authority. From her husband's duchy of Béarn, Marguerite wrote to her brother, François, about the cruelties perpetrated in the name of eliminating heresy: 'a poor woman whose baby was aborted by torture . . . and many other things that should be heard by you alone'. She was, as so often, however, carefully treading a fine line, protesting not about the principle but rather the extremities of the persecution.

Complaining of a local bishop who was preaching that both the king and his sister supported heretics, Marguerite made a point of dissociating herself from those who attacked the 'real presence' in the Mass: 'Thank God, my Lord, none of our people has ever been found to be sacramentarians'. But she and her husband believed the local monks had 'found a way of putting poison in the incense' and were trying to do away with them.

She found herself at odds with her former protégé, the austere French theologian John Calvin, over her protection for two mystic preachers.* By contrast, the pope, who had enjoyed discussions with Marguerite, was inclined to regard her as his spokesperson at François's court. All good Catholics had fresh reason to be hopeful in these years. The opening of the Council of Trent in 1545 signalled a new crusading spirit in the Catholic Church itself, discussing the reform of corrupt practices as well as doctrinal decrees. But inevitably, the 'Counter Reformation' would itself be the pretext for aggression against dissenters in the years ahead, and at the beginning of 1545 Marguerite had been horrified when François, at the pope's request, authorised the massacre of perhaps several thousand members (estimates vary wildly) of the unorthodox Waldensian sect.

---

* Calvin would later be best known for his reforming ministry in Geneva and for the doctrine of predestination, which held that all events, and the fate of all souls, have been preordained by God.

Marguerite may as so often have found refuge in writing, encouraging those around her to undertake translations of Plato's dialogues, while she herself began exploring the relationship between the kind of ideal love figured in the courtly romances and Plato's ideas. On her southern estates she surrounded herself with the talented and literary. Her writings, however, provide no clear answer to Marguerite of Navarre's continued ambivalence about her female role, an ambivalence the events of these years can have done little to diminish.

In 1544 she wrote to François of the desire she had had all her life to serve him not as a sister but as a brother. Conversely, she would write too of her wish that she might give birth to a hundred warriors to serve him. Perhaps that admixture of messages is something with which many women had to deal, in the sixteenth as in any other century.

28

NEW WINDS
ENGLAND AND FRANCE, 1544–1547

✳

I n England in 1544, Katherine Parr was, like Katherine of Aragon earlier, left regent when Henry went away to war against France. When England's ongoing affrays with the Scots set her at odds with Marie de Guise,
it was an echo in minor key of the events of 1513, when Katherine of Aragon
and Margaret Tudor had found their armies at enmity.

Katherine Parr's regency also allowed both her stepdaughters, Mary and
Elizabeth Tudor, to witness a woman successfully wielding power, a spectacle
familiar on the continent but one that had not always come England's way.

Even religious differences seemed, at first, to be subsumed into the new
Queen Katherine's reforming zeal. Katherine Parr had her own literary aspirations, producing first the anonymous *Psalms or Prayers* and then, under her
own name, *Prayers or Meditations*, which made her the first queen to be a published author in English, if not French, history. The ten-year-old Elizabeth
Tudor made Katherine a New Year's present of her translation of Marguerite
of Navarre's *The Mirror of Glass of a Sinful Soul*, but when Katherine Parr
commissioned the translation into English from the Latin of some of Erasmus's *Paraphrases upon the New Testament*, Katherine's other stepdaughter,
Mary, was one of the translators. Ill health prevented Mary from completing
her translation of the *Gospel According to John*, but the final version nonetheless included a lengthy dedication to Mary as a 'peerless flower of virginity'.

Katherine Parr would herself very nearly go the way of other of Henry's
queens, when she fell under suspicion for the extent of her reforming tendencies.* Mary Tudor, by contrast, was able to accommodate to her father's

---

* The Reformation in England had already produced female martyrs on both sides: Elizabeth
Barton, the 'Holy Maid of Kent', who prophesied against Henry VIII's marriage to Anne
Boleyn and was hung for it, and the Protestant Anne Askew, who was burned at the stake,
having first been shockingly racked.

religious policies, which still included the supremacy of the Mass, the celibacy of priests, and the necessity of confession. In her brother Edward's reign, it would be a different story.

At the beginning of 1544 Henry VIII—fifty-two, and with no sign of the longed-for second son—laid down another Act of Succession. If he had no further child, if his son, Edward, died without heir, then the throne would pass to Mary. If she too died childless, then it would pass to Elizabeth. Both sisters feature in the anonymous painting *The Family of Henry VIII*. In the centre sits Henry himself enthroned, with the young Edward at his right hand and at his left the long-dead Jane Seymour, as mother of the all-important boy. These three are framed in a network of gilded pillars. Pointedly outside the magic circle of legitimate royalty—framed by another set of rather less conspicuous pillars—stand the two royal daughters, separately, Mary as elder to Henry's right and Elizabeth to the left.

In December 1546, the message of the portrait was ratified by the king's will, which confirmed the place in the succession of both Mary Tudor and then (assuming neither her brother nor Mary had left any heirs) Elizabeth. But as 1546 turned to 1547, as Henry lay dying, that seemed an unlikely contingency.

THE YEAR 1547 SAW A general clearing of the decks. The death of the obese and ailing Henry VIII on 28 January 1547 was followed, barely two months later, by that of his old rival, the French king François.

Marguerite of Navarre had spent the last months on her own estates, in pain from arthritis and apprehensive of the future. At the time of her brother's death, she was on the road to try to meet—rescue, revive—him, an echo of her dash to Spain twenty years before. She was staying at a convent in Poitou when the news of his death reached her; it was several months before she could bring herself to leave. '*O death, who conquered the Brother, / come now in your great goodness / and pierce the Sister with your lance*', she wrote in the '*Chanson spirituelle*', and,

> *My life was filled with sugar and honey*
> *when it was sustained by his*
> *but now it is nothing but absence and bitterness*
>
> *("Le Navire")*

The last years had seen difficulties between brother and sister. But in the end, he had, as she had recently written to him, supported her 'in the office of king, of master, of father and brother and of true friend'. François's death was not only a bitter personal but also a practical loss: a loss of influence as well potentially of the pension François had given her. Small wonder that one source of friction between her and her daughter was the high expenses of Jeanne's household, which Marguerite found, as she wrote to Jeanne's financial controller, 'insupportable'.

In fact, the new king Henri II relieved Marguerite of her financial worries, but he wrote of her dismissively as 'my good old aunt'. The new king's solemn entry into Lyons saw Marguerite of Navarre, who had once taken pride of place in every procession, grateful for a place in Catherine de Medici's carriage. ('I share your distress, as I always knew you shared mine', Catherine had written to her.) Catherine, by contrast, was, of course, now queen of France.

The deaths of the men in this story brought all too often, for better or for worse, a dramatic change for their women. In England as in France, Henry VIII's daughters (and his widow) would have to trim their sails to a new wind. The effects of the powerful kings' deaths spread like ripples from a stone in a pond. They would be felt in Scotland, albeit that, for some years to come, the fate of Scotland would be bound to that of France ever more closely.

THE DEATH OF HENRY VIII brought no end to the Rough Wooing, which indeed, in September 1547, saw the disastrous Scottish defeat at Pinkie Cleugh. It was amid real fears that the young Queen Mary would be kidnapped by the English that Marie de Guise contemplated a suggestion by the new French king, Henri, that the four-year-old Queen of Scots should marry his three-year-old son, the Dauphin, and be raised in France. The plan was agreed, and on 7 August 1548, with a numerous Scottish retinue (including her famous contemporaries and future attendants the 'four Marys'), the little Queen of Scots set sail for France and what, it was assumed, would be her future country.

29

ACCOMMODATIONS

France, 1548–1550

Everyone, you might say, was having to make accommodations in these years. In Scotland Marie de Guise was certainly having to deal with the realities of practical politics. It was two years before in 1550 the relief of a peace treaty between England and France—one in which Scotland was included—allowed Marie, too, to return to France for an extended visit. She was lucky: she might well never have seen her daughter again.

The English envoy to the French court wrote that Marie's work in Scotland 'is so highly taken here as she is in this court made a goddess'. It had been suggested that the Scots governor Arran should be replaced by a French governor, which would have allowed Marie a comfortable retirement, but one account says she went to Henri and said she wanted to rule Scotland.

She had the immense distress, during her visit, of losing the one surviving son with whom she had so recently been reunited, the young Duc de Longueville. She also heard of a plot to poison her small daughter, the Queen of Scots. 'Our Lord must wish me for one of his chosen ones, since he has visited me so often with such sorrow', she wrote to her own mother, Antoinette. But as she prepared to return to Scotland, she had acknowledged where her own future lay.

The little Queen of Scots, meanwhile, was growing up very happily at the French court. The Scottish train with which she arrived had largely been sent away; the French complained the Scots were uncouth and dirty, and even the four Marys were sent to be educated at a convent near Poissy, since the aim was to make Queen Mary as French as possible. But she had come to a welcoming place. Henri II and his wife, Catherine de Medici, were devoted parents, constantly demanding reports and portraits when absent from their children, among whose number Mary was now included.

There are records of the endless chain of pets brought into the nursery—mastiffs and even a bear—and reports, as she grew, of Mary and her attendants taking pleasure in playing at cookery.

She shared a bedroom with Elisabeth, the eldest daughter of Catherine and Henri. The king often wrote to Marie de Guise with 'tidings of our little household'. More significantly, Mary and the French princesses shared the same educational curriculum as the Dauphin, François—history and rhetoric, languages and poetry.

From the first, care was taken to foster the idea of love in the Dauphin and his future bride (or in the slightly older and infinitely stronger Mary of protectiveness). Care was taken, too, to pay due tribute to Mary's rank. Henri II was enchanted with his future daughter-in-law and wrote that 'she should take precedence over my daughters. For the marriage between her and my son is decided and settled; and apart from that, she is a crowned Queen'.

With hindsight, it is too tempting to look back to Mary Stuart's childhood and ask what it was in her education that so signally failed to teach her how to rule. Mary had, after all, come to a country with a formidable tradition of female governance—for all that Catherine de Medici had not yet come into her own—and from one where her mother was already a leading player.

But the question may be a misguided one, the answer to do with Mary's own character and with those lessons that cannot be consciously taught. The branches of study in which Mary excelled were embroidery (in years to come she would often sit and sew through Scottish council meetings) and dancing. She was taught what were considered the skills of rule, but she never learned the edgy arts—the awareness of danger and opportunity—that Elizabeth Tudor in England learned during her difficult youth. She was expected to live her life less as ruler of Scotland than as consort of France, and it is hard not to feel that that expectation shaped her, to her ultimate danger.

It's a ready assumption that Mary Stuart's early consciousness of her status was a source of friction between her and Catherine de Medici, based on a tale that she spoke of Catherine as a merchant's daughter. But it has been largely the work of fiction (extrapolating backward, from the later conflict between Catherine and Mary's Guise relations) to suggest that Catherine regarded the child with unremitting hostility. Catherine must in any case have been largely preoccupied with her own continuous childbearing—ten children in twelve years, with Henri's mistress Diane de Poitiers assisting at the births.

In the first years of her husband's reign, Catherine de Medici had found that her new title in no way meant she could shift her husband's dependence on his mistress. (Many years later, in a letter concerning her daughter Margot's marital problems, Catherine wrote that she had only 'made good cheer' to Diane for Henri II's sake, 'for never did a woman who loved her husband succeed in loving his whore'.) In her capacity as overall superintendent of the royal nurseries, Diane would, of course, have been a figure in the life of the little Queen Mary. But as Henri's reign wore on, Diane's influence was perhaps beginning to fade, while just the opposite was happening with Catherine de Medici.

By the start of the 1550s, one observer noted that the king now treated his wife 'with so much affection and attention that it is astounding'. She had first been made nominal regent in 1548, when her husband needed to travel out of the realm to secure his interests in Italy. Four years later she was given rather more authority in a second regency, when the king went to war with the Habsburgs.

To her annoyance, she found she still had to share the power, but what is striking is the zest with which she took to the duties, writing to Constable Montmorency over her task of raising troops and money for Henri: 'I shall soon be past mistress, for I study nothing else all day long. . . . [Y]ou may count on me to press and push'. She was, in other words, beginning to assume the posture that would see her set against another woman in another clash-of-queens story.

THE QUESTION OF A MARRIAGE for Jeanne d'Albret had survived her uncle King François's death: it was indeed to be a source of friction between her cousin the new king and her parents, who were still secretly hankering after a Spanish match. It was, however, as before, the king's will that would prevail. On 20 October 1548 Jeanne was happy to be married to Antoine de Bourbon, France's premier noble, first in line of succession to the throne if Henri's sons should produce no heirs.

Antoine was an attractive man, whose bravery as a soldier perhaps masked a more fundamental lack of resolution in his personality. The hasty ceremonies were scanty compared to those that had marked the abortive Cleves match. But as King Henri noted, 'I have never seen a happier bride than this one, she did nothing but laugh', adding that Marguerite of Navarre, by contrast, was in floods of tears, which seemed not to trouble her daughter in the slightest.

A courtier noted that Antoine 'performs his marital duties very well both day and night. He says that the six couplings went off very gaily'. Contemporaries noted that Jeanne, later so austere and forceful, seemed besotted by her husband, and Marguerite wrote to Antoine in the summer of 1549 that her daughter had 'no pleasure or occupation except in talking about or writing to you'. Antoine, for his part, wrote to Jeanne with surprising tenderness. 'I would never have thought that I would love you as I do. I intend another time, when I have to take a long trip, to have you with me, for all alone *je m'ennuye* (I grow wearied)'. Nonetheless, his military duties kept him often away, and Jeanne meanwhile was spending time with her mother, in what would prove to be the last year of Marguerite's life.

Marguerite of Navarre had lived too long, perhaps like Anne de Beaujeu before her. Though still only in her fifties, she was the last survivor of her generation, with even those who, like Anne Boleyn, had been her protégées now gone. Retreating to a modest country estate, it was venturing outside on a damp night—possibly to watch a comet—that caused the chill that brought about her death on 21 December 1549.

There had clearly been a degree of rapprochement, if such were needed, with Jeanne. In those last months, mother and daughter exchanged a series of verse letters, expressing, albeit in highly stylised terms, ideas of love and loss when apart from each other. Jeanne d'Albret's reaction to Marguerite of Navarre's death is not recorded, but in the years ahead she would come to take on her mother's mantle, as arguably Marguerite had taken on Louise of Savoy's, promoting certain of her mother's causes, however, in ways Marguerite could not have foreseen.

30

'DEVICE FOR THE SUCCESSION'

ENGLAND, 1547–1553

✸

In England too, with Henry VIII dead and a new boy king on the throne, the question of accommodation to new political realities was coming sharply to the fore. Edward VI and his advisers were committed to the new faith in a way that would never have occurred to Henry VIII. Those who clung to the old faith would find the times growing ever more difficult— and notable among those was Edward's thirty-one-year-old half sister, Mary Tudor.

Conservative Catholics might be pernickety enough to query a marriage conducted outside the pope's authority, but when her father died, Mary Tudor showed no sign of querying that her nine-year-old brother, as a male, had a superior right to the throne.

Another woman had long been watching over Mary Tudor's safety, the Netherlands regent Mary of Hungary. After submitting to her father and acknowledging her own bastardy, Mary Tudor had been forced to write to Mary of Hungary, as well as to Charles V, declaring that she had done so freely. Mary of Hungary (like Charles's wife, Isabella of Portugal) would be sent reports as to Mary Tudor's welfare.

Now emperor and regent refused to acknowledge Edward until sure of Mary Tudor's position. As Mary of Hungary wrote to their ambassador, 'We likewise refrain from sending you any letters for our cousin, the Princess Mary, as we do not yet know how she will be treated'.

In fact, she was, at first, treated remarkably gently and given enough lands to make her one of the country's leading magnates, a generosity designed to buy her complaisance in the new regime. But nothing would buy her complaisance in the attacks on religious rituals that—under a regency council headed by Jane Seymour's brother Edward, soon Duke of Somerset—were shortly under way.

There is no doubt that the religious reforms had the active support of the young king himself. That fact, in a sense, gave Mary Tudor her opportunity. Writing to express her horror at the changes soon imposed on the celebration of the Mass (communion in both kinds for laity as well as clergy and a denial of the real presence), she insisted that she would 'remain an obedient child' to her father's ordinances, until such time as her brother should 'have perfect years of discretion': a waiting game. The more evangelical a doctrine was propounded, the more furiously Mary's household practised according to the old forms. But for a time at least, she was given a measure of leeway, with Edward's council ever conscious of her watchful Habsburg relatives.

When late in 1549 'Protector' Somerset was deposed from the preeminent position he had taken upon himself, there were even rumours Mary would become her half brother's regent. Instead, John Dudley—a successful military commander and fellow reformer—thrust himself into power. As the new forces on the council struck an alliance with France, sidelining the Habsburg interest, Mary was placed under increasing pressure to cease having Mass said, even in her private household.

Even before this, Mary had felt her own position sufficiently precarious that she told the Habsburg ambassador she might need to flee the country. In 1550 it seemed that would indeed become a necessity, with a plot hatched between Mary Tudor, the ambassador, and Mary of Hungary, who sent three ships to stand by off the Essex coast, just north of the Channel, ready to snatch her away.

Edward VI wrote indignantly of how 'you, our nearest sister', wished 'to break our laws and set them aside deliberately and of your own free will, . . . I will see my laws strictly obeyed'. By contrast, the Christmas celebration of 1550 brought the king's other sister, Elizabeth, to London 'with a great suite of gentlemen and ladies', escorted by a hundred of the king's horses and formally welcomed by the council, the point being, as the imperial ambassador bitterly pointed out, to show that she who had embraced the new religion had 'become a very great lady'. Elizabeth was preferred to Mary by the new elite, being 'more of their kidney'.

Elizabeth's image as a virtuous Protestant princess had been somewhat smirched, less than two years before, by the scandal of her 'affair' with Thomas Seymour, the brother of Protector Somerset, who had married the widowed Katherine Parr. It started out as merely a distasteful story of bedroom romps, where the forty-year-old Seymour smacked the teenage Elizabeth's bare backside. But when Katherine Parr died after giving birth to

Seymour's child, it became clear Seymour sought to marry Elizabeth, a girl with a claim to the throne.

The early months of 1549 had seen what must, for the fifteen-year-old Elizabeth, have been a terrifying official enquiry, with her servants—including her governess and surrogate mother, Kat Ashley—incarcerated in the Tower. But she herself had fought free, though Seymour went to the block. Elizabeth's famous comment that 'this day died a man of much wit and little judgement' is probably apocryphal, but she had shown that when danger threatened, she could act not from the heart but from the head.

The Seymour affair may have reinforced the lesson her mother's fate could have taught her: that sex is dangerous. But for the moment, she concentrated on displaying the kind of maidenly modesty that would speedily ensure her complete rehabilitation in the eyes of Edward VI's court. Kat Ashley's husband would recall the 'free talk' and 'trim conferences' that took place between Elizabeth and those she gathered around her, notably her tutor Roger Ascham. She appeared in the demure garb befitting Edward's 'sweet sister Temperance', deliberately positioning herself as a contrast to the Catholic Mary.

When in March 1551 Mary came to London, she rode through the streets escorted by a host of gentlefolk, each carrying their rosary. The council reacted, at first, merely with a war of attrition against members of Mary's household. Soon, however, she herself was under such pressure that Mary of Hungary was writing to the imperial ambassador that if they took the Mass away from Mary Tudor, she would have to endure it, but if they tried to force her into 'erroneous practices . . . it would be better for her to die than to submit'.

Once again, however, all the participants drew back from the brink. This was in part because of continental troubles that meant a need to secure England's wool trade with the Netherlands, though Mary of Hungary, afraid England would join with France, proposed invading England to place Mary Tudor on the throne and secure the precious trade that way.* Edward's councillors were no doubt conscious that Mary was still, by the terms of their father's will, her brother's heir. This consciousness was about to grow more acute as 1552 turned to 1553 and Edward caught first one cold, then another, that he failed to shake off.

---

* When in October 1551 Marie de Guise visited Edward's court on her way home from France, Mary was invited to help entertain her. Sadly, she declined on a plea of ill health, afraid, perhaps, of more pressure, one of several meetings in this story one only wishes could have taken place.

As his health worsened, the young king himself, committed to his position as defender of the reformed faith, was for obvious reasons determined his throne should not pass to Mary. If it did, Edward told a reluctant Lord Chief Justice, 'it would be all over for the religion whose fair foundation we have laid'.

Less obviously, he determined that Elizabeth had also to be excluded, despite her adherence to the new faith. Elizabeth, he explained, was the daughter of a disgraced woman 'more inclined to couple with a number of courtiers rather than reverencing her husband, so mighty a King'. Perhaps the truth was that Elizabeth Tudor was too much her father's daughter to consent to the overturning of his will, or that John Dudley, now running England behind the cloak of the royal council, knew she would never be his puppet.

More probably still, it was because, still unmarried, she could be married to a Catholic prince and (such was the perception) find her country returned to Catholicism that way. If Edward's sisters married abroad, their 'stranger' husband would, as Edward put it, work to have the laws and customs of his own native country 'practised and put in use within this our realm . . . which would then tend to the utter subversion of the commonwealth of this our realm, which God forbid'. Better the princesses should be 'taken by God' than that they should so imperil the true religion, thundered one of Edward's bishops, supportively.

Instead, it was Edward's intention 'to appoint as our heir our most dear cousin Jane'. Eldest daughter of Frances Brandon, herself the eldest daughter of Henry VIII's younger sister, Mary, Jane Grey not only was herself ardently Protestant but had also recently been married to Guildford Dudley, John Dudley's son.

Not that Edward had wanted to leave his throne even to Jane, this safely Protestant and safely married female. The irony is that he had little choice, specifically because of the efforts his father and grandfather made to clear the Tudor path of any potential rivals. With Edward's death imminent, questions of whether a woman could succeed were irrelevant. The only question was, which woman?

The paper in Edward VI's own handwriting, entitled 'My Device for the Succession', followed his father's will insofar as to exclude the Scottish line descended from Henry VIII's elder sister, Margaret Tudor, a line that was in any case now represented by the Catholic Mary Stuart. The line of Henry's younger sister, Mary, had likewise so far produced only females, since Frances Brandon had no sons. So Edward's original 'device' had been that the throne should pass not to Lady Jane herself but to her 'heirs male'.

Events, however, overtook him. In May, with the king's health visibly worsening, he altered 'the heirs male of the Lady Jane' to 'Lady Jane or the heirs of her body'.

The so-called gynocracy debate had not been silent in these years, as witness Sir Thomas Elyot's *Defence of Good Women*, written in the 1530s and published in 1540, defending Katherine of Aragon and her daughter's right of succession, and witness too the 1542 English publication of the volume Thomas Agrippa had dedicated to Margaret of Austria. But with the birth of Edward, the pamphlet debate had seemed an intellectual game rather than a real consideration of political possibilities.

What had been a game, however, was about to become reality.

PART V
1553–1560

A Queen ought to be chosen when she shall be wedded of the most honest kindred and people. For oftentimes the daughters follow the teachings and manners of them that they be descended from. . . . A Queen ought to keep her daughters in all chastity. For we read of many maidens that for their virginity have been made queens.

—WILLIAM CAXTON'S TRANSLATION OF JACOBUS DE CESSOLIS, *THE GAME AND PLAY OF THE CHESS* (1474?)

31

'HERCULEAN DARING'
England, 1553–1554

�֍

Mary Tudor's half brother Edward VI had died on 6 July 1553, having survived their father, Henry VIII, by only six years, and now another girl had been proclaimed queen. Lady Jane Grey, the granddaughter of Henry VIII's younger sister, had been nominated to the crown by Edward's will. But Mary Tudor, Henry's eldest daughter, was determined she should never be crowned.

What followed, wrote Robert Wingfield in his *Vita Mariae Angliae Reginae*, 'should have been judged and considered one of Herculean rather than womanly daring, since to claim and secure her hereditary right, the princess was being bold as to tackle a powerful and well-prepared enemy'.

For too many of her thirty-seven years, Mary Tudor had been able to mount only a passive, if stubborn, resistance to the blows life had dealt her. But in 1553 she had a chance to act. Act as her mother, Katherine, would have wanted—act as her grandmother Isabella had done.

Most of her contemporaries thought she was mad, when she unfurled her standard at the castle of Framlingham in Suffolk and had herself proclaimed queen. But everything in Mary Tudor's heritage told her the crown was a prize worth fighting for.

On the very day after the royal council proclaimed Jane queen, Mary set up her rival banner, and many were flocking to what they saw as the true Tudor monarchy. As Genoese merchant Baptista Spinola reported, 'The hearts of the people are with Mary, the Spanish Queen's daughter'. To cooler observers, the thing seemed impossible: the Habsburg ambassadors reported that all the country's forces were in the hands of the men who had proclaimed Jane Grey. But as Mary rode hard across the country, those hostile forces close behind her, the people were rallying to Mary's standard.

As it became clear King Henry's daughter would not passively accept what many saw as a perversion of the natural order, the magnates of East Anglia—Sir Richard Southwell and the Earl of Sussex, the nobles and the knights—came to join her, mustering their local forces. On 12 July she reached Framlingham, a castle she had only recently acquired. The great fortress might have been designed for just such an eventuality. And as the imperial ambassador triumphantly reported, 'A great concourse of people were moved by their love for her to come and promise to support her to the end'. Local justices, ordinary people bringing cattle instead of money. In Orwell Harbour, a squadron of five ships went over to her when the common sailors mutinied against their officers. Mary Tudor issued a proclamation, 'not doubting that all our true and faithful subjects will so accept us, take us, and obey us as their natural and liege sovereign lady and Queen'.

In London, meanwhile, even the members of the royal council who had pressed Lady Jane Grey to the throne were beginning to suffer 'a kind of remorse'. On 18 July the councillors holding the Tower, where Jane was lodged for safety, turned it over to the supporters of Queen Mary, only too relieved to abandon a policy of which they had never really approved. The next day Mary Tudor was proclaimed queen in London, and on the twenty-first John Dudley—Jane Grey's father-in-law, and the man behind her elevation to the throne—himself threw his cap into the air and hailed Mary as queen. In the Tower, the trappings of sovereignty had been stripped away from Lady Jane.

Enclosed at Hatfield, Mary's half sister, Elizabeth Tudor, had taken no part in the fray. Instead, she wrote to Mary, offering her congratulations. To have staked a claim of her own to the throne would have been neither a practical nor, for her, an ethical possibility. While many were supporting Mary out of civil loyalty rather than Catholic faith, many of the Protestant party might have followed Jane rather than Elizabeth. More important, by the dynastic rules to which Elizabeth herself subscribed, the throne did for the moment belong to Mary—their father had willed it so—even though Elizabeth may already have hoped that the much older Mary would not hold it indefinitely.

When Mary Tudor made her royal entry into London on 3 August—resplendent in purple velvet and satin, as a contemporary chronicle reported, 'all thick set with goldsmith's work and great pearls'—Elizabeth and her entourage rode directly behind her. There were also 'a great number of other ladies', a sign that under a female monarch, women, the ones directly around the monarch's person, would come more to the fore.

Even now Queen Mary's gender caused controversy. Some of Edward VI's councillors suggested the coronation should be postponed until

Parliament had confirmed Mary's legitimacy. England had never had a ruling queen, not since Saxon days. In 1135, when William the Conqueror's granddaughter Matilda had attempted to succeed her father, it sparked a long civil war with her cousin Stephen. Matilda was never crowned and had in the end to be content with the title 'Lady of the English' and an agreement that after Stephen's death, the crown would pass to her son, not his. The idea that women could thus transmit their claim to the throne, as Margaret Beaufort had transmitted hers to her son Henry VII, was much less controversial than the idea they might take it themselves.

The other powerful women in the first half of the sixteenth century had been regents rather than queens regnant, and the idea that a woman might deputise for (or exercise influence on) a man was more acceptable than the idea that she might rule in her own right. Even then, only a century before, the attempts of Margaret of Anjou to govern on behalf of her incapable husband had been met with chauvinistic horror.

Isabella of Castile represented a precedent that must have been ever present in her granddaughter Mary's mind, but four centuries after Matilda, the Aristotelian concept of society as a family, ruled over by a father, still held sway in most Western societies. There wasn't even the language: a queen was a king's wife.* Both Mary and Elizabeth Tudor would describe themselves as 'princes', while a successful woman was often described as being no longer wholly belonging to her sex.

In these puzzling first days of Queen Mary's rule, care would be taken to declare she had the same authority as a male ruler. But, reported Simon Renard, the new imperial ambassador, when Mary summoned all her council before embarking on the extensive coronation festivities, she sank on her knees before them. 'She had entrusted her affairs and person, she said, to them'. They were taken aback by this 'humble and lowly discourse, so unlike anything ever heard before'. So unlike anything they would have heard from Great Harry, her father, or even from his son.

But how to crown the queen, and with what rituals and festivities? With those of a king—nearly. The ceremonial was taken from the usual manual of such ceremonies, the *Liber Regalis*, but with again a curious admixture of messages. Whereas a king would ride through the streets on the day before his coronation, Mary Tudor was carried in a litter. Tudor women habitually kept their hair bound, but hers was loose, as a consort queen's

---

* A king's wife might, however, enjoy the status of *femme sole*, that is, of a woman able to conduct financial and legal affairs in her own right, without going through a male protector.

would be in token of her fertility. Mary wanted to invoke the idea that she was married to her country.

Another peer stood in for her at the ceremony that created fifteen new Knights of the Bath: it was obviously inappropriate for a woman to partake in the bathing and robing rituals that marked an important stepping-stone of masculine chivalry. But the next day, 1 October, Mary processed to Westminster Abbey with the Earl of Arundel, carrying the sword of state in front of her, the same militaristic symbol that had caused such controversy at the coronation of Mary's grandmother Isabella, some seventy years before.[*]

Mary's garments were not notably different from a king's ceremonial robes. Like any male king, she prostrated herself on the floor of Westminster Abbey; was anointed 'on the shoulders, on the breast, on the forehead and on the temples'; crowned; and presented with all the ceremonial regalia. But she merely touched the spurs, instead of attaching them to her heels, and while she was given the king's sceptre to hold in her right hand, she also held in her left 'a sceptre wont to be given to queens, which is surmounted by doves'. A queen consort, rather than regnant, had traditionally a pacific and intercessory role.

But, of course, this coronation was always going to be something of a mishmash of ceremonies, and not only because of the sovereign's gender. In religious terms, Mary Tudor was determined to put the clock back to where it had been before her father's break from Rome, but it would take time for her changes to come into effect.

An evangelical sermon preached one week outside St Paul's Cathedral was followed by a strongly Catholic one the next, the Catholic preacher having with difficulty to be rescued from the furious crowd. On 18 August Mary had issued a proclamation that while she herself would always practise the religion 'which God and the world knoweth she hath ever professed from her infancy', because 'of her gracious disposition and clemency her highness mindeth not to compel any her said subject thereunto unto such time as further order by common consent'.

No one can have thought it was going to rest there, however. Indeed, Mary was telling one foreigner she wished to restore papal authority, but

---

[*] The militaristic aspect of a monarch's role was not the only one to be problematic for female rulers. Like her male predecessors, Mary Tudor would make a point of 'touching' to cure scrofula, the King's Evil, and other diseases, and there was a huge symbolic importance in what was believed to be the monarch's healing touch. The French had used the monarch's supposed healing power as one justification for the Salic Law, in that it showed monarchy to be a quasi-priestly role, which self-evidently no woman could exercise.

as yet such matters should not be spoken publicly. In August she wrote to the pope, professing that 'his Holiness had no more loving daughter than herself'.

If Elizabeth Tudor would later describe the relationship between queen and country as a marriage, then in Mary's case the honeymoon was over almost immediately, as too was the brief community of interest between the sisters. The imperial ambassador Renard was soon reporting that Mary wanted to disbar Elizabeth from the succession because of her 'heretical opinion and illegitimacy, and characteristics in which she resembled her mother'. Anne Boleyn 'had caused great trouble in the kingdom', and Mary was all too sure Anne's daughter would do the same, 'and particularly that she might imitate her mother in being a French partisan'. Queen Mary, Renard noted, 'still resents the injuries inflicted on Queen Katherine, her lady mother, by the machinations of Anne Boleyn'.

As early as September 1553, Elizabeth felt it necessary to make the first move. Begging an interview with her sister, she pleaded mere ignorance of, rather than hostility to, the Catholic faith, 'having been brought up in the [Protestant] creed which she professed'. She requested instructors. A few days later she attended Mary's Chapel Royal, but made sure observers noted her ostentatiously 'suffering air'. Very soon, the Venetian ambassador noted that Mary was treating her sister with fresh hostility. As Mary Tudor had Parliament declare her parents' marriage valid, old wounds reopened. As for the succession, Mary must have hoped that the problem would resolve itself naturally. When Elizabeth left court in December, her absence must have been the more welcome for the fact that her sister, Mary, was about to marry.

Mary would declare that she had never as a private individual sought marriage, 'but preferred to end her days in chastity'. Nevertheless, Renard, at his first private audience, had told Mary that his master, Charles V, was conscious that 'a great part of the labour of government could with difficulty be undertaken by a woman' and advised her quickly to choose a husband. But the question of consort was seen, with some reason, as being one of the central problems for a female monarchy.

The book of Genesis gave it as part of Eve's punishment: 'Thy desire shall be to thy husband, and he shall rule over thee'. The fear was that the husband of a queen regnant would wind up mastering not only her but her country. Indeed, a preface to *A Glasse of the Truth* (a pamphlet in which Henry VIII was widely supposed to have had a hand, supporting his repudiation of Katherine of Aragon) had declared that if a woman shall chance to rule, 'she cannot continue long without a husband, which by God's law must then be her governor and head, and so finally shall direct the realm'.*

Mary Tudor faced the same arguments that would later revolve around the famously vexed question of Elizabeth Tudor's marriage: the dangers of faction if she married within the realm and the danger that if she married out of it, England would be subjugated to a foreign power. But in Mary's case, the clamour seems to sound less loudly. Not only if but whom Mary would marry was decided so quickly.

In her childhood Mary Tudor had, of course, been betrothed to her cousin Charles V himself, but though Charles was now a widower, his health made another marriage unlikely. Charles's son Philip, his father's regent in Spain, was a widower, having made a first marriage with his cousin, the short-lived Maria of Portugal. More than a decade younger than Mary, he was, however, as Catholic as she. This last was important: the Counter Reformation had given a new impetus to the international Catholic community. But Protestantism, too, was now more forceful. Lutheranism was looking like yesterday's creed, and 'the wolves' were coming out of Geneva, with the harsher doctrines of Calvin on their lips.

Charles V proposed Philip as Mary's husband almost before the ink was dry on the letters that announced her accession, and at the end of October 1553, Mary agreed. The Venetian ambassador reported that 'being born of a Spanish mother she was always inclined towards that nation, scorning to be English and boasting of her descent from Spain'. The imperial ambassador Renard was quickly established as her secret counsellor, Mary begging him ('If it were not too much trouble for you . . . ') to come secretly to her privy rooms under cloak of darkness. It had been Mary of Hungary who sent the able and ingratiating Renard to speed the matter and who sent to England Titian's portrait of Philip.

But only a fortnight after Queen Mary agreed to marry Philip of Spain, Parliament presented a petition that she would reconsider and marry within the realm. Mary's reply was singular, based less on the protection of a powerful Spanish alliance than on her personal preference. 'Where private persons in such cases follow their own private tastes, sovereigns may reasonably challenge an equal liberty'. In November a deputation of members of Parliament tried unavailingly to dissuade Mary from the Spanish marriage.

---

* Back in the twelfth century, Henry I, trying to ensure the succession of his daughter Matilda, had attempted to decree that her country would not be subjected to her husband.

There were, everyone agreed, to be provisos to the match. Mary had told Renard that in her private capacity she would love and obey her husband, 'but if he wished to encroach in the government of the kingdom she would be unable to permit it'. This was essentially the deal Isabella of Castile had made, but it would inevitably have practical difficulties. Isabella's partnership with Ferdinand of Aragon had worked not only because of personal compatibility, but also because hers was by far the larger kingdom. Here, the balance of power was all Philip of Spain's way.

In France Henri II said that once Philip was married to Mary, 'he shall be King himself, and then what councillors will or dare counsel against his King's pleasure and will?' Henri told Mary's ambassador that 'a husband may do much with his wife' and that it would be hard for a woman 'to refuse her husband anything that he shall earnestly require of her', adding that he knew marital authority to be 'very strong with ladies'.

Henri, of course, was partisan. It was the old problem: an Anglo-Habsburg alliance was a dangerous prospect for France, which would thus be surrounded. But his opinion was shared by many. Mary's ambassador was accordingly instructed by her council to stress that 'if the marriage took place the government of the realm should always remain in her Majesty and not in the prince'. Mary's bishop Gardiner preached that Philip 'should be rather a subject than otherwise; and that the Queen should rule all things as she doth now'.

The final terms of the marriage treaty—published in January 1554 to allay popular concern and ratified by Parliament in April—stipulated that Philip could not introduce foreign office holders or involve England in foreign wars. If Mary died without children, he would have no further role in English affairs. Should a child be born of the marriage, it would inherit not only England but the Low Countries. (Spain would go to Don Carlos, the son of Philip's first marriage.) Highly advantageous to England, in theory. But the practice might be a different story. The more so since Philip, when he saw the terms, made a secret but solemn vow not to consider himself bound by them.

From the start, the Spanish marriage met with the deepest public hostility. When an imperial embassy arrived in London in the first days of 1554, even the schoolboys in the streets threw snowballs at the ambassadors. Within weeks came news of the so-called Wyatt rebellion—a series of co-ordinated risings planned to take place across the country, the aim of which was to dethrone Mary and replace her on the throne by Elizabeth. But the plots were leaked in early January, and it was only Sir Thomas Wyatt himself (the son of the poet, Anne Boleyn's admirer) who, at the end of that month, marched on London with a Kentish army.

Some of Mary's own troops, even, went over to Wyatt rather than be ruled by 'Spaniards or strangers'. But Queen Mary herself showed to advantage in this crisis, even asking to go and fight in person. Riding to rally her troops in the City, she had, she said, been wedded to her realm at her coronation, 'the spousal ring whereof I wear here on my finger, and it never has and never shall be left off'.

'I cannot tell how naturally the mother loveth the child, for I was never mother of any. But certainly, if a prince and governor may as naturally and earnestly love her subjects, as the mother doth the child, then assure yourselves that I, being your lady and mistress, do as earnestly and tenderly love and favour you'. In the same sentence, Mary was figuring herself as a mother and as a prince. It was the same sense of a monarch's being above gender that allowed a king to be described as a nursing father. Mary promised, furthermore, that unless both houses of Parliament were content that the marriage would be for the benefit of the whole realm, 'then I will abstain from Marriage while I live'.

London stood; Wyatt surrendered his arms and was taken to the Tower. In February Mary reluctantly consented to the execution of the girl who had so briefly been raised up to supplant her, the hapless Jane Grey. In March Elizabeth Tudor—the intended beneficiary of the Wyatt plot—was charged as an accessory and found herself, too, a prisoner in the Tower. She must have felt she was following in her mother's footsteps, in the most horrifying way.

But she admitted nothing. What written evidence there was proved nothing, really, and when Wyatt was executed on 11 April, his speech from the scaffold exonerated her completely. The terms of her imprisonment became lighter. When fresh guards appeared at the Tower early in May, she was still in a state to be terrified, asking whether Jane Grey's scaffold had been taken away. But in fact, the guards were there to escort her away from the Tower, to house arrest in Woodstock where, warmed by the popular support that was shown her on the journey, Elizabeth would spend a year in comfortable captivity.

THE PARLIAMENT OF APRIL 1554 had confirmed that the status of a ruling queen was identical to that of a king and that Mary would remain 'sole and solely queen' after her marriage. But when at the end of July Mary married Philip in Winchester Cathedral (the ceremonies based on those that had tied Katherine of Aragon to Prince Arthur in an earlier Anglo-Spanish alliance), the old Catholic marriage service saw her promising 'to be compliant and obedient . . . as much in mind as in body'.

Once again, though, the messages were infinitely mixed. At the feast that followed the ceremony, Mary Tudor was served on gold plate and Philip of Spain merely on silver. But she endowed Philip with her worldly goods, while he endowed her only with his movable ones, that is, not his territories.

But as Philip moved into the rooms once known as the queen's apartments, Mary taking the king's, it seemed, too, as if Philip and his Spanish entourage were determined to prove that the worst fears of the English would not be fulfilled and to use his position as queen consort tactfully. On a personal level, his behaviour was positively emollient; he had been warned to 'caress' the English gentry. Two days after his marriage, he assured the council that he was there to advise but that on any question, 'they must consult the Queen, and he would do his best to assist'. But Mary, for her part, insisted that, in his advisory capacity, Philip should always be informed of the council's discussions (by a note in Spanish or Latin, since he spoke no English) and that all council papers were to be signed by him as well as herself.

Habsburg negotiators insisted that his name should precede hers on official documents—'Philip and Mary by the grace of God King and Queen of England'. They claimed that 'no law human or divine, nor his highness's prestige and good name' would allow otherwise. A newly minted coin featured both their images, at the same height, with a single crown floating above their heads. It was the Spanish belief that Philip would provide an element necessarily lacking in Mary's female monarchy, that he would 'make up for other matters which are impertinent to women'. But Parliament would never grant Philip a matrimonial crown or any official authority. Philip himself was angered by this, though Mary seems to have understood that her people would never accept any alternative.

In the autumn of 1554, Mary, ecstatic, was convinced she was pregnant with a child who would consolidate her marriage, confirm her husband's status, and ensure a Catholic future for the country. The Parliament of November, however, confirmed measures to define, and limit, Philip's powers as regent should Mary leave a living child but herself die in childbirth. Advised by a council of peers, he could have 'rule order and government' of child and country during the child's minority, but could not call Parliament, declare war, or arrange the marriage of the child without the consent of the peers. It was the deal Margaret Tudor had seen in Scotland, effectively. Should both mother and child die, the default heir was Elizabeth. Mary herself was said to prefer Margaret Douglas (yet another woman), the child of Margaret Tudor's second marriage, but perhaps that was seen as an over-throw of the natural order, on the scale of Jane Grey.

One of the matters on which Philip wished to help his wife was the full restoration of Catholicism and of the pope's authority, and that was in part why he stayed in the country a full year, considerably longer than had at first been expected. But here too Mary's own signals were considerably less simple than her later reputation might lead us to expect.

Mary was not, after all, the backward-looking bigot of legend. She had been reared in the humanist tradition that pushed for reform with a small *r*—reform from within the Catholic Church. Now her concern to restore the Latin service, and the centrality of the Mass did not prevent her plac-ing more emphasis on preaching, education, and the importance of good works than Catholic hard-liners, who stressed the transformative power of religious ceremony alone, would allow. At the end of her reign, she was still encouraging plans for a new English translation of the New Testament. She employed a number of Protestants in her service and would remain close to Lady Anne Bacon, a noted Protestant.

One huge sticking point was the question of church lands. Those who had profited from the Dissolution of the Monasteries were in no hurry to give back their booty, and that went for the Crown itself, to a degree. Here, Mary Tudor differed even from the man who became known as her chief adviser. Reginald Pole was her kinsman, with Plantagenet blood in his veins. Long exiled for his faith, he had in Italy years before been one of the group that hoped to bring about an accommodation between the Lutherans and the Catholic Church. But by the 1550s, his own view had probably hard-ened; certainly, *spirituali* views were out of synch with the tougher times. Now Pole was insisting, from abroad, that all ecclesiastical property should be returned, that Parliament should instantly restore papal supremacy. Mary understood that this was a political impossibility. It was November 1554 before Pole was allowed to return to England as papal legate; by this time, it was possible for a prayer for the pope to be included in Parliament's opening ceremonies.

When Pole attended the court ceremonies that celebrated the country's return to the Catholic fold, he made a speech praising Philip as a king of 'great might armour and force' and spoke of how miraculously God had pre-served 'a virgin, helpless, naked and unarmed'—Mary. A few days later, at

St Paul's, Bishop Gardiner preached a sermon with an interesting take on the same theme. 'When King Henry was head perhaps there was something to be said for it, but what a head was Edward. . . . Nor could the Queen, being a woman, be head of the Church'. Women were openly assuming rule as never before; women were finding themselves at the forefront of opposing sides of the religious divide. But the two positions did not necessarily agree.

32

'NOT ONE YEAR OF REST'

SCOTLAND AND THE NETHERLANDS, 1554–1558

✳

As Mary Tudor came to the throne, two women, Marie de Guise and Mary of Hungary, were already occupying positions of great power in western Europe. Neither, however, was finding her position easy.

Inevitably, the effect of Mary Tudor's accession and marriage was felt north of England's border. Marie de Guise wrote politely to the new English queen, expressing the hope for a continued peace, and Mary Tudor answered in kind. But that was far from the whole story. They shared a Christian name and a faith, but in terms of the great power struggle of Europe, their allegiances were very different: Marie's to France and Mary's to the Spanish Habsburg family.

While Marie de Guise was trying to steal support away from the governor of Scotland, Arran, and seeking to recruit a powerful Scottish noble, the Earl of Lennox, to her side, Mary Tudor's government was urging Lennox to double-cross her, to 'secretly enter into communication with the Regent [Arran] against the Dowager, with a view not only to driving her from the country, but to making himself King if possible and throwing Scottish affairs into confusion'. So much for the sisterhood of queens.

But it was Marie who would be the winner here. In December 1553 she sent an envoy to the French court to consult about the Scottish situation. France, too, needed to ensure that Scotland was ruled by an ally more secure than the ever-uncertain Arran. The result was that increasing pressure was placed on Arran to resign and cede to Marie the regency, and on 19 February 1554 he signed an agreement to do so.

There were questions, also, as to the precise status and household of Mary, Queen of Scots, in France, as she entered her teenage years. Marie's brother, the Cardinal de Guise, proposed that at just eleven (considerably younger than the usual age) she should be declared of age and 'take up her rights', including the right to appoint her own deputy—her mother, naturally.

On 12 April 1554 Marie de Guise processed up from the palace of Holyrood to the Tolbooth, there to be solemnly invested with the Honours of Scotland: the sword, the sceptre, and the crown. In France young Mary, Queen of Scots, wrote a neat showpiece letter to Queen Mary of England. 'May it please God, there shall be a perpetual memory that there were two Queens in this Isle at the same time, as united in inviolate amity as they are in blood and near lineage'. In Scotland Marie de Guise—now officially her daughter's alter ego and queen regent of Scotland—rode back to Holyrood accompanied by all the accoutrements of male authority.

It had been, significantly, the French ambassador, the Sieur d'Oysel, as King Henri's representative, who performed the ceremony. One of Marie's first acts—replacing Arran's choices with her own, mostly French, appointments—was to make d'Oysel lieutenant governor. Once again, a royal wife had to juggle the demands of her natal and her marital countries; once again, she saw them as identical. But, once again, her Scots subjects would prove to disagree.

Marie's concerns were to restore royal authority to a faction-ridden country, centralise government, and improve the administration of justice (though she complained that Scotsmen, convinced the old ways were best, 'would not endure it'). As Marie would later write to her brother, the Cardinal de Guise, in France, 'It is no small thing to bring a young nation to a state of perfection and to an unwonted subservience to those who wish to see justice reign. . . . I can safely say that for twenty years past I have not had one year of rest, and I think that if I should say one month I should not be far wrong for a troubled spirit is the greatest trial of all'.

IN 1555, ON MUCH THE same note, another woman resigned her post. The last years had been hard ones for Mary of Hungary, the regent of the Netherlands, forced increasingly to act as amanuensis to her depressed and ailing brother Charles V, who was planning to set aside his titles and responsibilities and retire to a religious life. Mary had to assist him in his struggles to determine how best to bequeath his immense lands and to attempt to heal the breach this issue was making within the Habsburg family.*

---

* In the event, Charles's son Philip would get Spain and its New World territories and the Netherlands as well; the Holy Roman Empire as well as the Austrian lands would go to Charles's brother Ferdinand's branch of the family. This had not, however, been Charles's original plan—he'd wanted Philip to succeed him also as Holy Roman Emperor—and the

Now, knowing that Charles's and her own widowed sister Eleanor, the dowager queen of France, would join him in his retirement, Mary of Hungary was determined to make a third. Once familial duty (to which she and Eleanor both subscribed) had seen them placed on opposite sides of Europe's great political divide. But now sisterhood trumped politics at last. Mary had asked to resign her position before, but now she argued her case in an extraordinary letter:

> It is impossible for a woman in peacetime, and even more in time of war, to do her duty as regent towards God, her sovereign, and her own sense of honour. For in peacetime it is unavoidable, in addition to all the meetings and cares of daily affairs which any government brings with it, that whoever guides the government of these provinces must mix with as many people as possible, in order to win the sympathy of both nobility and middle classes. . . . For a woman, especially if she is a widow, it is not feasible to mix thus freely with people. Of necessity I myself have had to do more in this respect than I really wanted. Moreover, a woman is never so much respected and feared as a man, whatever her position.
>
> If one is conducting the government of these countries in time of war, and one cannot in person enter the battle, one is faced with an insoluble problem. One receives all the blows and is blamed for all mistakes made by others.

It was a theme to which she would return, that 'as a woman I was compelled to leave the conduct of war to others', and it was one other female rulers knew.[*]

Mary of Hungary—'a woman of fifty who has served for at least twenty-four years', she wrote, and served, moreover, 'one God and one master'—was finally allowed to have her way. Her brother was retiring, and to serve his son Philip would be to find herself 'learning my ABC all over again'. Philip of Spain had been slow to visit his Netherlands territories, and Mary had already written to him tartly: 'Anything is better than to wait until your lands are lost to you, one by one'.

The ceremony by which on 25 October Mary quit her post and Philip took possession of the Netherlands was an emotive one. Mary told the Estates-General with whom she had so often been at odds that 'if my

---

painstaking memorandum Mary drew up concerning the future allocation of power, and defence of the Habsburg interests, shows just how divisive this issue was.

[*] It would be one motive behind Elizabeth Tudor's famous pacifism.

capacities, my knowledge, and my powers had been equal to the good will, the love and the devotion with which I have given myself to this office, I know for certain that no ruler could have been better served and no land better governed than you'.

Preparing to leave the country she had governed for almost a quarter of a century, Mary of Hungary made her will. She concluded by requesting, with unexpected softness, that a certain gold heart she wore, which had been left her by her long-dead husband, should be melted down and the proceeds given to the poor. It had been worn by two people who 'though parted for a long time in body have never been so in love and affection', so it was fitting that on her death, 'it should be consumed and change its nature as the bodies of these lovers have done'.

The following autumn Mary travelled to Castile with her siblings (not without qualms, since Spain to her was foreign territory), but only eighteen months later, in February 1558, Eleanor died and left her lonely. Bereft, and despite her conflicted feelings about the responsibilities of public life, Mary sought to find herself another role as adviser to her niece Juana, Philip's sister, who was acting as regent of Spain while he was in the North. But Juana rejected Mary's offer with some coldness, saying—probably with truth—that Mary's character would make it impossible for her to take that backseat role.*

Charles V and Philip now sought to persuade Mary of Hungary to resume the regency of the Netherlands. 'Explain to her what a support her presence will mean', Philip wrote to an intermediary. 'Finally offer her a large income and great authority, and give her hope there will be peace, and that this will last a long time, as the rulers are all exhausted'. Mary's reluctant agreement was rendered irrelevant by her own death, eight months after her sister's.

---

* Married off to her first cousin João, the heir of Portugal, Juana had been summoned back to take the Spanish regency after João died and three weeks after the birth of their only son, whom she left behind in the care of his grandmother Catalina, herself a former princess of Spain, Juana the Mad's youngest daughter, and regent of Portugal. Charles V wrote to his son that Juana's instructions should be based on those given to Mary of Austria, 'but as [Juana] is of a more active disposition . . . be sure to insist upon it that she and her advisors . . . forbear from those new interpretations of their instructions of which they have sometimes been known to be lavish'. Founder of the Convent of the Descalzas Reales, the Barefoot Royals, in Madrid, Juana is believed also to have been admitted to the Jesuit order under the pseudonym Mateo Sanchez.

33

SISTERS AND RIVALS

ENGLAND, 1555–1558

✳

Mary of Hungary died on 18 October 1558, and by that time, in England, another and far from reluctant woman would be preparing to assume power. The second half of Mary Tudor's reign was in some sense a battle between Mary and her sister, Elizabeth—between Catholic and Protestant—and it was far from clear who would win.

In the spring of 1555 Elizabeth Tudor was summoned from her imprisonment at Woodstock to Hampton Court, where her sister, Mary, triumphant, awaited the child who would sweep Elizabeth herself out of the succession. There were rumours, at the end of April, that the queen had been delivered of a son; the bells actually rang out in joy. But it was a miscarriage—or worse, a mistake, a phantom pregnancy. Early in May the French ambassador heard that all the thirty-nine-year-old queen's symptoms had been the result of 'some woeful malady'.

Mary Tudor's mistake has been used to the detriment of her reputation—a sign of her obsessive personality, even a cause of comedy. But actually, it would be fairer to blame the medical knowledge of the sixteenth century. Mary herself had only slowly been convinced by her doctors that she was pregnant, just as her mother, Katherine, had been convinced, on the occasion of her first miscarriage, that she was still carrying another baby.

Through May, June, and July, Mary waited in her birthing suite, quietly emerging in August to hear that her husband, Philip of Spain, was going away. The Habsburg empire was once again at war with France, and Philip was to assume his father's duties. As Emperor Charles V resigned to Philip first the lordship of the Netherlands and then the two Spanish crowns of Castile and Aragon, he sent a message of congratulation to Mary on 'being able for the future to style herself the Queen of many and great crowns, and on her being no less their mistress than of her own crown of England'. But this was, of course, to make no distinction between the role of a queen regnant and of a consort.

It was beginning to look likely that Mary Tudor would die childless, which left the succession in jeopardy. Ironically, Elizabeth (heretic though she may be) was from Spain's viewpoint a better candidate than the French-dominated Mary, Queen of Scots. A female could, after all—her brother Edward's point—be safely married to a Catholic prince and converted that way.

In November 1556 Elizabeth Tudor was invited to come to court for Christmas, but by the first week of December she was on her way back to Hatfield. She had almost certainly been instructed to marry a suitor of her brother-in-law Philip's choosing—the titular Duke of Savoy, cousin by marriage to Philip of Spain, whose dukedom, however, had been seized by the French in 1536.

Elizabeth seems swiftly to have refused. She never even met the two Habsburg relatives whom Philip sent over to persuade her, his cousin Christina of Denmark and his illegitimate half sister Margaret, the Duchess of Parma. (Christina had—after her refusal to marry Henry VIII and despite being in love with another man—in 1541 been married off by her uncle Charles V to the heir to the duchy of Lorraine. Her husband had died early, however, and though Christina had been left as regent for their young son, in 1552 the French had invaded Lorraine, taking the boy back to be raised at the French court and causing Christina to flee back to the Netherlands and her aunt Mary of Hungary's protection.)

But Philip still saw Elizabeth as a valuable pawn in Habsburg policy, and his protection would shield Elizabeth for the rest of her sister's reign. That protection was increasingly necessary. Whether Mary believed the failure of her pregnancy was God's sign of displeasure, a sign her country had to be cleansed, the fires of Smithfield (where heretics were burned at the stake) have defined 'Bloody' Mary's posthumous reputation.

It was, of course, the Protestants who had the chance to write the history, but the facts cannot be denied. The reigns of Protestants Edward and Elizabeth each saw two heretics burned (though others died for other religion-related crimes, some two hundred Catholic priests or sympathisers under Elizabeth). Mary burned almost three hundred. That obdurate heretics, who refused to recant, should die was an all but universal tenet. The former Archbishop of Canterbury Cranmer, who himself famously died in Mary's fire, had prepared measures, at the end of Edward's reign, to punish obstinate Catholics in the same way.

The first man had died in the fires on 1 February 1555. (There would be women too, some fifty-odd, with the nightmare story of the pregnant woman in the Channel Isles who gave birth at the stake, only to have her baby flung back into the flames.) Nonetheless, Mary's initial instruction had been that the penalty should be exacted 'without rashness'.

But the crunch for Mary (as for Elizabeth after her) may have been the question of conformity to the law. Unfortunately, Calvin was at this moment urging true believers to declare their beliefs openly. And there was also a political element to the story. Some who claimed to act for the Protestant cause had found an unlikely ally in Catholic France.

At the start of her reign, Mary refused to accept that the interests of France and of the Habsburg empire could never agree for long. Like the ladies of an earlier generation, she had, within weeks of her accession, offered herself as a mediator. The French responded derisively, but a year later, in 1554, Mary had by no means abandoned the idea, and early in 1555 the French ambassador de Noailles believed her health had even been improved by hopes of a European peace. But when France and the Habsburgs did finally agree to a short-lived truce in February 1556, Mary had played no role in the discussions, and now France was active in support of rebellion against Mary.

By the autumn of 1556, France and the Habsburgs were once again at war, with a French army attacking the Netherlands. By March 1557 Philip had urgent reason to seek English support. He arrived at Greenwich on 19 March, to resume his marital duties—and to persuade England into the war. Parliament and council had long opposed Mary's desire to send troops and money to her husband's fight, exactly what the terms of the marriage treaty had been designed to prevent. But French support for yet another minor rebellion in England helped to change the minds of the English government: a support so ill-timed that it has been suggested the whole thing was the work of Spanish agents provocateurs.

War against France, at this point, was war also against the pope; small wonder that the French ambassador commented that a distraught Mary was on the eve 'of bankrupting either her own mind or her kingdom'. But some of the rhetoric around the war was interesting. Thomas Stafford, the rebel leader, used as justification for his act the theory that Mary had broken the terms of her father's will by marrying without the declared consent of the councillors Henry had appointed for the underage Edward. (Absurd—but, noteworthy, in that it is not a charge ever likely to be levelled against a male monarch.) And Mary, speaking to her own council, 'expounded to them the obedience which she owed her husband and the power which he had over her as much by divine as by human law'.

In June a herald was sent to the French court, literally to throw down the gauntlet. Henri II dismissively declared that 'as the herald came in the name of a woman it was unnecessary for him to listen to anything further, as he would have done had he come in the name of a man to whom he would have replied in detail. . . . "Consider how I stand when a woman sends to defy me to war"'.

But Philip was able to send to France a six-thousand-strong English army. He himself sailed from Dover on 6 July, never to return. The siege of Saint-Quentin was considered a notable Anglo-Spanish victory. But the campaign would go sour when in January 1558 the French took Calais. England's last remaining continental outpost had been in her possession for two centuries, and its loss was a humiliation for England abroad and a personal failure for Mary. Protestant martyrologist John Foxe would report that she told her trusted lady Susan Clarencius, in her unhappy latter days, that though she regretted the absence of her husband, Philip, it was Calais the embalmers would find engraved upon her heart. It was another lesson (one Elizabeth Tudor was surely learning) that war was an evil to be avoided at all costs, a reason to be wary of foreign alliances, and foreign allies.

In January 1558 Mary once again informed her husband that his last visit had left her pregnant. He expressed proper delight, but perhaps few this time thought that it was anything other than a phantom pregnancy. By April Mary herself knew she had been mistaken, and everyone knew her half sister, Elizabeth, was likely to be her heir. The Venetian ambassador had written the year before that 'all eyes and hearts' were turned toward Elizabeth as Mary's successor, that she or her people were found behind every plot. When, in the late summer of 1558, it became clear that Mary was very ill, Elizabeth had a network waiting, ready.

At forty-two Mary Tudor had endured a lifetime of difficult health beset often by stress-related problems, something that was true of many of the women in this latter half of the story. But in early October the queen's condition worsened, and on 28 October Mary added a codicil to her will. If she continued to have no 'fruit nor heir of my body', she would be followed by 'my next heir and successor by the Laws and Statutes of this realm'—Elizabeth.

Philip's special ambassador, De Feria, rushed to Hatfield, where he found Elizabeth impatiently waiting. Wanting Elizabeth to acknowledge her debt to Philip and Spain, he heard instead Elizabeth declare that the affection of the people would bring her to the throne, an affection Mary had lost 'because she had married a foreigner'. De Feria warned that 'she is determined to be governed by no one', and so it would prove to be.

In the early morning of 17 November, Mary Tudor slipped quietly away. The blame game would quickly take over her memory. Protestant exile Bartholomew Traheron in 1558 could already write that she was 'spiteful, cruel, bloody, wilful, furious, guileful, stuffed with painted processes, with simulation and dissimulation, devoid of honesty, devoid of upright dealing, devoid of all seemly virtues'. Five years after Mary's death, in what became known as his *Book of Martyrs*, John Foxe would have his say.

Venetian ambassador Michieli had written of Mary Tudor that 'in certain things she is singular and without an equal; for not only is she brave and valiant unlike other timid and spiritless women, but so courageous and resolute, that neither in adversity nor peril did she ever display or commit any act of cowardice or pusillanimity, maintaining always, on the contrary, a wonderful grandeur and dignity'. But his description was coloured by the fact he believed her sex 'cannot becomingly take more than a moderate part in government'.

The gynocracy debate, moreover, had just seen its most famous contribution. In the spring of 1558, Scottish reformer John Knox had published his *First Blast of the Trumpet Against the Monstrous Regiment of Women*, claiming that to put a crown on a woman's head was as inappropriate 'as to put a saddle upon the back of an unruly cow', 'the subversion of good order, of all equity and justice'. It is, he wrote, 'a thing most repugnant to nature, that women rule and govern over men'.*

Women in general, Knox declared, were 'weak, frail, impatient, feeble and foolish: and experience hath declared them to be inconstant, variable, cruel and lacking the spirit of counsel and regiment'. Mary Tudor was the 'horrible monster Jezebel'. Nor was Knox's the only voice: other writers, such as Christopher Goodman, Anthony Gilby, and Thomas Becon, likewise linked their attacks on Mary's Catholicism with her gender.

But perhaps facts speak louder than words, and the fact was that Mary Tudor had ruled England with a successful assumption of authority. As John Aylmer wrote in his 1559 refutation of John Knox (*An harborowe for faithfull and trewe subiectes, against the late blowne blaste, concerning the*

---

* Knox had earlier spent several years sentenced to row the French galleys as punishment for his part in an anti-French rebellion, something that surely helped harden his attitude.

government of women), 'It is not in England so dangerous a matter, to have a woman ruler, as men take it to be'. Mary Tudor, granddaughter to Isabella of Castile, had proved it was a possibility. That was her legacy, her gift to the women who came after her, though she never wanted it to be her Tudor half sister, Elizabeth, who would benefit most immediately.

34

'IF GOD IS WITH US'

FRANCE, 1558–1560

✳

As Mary Tudor died and Elizabeth Tudor came to the throne, in France, by contrast, all three of the women who would one day be called upon to take charge of a realm still saw their future as subsumed into a husband's authority. But Europe's religious divides were already underpinning the fabric of their lives, whether the process was plain to see or not.

In April 1558 the fifteen-year-old Mary Stuart achieved the destiny for which she had been reared: marriage with François, the fourteen-year-old French Dauphin. The recapture of Calais had been a victory led by Mary's Guise family, and this was their reward. The ceremonies were spectacular, albeit that Mary's vivid white-clad beauty showed up her puny new husband's frailty.* 'These nuptials really were considered the most regal and triumphant of any that have been witnessed in this kingdom for many years', wrote the Venetian ambassador, 'from the pomp and richness of the jewels and apparel both of the lords and ladies; or from the grandeur of the banquet and stately service of the table, or from the costly devices of the masquerades and similar revels'.

At the state banquet that followed the ceremony, six mechanical ships with silver masts sailed in by clockwork over the billowing cloth waves of a painted sea. Each was captained by a royal male, who invited in the lady of his choice, King Henri II choosing Mary herself, and the Dauphin his mother, Catherine de Medici. Marie de Guise, unable to leave Scotland to be present at the ceremony, appointed her own mother her representative in the negotiations, but the important deal was the one done behind the scenes.

---

* She broke with tradition in wearing the white that suited her so well—it was, all too prophetically, the colour not of marriage but of mourning in the French royal family.

The official marriage treaty (like those of Mary Tudor and of Isabella of Castile before her) carefully preserved the independence of the Scottish nation. But on the instruction of her Guise uncles, this fifteen-year-old queen had already some days earlier signed another, secret, treaty by which Scotland, should she die childless, would become the property of France. Would Elizabeth Tudor, even at fifteen, have signed away her country so blithely?

François would now be called King Dauphin. Even more problematic, at the end of the year after Mary Tudor in England died would be the decision to blazon the heraldic arms of England with those of France and Scotland on all Mary Stuart and François's goods. It was a clear declaration that France did not recognise the Protestant Elizabeth—a bastard, to Catholics—as queen. Instead, they saw Mary Stuart, Henry VII's true-born great-granddaughter, as Mary Tudor's heir. By the following summer, ushers were calling out to 'make way for the Queen of England' as Mary Stuart went to chapel.

In fact, where the French government was concerned, cooler diplomatic counsels would prevail, and they would soon be dealing with Elizabeth Tudor as England's queen. But between the two royal kinswomen themselves, the question of Mary Stuart's rights to the English throne would continue to be an issue until their dying days.

CATHERINE DE MEDICI'S STAR HAD continued to rise through the 1550s. When Henri II backed Catherine's claim to inheritance in Tuscany, Venetian ambassador Michele Soranzo wrote that 'the Queen will have all the merit should Florence be liberated'. (The same man also wrote that she was 'loved by all'.) When northern France was itself invaded in 1557, Catherine—once again regent while Henri pursued France's war with Philip of Spain—did much to calm the people of Paris and persuade them to give Henri men and money.

But all of Europe was growing tired of war. And the vital peace that was negotiated at the end of the decade would have another woman's fingerprints all over it. Christina of Denmark, the widowed Duchess of Lorraine (and one of the nieces Mary of Hungary raised), had, she claimed, for several years been trying to bring about a peace between the two great powers. She had, after all, felt the effects of the conflict firsthand—suspected in Lorraine because of her Habsburg connection and then forced into exile as a result of French action. In October 1558 she wrote to her cousin Philip of Spain that she was happy, as suggested, to act as mediator in any peace negotiations, but that he must provide for her safety 'not only because I am a woman, but because, as you know, I am not in the good graces of the French'.

The talks begun that autumn had to be broken off, not least because of the need to mark Charles V's funeral and the deaths of Mary of Hungary and Mary Tudor. But in the spring of 1559, shortly after Christine's son, the young Duke of Lorraine, was married to the French king's daughter Claude, they began again in the small town of Cateau-Cambrésis, some twenty kilometres from Cambrai, where three decades before Margaret of Austria and Louise of Savoy had negotiated the Ladies' Peace.

As her kinsman and representative, Howard of Effingham wrote to Elizabeth Tudor, 'The assembly hath been entirely procured by the Duchess's labour and travail . . . and she is continually present at all meetings and communications'.

Christina of Denmark sat at the head of the table, the French on her left, the Spanish opposite her, and the English on her right-hand side. Just as at Cambrai all those years ago, the talks almost stalled several times, with Christina catching the ambassadors at the very door to prevent a walkout. As the Venetian Tiepolo wrote, 'The Duchess, regardless of personal fatigue, went to and fro between the Commissioners, with the greatest zeal, ardour, and charity, imploring them to come together again'. In April, finally, a deal was agreed.

The Treaty of Cateau-Cambrésis brought an end to decades of the Italian Wars. France essentially agreed to abandon its historic claims in the peninsula. This was, of course, greatly to Spain's favour, but there was a downside to the agreement for Habsburg interest as a whole, since the concessions made to France cut the Holy Roman Empire off from Spain, but Spain itself emerged the stronger.

Christina wrote to the French king that 'I feel the utmost satisfaction in having been able to bring about so excellent an arrangement, and one which cannot fail to prove a great boon to Christendom'. She returned to the Netherlands a heroine—a worthy 'daughter' to Margaret of Austria, and Mary of Hungary, surely?

But ironically, it was probably her very roots in the Netherlands, her independent popularity in that country, that militated in Philip's eyes against her getting the regency there, the post that had been up for grabs since Mary of Hungary's retirement and that would in June be given instead to Margaret of Parma. Christina of Denmark would spend the next nineteen years as adviser to her son in Lorraine, another dozen after that in a fiefdom of her own in Italy, never ceasing to keep a wary eye out for undue pressure being placed upon either territory by either Philip of Spain or France, in the person of Catherine de Medici.*

THE TREATY OF CATEAU-CAMBRÉSIS SAW Catherine de Medici and Henri II's eldest daughter, thirteen-year-old Elizabeth de Valois, promised in marriage to Philip of Spain (and the French king's sister, Marguerite, to the Duke of Savoy). But indirectly, the treaty would soon bring tragedy to the French royal family.

In the summer of 1559, at a joust to celebrate his daughter's marriage to Philip, his opponent's lance struck Henri II in the face. His visor shattered, a splinter entered his eye, and after nine days of agony, he died.

It was unquestionably a personal tragedy for Catherine de Medici. The perceptive Venetian Soranzo had noted that 'more than anyone else she loves the King'. But arguably it was also an opportunity, or, to put it more kindly, a challenge to which she dared not fail to rise. Had Anne de Beaujeu, holding the throne for another boy king of France a half century before, not singled out widowhood as the time of a powerful woman's greatest responsibility—and autonomy?

The new king, Catherine de Medici's eldest son, François II, was a sickly teenager, susceptible to influence. But Catherine's was not the only voice in his ear, and Catherine could now, in the first days of her son's reign, take a seat at the table of power only by allying herself with the new queen Mary's Guise family. As the Guises moved swiftly to take possession of the fifteen-year-old king, Catherine abandoned her husband's body to join them. Her presence lent them legitimacy; the others who might have hoped to seize a measure of power—notably the Guises' great rival, the Constable of France, Montmorency—were left lamenting.

Once installed in the Louvre, Catherine de Medici allowed herself to relapse into the mourning seclusion expected of a French queen dowager, her daughter-in-law Mary frequently joining her in apartments shrouded in black silk. In a letter to her 'true friend, good sister and cousin' Elizabeth of England, Catherine wrote that her loss was 'so recent and so dreadful and brings such pain, regret and despair that we have need of God, who has

---

* Christina's ambitions in another direction were also thwarted. On the death in prison of their father, Christian of Denmark, his rights had devolved on her elder sister, Dorothea, who, however, as a childless ageing woman, was persuaded to cede them to Christina. She would never win the help she needed to recover that throne but, from 1561, would style herself as rightful queen of Denmark, Norway, and Sweden. Her daughters would also be women of influence, the elder becoming governor of Siena and the younger regent of the Tyrol.

visited us with this affliction, to give us the power to endure it'. A visitor described her as so 'wept out' as to bring tears to their own eyes.

Under Guise influence, the new king told Montmorency that he was 'anxious to solace thine old age'—effectively, that he was being pensioned off. Jeanne d'Albret's husband, Antoine de Bourbon, would as first Prince of the Blood have expected to head a regency council, but instead he too found himself sidelined, to the point where Catherine de Medici commented that he was 'reduced to the position of a chambermaid'. Catherine herself, by contrast, got a speedy and lavish financial settlement, and the title she claimed for herself—Queen Mother rather than the conventional Dowager Queen—showed clearly that she considered her part to be about the future, not merely the past.

Although English ambassador Sir Nicholas Throckmorton had declared, in the first days after Henri II's death, that the 'House of Guise ruleth', a fortnight later he opined that Catherine had 'though not in name, yet in deed and in effect th'authority of Regent'. From the early days of her son's reign, his official acts opened with the words 'This being the good pleasure of the Queen, my lady-mother, and I also approving of every opinion that she holdeth, am content and command that'. The challenges facing France—faction, the terrible debt caused by Henri's wars, and religious controversy—were enough to employ the talents of all François's possible advisers.

Protestantism by now had reached tentacles into every level of French society. Within a few years, as many as two million would worship in a thousand congregations, while two of Constable Montmorency's nephews had converted: notably (and this a name that would resound later in French history) Gaspard, Admiral de Coligny. King Henri II had taken a hard line against the dissidents, but now it was not so easy.

The new faith was gaining a particular hold in the Southwest and in the territories of Navarre and Béarn. The seeds were also being sown (in France as in the British Isles) of a clash of two ruling women, Catherine de Medici and Jeanne d'Albret, one on either side of the religious divide.

IN 1555 ANOTHER FEMALE RULER had ascended a throne on France's southern borders. The first half of the 1550s had seen Jeanne d'Albret, heiress of Navarre, as a wife and a mother, her first child having been born in 1551. Sadly, that son died just before his second birthday, but by that time Jeanne was pregnant again, with Henri, born on 14 December 1553, in the family seat of Pau.

The family legend surrounding his birth has Jeanne d'Albret's father promising to hand over a will in her favour if she sang, while giving birth, a local song to the Virgin and if her baby was born without a cry. His conditions being fulfilled, he handed over the will but took the baby, saying, 'That is for you, my girl, but this is for me'. When Jeanne had been born a girl, the Spanish had sneered that the 'the bull has sired a lamb'. Now, showing the baby to the people, 'The lamb has given birth to a lion!', he proclaimed triumphantly.

Jeanne's marriage to Antoine de Bourbon was still a loving one, troubled only by Jeanne's insecurities. Antoine's letters are full of reassurance and perhaps a touch of exasperation: 'No husband ever loved a wife as I love you. I hope, my dear, that in time you will realise it, more than you have up to now'. She should rid herself of her fears, concerning both his safety and his fidelity: 'I am saving everything I have for my spouse, praying her to do the same'. On another occasion, he wrote that 'I have offended neither God nor you, and have no desire to begin now. I am surrounded by trotting horses every day, I feel fine and feel no need for a mare'.*

Antoine's letter to Jeanne during what proved to be her father's last illness still breathes warmth, if a clear measure of apprehension: 'I fear that your nature will cause you to *faire une demonstration* [to make a fuss] and I beg you to keep calm. I assure you that [if need be] you have a husband who will be father, mother, brother, and husband to you'. Her father's death in the spring of 1555 made her Jeanne III.

Jeanne d'Albret's marriage to Antoine—a prince expected to rule on her behalf—might well have been seen as one way to circumvent the anomaly of female rule. This was indeed how things had worked for the country's first reigning queens, for Navarre did have some tradition of female sovereignty (even before the troubled reign of Jeanne's grandmother Catherine de Foix). But in fact, the equation worked out differently. Jeanne indeed instructed the Estates of Béarn that she wished to rule jointly with her husband, since 'if she, who was their Queen and sovereign lady, regarded him as her lord, they should do the same, because the husband is lord of the person and property of his wife'.

It was, by contrast, the Estates (who had to ratify by vote the selection of a new sovereign) who declared that Jeanne was their 'true and natural Lady', while her husband, by their law, had only stewardship of her goods.

---

* Less happily but perceptively he wrote to Jeanne that 'it is your natural tendency to torment your husband and all who love you'—to test them, in terms of pop psychology.

It took them five days of debate to give in and accept a joint sovereignty. The ceremony that crowned Jeanne III was based on that of Jeanne II and her husband in 1329.*

The marriage was still a devoted one. 'You say you want to wear a coiffe next summer and I think you could not do better, it became you very well last year. I am sending by the bearer a golden chain', Antoine wrote.

Jeanne tried to smooth over concerns at the French court that Antoine (through the ubiquitous Descurra, the spy who had reported on Jeanne's first, Cleves, marriage) was intriguing with the emperor over the restoration of the part of Navarre that Spain had annexed, just as her mother, Marguerite of Navarre, had tried to smooth over her husband's intrigues. Antoine was as desperate to do the deal as his father-in-law had been, but the Habsburgs played him in the same way. Finally, he began looking for another source of support and found it in the Protestant faction.

It is impossible to be sure, now, whether it was Jeanne or her husband who first began the move toward Protestantism. It was Antoine, at this stage, who conducted the correspondence with Calvin, Antoine to whom the French Protestant (or 'Huguenot') community looked. Brantôme famously wrote of Jeanne that she 'loved a dance more than a sermon' and that he had heard 'on good authority' she reproached Antoine for his interest, saying that 'if he wanted to ruin himself she did not wish to lose her possessions'.

But some Protestant contemporaries were already thinking of Jeanne. On 19 July 1559 the new queen Elizabeth of England (prompted by her minister William Cecil) wrote to both king and queen of Navarre. To Antoine, she expressed herself 'anxious to please and serve'. To Jeanne, her tone is at once more encouraging and more that of one beleaguered sister addressing another: '*Si Deus nobiscum quis contra nos?*' (If God is with us, who can be against us?). Elizabeth had been anxious to have the pleasure of Jeanne's acquaintance, but since distance had not permitted that, it would have to be done in spirit and goodwill, honouring Jeanne 'not only for [your] rank in the world but even more for the true profession and sincerity of your Christian religion, in which [I] pray the Creator may keep [you] by His grace, and that [you] may continue a supporter of His Holy Word'. Religion was making bonds between powerful women, just as it would divide them, ultimately.

---

* The concern of the Estates was that in the event of Jeanne's death, Antoine should not become their ruler and that only Jeanne's children should inherit. It was the same distinction between king and king consort that had plagued Mary and Philip in England, that would deny the Crown Matrimonial to Lord Darnley, husband of Mary, Queen of Scots.

35

'MAIDENLY ESTATE'

ENGLAND, 1558–1560

✳

Elizabeth Tudor's gender (as well as her Protestant religion) from the first set the terms of her rule, a perceived weakness the 'Virgin Queen' would manage to make a strength. On the one hand, the long game she played, dangling the tantalising possibility of her hand in marriage, would prove to be one of the best tools of her diplomacy.

On the other hand, like other reigning queens, Elizabeth did not present herself as a woman when it suited her not to. The doctrine of the monarch's two bodies had been implicit at her sister Mary's funeral when the Bishop of Winchester described her thus: 'a Queen, and by the same title a King also'. But the idea got its clearest expression in Elizabeth's reign. Just three days after her sister's death, she told Parliament, 'I am but one body naturally considered though by [God's] permission a body politic to govern'. A few years later (in relation to an obscure piece of property dealing), her lawyers spelled it out for her. A monarch, they said, was 'utterly devoid of Infancy, old Age, and natural Deformities or Imbecilities, which the Body natural is subject to'—including mortality. Or, presumably, femininity.

The very ideal of government—'the king counselled'—gained added impetus from the ruler's being a woman. Even the supportive John Aylmer had written in his refutation of John Knox's tirade against women rulers that Elizabeth's sex mattered the less because England was not 'a mere monarchy' or yet a mere oligarchy or democracy, but 'a rule mixt of all three'. In other words, Elizabeth's gender did not matter, because she was not that powerful anyway.*

Knox's work, originally written to take aim at the Catholic rulers Mary Tudor and Marie de Guise, was now all too obviously also potentially a slur

---

* Aylmer's treatise memorably contrasted Elizabeth with the bulk of womankind: 'fond, foolish, wanton, flibbergibs . . . in every way doltified with the dregs of the devil's dunghill'.

on the Protestant Elizabeth. John Calvin wrote a private letter to William Cecil in which he admitted he and Knox had discussed the problem. Calvin's own feeling was still that a female sovereign was 'a deviation from the original and proper order of nature . . . to be ranked no less than slavery'. But there was, Calvin admitted, the biblical Deborah; there was the idea derived from the prophet Isaiah that 'queens should be nursing mothers of the church'. Indeed, the idea Knox—and others—now employed was to figure Elizabeth as a reincarnation of the biblical Deborah, an 'extraordinary' woman, exempted from the 'proper order of nature' only by the 'special providence' of God.

IT WAS, MOREOVER, ASSUMED FROM the first that Elizabeth would, for better or worse, soon be sharing her authority with a husband. On 21 November 1558, within four days of the old queen's death, the Spanish ambassador De Feria was writing to King Philip that 'everything depends upon the husband this woman may take'. Meanwhile, every decision taken was in a sense provisional. Even Elizabeth's mainstay William Cecil could in these early days be found reproaching a messenger for having taken papers directly to the queen, 'a matter of such weight being too much for a woman's knowledge'. Cecil would be only one of the influential voices urging now and later that a husband was her and the realm's 'only known and likely surety': 'God send our mistress a husband, and by him a son, that we may hope our posterity shall have a masculine succession'. At the time, it still seemed likely.

Both Elizabeth and 'her people', De Feria warned, 'will listen to any ambassadors who may come to treat of marriage'. Three weeks later, on 14 December: 'Everybody thinks that she will not marry a foreigner, and they cannot make out whom she favours, so that every day some new cry is raised about a husband'. Besides Philip of Spain himself (reluctant but resigned), there was the persistent Eric of Sweden. Charles V's brother, Ferdinand, the Holy Roman Emperor, offered one of his younger sons; Scotland proposed the Earl of Arran. Homegrown candidates included the Earl of Arundel and Sir William Pickering, or, of course, that perennial frontrunner (as the next two decades would prove him to be), Elizabeth's Master of Horse, Robert Dudley.

Certainly, it was assumed that she must and would marry someone. There was, Elizabeth Tudor herself observed, 'a strong idea in the world that a woman cannot live unless she is married'. The Holy Roman Emperor's envoy agreed that she should ('as is woman's way') be eager 'to marry and be provided for. For that she should wish to remain a maid and never marry is inconceivable'. She herself, of course, would say that 'I have already joined myself to an husband in marriage, namely the kingdom of England'. It was the rhetoric her sister had already used, but Elizabeth would prove to take it more seriously.

The example of Mary Tudor offered Elizabeth a dreadful warning, just as Mary Stuart would later do. Again, any marriage of a queen regnant offered an insuperable problem: Whose would be the mastery? Elizabeth Tudor herself wrote hastily to fellow sovereigns on her accession to explain that she would not necessarily continue the quarrels of her sister's day. Then, after all, 'nothing was done on the part of England but with the privity and direction of the Ministers of the said King [Philip]', Mary's husband. The unmarried Elizabeth, by contrast, was 'a free princess'.

John Aylmer had tried to argue: 'Say you, God hath appointed her to be the subject to her husband. . . . [T]herefore she may not be the head. I grant that, so far as pertaining to the bands of marriage, and the offices of a wife, she must be a subject: but as a Magistrate she may be her husband's head'. She could be his inferior in 'matters of wedlock' yet his leader in 'the guiding of the commonwealth', he claimed. But such a distinction would be almost impossible to make, in practical terms.

On 4 February 1559, nonetheless, Parliament drafted a petition, urging Elizabeth to marry quickly, in order to ensure the succession. If she should remain 'unmarried and, as it were, a vestal virgin', it would be 'contrary to public respects'.

She answered them that 'from my years of understanding', that is, since she first was old enough to understand herself a servant of God, 'I haply chose this kind of life in which I yet live, which I assure you for mine own part hath hitherto best contented myself and I trust hath been most acceptable to God'. In the end, she said, 'this shall be for me sufficient: that a marble stone shall declare that a queen, having reigned such a time, lived and died a virgin'.

Where other powerful women accepted their coding within the usual social framework—as surrogates for or in at least some ways subordinate to a man—the unmarried Elizabeth Tudor would be challenging preconceptions to an almost unprecedented degree, Isabella of Castile being ironically the great exception to that rule. Perhaps it was in part her controversial position as an unmarried, Protestant queen regnant, however, that drew Elizabeth toward a centuries-old established image, albeit one so central to the Catholic Church, that of virginity.

Virginity—chastity—had at various points in both ancient and medieval times been seen as offering entry into what was almost a third sex. Its importance had been confirmed by Saint Augustine and Saint Jerome (as well as by the whole monastic convention) and by early modern writers from Malory, stressing the (male) chastity of the *Morte d'Arthur*, to Petruccio Ubaldini, whom Elizabeth patronised and whose book on six celebrated women included an early female warrior queen whose virginity, like Samson's hair, was crucial to her military success. (Medieval Scandinavia likewise had tales of maiden-kings who dressed as men and successfully led armies, until finally overcome by the man they would marry.)

Elizabeth Tudor herself would seem to subscribe to this view of virginity, later writing to Ivan the Terrible (who had dared suggest that 'there be other men that do rule in England' while 'you flow in your maidenly estate like a maid') that 'we rule ourselves with the honour befitting a virgin queen appointed by God'. It was only later in Elizabeth's reign that her status as the Virgin Queen would reach its apogee. But even now, at this vulnerable early moment in her reign, she needed something to set herself apart from other women, even if it was the Catholic image of the Virgin Mary.

The religious question distinguished Elizabeth's rule from that of not only her sister but also any previous female ruler of Christian Europe (unless you are to count Jane Grey). She was not only a queen regnant but one who did not see herself as subject in any way to the pope's authority and thus with an almost unprecedented autonomy.

It was from the start obvious, moreover, that the religious aspect of her role might be a particular stumbling block. The first version of a frankly reforming bill Cecil prepared in the first months of her reign met with outrage, not least because of the role it accorded to Elizabeth herself. As Archbishop of York Nicholas Heath put it, 'Preach or minister the holy sacraments a woman may not, neither may she be Supreme Head of the Church of Christ'. (Heath was a moderate Catholic and an appointment of Mary's who was soon eased out of his role, albeit without too harsh a penalty.) The subsequent amendment declared that Elizabeth in her humility wished to be known not as Supreme Head of the church, but as its Supreme Governor.

Meanwhile, Elizabeth Tudor was about almost to fall into the trap that lay in wait for any powerful woman, if (as Anne de Beaujeu had warned, as Anne Boleyn had found) she was even the least bit unwary.

FROM THE START OF ELIZABETH'S reign, ambassadors reported her closeness to Robert Dudley. His rise in those first months of Elizabeth's reign had been extraordinary, so much so that by November 1559 the outgoing Spanish ambassador, De Feria, was reporting that the pair had 'a secret understanding', and his successor, De Quadra, two months later was describing Dudley as 'the King that is to be'.

But the idea was a dangerous one, for a queen who needed to preserve her reputation, her support base among the English nobility, and her foreign allies. Feria had put it plainly: 'If she marry the said Mylord Robert, she will incur so much enmity that she may one evening lay herself down as Queen of England and rise up the next morning as plain Madam Elizabeth'. De Quadra said there was not a man in England who did not 'cry out upon him [Dudley] as the Queen's ruin'. Other factors apart, of course, Robert Dudley was already a married man, even though he lived largely apart from the girl, Amy Robsart, with whom he had made a youthful match.

The extraordinary thing is how ready everyone seems to have been, as the first year of Elizabeth's reign turned into the second one, to assume that Amy Dudley was a problem that could be resolved. De Feria had reported rumours that she had 'a malady in one of her breasts', and natural causes (or the effects of sixteenth-century medication) remain one possible explanation for what was to come. On a more sinister note, De Quadra spoke of Amy's being sent into Eternity. It all set the scene for what was to prove the first defining moment of Elizabeth's rule. On 8 September 1560, Amy Dudley was found dead at the bottom of a staircase in the Cumnor house where she was staying, her neck broken and with wounds to her head.

She may conceivably have fallen, through sheer misadventure or ill health, though the shallow nature of the steps makes the former unlikely. She may have committed suicide; there is circumstantial evidence that she was in a state of desperation, though the same cavil concerning the stairs applies. Or she may have been murdered, either by someone anxious to see Robert Dudley take the blame, or simply by Robert Dudley. No case can on existing evidence be proven, but what matters in this context is the effect on Elizabeth's reputation.

If sexual scandal was the obvious way to attack a powerful woman, no powerful woman could give better excuse for an attack than this. The English ambassador in Paris, Sir Nicholas Throckmorton, wrote of how his very hair was standing on end at the 'dishonourable and naughty reports' that were being relished by 'the malicious French'. The French queen, he reported, had joked that the queen of England was to marry her horse master, who had murdered his wife to make way for her. More seriously, 'The cry is that [the English] do not want any more women rulers'.

In this situation, Elizabeth's reaction was crucial. In the short term, she sent Robert away from court, pending an enquiry. And after a coroner's court had found Amy dead by misadventure—after the scandal too had finally died away—she still did not marry him. The question, of course, is why.

In 1560 contemporaries certainly assumed that Elizabeth Tudor wanted to marry Robert Dudley. It is only hindsight that encourages us to ask whether, when it came to it, she really found marriage an emotional possibility. Whether she had been too deeply scarred by the scandal of her youthful relationship with Thomas Seymour, by her mother's fate, by the deaths in childbirth of two of her stepmothers and several of her leading courtiers' wives, or whether she simply saw no way to combine wedlock with the retention of her own authority.

Certainly, she would over the years speak with what sounds very much like a visceral fear of marriage and of childbirth, while in the short term she behaved now toward Robert Dudley with an increased freedom, as if the very fact she could not for the moment marry him had perversely given her the freedom to enjoy him more completely.

But in objective terms, Elizabeth had behaved correctly, authoritatively, impeccably. Behaved as Margaret of Austria had done over the scandal with Charles Brandon. Behaved in a way designed to set her aside from the scandalous sisterhood John Knox had so vividly described.

36

TROUBLE IN SCOTLAND

SCOTLAND, 1558–1560

✳

When Elizabeth Tudor acceded to England's throne, once again English affairs had an effect in Scotland. Marie de Guise's French-backed rule had already become deeply unpopular. (When back in 1557 Henri II declared war on England's ally Spain and told Marie he required her to invade the North of England as a diversionary tactic, she had had no choice but to agree. She and Mary Tudor, who had been forced into war by her own Spanish allegiance, had been caught in the same trap at the same moment, essentially.) Ironically, when in April 1558 Mary, Queen of Scots, married the French Dauphin, some Scots even hoped that in Mary's teenage husband, they would find an alternative to her mother Marie's governance.

As the Protestant Elizabeth took the English throne, Scottish Protestants took courage. Marie de Guise was convinced that their demands—the right to hold services in the vernacular, to take both bread and wine at Mass—had a political motivation. She had herself, like so many of these women, long been in favour of internal reform of the Catholic Church. Indeed, in 1557 she had appealed for the pope to send a cardinal to reform Scottish abuses. But this was different and, in her eyes, a piece of English-inspired meddling. As her adviser the Sieur d'Oysel wrote, 'You can never know here who is the friend or the enemy, for he who is with them in the morning is against them after dinner'. Both sides felt betrayed, the lords by what they saw as Marie's determination to make Scotland a virtual French province, Marie by the readiness of those closest to her to side with her enemies.

The winter of 1558–1559 saw a series of petitions from the Protestants, including the so-called Beggars' Summons that, pinned on the doors of the Scottish friaries, called on the inhabitants to vacate the properties. At this all too opportune moment, at the beginning of May 1559, John Knox arrived back from continental exile, declaring that the deeds of the French queen regent 'did declare the venom of her heart'. The sermon he preached at Perth on 11 May provoked a storm of rioting that saw locals smashing the church's images.

Marie de Guise summoned Châtelherault (the former Arran, a title now accorded to his son), saying that it was for him, as 'second person of Scotland', to act, since the lords 'stand in no awe of me because I am but a woman'. Her mixture of force and flattery did the trick, despite Châtelherault's rumoured Protestant sympathies, and they rode out together at the head of a small army, too small, as it turned out, to face the forces mustered by their Protestant foes.

A deal was struck, but the trouble was not really to be put down in Marie de Guise's lifetime. Now effectively banned from using French troops, fleeing from Edinburgh to Dunbar on the coast, she had to worry more about her actual safety than about the dwindling chance of exerting her authority.

A fresh deal gave Protestants freedom of worship in exchange for their bowing to Marie's civil authority. But Marie was shocked when (in line with the austere tenets of the reformed faith) a revered statue of Saint Giles was stolen, hurled into the Nor' Loch, and then dragged out and burned. She might have been even more distressed had she known that Elizabeth of England was instructing her agent Ralph Sadler to stir up faction and force her to sign a treaty of perpetual peace with England, thus stymieing the French.

Throughout the autumn the number of Marie de Guise's followers diminished almost daily, with Châtelherault chief among the quitters. In October Marie was forced to flee to Leith, her regency—so the lords declared—suspended. In November, however, she was back in Edinburgh, but fell ill with what was probably chronic heart disease, though Sadler reported that rumours of her death 'are too good to be true'. Her doctors advised her to shun cold, damp climates (in Scotland!) and to avoid worry.

In January 1560 eight English warships sailed into the Firth, and while Marie ordered Scotsmen to prepare for war with England, the Scottish Lords of the Congregation had other plans. They went south to meet Elizabeth Tudor's representative and on 27 February signed the Treaty of Berwick, by which Elizabeth took Scotland under her protection and promised military help for the Scottish to expel the French. But Marie was never going to accept a treaty that sidelined her completely.

As an English force crossed the border, on 1 April Marie de Guise entered the security of Edinburgh Castle, the safer for the fact that Elizabeth's lieutenant the Duke of Norfolk believed Elizabeth would never countenance so directly personal an attack on a fellow queen. Stalling for time, writing desperately for French military aid, Marie met with the English envoys. 'Madam, you have composed so many great differences, I beseech you to bring to the settlement of this one all the means in your power', one of them said.

The Protestant Scots 'think the Dowager does more harm than five hundred Frenchmen', the Duke of Norfolk said. But Marie (writing to her Guise brothers that 'our troubles and affairs increase here by the hour') found the strain telling badly on her health. Her leg so swollen that 'if any lay his finger upon it, it goes in as with butter'—with, it was said, only her tears keeping the watery swelling of dropsy at bay—she was losing lord after lord to the other side.

Her health was rapidly worsening. Just after midnight on 11 June, Marie de Guise died, with several of the Scottish lords she had seen turn from friend to enemy at her side.

On 6 July Scotland and England (with France represented by the Guises) signed the Treaty of Edinburgh. All English and French troops were to withdraw, while in France the young Mary, Queen of Scots, would cease using English arms.

For the duration of Mary Stuart's absence in France, Scotland would be ruled by a council of twelve lords, chosen jointly by the queen and by the Scottish parliament (one of whose first actions was to declare Scotland a Protestant country). If Mary and her husband, François, refused to ratify the treaty, then England would intervene to protect the Scottish Reformation, a refusal the likelier for the fact that Mary, frantically mourning her mother, had never been consulted as to the treaty's terms.

Nonetheless, with Mary apparently permanently based in France, it seemed as if the council—headed by Châtelherault and Mary's increasingly ambitious half brother Lord James—had things satisfactorily under their own control. But fate, of course, had a twist in store.

In her last letter, Marie de Guise had written that of her health, 'I do not know what will happen'. In fact, as regards her own impending death, she probably did have some idea. But she could not possibly have foreseen the overthrow that was about to come to her daughter, Mary Stuart.

PART VI
1560–1572

The greater and better parts of Christendom would be very wrong to complain, seeing themselves presently governed by princesses whose natural intelligence, seasoned by long experience of good and bad fortune both in wars and domestic matters, have put a great many kings to shame.

—Pierre de Ronsard, *Mascarades et Bergeries* (1565)

37

'RANCOUR AND DIVISION'

FRANCE, 1560–1561

✳

France was becoming the theatre in which the religious conflicts of Europe played out most clearly. In March 1560 came the Conspiracy of Amboise, a Protestant plot to overthrow the Guises and the government. It may or may not have been supported by Elizabeth Tudor of England—some of the conspirators, under torture, implicated the Prince de Condé, the committedly Protestant brother of Jeanne d'Albret's husband, Antoine—and there were suggestions about Antoine, too.

That summer Jeanne and Antoine (home at Nérac, accompanied by Condé) requested Calvin to send them a preacher, Theodore Beza. Another minister wrote ecstatically of the atmosphere that awaited him in their territory: 'Preaching is open—in public. The streets resound to the chanting of the Psalms. Religious books are sold as freely and openly as at home [in Geneva]'.

A letter from Beza to Calvin on 25 August says that 'the ladies commend themselves warmly to you'. The importance of great ladies in spreading the reformed faith was universally acknowledged: Condé's wife, Eleonore de Roye, was another significant figure. Nothing, however, was yet to be done openly; indeed, Antoine and Jeanne were still sending an envoy to the pope, to assure Rome of their orthodoxy.

Catherine de Medici, meanwhile, was arguing forcefully that the way to forestall any more religious troubles would be to allow a measure of toleration to the French Protestants. Catherine was on the rise. Mary, Queen of Scots, was now also Queen Consort of France, but by the start of 1560, there were mutters of discontent about the hold her Guise family had over its young king. Catherine de Medici's policy of allowing the Guises to take the political foreground, while herself remaining aloof as the sorrowing widow and mother, was paying off.

It was Catherine who sought to make a distinction between those genuinely committed to the new faith and those disaffected with the Guise regime, between, even, those of Protestant beliefs and those prepared to rebel to promulgate them. The Edict of Romorantin in May 1560 was Catherine's doing, an edict that confined the trial of religious cases to the ecclesiastical courts, which could not impose the death penalty. She also urged, successfully, for peace with England and for France's withdrawal from active participation in Scottish affairs, the latter decision perhaps the easier for the death of Marie de Guise.

On the advice of the leading Protestant Admiral de Coligny, Catherine de Medici also called a meeting of the full council for August, a discrete move to curb the exclusive influence the Guises had at first enjoyed. She herself made the first speech, hoping the councillors might find a policy whereby the king 'could conserve his sceptre, his subjects find relief from their suffering and the malcontents find contentment'. But events would overtake the peaceable plan.

The first of these events involved the Bourbons, Antoine and particularly Condé preferring to put their faith in military might rather than in Catherine's assemblies, prepared through the autumn for armed confrontation. Condé was arrested, his wife imprisoned, while there were stories the Guises in league with the Spaniards planned to seize Jeanne d'Albret and her son. But the second event was more definitive still. Young King François II had always been frail and sickly (his passion for hunting notwithstanding); on November 9, after riding out in the cold, he fell ill.

It soon became clear that his condition was serious. Catherine de Medici wrote of how hard it was 'to see the terrible and extreme pain that the King, my son is suffering'. François II had an abscess in the ear, and sepsis set in. Everyone, even François's mother, had to think of what would happen if the worst befell.

The next heir—Catherine's next son, Charles—was only ten, so the Estates-General would have to vote on a regency. Their choice was likely to fall on Antoine de Bourbon, because his brother Condé was now under sentence of death. This would leave no great place for Catherine. Boldly, she called Antoine de Bourbon into her presence (and that of the Guises) and accused him of having plotted, treacherously.

Terrified that the same sentence would fall on him as on his brother, Antoine weakly offered to give up his rights in the regency to Catherine de Medici, an offer with which she was quick to close, citing examples of other queen mothers who had ruled on behalf of a young son, notably the thirteenth-century Blanche of Castile, mother of the revered Louis IX. The Guises too were alarmed that they would be called to account for their dubious part in prosecuting Condé (and all too aware that their influence would suffer once their niece Mary was no longer queen). Catherine placated both parties and made them embrace. Pitting her rivals against each other, she had herself emerged seemingly above the fray. She had become an operator. It was a triumph of her personal diplomacy.

François II died on 5 December 1560, after a reign of only sixteen months. This was Catherine de Medici's moment. An English diplomat even wrote that 'the Queen was blithe of the death of King Francis her son, because she had no guiding of him'. Calling a meeting of the council, she told them, 'Since it has pleased God to deprive me of my elder son, I mean to submit to the Divine will and to assist and serve the King, my second son [Charles IX], in the feeble measure of my experience'.

She had decided, she told the council, 'to keep him beside me and to govern the state, as a devoted mother must do. Since I have assumed this duty, I wish all correspondence to be addressed in the first place to me; I shall open it in your presence and in particular in that of the King of Navarre [Antoine de Bourbon], who will occupy the first place in the council as the nearest relative of the King'.

Antoine gave his assent, protesting his loyalty, and the Guises did, too. Both parties now ascribed the actions that had produced their former enmity to the orders of the dead François II, and Catherine de Medici colluded in the pretence, content with the situation she had set up. At forty-one she had attained immense authority. The Venetian ambassador wrote that her will was supreme: 'It is she who will henceforth have her hand upon the most important negotiations'. Before the year was out, she had herself proclaimed Governor of the Kingdom—'Catherine by the grace of God, Queen of France, Mother of the King'.

FRANÇOIS II'S EARLY DEATH WOULD have huge consequences for his widow, Mary Stuart, and thus, indirectly, for Elizabeth in England. Mary Stuart had been raised in the expectation that her role as queen consort of wealthy France would outrank that as queen regnant of obscure Scotland. But now, less than two years into her marriage, as she sat in the darkened room custom prescribed for a mourning queen, she must have known her future had changed, completely and unexpectedly.

And there was yet another woman, also in France, whose future would be profoundly affected by the ramifications of François's death. It was clear

Catherine de Medici had used Antoine de Bourbon as pawn and cat's-paw. Did the word of his humiliation, and his vacillation, persuade Jeanne d'Albret that she, at least, should take a stand? Calvinism, with its authoritarian logic, its insistence on a black-and-white simplicity, must have made an emotional appeal to her. At Christmas communion, at Pau, she publicly forswore Rome and, as her personal historian, Nicolas de Bordenave recorded, 'having made a confession of faith, partook of Holy Communion according to the rites of the said Reformed Religion'.

Bordenave recorded that once the previously reluctant Jeanne had 'put everything in God's hands', she did so 'with such constancy that never again could she be turned from her course, no matter what assaults Satan and the world made upon her'.*

Jeanne d'Albret was hailed by other Protestant players on the international board. Calvin first wrote to her in mid-January 1561, declaring that he had no need to advise her, for 'when I see how the spirit of God rules you I have more occasion to give thanks than to exhort you'. Queen Elizabeth's ambassador Throckmorton had been told to congratulate Jeanne on her 'affection for the true religion', commenting that the time offered 'great opportunities to encourage those well-disposed'.

Both Calvin and Queen Elizabeth regretted the defection of Antoine, now declared Lieutenant-General of France, as Catherine had promised he would be. The Florentine ambassador took his appointment as a sign of Catherine's weakness, declaring that she had 'finally proven that she is only a woman'. But Antoine's reward was less than he hoped. When he suggested that in the event of Catherine's illness, her responsibilities should be agreed to devolve on him, her reply was uncompromising: 'I shall never be too ill to supervise whatever affects the service of the King my son'.

In the middle of 1561—delayed by the need to settle affairs in Béarn before she left, not least the protection of her Calvinist ministers—Jeanne d'Albret set out to join her husband at the French court. She hoped, perhaps, to stiffen his commitment to the Protestant faith.

The Spanish ambassador wrote that along the way, 'everywhere the heretics await her coming as if she were the Messiah, because they are certain

---

* Jeanne commissioned Bordenave to write a history of her provinces. She would also commission a volume of *Mémoires*—or, more accurately, 120 pages of self-justification—to be written for her in the first person. Two lines in particular stick in the memory: that 'if I wished to undertake the defence of my sex, I could find plenty of examples'; and the opening line: 'I have always considered that if a person is not satisfied with herself in herself, the contentment that others can have of her is only a half in her conscience'.

she will perform miracles on their behalf. Personally I do not doubt it, for wherever she goes she meets with no resistance'. Throckmorton told Elizabeth's minister Cecil, after Jeanne had moved on from Orléans, of how twenty-five religious ladies, 'the fairest of sixty', threw aside their habits and scaled the walls, so convinced were they now of 'the superstitions of the cloister, and the pleasures of secular company'. The Venetian ambassador called Jeanne a woman *di terribile cervello*, of a frightening brain. Catherine, noted the Spanish ambassador, 'will have a hard time living with her'.

Jeanne d'Albret made herself a focus of Protestantism at the French court, setting up a religious council, welcoming new evangelists, winning a certain following among other young court ladies, and regularly attending Protestant services 'with the doors open'. She also sent word to England that Elizabeth Tudor's 'credit is great, and the more so for standing so firmly in God's cause. [Jeanne] was glad to hear that the candles and candlesticks were removed from the Queen's chapel'. Her husband, Antoine, by contrast, attended both Protestant and Catholic services over these months.

And Antoine (as even Calvin in Geneva heard with profound disapproval) was now notorious as a ladies' man, involved with one of the pretty young attendants around Catherine (which, her enemies alleged, she would purposely deploy where necessary). Even Calvin became drawn into the attempt to heal Antoine's marriage to Jeanne, but nothing could weigh against the inducements held out by the other side. Spain even offered him ('in principle') another kingdom to compensate for the loss of Navarre.

'I have always worked for the advancement of [the Religion]', Jeanne d'Albret declared later in her memoirs. Her husband, 'having withdrawn from the first zeal that he had had for it, was for me a tough thorn, I won't say in the foot, but in the heart'. By contrast, 'I have always, by the grace of God, followed the straight path'.

The Venetian envoy wrote that Jeanne was harassing Antoine 'night and day', while he was trying to force her into at least outward conformity. Forbidden Calvinist services in her own apartment, she went to those in Condé's, and when Antoine confronted her as she was about to step into the carriage, the rows were 'so loud everyone in the château could hear'.

While Jeanne d'Albret's ever-fragile health gave way, Antoine changed tactics and began seeking to separate himself from her. A year after his wife's conversion, he would openly set his face even against the measures of toleration now proposed by Catherine de Medici, declaring his determination to 'live in closest friendship with the Guises'. His brother Condé, however, would take his place as leader of the threatened Huguenots. Meanwhile, the anti-Protestant alliance of Guises and Montmorency in the spring of 1561 had the support also of Spain, of the emperor, and of the pope: an all-male conspiracy to which they were eager to recruit also Antoine.

Catherine de Medici, by contrast, was strongly behind the Colloque de Poissy, which met that summer in what proved a vain attempt to reconcile religious divides. She was issuing an amnesty for all religious offences committed since her husband's death, delaying French churchmen from attending the Counter Reformation's Council of Trent, but Catherine's toleration was a pragmatic measure aimed at preserving her son's monarchy. As she wrote to her reproachful son-in-law Philip of Spain, the experience of decades in France taught that 'violence only serves to increase and multiply [this infection], since by the harsh penalties which have constantly been enforced in this kingdom, an infinite number of poor people have been confirmed in this belief'.

Her edict in January 1562 allowed Protestants to practise their faith so long as it was outside town walls. But it was greeted with horror by domestic and foreign Catholic powers, despite her continued assurance that she and her children 'wished to live in the Catholic faith and obedience to Rome'. The Parlement of Paris at first refused to register the edict, specifically linking their refusal to Catherine's gender in their formal remonstrance: 'Laws both sacred and profane insist that the woman is in holy bond to her husband and children in holy bond to their father, which is to say that the entire family is of the same religion as the father of the family', that is, of the religion Henri II had followed. Failing to follow this, they said, produced 'nothing but contention, rancour, and division'. Deliberately, Catherine now displayed herself, with her children, at every Catholic ritual.

To her daughter Elisabeth, Philip's wife, Catherine wrote word to ignore any rumours: 'I do not mean to change my life or my religion or anything. I am what I am in order to preserve your brothers and their kingdom'. But Jeanne d'Albret was cut from very different cloth. When Catherine de Medici asked Jeanne to moderate her Protestant behaviour, Jeanne's reply was uncompromising: 'Madame, if I had my son and all the kingdoms in the world within my hands, I would rather cast them to the bottom of the sea than lose my salvation'.

Catherine de Medici did not give up. She was still cultivating Jeanne d'Albret to a marked degree. As Jeanne prepared to leave the French court in the spring of 1562, Catherine was keeping Jeanne close as she and her son received foreign ambassadors, going out shopping in Paris together for a day, 'disguised as bourgeois ladies in simple headdress'. Indeed, Catherine was identified with Jeanne's interest to the point where Elizabeth Tudor could instruct Throckmorton 'to encourage the Queen Mother, the Queen of Navarre, and the Prince of Condé to show their constancy [and to convey] her intention to stand by them'.

But it was no longer possible to resist the demands of Antoine and of the Spanish ambassador that Jeanne should be sent away from court. Her son Henri had been taken away from her, to be educated under his father's charge and by conservative Catholic tutors. Jeanne, allowed to say goodbye to him, told the child that if ever he went to Mass she would disinherit him—or so the Cardinal of Ferrara said. The eight-year-old held out for several months before finally, predictably, being seen at Mass with his father and the royal family. But by that time, the temperature of the religious conflict had risen in an alarming way.

On 1 March 1562 the Duc de Guise—visiting family estates in the Champagne region—was riding to Mass through the small town of Vassy, property of his niece Mary Stuart, when he heard the provocative sound of a Protestant service coming, illegally, from a building within the town walls. Whether his armed escort actually began what came to be called the Massacre of Vassy, it left more than seventy Protestants dead and more than a hundred wounded. Small wonder that Jeanne d'Albret fled secretly southward to her own territories. The First War of Religion, as it would become known, was under way, with women prominent on either side.

38

'TWO QUEENS IN ONE ISLE'
SCOTLAND AND ENGLAND, 1561–1565

✳

Events in France had radically altered the life of one young woman who had expected to live out her life in that country. Now that Catherine de Medici was the power in the land where Mary Stuart had expected to be queen, the Queen of Scots' eyes turned another way. After her young husband, King François, died, Mary, as a childless widow, had now no role in France, while Scotland had no royal visible on the throne.

In August 1561 Mary, Queen of Scots, landed at Leith with the intention of governing her country. Just what kind of a fist she made of it is hotly disputed by historians. The question goes right to the heart of the notion of the female ruler in the sixteenth century.

Mary made no attempt to consolidate her position in France. On the first day of her widowhood she handed the queen's jewels back to Catherine de Medici. A Scottish contemporary mentioned her next move as being motivated by Catherine's 'rigorous and vengeable dealing'. But the forty days' seclusion may have given Mary the thinking space she needed. Her Guise relatives were pushing for another marriage, pushing hard (through her aunt Louise, who had many Spanish connections) for the Spanish heir Don Carlos and receiving offers from the kings of Denmark and Sweden, from the dukes of Ferrara and Bavaria. Holy Roman Emperor Ferdinand offered one of his sons, while the Scots offered their leading noble, Arran, Châtelherault's son. Philip's son Don Carlos was the prize, but this was blocked by Catherine de Medici, who was writing in code to the queen of England (who had likewise no wish to be caught between two jaws, northern and southern, of a Spanish vice) that this should be circumvented. Catherine's daughter Elisabeth, Mary's old playfellow, had, after all, married Philip II but still was as yet childless, and Catherine did not want a rival at her court.

But Mary herself was determined on returning to Scotland. The English envoy Throckmorton reported that Mary felt she could count on her family there, that she 'holds herself sure of Lord James and all the Stuarts'. It was perhaps a mark of her political naïveté. Her half brother Lord James Stuart—able, ambitious, and fast gaining control of a country where he was barred only by illegitimacy from himself succeeding his father, James V— would surely have preferred to see his legitimate but wholly inexperienced half sister stay well away.

There was, of course, a perverse benefit in the very fact of Mary's being a young woman, whom the lords thought they could manipulate. Mary agreed that she would maintain the religious status quo, with Protestantism the official (if far from the universal) religion, while she herself should be allowed to hear the Catholic Mass in her own chapel at Holyrood. It is unlikely, however, that she altogether understood the deal she was making. (On her very first progress, it would become clear that Lord James regarded the deal as extending only to Holyrood itself, not even to any other of her palaces where Mary might happen to be staying.) And the problem was more fundamental than that. After the death of Marie de Guise in 1560, Scotland had reorganised itself into a country run by its lords, together with a Reformation Parliament that abolished the Mass and refuted the pope's authority. In England letters were now being filed as coming from 'the States of Scotland', as if from a Scottish republic.

This was the rub. In the centuries ahead, it would be speculated why Mary Stuart failed in Scotland while Elizabeth Tudor in England succeeded. One answer surely lies in the fact that Mary was eighteen when she began to rule; Elizabeth Tudor had been an unusually experienced twenty-five when she ascended the throne and her sister Mary thirty-seven. But too much altogether may be put down to personality, ability, and training, too little to the fact that the Scottish nobles, and the Scottish church, had a very different concept of their relation to their monarchy.

There is too the issue of her ministers. It is sometimes regretted that Mary had no minister as able as Elizabeth's Cecil. That's not altogether true; in William Maitland of Lethington, she had 'Michel Wylie', the Scottish Machiavelli, who would become her one of her chief ministers. But Maitland, like Lord James, was a Protestant, and his devotion to an increasing rapport with England would eventually put him at odds with his queen, though for the first half of her reign, Mary's own eyes were turned England's way.

On the death of her husband, François II, Mary Stuart told the Earl of Bedford, who brought Elizabeth's letters of condolence, that Elizabeth 'shows the part of a good sister, whereof she [Mary] has great need'. She reiterated the fact that she and Elizabeth were (as she had written of Mary Tudor) 'two Queens in One Isle, both of one language, both the nearest kinswoman that each other hath and both Queens'. She failed to realise that though Elizabeth told Maitland she was 'obliged' to love Mary ('as being nearest to me in blood of any other'), for the English the question of Mary's claim to the English throne stood—and would continue to do so— in the way.

That is why Elizabeth, asked to grant Mary safe conduct to travel home through her realm rather than face the journey by sea, refused, unless Mary ratified the Treaty of Edinburgh made between Elizabeth and the Scottish lords. (Typically, Elizabeth changed her mind, offering the necessary conduct only too late.) William Maitland, for one, ever aiming at securing Mary's place in the future English succession, had been as anxious as Mary herself to bring about a meeting between the two queens, which, he said, 'shall breed us quietness for their times'. The meeting, of course, would never happen—though fictional writers have often imagined it—and Mary would continue to plead for it almost until her dying day.

Mary Stuart landed at Leith on 19 August 1561. As she made her official entry into Edinburgh a fortnight later, the welcoming pageantry suggested genuine pleasure at a queen's return, coupled with violent hostility to the Mass, a doctrine of hostility not necessarily felt by all the people, but urgently propounded by men like Protestant reformer John Knox.

On her first Sunday at Holyrood, Mary's own Mass in her private chapel was interrupted by a noisy demonstration. She summoned John Knox, tackling him on his statement that a woman ruler was 'a monster in nature', and this was Knox's idea of an emollient reply: 'If the realm finds no inconvenience from the rule of a woman, that which they approve shall I not further disallow . . . but shall be as well content to live under your Grace as St Paul was to live under Nero'.

'I perceive that my subjects shall obey you, and not me', Mary told him, managing to wait until he left before bursting into tears. Small wonder that English ambassador Thomas Randolph noted what would become a regular feature of Mary's life, a failure in health he called one of the 'sudden passions' that overtook her 'after any great unkindness or grief of mind'.

Nonetheless, when Mary Stuart named her first council, it was an inclusive blend of men. Seven out of twelve were Protestants. Randolph wrote home: 'I see the Lord James and the Laird of Lethington, Maitland, above all others in credit. . . . She is patient to hear, and beareth much'. Maitland wrote to William Cecil in England that 'the Queen my Mistress behaves herself so gently in every behalf as reasonably we can require', adding that she 'doth declare wisdom far exceeding her age'. He thought that 'the Queen your sovereign [Elizabeth] shall be able to do much with her in religion, if once they enter into a good familiarity'. A meeting was still Mary's own passionate hope.

In the early spring of 1562, plans for a late-summer meeting at York got as far as arrangements about the *bureau de change* to convert Scottish currency and agreement that Mary Stuart might bring a thousand attendants and practise her religion in private. There were advantages on both sides. Elizabeth's approval would ratify Mary in the eyes of her Protestant subjects, besides holding out hope of the succession. But Mary's stock with Elizabeth Tudor was also high. Her rival in the English succession stakes, Lady Katherine Grey, sister of the nine-day queen Lady Jane, had recently blotted her copybook by contracting a secret marriage with the Earl of Hertford.*

But the plan fell through on news of the Massacre of Vassy at which the Duc de Guise's men killed a party of Huguenots. In the ensuing first outbreak of the French Wars of Religion, Elizabeth threw in her lot with the Huguenots, spurred thereto by the hope of regaining Calais, which had been lost through her sister's Spanish sympathies.

Baulked of the trip to York—which news put Mary Stuart 'into such a passion as she did keep her bed all that day'—she set off on another, a progress into the North of Scotland. The Catholic Earl of Huntly, the so-called Cock of the North, had made no secret of his disapproval of any pro-English policy and showed, moreover, no disposition to bow to his queen's authority. The progress turned into something like a punitive expedition, and one in which Mary showed to advantage.

'In all these broils I assure you I never saw the Queen merrier, never dismayed, nor never thought that stomach to be in her that I find. She repented nothing but that she was not a man, to know what life it was to lie all night in the fields, or to walk on the causeway with a jack and knap-scall [a soldier's tunic and helmet], a Glasgow buckler, and a broad sword', Randolph wrote to Cecil that autumn of 1562. When one of Huntly's captains ordered Inverness Castle closed against her, she had him hanged from the battlements; when one of Huntly's sons set out to kidnap Mary (and

---

* For much of Elizabeth's reign, all the possible candidates to succeed her were female. The Grey sisters and Margaret Clifford were descended from Henry VIII's sister Mary, Margaret Douglas and her granddaughter Arbella Stuart from Henry's sister Margaret.

perhaps marry her by force), she had him too executed. But the stress told: when she arrived back at Holyrood, it was to a bout of illness, and to news from England that put a different perspective on many of her policies.

Elizabeth Tudor too was ill, with an attack of smallpox so serious her councillors were clustered around her bed in expectation of her death, terrified for the future of her country. 'Death possessed every joint of me', she later wrote. Mary Stuart was genuinely concerned, ordering her ladies to look up the recipe for a lotion used when she herself had had the disease in youth, which had prevented the scarring every woman dreaded. But she must also have thought—what if?

When the answer came, however, it was devastating. 'I have heard it whispered that in this late storm of yours a device was intended to prefer some other in the succession to my mistress, which I cannot think to be true, seeing none is more worthy', wrote Maitland to Cecil, disbelievingly. Elizabeth recovered from the smallpox, but when the lords had felt impelled to discuss her successor, only one voice had been raised in favour of Mary.

This, in all its aspects, was the situation that would continue to bedevil Elizabeth and Mary's relationship. The succession was always the problem for Elizabeth. As she told Maitland, 'Princes cannot like their own children. Think you that I could love my own winding-sheet?' Over the years ahead, the two queens would never cease to eye each other, and their relationship continued to employ a complex rhetoric.

Mary Stuart wrote of Elizabeth Tudor that 'I honour her in my heart and love her as my dear and natural sister'. At other moments, they were mother and daughter; at other times again, they sent jewels, exchanged ardent verses, as lovers might do. In the hopes of meeting with the English queen, Mary put all talk of suitors and a new marriage aside, joking that she would have no one but Elizabeth. There seems to have been a recurring fantasy current at both courts that the two might marry, and though one thinks of Elizabeth as the masculine partner here, it was tall Mary who liked to roam the streets in male clothing.

But in the first days of 1563, Mary heard that Cecil was planning to have Parliament bar her from the English throne by an Act of Exclusion. Mary was forced to think of other plans—of marriage. But what seemed like a fresh possibility to her loomed as a threat for Elizabeth.

ELIZABETH TUDOR HAD HERSELF LONG been coming under increased pressure from her council to marry and produce an heir, assuring Parliament she would do so as soon as it might be done 'conveniently'. Her ambivalence is understandable. When Mary Stuart had first been widowed, and the question of her remarriage mooted, Elizabeth's own ambassador Throckmorton had written of the Scots' queen, 'During her husband's life there was no great account made of her, for that, being under band of marriage and subjection to her husband (who carried the burden of care of all her matters) there was offered no great occasion to know what was in her'. It must have sounded more like a warning than an invitation.

Elizabeth was still toying with her chief favourite, Robert Dudley. In the spring of 1561, Cecil had been able to write in confidence to Throckmorton, 'I know surely that my Lord Robert [Dudley] hath more fear than hope, and so doth the Queen give him cause'. But that same season Elizabeth could tell the Spanish ambassador De Quadra that she 'could not deny that she had a strong regard for the many excellent qualities which she saw in Lord Robert. She had not indeed resolved to marry either him or anyone; only every day she felt more and more the want of a husband'.

By the summer of 1562, rumours were rife that Elizabeth had actually married Robert secretly. But weeks later, Swedish diplomat Robert Keyle was reporting the queen as telling Dudley with 'a great rage and great checks and taunts' and in the presence of all the nobility that 'she would never marry him, nor none so mean as he'.

This was in a sense a game, but it was play with a point, as all Elizabeth's marital games tended to be. In the decade ahead, Elizabeth Tudor would use Robert Dudley, with his enduring pretensions to her hand, as a stalking horse, an alibi for when any other, foreign, suitor got too close, to be safely spurned again once they had retreated.* But the scare of her smallpox meant that, for the moment at least, her councillors were in no mood to play. The crisis had shown up the danger of the situation, the queen a childless woman with no near relations. The Parliament that met in January 1563 was determined Elizabeth should marry. Both houses united in sending petitions urging on Elizabeth the delight of beholding 'an imp of your own', whoever the father of the imp might be.

'Whomsoever it be that your Majesty shall choose, we protest and promise with all humility and reverence to honour, love, and serve as to our most bounden duty shall appertain'. It was effectively a mandate for Robert

---

* She would use him as a foil through which to show up her own resolute chastity. As Anne de Beaujeu had written: 'Suppose a castle is beautiful and so well-guarded that it is never assailed—then it is not to be praised, nor is a knight who has never proven himself to be commended for his prowess. To the contrary, the thing most highly commended is that which has been in the fire yet cannot be scorched'.

Dudley. But Elizabeth did not avail herself of the permission. Instead, it was at this moment that she first broached with Maitland a far stranger plan, the possibility of Dudley's marrying the Scottish queen, though it would be another year before anyone dared mention it to Mary.

THE QUESTION OF MARY STUART'S remarriage had never gone away, but (as was true also at Elizabeth's court) her councillors could never all agree on whom she should marry. Maitland was willing to promote a match with Philip of Spain's son Don Carlos, since the threat of this grand alliance, of Spanish power on their northern border, might surely push England into making Mary the counteroffer of a secure place as Elizabeth Tudor's heir. Mary herself wrote to the pope, expressing herself as his 'most devoted daughter' and effectively seeking a sign of warmth that would make her a more attractive proposition to Catholic suitors. Her Guise relatives, however, were now trying to promote another match, with the emperor's third son, the Archduke Charles of Austria, while Catherine de Medici still used her influence as Philip of Spain's mother-in-law to oppose it, just as she opposed the idea of Mary marrying her youthful brother-in-law Charles IX, the new French king. Maitland wrote to Mary from the French court that the powers there 'care not greatly of your marriage or with whom it be, provided it bring with it no peril to this crown'.

In fact, the marriage with Don Carlos would eventually founder on reports of his insanity. But before that, two other individuals had decided to take a hand. One, with an unusually broad view of a subject's remit, was John Knox. Hearing that he had been speaking from the pulpit against her marriage plans, Mary sent for him and furiously demanded, 'What have ye to do with my marriage?' Alas, he was only too willing to tell her, declaring that if she married a Catholic, the realm would be 'betrayed'.

When Mary had first been widowed, Throckmorton had written admiringly of how Mary 'more esteemeth the continuation of her honour, and to marry one that may uphold her to be great, than she passeth to please her fancy'. But now Mary's Stuart Catholicism was being equated with the lustful urge to marriage (whence came that stereotype that she ruled from the heart not the head). Knox told his congregation at St Giles Kirk that the dogs would 'eat the flesh of Jezebel'. Dancing, of which Mary was so fond, 'is the vanity of the unfaithful, which shall cause the people to be set in bondage to a tyrant'.

But soon Knox had a more reasonable cause of suspicion in the behaviour of one Chastelard, a French poet whom Mary had admitted to her court. Chastelard's sighing devotion to Mary came straight from the fantasy of courtly love, but perhaps Chastelard himself (like Knox, who claimed that while dancing, Mary would steal a kiss from the poet's neck) confused fantasy with reality.

In those first weeks of 1563, he was twice found hiding under the queen's bed. The first time it was passed over as perhaps a drunken prank, the second, he was tried, sentenced, and executed. Chastelard had been found with sword and dagger, and one theory held he had been sent to assassinate Mary. Another held that he was an agent provocateur, intent on compromising her reputation. But Mary had behaved as a queen should do, behaved as Elizabeth in England had behaved, over the death of Amy Dudley.

The other meddler, of course, was Elizabeth herself. Elizabeth Tudor wanted Mary Stuart married off—an interesting sidelight on her view of the institution—but only under such conditions as she herself had, as Maitland put it, 'least cause to stand in fear'. Never mind the fact that Mary's marriage, and any alliance it might bring, had huge implications for the security of England's northern border, the more so since Mary's claim to the English throne might well be taken as the most important part of her dowry.

Mary, however resentfully, seemed prepared to allow herself to be driven, demanding sarcastically just which husbands Elizabeth felt might be 'sortable' for her. Scotland had never been able safely to defy England without the French aid Catherine de Medici was now unwilling to provide, and Mary wanted that place in the succession to the English crown.

In November 1563 England's description of the 'sortable' candidate arrived. He should ideally be an English nobleman, committed to Scotland's friendship with that country. Failing that, a foreigner might, subject to specific English permission, be acceptable so long as he was prepared to live in Scotland after the marriage—and did not come from Spain, France, or imperial Austria. Only then could Mary be treated as Elizabeth's 'only sister or daughter'. No wonder if, in the ensuing months, Mary began formulating her own plans.

She neither acceded to nor refused Elizabeth's demand. Instead, she would call out to her courtiers that the English ambassador wanted her to marry in England. 'Is the queen of England become a man?', the courtiers would call back in mocking query. She also asked, who exactly was it Elizabeth did want her to marry? When the answer came, she was never going to be pleased.

It had been back in 1563 that Elizabeth had first broached with Maitland the incredible idea that Mary should marry her own favourite, Robert

Dudley, but no one had felt it necessary to try the insulting idea on Mary. When in the spring of 1564 Thomas Randolph did bring himself to declare Dudley's name, Mary entered into the discussion with apparent seriousness, but really she was never likely to 'so far abase my state'.

Mary Stuart was surely closer to reality than Elizabeth Tudor here, especially when Elizabeth suggested that she, Mary, and Dudley might all three live at the English court, at Elizabeth's cost, and as one 'family', a virtual *ménage à trois*. But from Elizabeth's viewpoint, the idea was perhaps logical: a loyal, Protestant candidate of her own on Scotland's throne and perhaps, just perhaps, a way for Elizabeth to avoid actually marrying her favourite. If Elizabeth had ever wanted a husband, she told Sir James Melville, the urbane diplomat sent south from Scotland, 'she would have chosen Lord Robert, her brother and best friend, but, being determined to end her life in virginity, she wished that the Queen her sister should marry him'.

Melville, during his stay at the English court, was called upon to prove how well he deserved the name of diplomat. Elizabeth quizzed him as to who was the fairer—Elizabeth was the fairest queen in all England, Mary in all Scotland, he said. Elizabeth's skin 'was whiter, but my Queen was very lovely'. Who made music more skilfully? Melville said that Mary played the lute and virginals 'reasonably, for a queen'; Elizabeth made sure he came upon her playing like an expert the next day.

More seriously, in one of their conversations Elizabeth had told Melville that 'it was her own resolution at this moment to remain till her death a virgin queen'. He told her the information was unnecessary. 'I know your stately stomach. You think if you were married, you would be only a queen of England, and now ye are king and queen both. You may not endure a commander'. In Robert Dudley, she had a man—a subject—she could enjoy without fear of mastery.

Mary refused a proposal made by Catherine de Medici that while Elizabeth married King Charles IX, Mary should marry his brother Henri. Neither of the adult queens (thirty and twenty-one, respectively) were eager for matches with boys of fourteen and thirteen, and having been a queen in France, Mary said, she could never return there in a lesser role. Through 1564 she pretended to be considering Dudley, now raised a little closer to her own status when Elizabeth created him Earl of Leicester, though Melville spotted her tickling his neck during the ceremony. But even the new Earl of Leicester, Dudley, was not eager for the match. The plan had been a failure; now Mary was eyeing up other possibilities.

Mary Stuart's experience had taught her that marriage was a necessity, albeit that Elizabeth Tudor in England was drawing a different lesson. As Mary told Randolph early in 1565, 'Not to marry, you know it cannot be for me. To defer it long, many incommodities ensure'. But who was the lucky man to be?

He had already appeared on the scene. The way was clear for another candidate, not Dudley but another Englishman, newly arrived in Scotland. He was the son of Margaret Douglas, and like her mother, Margaret Tudor, Margaret Douglas dreamed of uniting England and Scotland. But she dreamed of doing it in the person of her son—Henry, Lord Darnley.

39

CHALLENGE AND CONCILIATION

France, 1562–1565

※

In France, two other women also dreamed of unity. They were facing each other across the religious divide, but neither had abandoned the idea that something (their gender?) might still be a bond between them.

Jeanne d'Albret fled the French court in 1562, amid rumours that her husband, Antoine, was preparing even to capture and imprison her. But Jeanne had, she would later insist in her memoirs, still the covert support of Catherine de Medici, herself anxious to escape from the influence of the Guises.

Catherine, Jeanne wrote, 'approved everything I had done and made an infinity of complaints against my husband'. Jeanne was the one who now withdrew, refusing to assist Catherine's negotiations with Antoine's committedly Huguenot brother Condé. For the next few years, she would be occupied chiefly in her own lands. 'God . . . has always granted me the grace to preserve this little corner of Béarn, where little by little, good increases and evil diminishes'.

Diplomatically, she would attempt to steer something of a neutral path: her son Henri, after all, was still in French hands, and still an heir to the French throne, while the Huguenots had yet no military strength to stand against the royal armies. But within her own fiefdom, she made her stance clear.

Antoine, she said, had sent orders to Pau that the Parlement should now cease all exercises of the Reformed religion and exile any officials not Catholic. She in turn withdrew her permission for him to negotiate with Spain about exchanging Navarre for Sardinia, saying it had been 'given through force and fear, not having dared refuse a husband'. 'When I learned this, I used the natural sovereign power God had given me over my subjects, which I had ceded to my husband for the obedience which God commands; but when I saw that it was a question of my God's glory and the purity of his worship'. One way or another, the marriage was coming to an end.

The violence that followed the Massacre of Vassy in 1562 had forced Catherine de Medici, however reluctantly, to put herself under the protection of the Duc de Guise, who arrived at Fontainebleu with a thousand cavalrymen. As the Protestants appealed to their coreligionists in Geneva, to the German Protestant princes, and to Elizabeth of England, Catherine with the Guises was forced to find aid both from Philip of Spain and from the papacy. Despite the wreckage of her policies, her personal courage remained high as she appeared on the ramparts above Rouen. 'My courage is as great as yours', she told the men.

Another, too, showed bravery in these wars: whatever his vacillations of policy, no one had ever doubted Antoine de Bourbon's physical courage. But in fact, he had merely wandered into the bushes to relieve himself when he was hit in the shoulder. The wound became gangrenous, and he died a few weeks later, on 17 November. Catherine now allowed Antoine's widow, Jeanne, to take control of her son's education, though for the next few years he would remain effectively a hostage at court.

In the following spring of 1563, Jeanne d'Albret wrote a long letter to Catherine de Medici:

> I trust, Madame, that you will not find that I have exceeded my duty by addressing myself to you on wings that fly above the heads of others. . . . I am fully aware, Madame, of your perfect good will and friendship, and of your desire to further my son's welfare and my own, and I cannot ignore your acts, so praiseworthy that I kiss the ground where you walk. But forgive me, Madame, if I write as I spoke to you at St Germain, where you did not seem to mind. Your good intentions are obstructed by the interference of those whom you know too well for me to describe them.

The letter also makes reference to a recent 'pitiful event'.

Antoine's had not been the only important death this season. In February 1563 (to the grief of his niece Mary in Scotland), the Duc de Guise was assassinated. Catherine was suspected: she is said to have told Condé (who had been captured by her royalist party) that Guise's death 'released her from prison'. Ironically, however, it also made her by default the leader of the Catholic faction, while the Protestant one was led by Condé and Admiral de Coligny, supported by the emotive figure of Jeanne d'Albret.

There was, however, a brief breathing space for all concerned. In March the Edict of Amboise gave freedom of conscience, and limited freedom of worship, to Huguenots. And in the summer of 1563, Catherine de Medici adopted the device that had earlier been used to confirm Marie de Guise's authority in Scotland. She had her thirteen-year-old son, Charles IX, declared of age (despite the opposition of the Paris Parlement).

The first act of the young king was to hand his mother the 'power to command', declaring that she 'would continue to govern as much and more than before'. When, some months later, Charles IX also issued a decree maintaining a fragile peace between the Guises and the Coligny clan, his mother boasted that he had done so 'without anyone's prompting'. But that seems, to say the least of it, unlikely.

JEANNE D'ALBRET, MEANWHILE, WAS ALSO consolidating her authority. The year 1563 saw the abolition in her lands of the traditional religious processions and the arrival of the extra ministers she had requested from Calvin. 'The Queen of Navarre has banished all idolatry from her domains and sets an example of virtue with incredible firmness and courage', wrote one. Many of Jeanne's nobles and officials, however, were against her reform, and the reformer Jean-Raymond Merlin fretted that 'she is inexperienced . . . having always been either under a father who managed affairs, or under a husband who neglected them'.

A few months after Jeanne's imposition of Protestantism, she was, he said, *épouvantée* (aghast) at news the Spanish had stationed troops on her frontier and that though he had pushed her into forbidding the Mass in one town, she was hanging back ('paralysed by fear') from repudiating the papacy entirely. The Spanish envoy, once again Descurra, had brought her a letter of remonstrance from the king of Spain. 'Although I am just a little princess, God has given me the government of this country so that I may rule it according to His Gospel and teach it His laws. I rely on God, who is more powerful than the King of Spain', she replied. Philip had been attempting to neutralise the widowed Jeanne by marrying her into his house, but now he told his secretary of state that 'this is quite too much of a woman to have as a daughter-in-law'.

Next, frighteningly, Jeanne d'Albret received a letter from an emissary of the papacy, a Cardinal d'Armagnac sent from Trent to warn her away from the reformist path. But to that too Jeanne replied with mounting indignation.

I condemn no one to death or imprisonment, which penalties are the nerves and sinews of a system of terror—I blush for you, and feel ashamed when you falsely state that so many atrocities have been perpetrated by those of our religion. Purge the earth first from the blood of so many just men shed by you and yours. . . . As in no point I have deviated from the faith of God's Holy Catholic church, nor quitted her fold, I bid you keep your tears to deplore your own errors. . . . I desire that your useless letter may be the last of its kind.

On 28 September 1563 Pope Pius IV summoned Jeanne to appear before the Inquisition in Rome, on a charge of heresy. If she failed to appear, she would be excommunicated and her lands declared free to anyone who could take them. She had six months to comply.

From this predicament she was once again rescued by Catherine de Medici, albeit that Catherine's motives were not solely sisterly. The papacy's intrusion on French sovereign power had long been a bone of contention. In December Catherine sent a special envoy to Rome, protesting that the pope's actions were 'against the ancient rights and privileges of the Gallican Church'.

Philip of Spain, meanwhile, planned to kidnap Jeanne and deliver her to the Inquisition in Spain. But elements of the plan leaked out when an embroiderer employed by Catherine de Medici's daughter Elisabeth—also Philip's wife—passed on word of what one of the agents had said in his cups. The former French princess passed word to her mother's ambassador, an example of natal winning out over marital loyalties, or even of female solidarity.

'I put myself wholly under the wing of your powerful protection', Jeanne d'Albret wrote gratefully to Catherine de Medici. 'I will go to find you wherever you may be and shall kiss your feet more willingly than the Pope's'. Protection, however, had a price. Jeanne was summoned to the French court, and Catherine wrote that she must moderate her religious policy 'in such a way that her subjects will not be led to rebel nor her neighbours to support them'. Jeanne should let her subjects 'all live in freedom of conscience and in the exercise of their own religion without forcing of any'. Jeanne's edict of February 1564 did indeed permit a measure of Catholic as well as a measure of Calvinist worship and the pardon of all religious crimes that could not be considered lèse-majesté.

Jeanne d'Albret dawdled in obeying Catherine de Medici's summons to court; she had, after all, to arrange for her land to be ruled in her absence.

But by the spring of 1564, it was Catherine herself who was setting out, taking her court and her son the king on a progress through France that would last for more than two years, ten thousand people on a twenty-seven-month journey, equipped with everything from portable triumphal arches to a travelling zoo. At the beginning of June, in Mâcon, Jeanne at last joined the royal tour, herself accompanied by three hundred cavalry and eight Calvinist ministers. From the start, her intransigence was clear.

The day after Jeanne's arrival, as the Corpus Christi procession passed under her windows, members of her suite shouted lewd remarks. At Lyons a few days later, she attended Huguenot sermons in the city, taking her son with her, until a provoked Catherine stopped the Calvinist services, took Jeanne's son Henri back into her own hands, and swore she would cut off the head of anyone who did not attend Mass. But in some ways, the progress was having the unifying effect Catherine had hoped: at Lyons a joint procession of Catholic and Protestant children was staged, to celebrate the current state of religious harmony.

As the journey wore on, however, Jeanne d'Albret often requested to be allowed to return to her own lands and to take her son with her. This was refused. Henri would continue to accompany the court. Jeanne, as a compromise, was instructed to retire to Vendôme, also her own land but closer at hand and held in fief to the French crown.

Even Vendôme had seen conflict between the Calvinist lieutenants Jeanne had appointed and the royal agent the Protestants claimed was persecuting them. But in those environs, Jeanne was to remain for some months. Everyone wanted her out of the way for the meeting that was looming at Bayonne, on the Spanish border.

There Catherine de Medici would once again meet her daughter Elisabeth, a longed-for personal as well as a vital diplomatic encounter. But Philip of Spain, already annoyed with Catherine's tolerant religious policy, and refusing to attend the meeting himself, had refused even to let his wife attend if Jeanne d'Albret and Condé were present, not wishing, he said, his wife to meet 'with rebels and fomenters of sedition'.

The meeting was a grand diplomatic spectacle, and no doubt a rare personal pleasure for both Catherine de Medici and her daughter. But even here there was a conflict of interests. 'How Spanish you have become, my daughter', Catherine said to Elisabeth, observing the latter's wholesale adoption not only of Spanish dress and manners but also of her husband Philip's opinions. Philip had sent with his wife the notorious hard-liner the Duke of Alba, an ardent Catholic, to dragoon Catherine into clamping down on the Huguenots. He failed, but, conversely, the very fact of Catherine's having met with him was taken by the Huguenot leaders to be a worrying sign.

But right after Bayonne, Catherine de Medici, characteristically, set once more about appeasing the Protestant leaders. In the summer of 1565, Jeanne was allowed to leave Vendôme for Nérac (capital of the duchy of Albret, which gave Jeanne her name), there to receive the court on its homeward journey. Catherine urged Jeanne to return to the Catholic faith; Jeanne used the time to introduce her son Henri to leading Huguenots. When the royal circus finally reached Paris in early summer 1566, Jeanne d'Albret would be with them, but still—so the Spanish ambassador complained—behaving intransigently.

40

'MAJESTY AND LOVE DO NOT SIT WELL TOGETHER'

Scotland, 1565–1567

❋

In the summer of 1565, Mary, Queen of Scots, married her kinsman Lord Darnley, and what followed is one of the better-known tales in British history, a catastrophic chain of events and errors. Was Mary Stuart, like Jeanne d'Albret, a rebel against what those around her saw as good order and authority? Was she a fool for love? Or was she, by contrast, making what she saw as her best bid at keeping in her own (and a husband's) hands the rule of her country, however misguided her gamble proved to be? From the start, contemporary opinions were contradictory.

When Mary Stuart met and to all appearances swiftly fell for Henry, Lord Darnley, she seemed to be fitting into the very stereotype John Knox had used to discredit the whole idea of women's rule. Infatuated, a prey to unbridled sensuality. As she told the English ambassador Randolph: 'Princes at all times have not their wills, but my heart being my own is immutable'. At eighteen Darnley was tall (taller even than Mary's six feet), elegant, an expert in manly arts, and educated in a way that gave him at least the veneer of courtly civility, however illusory that would prove to be.

But when in February 1565 Mary went to greet Darnley on the Scottish coast, there was a subtext to any possible love story. The English Parliament had objected to Mary's claim to the English throne that she was a foreigner as well as a woman. But if she could ally her claim to that of the English-born Margaret Douglas—Margaret Tudor's daughter as well as Darnley's mother—or to that of her son, it might be a different story.

This, of course, begs the question of why Elizabeth Tudor had agreed to let Darnley and his father, Lennox, go north to Scotland when they had asked permission the year before. The plausible pretext was that Lennox needed to deal with his Scottish lands, but surely Elizabeth must have guessed what might happen? The idea of a match between Mary and Darnley had first been mooted long ago. Is it conceivable even that Elizabeth was purposely handing Mary a poisoned chalice, knowing that Darnley would make Mary the worst of husbands?

It was Elizabeth Tudor herself who now—inadvertently or otherwise—put the seal on the affair. Mary Stuart had been pressing for some definite commitment from Elizabeth regarding her place in the succession. In the middle of March, Elizabeth's answer arrived, that 'nothing shall be done until her Majesty (Elizabeth) shall be married, or shall notify her determination never to marry'. No wonder it took English ambassador Thomas Randolph two days to brace himself to deliver the message.

Within weeks Mary and Darnley were openly courting, with Mary defying convention to nurse him herself when he fell sick. When Elizabeth sent orders recalling Lennox and Darnley to England, Mary commanded them instead to remain. She was strengthened in her resolve by France's support and that of her former mother-in-law, Catherine de Medici, whom it suited to have Elizabeth under pressure at this time.

Before the marriage, Darnley began to show himself as 'proud, disdainful and suspicious', drunken and violent. The question is whether Mary knew it, whether any infatuation she felt for him had already died. Throckmorton, sent to the Scottish court to bring Darnley home, found a queen 'seized with love in fervanter passions than is comely', even for 'mean persons'. But Randolph wrote to Robert Dudley, the Earl of Leicester, that Mary showed so much change in her nature that 'she beareth only the shape of the woman she was before'. A fool for love—or one already seeing love slip away?

'What shall become of her, or what life with him she shall lead, I leave it to others to think', Randolph prophesied gloomily. As Throckmorton quoted to Leicester and Cecil: 'Majesty and love do not sit well together, nor remain on one throne'. But Randolph was a partial witness—and royal marriages weren't made for pleasure—and it was going ahead whatever anybody said. Mary was unmoved by the disapproval of her half brother Lord James (now Earl of Moray) and Maitland. She was understandably disenchanted with their pro-English policy, while the fickle and ambitious Earl of Morton, another powerful player in Scottish affairs, was actually a kinsman of Darnley's.

'Greater triumphs there never were in time of popery than were this Easter at the resurrection and at her high mass', reported Randolph grimly to Cecil at the end of April. 'She wanted now neither trumpet, drum, nor fife, bagpipe nor tabor. . . . Upon Monday she and divers of her women apparelled themselves like burgesses' wives, went upon their feet up and down the town, and of every man they met they took some pledge of money towards the banquet'. Mary was riding high.

Elizabeth Tudor's own attempt to forbid the match was countered by Mary Stuart with a mixture of wilful misunderstanding—Elizabeth had always said that Mary should marry an Englishman, hadn't she?—and outright anger. 'You can never persuade me that I have failed your mistress', Mary told Randolph, 'but rather she to me; and some incommodity it will be as well for her to lose my amity as hers will be to me'.

The wedding took place on 29 July 1565, in Mary's private chapel, with Mary wearing the white dress of her widowhood. The ceremony was a Catholic one, though Darnley removed himself before the nuptial Mass, and the heralds proclaimed him now king of Scotland. 'This Queen is now become a married wife', Randolph wrote to Leicester, 'and her husband, the self same day of his marriage made a king'. A king, however, 'so proud and spiteful, that rather he seemeth a monarch of the world than he that no long since we have seen and known the Lord Darnley'.

And Darnley's kingship was in many ways an empty title. Mary would never manage to procure him the Crown Matrimonial, which would have secured his position as a monarch of Scotland, independent of Mary and even in the event of her death. The great problem for reigning queens—the position of a consort—had caught out Mary. But it had also caught out Darnley.

In the first months of their marriage, however, Mary and Darnley were able to subsume any anxieties into activity. They set out in force (and, in Darnley's case, in a specially made gilt breastplate) to pursue and punish those lords who, under the leadership of her half brother Moray, were now in open rebellion. Since battle was never really engaged with a fleeing foe, this became known as the Chaseabout Raid, but again Mary showed to advantage, with loyal Scotsmen flocking to join her cause, and more of them every day.

She sent Elizabeth word that she wanted no more interference in the affairs of her country, that she hoped she and her cousin could be the best of friends once more, but only after Elizabeth had declared Mary her heir, she and Darnley. She reconciled most of the lords to her, split off the few rebels who held with Moray. When at Mary's invitation the Earl of Bothwell returned to the country and took command of the army, the rebels simply melted away. This, however, left the divisions in the royal marriage itself all the plainer to see.

On the one hand, Darnley was pressing not only for more power, but also for Europe's rulers to acknowledge his rights to hold the reins of the country. On the other, his unfitness for the role was becoming clearer every day. (Both his ambition and his outrages were reminiscent of the comportment of Margaret Tudor's husband Angus.) And there were two more jokers in the pack. One was that before the end of 1565, Mary Stuart must have known that she was pregnant. The other was that people were starting to talk about the favour Mary was showing to her Piedmontese private secretary, David Rizzio. 'To be ruled by the advice of two or three strangers, neglecting that of her chief councillors, I do not know how it can stand', Randolph wrote disapprovingly, calling Rizzio 'a filthy wedlock breaker'. Randolph warned Leicester, 'Woe is me for you when David son shall be a King of England'. This was surely an unfounded slander, but Mary's attitude toward Rizzio could not but show up her very different feeling toward Darnley.

On 13 February 1566, Randolph told Leicester that 'I know now for certain that this Queen repenteth her marriage, that she hateth the King [Darnley] and all his kin' and that Darnley would be seeking to find a reason for that hatred. Darnley (prompted by a disaffected Scottish faction) had driven himself into a jealous fury, convinced Rizzio was the father of the child Mary now carried. Darnley's suspicion of Rizzio was only heightened by the fact that some believed he himself to have been sleeping with the Piedmontese secretary.

'I know that, if that take effect which is intended, David, with the consent of the King, shall have his throat cut within these ten days', Randolph predicted. It took a little longer, but on 9 March 1566 a party of nobles, Darnley among them, burst into Mary's chamber and hacked Rizzio to death almost before her eyes.

'Be it known to all men by these present letters: We, Henry, by the grace of God, King of Scotland and husband to the Queen's Majesty . . . have thought pity to suffer her to be abused or seduced by certain privy persons, wicked and ungodly, especially a stranger Italian called Davie', declared the bond signed by Lord Darnley. He and a group of lords had accordingly 'devised to take these privy persona, enemies to her Majesty, us, the nobility and commonwealth, to punish them according to their demerits, and in case of any difficulty, to cut them off immediately'. In this as in many things, Darnley was the dupe of other, more resolute, men. But what was extraordinary was the insult to Mary.

Mary rallied sufficiently to persuade Darnley that his life as well as hers would ultimately be in danger from his collaborators, overmighty subjects who had dared to kill her servant, almost in her very presence. Slipping out of the palace of Holyrood, she escaped, taking him with her, a daring ride across the country, despite her pregnancy, reminiscent, again, of that her grandmother Margaret Tudor had undertaken. With Bothwell swiftly at her side, she returned to Edinburgh in triumph and managed to regain a measure of control.

ELIZABETH TUDOR WAS GENUINELY HORRIFIED when she heard of the insults heaped upon Mary Stuart, telling the Spanish ambassador that Rizzio's killers had broken into Mary's chamber 'as if it were that of a public woman'. If this could happen to one of the two queens in the isle, it was all the harder for the other to preserve any sense of invulnerability.

While urging Robert Dudley on Mary, Elizabeth had still been half-heartedly contemplating her own marriage to the Archduke Charles, the emperor's son, though braced only for marriage 'as Queen and not as Elizabeth'. Then had come that suggestion of a French match . . . and meanwhile, there was always Robert Dudley. Even while Mary Stuart was ordering her wedding clothes, Elizabeth Tudor was telling the Spanish ambassador that she would marry Robert, if only he were 'a king's son', while the Holy Roman Emperor was sending another envoy. It seems likely that by 1566 Robert must have been suspecting he would never get anywhere with his hopes of marriage to the queen, but, with him and with at least one other, Elizabeth's matrimonial game had still some moves to be played.

The tempting possibility of her hand had, of course, become one of the best tools of her diplomacy. Almost forty years before, a Venetian observer had noted that the English used the young Princess Mary as a hunter uses a lure to draw in birds. Now Elizabeth used her own hand the same way.

IN SCOTLAND, INCREDIBLY, THINGS WERE patched up after the debacle of Rizzio's death. With Mary expecting Darnley's child, they had to be. When in June she took to her birthing chamber, however, it was in Edinburgh Castle rather than any of her more commodious palaces, a place steeped in Scottish history, indeed, but also one of oft-proven security.

On 9 June she summoned the lords to hear her will, a sensible precaution for any woman embarking on childbearing. The birth was indeed long and difficult, so much so that Mary, in the throes, cried out that had she known the whole, she would never have gotten married, while her ladies tried by witchcraft to cast her pains onto another woman. But on 19 June the birth of a healthy baby boy, Prince James, set the seal on Mary's monarchy.

The Scottish ambassador to England took care to give Elizabeth all the gory details of the birth, telling her his mistress had been 'so sore handled that she wished she had never been married'. He did it, he said, 'to give her a little scare' off any marriage of her own. (It was obviously in Scotland's interest that Elizabeth Tudor should die unmarried, leaving Mary Stuart, or Mary's son, as her heir.) But that October, when Elizabeth, in order to raise funds, was forced to summon Parliament back after a three-year absence, the members returned to London even more determined to tackle the question of the succession than when they had gone away.

Mary, when Darnley came to see his son, declared before witnesses that the baby was his. The extraordinary thing was that she should need to. Nonetheless, the summer of 1566, as Mary took time off to recover, saw some attempts at amity—sabotaged by the impossible Darnley. At Traquair there were plans for the royal couple to stag hunt the next day, but Mary whispered in Darnley's ear that she preferred not to ride out. Another pregnancy was already a possibility. Darnley said loudly that never mind, if she lost this baby they could make another. It was a tiny incident that dramatised Mary's difficulties. And his intransigence could only make her look favourably at other, more supportive, figures.

In the autumn Queen Mary went to Jedburgh to preside over the justice assizes, one of those tasks she regularly undertook that showed she still aspired to be more than a pretty figurehead. While there, in the middle of October, she rode over to the stronghold of the Hermitage, where Lord Bothwell was lying sick, having been injured by Border raiders. The incident was later used to blacken her name, with the suggestion of an illicit affair between the pair, but in fact Mary took a large party with her (including her half brother Moray). The journey back, however, was marred by Mary's horse throwing her into a bog. The next day she fell ill, and soon her life was despaired of. The Bishop of Ross described it vividly: 'Her Majesty became dead, and all her members cold, eyes closed, mouth fast, and feet and arms stiff and cold'.

She was brought around. But what is interesting is what the Venetian envoy in France heard as she recovered: 'The illness was caused by her dissatisfaction at a decision made by the King, her husband'. Someone was going to have to do something about Lord Darnley.

As Mary began to recover her strength, she moved, with a number of her lords, to Craigmillar, outside Edinburgh, and it was probably there that a conspiracy was launched. Or even, perhaps, several different conspiracies. Mary was now persuaded to pardon even the Rizzio plotters. There was, after all, now only one real enemy. When his son was baptised on 17 December at Stirling Castle, Darnley, although present in the palace, did not attend the ceremony. Instead, foreign guests were welcomed by Lord Bothwell, who was gaining an ever-increasing ascendancy.

The first weeks of 1567 saw Darnley ill and undergoing medical treatment in Glasgow, heartland of his family's territory. (His illness was almost certainly syphilis, and the fact that she might soon be called on to resume sexual relations with him was a factor in Mary's determination to be free.) When Mary went to visit him there, there were huge concerns about her security. There had long been talk that Darnley might try to kidnap the baby James, so as to rule as regent himself while holding Mary in captivity.

Just how far Mary's desire to be free carried her was and is a source of huge controversy. The bare facts are easily stated. At the end of January, Queen Mary persuaded Darnley to return with her to Edinburgh, where, his own choice of venue, he was lodged at the nearby house of Kirk o'Field until his cure was complete. Mary visited him frequently, doing so on 9 February with a cheerful company, leaving early, however, to attend a page's wedding party.

At two in the morning on 10 February, Edinburgh was rocked by the sound of an explosion. Mary, at Holyrood, sent at once to enquire what had happened and soon heard that Kirk o'Field was rubble. It was only the day's light, however, that revealed Darnley's dead body not in the house itself but, strangled, in the garden, whence he had apparently been trying to flee.

Volumes have been devoted to the murder of Lord Darnley, and this is no place to weigh the evidence. Two things are important here: that Bothwell was immediately suspected on all sides of having cleared his rival out of the way and that Mary was widely suspected of complicity. And perhaps a third: that most historians today consider she was innocent at least of precise knowledge of the plan . . . though that said, one of the skills of medieval or early modern monarchy might be to express a desire that some obstacle might be removed and take care not to know how it would happen, precisely.

Maitland at Craigmillar had suggested a divorce or annulment, but Mary had been concerned that might impact on her son's legitimacy. When Maitland had then seemed to say another way would have to be found, she had cried out that nothing could be done against her reputation or her honour. To have failed subsequently to prevent what she should surely have guessed her lords were thinking was, if not a sin of omission, then at least an act of folly. But of folly, most would in the end have to declare Mary Stuart guilty.

Certainly, Mary did now act foolishly. Her very unpreparedness to deal with this crisis perhaps suggests she had not anticipated it precisely. Instead of observing the strictest mourning as a wife, and as queen distancing herself from those suspected of the deed, she . . . vacillated, basically. She ordered black drapes for her chamber at Edinburgh Castle, but stopped off as she went there to attend another wedding party. She set out to nearby Seton, several times, for a few days' holiday. She was observed, with the ever-present Bothwell, to be disporting herself at archery. Her mood was volatile, though she was distressed and angered by the placards blaming Bothwell for Darnley's death. One would depict Mary herself as a mermaid, that notorious symbol of harlotry.

Elizabeth in England wrote to her with extraordinary vehemence:

> My ears have been so astounded, my mind so disturbed and my heart so appalled at hearing the horrible report of the abominable murder of your late husband and my slaughtered cousin, that I can scarcely as yet summon the spirit to write about it. . . . I will not conceal from you that people for the most part are saying that you will look through your fingers at this deed instead of avenging it. . . . I exhort you, I counsel you, and I beg you to take this thing so far to heart that you will not fear to touch even him who you have nearest to you if he were involved.

Elizabeth was clearly afraid that Mary's actions might have compromised the whole sisterhood of queens—a sorority from which Mary might yet be barred. If Mary failed to use such sincerity 'and prudence' that the world should pronounce her innocent, wrote Elizabeth on another occasion, then she would 'deserve to fall from the ranks of princesses and rather than that should happen to you, I would wish you an honourable burial rather than a soiled life'.

But on 12 April Bothwell was acquitted in a show trial, the verdict the surer for the fact that Edinburgh was so packed with his men that Lennox, Darnley's father, dared not appear—and that Mary had waved him off to the hearing. A week later Bothwell went further, summoning the lords to a supper at Ainslie's Tavern. There he demanded that they should all sign a bond. It called on the queen to marry, and to marry a Scotsman, and who better than Bothwell himself?

Mary's next action was that of both a queen and a mother. She went to Stirling, where her son was being raised, to try to get possession of the baby. When Prince James's official guardian refused to give him up, Mary was forced to set out once again toward Edinburgh. On 24 April she rode out from her own birthplace of Linlithgow to return to the city. Spanish ambassador Guzman de Silva (writing home on 3 May) described what came next: 'On arriving six miles from Edinburgh, Bothwell met her with four hundred horsemen. As they arrived near the Queen with their swords drawn they showed an intention of taking her with them. . . . She was taken to Dunbar, where she arrived at midnight, and still remains. Some say she will marry him'. Crucially, the ambassador continued: 'It is believed that the whole thing has been arranged, so that if anything comes of the marriage the Queen may make out that she was forced into it'.

Therein lay the rub. Though Mary's first reaction—ordering her men to ride for help—suggests she had genuinely been ambushed by Bothwell, her subsequent reaction is harder to understand. She remained at Dunbar twelve days, by the end of which, from later evidence, she would seem to have been pregnant. Bothwell himself was absent for a part of that time, arranging a hasty divorce from his wife, so as to free himself for a more advantageous marriage, and the conditions of her 'captivity', if such one can call it, were not such as to preclude Mary's having escaped, if she had really wished to do so.

The dark suspicion, as Maitland's friend Kirkaldy of Grange put it, was that Mary 'was minded to cause Bothwell to ravish her'. That to avoid the blame she would incur if she openly took up the man believed to be her husband's murderer, she had helped to set up what was to be passed off as an abduction and ravishment.

But perhaps a more likely explanation is that Mary was indeed surprised and outraged by Bothwell's abduction, but that he then won her around. She had, after all, come to feel in the last months that he was the only man in Scotland on whom she could really rely, who seemed to answer her desperate need for support and protection.

If he told her he'd been impelled to seize her for her own safety, that her only hope lay in marrying him, if he showed her the Ainslie Tavern bond, that indeed is the explanation Mary herself sent to her ambassador at the French court, and the long circumstantial story makes convincing reading.

Seeing ourselves in Bothwell's power, sequestered from the company of our servants and others, of whom we might ask counsel . . . left alone, as it were, a prey to him, many things we resolved with ourself, but never could find a way out. And yet he gave us little space to meditate with ourself, ever pressing us with continual and importunate suit. In the end, when we saw no hope to be rid of him, never man in Scotland making a move to procure our deliverance we were compelled to mitigate our displeasure, and began to think upon that which he propounded.

. . . Albeit we found Bothwell's doings rude, yet were his words and answers gentle. As by a bravado in the beginning he had won the first point, so ceased he never till by persuasions and importune suit, accompanied not the less with force, he has finally driven us to end the work begun at such time and in such form as he thought might best serve his turn.

The conclusion that would best serve Bothwell's turn was marriage with the queen, but she had also her own reasons for agreeing to the idea. Scotland 'being divided into factions as it is', she wrote (and it might have been her grandmother Margaret Tudor speaking), 'cannot be contained in order unless our authority be assisted and set forth by the fortification of a man'.

On 6 May they rode back into Edinburgh through sullen crowds, Bothwell leading Mary's horse. On 12 May she formally pardoned him for abducting her and raised him to be Duke of Orkney. On 15 May they were married, in a Protestant ceremony.

But once again, as with the marriage to Darnley, Mary's feelings appear to have been conflicted. Within days, the French ambassador Du Croc was writing to Catherine de Medici, 'The Queen's marriage is too unhappy and begins already to be repented of'. Mary had sent for him, after he had seen her and her husband at odds, and told him that 'if you see me melancholy, it is because I do not choose to be cheerful; because I never will be so, and wish for nothing but death'.

'Yesterday, when they were both in a room, she called aloud for a knife to kill herself; the persons in the ante-chamber heard it', De Croc reported. Bothwell—like Darnley, but with greater force and abilities—was another man determined to rule as king. But the court was becoming a travesty, from which daily men like Maitland slipped away.

On 6 June, knowing the Earl of Morton and the lords were planning an attack, determined on his overthrow, Bothwell took Mary away from Edinburgh to a place of greater safety. On 15 June, a scorching day, the royal forces and those of the lords faced each other at Carberry.

Bothwell was ready to decide the matter by single combat. It was Mary who finally intervened, knowing, surely, that this was no way to regain any useful control of her country. A deal was struck, whereby she would be taken into honourable custody, while Bothwell was allowed to go free. But Mary was appalled by the reaction of the soldiers and, as the lords led her into Edinburgh, of the citizenry. Her dress torn, alternately sobbing and threatening, she listened to the crowds yelling 'Burn the whore'. Was this the real romance gone wrong—the love Elizabeth never wholly lost in all her long marriage to her country?

On 17 June Queen Mary was taken, captive, from Holyrood to the island castle of Loch Leven, where she almost immediately miscarried, reportedly of twins.* On 24 June, still weak, Mary was forced to sign a document of abdication. Five weeks later her baby son would be crowned James VI, with her half brother Moray to act as regent during his minority.

Queen Elizabeth wrote yet again to her 'sister Sovereign': 'Whatsoever we can imagine meet for your honour and safety that shall lie in our power, we will perform the same [so] that it shall well appear you have a good neighbour, a dear sister, and a faithful friend'. Elizabeth was indeed aware that a blow to one monarch—and female monarch—damaged any monarchy. 'You shall plainly declare to the lords that if they shall determine anything to the deprivation of the Queen their sovereign lady of her royal estate. . . . [W]e will make ourselves a plain party against them, for example to all posterity', she wrote to her ambassador in Scotland.

It may even have been the fear of Elizabeth's wrath that kept Mary's lords from proceeding to any lethal extremity against her. Nonetheless, in Elizabeth Tudor's eyes, Mary Stuart had indeed committed an unforgivable crime. She had made all female rulers look foolish—exactly as men like John Knox had always suspected them to be.

---

* This has been used as evidence that she must (as her enemies alleged) have been sleeping with Bothwell before Dunbar, since otherwise the foetuses could not have been sufficiently developed to have shown themselves a pair.

41

'DAUGHTER OF DEBATE'

The Netherlands, France, and England, 1566–1571

In continental Europe too, religious divisions were hardening. In the Netherlands Margaret of Parma, acting as regent for her half brother, Philip of Spain, had from the start faced a situation even more difficult than that which had plagued her aunt Mary of Hungary when she was regent for *her* brother Charles V.*

Charles V (who had, after all, been raised in the Netherlands) spent much of his reign moving around his vast territories. Philip, though too painstaking not to pay due tribute to the Netherlands and its culture, was every inch a Spaniard, determined to rule from Madrid, or from the vast new palace he was raising nearby, the Escorial. This left the Netherlands dissatisfied with their position as, effectively, a mere colony and left Philip with little real understanding of the seventeen very different provinces that made up his northern holding. But it also left Margaret of Parma, given far less authority than her predecessors, trying to implement instructions sent from Philip, many weeks' journey away.

No one as yet was speaking of the dissent in the Netherlands as a struggle for independence. Instead, the trouble was cast in religious terms. The Netherlands Council of State was coming under the leadership of the Stadtholder William of Orange, who had been raised in part under the influence of Mary of Hungary and was much trusted by her and by Charles V. But now William (brought into alliance with the German Protestant princes through a marriage with Anna of Saxony) electrified the council by expressing his continued opposition to Philip on religious grounds. Himself a Catholic, he could not concede that a monarch had the right to decide his

* Margaret of Parma was unusual among female regents in that her (second) husband, Ottavio Farnese, was still alive. He, however, remained in Italy to govern his duchy of Parma, while their son, Alexander, accompanied Margaret to the Netherlands.

subjects' beliefs. Philip, horrified by the growing power of the Protestants in France, had earlier ordered Margaret of Parma strictly to enforce Charles V's *Placarten*, edicts imposing harsh penalties against heresy. William now told the council that 'the king errs if he thinks that the Netherlands, surrounded as they are by countries where religious freedom is permitted, can indefinitely support the sanguinary edicts'.

In April 1565 a confederacy of noblemen, William's younger brother Louis prominent among them, presented a petition to Margaret of Parma, requesting an end to the persecution of Protestants. The next year saw a wave of iconoclasm, as Protestants of various denominations swept through the Netherlands, destroying Catholic images, exactly the kind of news most certain to appall Philip of Spain. Religious discontent was fostered by economic hardship: as one observer put it, 'It is folly to enforce the edicts while corn is so dear'.

Margaret's instinct was to agree to the demands of the confederacy, as long as its members joined her in restoring order. Back in Italy, the counselling of the Jesuit founder, Ignatius Loyola, had mediated in Margaret's troubled marriage to Farnese, and her patronage had been vital in getting Loyola's nascent Society of Jesus off the ground. But she seems—like Catherine de Medici, like Elizabeth of England—to have made a distinction between religious belief and civil disobedience. Like Catherine de Medici, however, she would be thwarted in the attempt to act on any such belief. (Elizabeth in England would hold out for longer.)

The report Margaret of Parma sent to Philip sounded a despairing note: 'Everything is in such disorder that in the greater part of the country there is neither law, faith nor king'. But despite the sound of panic, she was taking steps successfully to deal with the situation. The noblemen, content their petition was to be forwarded to Philip, had for the most part rallied behind the regent and the country was calmed—and the effect of her words was surely not what she desired. Even as Margaret caused to be struck a triumphal medal, figuring her as an Amazon wielding both sword and olive branch, the hard-line Duke of Alba was despatched north from Spain to deal with what Philip saw as a rebellion, while the request that something from ten to twenty thousand Spanish troops should be allowed to march through France, Netherlands bound, was another source of alarm to the French Protestants and another thorn in the side of Catherine de Medici.

On his arrival Alba set up the Council of Troubles, a body directly under his control, to enforce the Placarten with utmost stringency. More than three thousand people would be executed over the next five years or so. In June 1568 sixty Netherlands nobles, including a cousin of the French Admiral de Coligny were put to death on the Grand Place in Brussels. But by then, in September 1567, Margaret of Parma had resigned her regency.

Margaret's resignation was a protest against Alba's powers, which were greater than her own, and perhaps also against his policies, though it might be a mistake to assume hers were humanitarian motives. Margaret soon retired to L'Aquila in Italy, where she was appointed governor of Abruzzo, but she was still identified with the harsh rule of Spain. A 1622 picture in Berlin's museum of history, *The Tied-Up Dutch Provinces Before Duke Alba*, shows Alba enthroned in judgment above seventeen chained women, representing the provinces. Cardinal Grenville wields bellows to inflate Alba's fury, while behind him Margaret of Parma fishes for their goods in a river of blood.*

EVENTS IN THE NETHERLANDS REVERBERATED throughout Europe. In England, at the end of 1567, it was word of the Spanish activities that finally saw an end to the proposal of a marriage between Elizabeth and the Habsburg archduke, the emperor's son. Moreover, William of Orange—now escaped to Germany—sought to drive the Spanish from the Netherlands. He would look not only to the German princes but also to the French Protestants for help in raising an army. As the French court arrived back from its 'Grand Tour', it became clear that one major source of dissension was going to be the desire of the Huguenots (and particularly of Admiral de Coligny, who had soon gained a quasi-paternal ascendancy over the young king Charles IX) to aid their fellow Protestants across the border.

The clampdown in the Netherlands affected even Jeanne d'Albret. Through 1566, after the court's return, she remained in Paris (possibly in a house of her own rather than in the uncongenial atmosphere of the court itself; eyeing the sexual license of the French court, 'It is not the men who invite the women but the women who invite the men', she wrote disgustedly). She was increasingly ill, and increasingly at odds with other ladies of the court, notably Anne d'Este (the former Duchesse de Guise), and thus also with Anne's mother, Renée, Marguerite of Navarre's former protégée. But she was also taking her son Henri on brief, seemingly innocuous, visits to lands of her own nearby.

---

* Later Margaret would be adviser to her much younger bastard stepbrother, Don John, appointed governor-general of the Netherlands in 1576, and to her son, Alexander Farnese, who succeeded him. She would indeed be asked to act as coregent with her son, dealing with civil administration while he, a commander of genius, took care of what was by now a full-scale military campaign, but the two could not work together, and Margaret retired again.

It apparently came as a surprise to Catherine de Medici when the Spanish ambassador told her, in the middle of February 1567, that Jeanne, with her son, had slipped away back to the Southwest and out of French control. 'This woman is the most shameless [*dévergondée*] and passionate creature in the world', raged Catherine.

Jeanne d'Albret recorded in her *Mémoires* how often she had cried for peace, and how often Catherine and her son had tried to lure her back to court, 'under the pretext of doing me the honour of making me the mediator between the King and his subjects of the Reformed religion'. But Jeanne's path led another way.

IN SEPTEMBER 1567 THE HUGUENOT leaders Condé and Coligny, mistrusting the French crown's promise of religious toleration, made an unsuccessful attempt to capture the young king. Six thousand Swiss guards were hired to escort Catherine and her son back to Paris, but Condé and Coligny then embarked on a siege of the city. Their assaults were unavailing, and they were forced to retreat southward, but small wonder that in May 1568, weeks after a peace had finally been negotiated with the rebels, Catherine de Medici fell gravely ill. When she recovered, it was to find Coligny and Condé in flight, and Catherine's intentions now were to 'run them to earth, defeat them and destroy them'. Would she include Jeanne in her hostility?

For that autumn, as Condé and Coligny rode toward the Huguenots' stronghold of La Rochelle, on the coast toward the Southwest of France where Protestantism had gained the greatest support, Jeanne d'Albret set out to join their party, with her daughter, Catherine, and fifteen-year-old Henri. 'Do not think . . . that I undertook this journey lightly', she said in the *Mémoires* she caused to be written some eight weeks into her stay. 'Believe me, it was not without conflict, with others and with myself. . . . I not only had to fight outside enemies, I had a war in my entrails. Even my will was in league against me'. But in La Rochelle, 'deprived of the pleasure of my own houses, but only too happy to suffer for my God', she was to be based for almost three years. She was, she wrote to Catherine de Medici, in 'the service of my God and of the truth faith', but Catherine was unlikely to be mollified.

Jeanne d'Albret wrote also to Elizabeth of England, whose 'good will' she continued to laud. She also wrote propaganda pamphlets and ran a body called the Council of the Queen of Navarre, charged with administration of the town and all aspects of the campaign not strictly military. She set the troops she had brought to work, strengthening La Rochelle's fortifications.

At the end of 1568 the Spanish ambassador was reporting that she 'continued to share the leadership' with Condé.

Then, at the battle of Jarnac on 13 March 1569, the Prince de Condé was taken prisoner and then slain, leaving nominal command of the Huguenot cause to two fifteen-year-olds, Jeanne's son Henri of Navarre and his cousin, the son of Condé. It was Jeanne who led the boys out to receive the acclamation of the Huguenot troops. It was Jeanne too who wrote begging that Elizabeth of England would 'continue the affection you bear to so just and legitimate a cause. . . . Amongst us, great and small are resolved to spare neither our lives nor our fortunes in the service of God's quarrel'. Though Catherine de Medici referred to her as 'marching with the Admiral', as Coligny and the boys went out on campaign, Jeanne was actually left behind to cope with as many as sixty thousand refugees now pouring into La Rochelle.

Most among the Huguenot leadership were now thinking of peace. Not so Jeanne d'Albret, who was almost taken prisoner while outside the walls overseeing the construction of new fortifications. By the spring of 1570, it was Jeanne's determination that was continuing the fight. (It would be Jeanne who, later, held out for freedom of worship as the price of peace rather than Catherine's subtler and more pragmatic offer of freedom of conscience, with its suggestion of outward conformity.)

Jeanne wrote to Catherine de Medici, 'I can scarcely persuade myself having once had the honour of knowing Your Majesty's sentiments intimately that you could wish to see us reduced to such an extremity or to profess ourselves of no religion whatever, which must be the case if we are denied the public exercise of our own ritual. . . . We have come to the determination to die, all of us, rather than abandon our God, the which we cannot maintain unless permitted to worship publicly, any more than a human body can live without meat or drink'.

The war, in every direction, was becoming ever more bitter. Outside La Rochelle, Catherine's son Henri, Duc d'Anjou, leading the fighting on the crown's side, was behaving with terrifying savagery. There were rumours that Catherine, earlier in the troubles, had tried to kill Condé by means of a poisoned apple (the Snow White touch), and now a man was indeed arrested on his way to Coligny's service and carrying a packet of poison, while the Spanish ambassador reported Catherine had been trying to rid herself of the Protestant leaders by sorcery.

Catherine had been greatly saddened when her daughter Elisabeth, Philip of Spain's wife, died in childbirth in October 1568. This also meant she had no longer any special hold on Elisabeth's widower, Philip of Spain, who had long been disgusted by her pragmatic religious stance. Catherine had written that she envied Elizabeth of England, because 'all the subjects share the Queen's religion; in France it's quite another matter'. But in fact, Elizabeth Tudor might have greeted that with an 'if only'.

AT THE BEGINNING OF MAY 1568, the imprisoned Mary Stuart had escaped from Loch Leven and from her lords' custody. Her supporters were defeated at the battle of Langside on 13 May, and on 16 May she crossed the Solway Firth and fled across the border into England.

Mary had believed all Elizabeth Tudor's protestations of sisterly solidarity, believed Elizabeth would immediately restore her to her throne. In many ways, that was Elizabeth's first instinct, queenship called to queenship. But this met with disagreement from most of Elizabeth's councillors, especially from Cecil, and Elizabeth's own attitude was a complex one. As Mary sent an appeal to Elizabeth's fellow feeling 'not from a queen, but from a gentlewoman', Elizabeth was gloating over the purchase of Mary's famous black pearls—twenty-five of them, the size and colour of grapes—for which she had outbid Catherine de Medici.

Mary reluctantly agreed to Elizabeth's suggestion of an enquiry into her conduct and into the rumours she had been involved in her husband Darnley's death, which opened at York that autumn. The Scottish lords tried to ensure a 'guilty' verdict by producing the infamous 'Casket Letters', letters purporting to prove Mary a murderous adulteress but were almost certainly faked. But even with these dubious documents before them, the commissioners failed to reach any real verdict, leaving Mary to remain as 'guest' to her 'dear cousin and friend' Elizabeth, locked into an indefinite genteel captivity.

But the enquiry had repercussions of a different sort. The commissioners had been led by Thomas Howard, Duke of Norfolk, Elizabeth's kinsman and premier peer, and thus a man with his own stake in the English throne. Norfolk had at first been horrified by the letters that seemed to prove Mary's 'inordinate' love for Bothwell. Norfolk's instructions from Elizabeth's government had moreover included the clause that anyone plotting Mary's marriage 'shall be *ipso facto* acknowledged as traitorous and shall suffer death'. But when one of Mary's lords suggested to him that the best way of neutralising Mary, and providing for the English succession, was for he himself to marry her, the idea took root in his mind.

The story of the next few months is an uncertain one, but Norfolk's aspirations were clearly something of an open secret at the English court. Dangerously, they became linked to the discontent felt by peers in the North of England, many of whom had never lost their Catholic faith. The result was the so-called Revolt of the Northern Earls in the autumn of 1569, aiming to free Mary, if not actually to place her on Elizabeth's throne.

The rebellion failed, and the rebels (especially the wretched, ordinary men among them) suffered the harshest punishments. Norfolk was sent to the Tower, where he languished for some months—but what of Mary? The Queen of Scots had written to Norfolk as to her future husband, had made and sent him embroideries depicting a fruitful vine (Mary herself) and a hand clipping away the barren branch (Elizabeth). No direct reprisals were taken against Mary Stuart, but she was kept in closer captivity.

In February 1570 the pope issued the bull *Regnans in excelsis*, depriving Elizabeth of 'her pretended right to her realm' and sanctioning any Catholic who attempted to depose her. This greatly raised the level of tension in England, both increasing and highlighting Elizabeth's vulnerability. In a poem she wrote probably in 1571, Elizabeth Tudor described Mary Stuart:

> *The daughter of debate*
> *That discord aye doth sow*
> *Shall reap no gain where former rule*
> *Still peace hath taught to know.*

Her words would prove prophetic.

IN FRANCE, CATHERINE DE MEDICI had every cause to regret the bull against Elizabeth. Her goal, after all, was the reduction of tension, not its increase. On 8 August 1570 the Treaty of St Germain finally brought peace: freedom of conscience and freedom of worship limited to certain locations. But there had been other peace treaties, and none had lasted. Jeanne d'Albret for one, during the long negotiations, had called this 'a peace made of snow this winter that would melt in next summer's heat'. Now Catherine had a plan to cement it. As early as May 1569, Sir Henry Norris had been telling Elizabeth of England that Catherine de Medici planned 'to practice to withdraw the Queen of Navarre' by offering her daughter Margot in marriage to Jeanne's son Henri. Marriage, of course, was always Catherine's favourite way out of any diplomatic difficulty.

And Catherine had also another marriage in mind. England had more reason than ever to pursue the safety of a French alliance against the increasing power and aggression of Spain. The summer of 1571 saw the 'discovery' of the Ridolfi Plot (of which Elizabeth's ministers may in fact long have known) to place Mary Stuart and the Duke of Norfolk on England's throne, with Spanish support and an invasion force headed by the Duke of Alba.

So Queen Elizabeth was amenable to Catherine's suggestion, in December 1571, that she might marry François, the Duc d'Alençon, instead of his elder brother, the reluctant Anjou. François (so his mother Catherine coolly observed) was 'much less scrupulous' than his brother in matters of religion—sympathetic, even, to the Huguenots. Altogether less 'like a mule', as Elizabeth's envoy chimed in enthusiastically, and 'more apt than th'other' when it came to getting children.

England and France concluded the Treaty of Blois, whereby they agreed to support each other against the Spanish enemy. It now seemed more desirable than ever that this alliance should be cemented dynastically. In June came the formal offer of Alençon's hand. Elizabeth's ambassador (and later spymaster) Francis Walsingham for one feared that the small and pockmarked seventeen-year-old Alençon would never pass the crucial test, given 'the delicacy of Her Majesty's eye'. Nonetheless, as the court set off on its annual summer progress, the thing seemed still a real possibility.

England and France had both seen trouble, but both might now hope the trouble had been successfully resolved. But that hope would prove deceptive.

42

THE MASSACRE OF SAINT BARTHOLOMEW'S DAY

FRANCE, 1572–1574

✳

Queen Elizabeth was at Robert Dudley's great castle of Kenilworth when she had news of an event that shook her world—one of those events that really do change history—the Massacre of Saint Bartholomew's Day. The story had seemed at first to lie between Catherine de Medici and Jeanne d'Albret. But in the end, the repercussions would reach out to touch everybody.

In those early months of 1571, William of Orange, the exiled leader of the Netherlands Protestants, was trying to orchestrate an armed invasion of the Netherlands from Germany. Though his brother was with the Huguenot rebels in La Rochelle, Orange needed to draw the French crown also to his side, invoking an old anti-Spanish hostility still arguably more potent than religious division. The idea had immense appeal for a young king anxious to prove his mettle in battle, and soon Charles IX was to be heard complaining that Catherine was 'too timid'. Newly wed to Elizabeth of Austria, devout young daughter of the Holy Roman Emperor, Charles was beginning to resent his mother's dominance.* A few days after the formal entry into Paris that celebrated his marriage in March 1571, Charles made a speech to his Parlement commending Catherine's 'tireless work, energy and wisdom' in taking care of affairs of state for all the time he had been too young to do so himself, the implication being perhaps that such days were coming to an end.

Catherine de Medici herself was temperamentally opposed to expensive warfare (yet another thing on which she agreed with Elizabeth of England).

---

* The Holy Roman Emperor was now no longer Ferdinand, who had died in 1564, but his son, named Maximilian, for his grandfather.

But she was prepared to use the possibility of French support for the Dutch Protestants as a lever to induce Jeanne d'Albret to agree to the marriage of her son Henri with Catherine's daughter Margot. (No one cared about Margot's reluctance to marry a heretic. Catherine threatened to make her daughter 'the most wretched lady in the kingdom' if she refused—but Jeanne's reluctance was another story.)

There was still in theory at least a personal bond between Catherine de Medici and Jeanne d'Albret. At the start of 1571, Jeanne wrote to Catherine of her reluctance to bring her son to the French court. 'I have a suspicious nature, Madame, as you well know, which makes me fear that, although your intentions are good—which I do not doubt—those who have been able to alter them in the past in regard to us . . . continue to have credit with you. . . . I would fear to anger you by these words, Madame, if your kindness to me in my youth had not accustomed me to the privilege of speaking frankly and privately to you'.

Touchingly, she wrote *Je suis ung pettite glorieuse* (I am a proud little thing, or a bit of a proud one). She was indeed: Biron, one of the envoys sent to negotiate with her, described to a colleague 'the scowling face in front of me'. An Italian wrote that 'the temper of this Queen is *molto fantastico* [very fantastical]. . . . She changes often and eludes you every minute. In the end she hopes to manage everything her own way'.

Jeanne d'Albret was under considerable pressure, not least from some of her own side. Admiral de Coligny's prime goal was to get French help for the Dutch Protestants, Jeanne's to preserve her inherited territories and her son's place in the French succession. On 31 August the papal nuncio was reporting that 'there is great discord between them because the Queen [Jeanne] wishes to conduct her own affairs by herself, without interference from the Admiral, while he seeks to make her obey the King'. While she was dubious about marrying her son to the Catholic Margot, she must have been alarmed, too, by Coligny's attempts to marry him elsewhere, even, for a few weeks in 1571, to Elizabeth of England.

That autumn Coligny arrived at court to negotiate, his safe conduct signed by Charles IX, by Catherine de Medici, and by her next son, Anjou. Nonetheless, his friends had warned Coligny not to go. His reception, however, went almost too smoothly. Coligny even accompanied Catherine to Mass, though he made a point of neither removing his hat nor bowing to the host. The young king Charles, indeed, was soon back under Coligny's sway. The Spanish envoy described how Coligny told the king not to discuss his Netherlands plans with his mother, because these were 'not questions to be discussed with women and clerks. When the Queen Mother heard of this, she was on very bad terms with the said Admiral'.

Ever more pressure was being placed on Jeanne that she too should come to the French court. One indirect form of blackmail was the fear that her youthful marriage to Cleves could be recalled to discredit her marriage to Antoine de Bourbon and thus cast doubts on her son Henri's legitimacy.

Through the summer of 1571, Jeanne's health had given her a pretext to stall. 'I can never thank you enough for the honour you do me in wishing to see me', she wrote to Charles. 'But, to my great regret, Monseigneur, I have been obliged to yield to the exigencies of my health'. If she could no longer reasonably remain in La Rochelle, she could and did go to take the water cure at Eaux-Chaudes.

To Catherine de Medici's endless assurances of her safety if she entrusted herself to the French court, Jeanne d'Albret had written testily from La Rochelle, 'I cannot imagine why you should find it necessary to say that you want to see me and my children, but not in order to do us harm. Forgive me if I laugh when I read these letters, for you are allaying a fear I never had. I have never thought that you fed on little children, as they say'.

But finally, her historian Bordenave related, Jeanne could no longer hold out. 'The leaders of her own religion were those who most urged her to do it'. She 'bowed to their will in order that they might not blame her stubbornness for keeping so many good things . . . from coming to pass'.

Jeanne said she would come to court—on conditions. One was that she wanted to negotiate directly with Catherine. Was it to be another kind of ladies' peace?

THERE WERE CONDITIONS, TOO, ON the other side, of course. The pope vowed he would lose his last drop of blood rather than grant the necessary dispensation for the marriage before the groom had returned to the Catholic Church. But his envoy told him that most French, even Catholics, desired the marriage, 'comparing it to that of Clovis and Clothilde' (the Frankish king and the wife who persuaded him to convert to Christianity), while Catherine de Medici warningly invoked the example of Henry VIII.

In January 1572, in a carriage the size of a house, with a stove burning inside, and in no particular hurry, Jeanne d'Albret reluctantly set out to join the French court at Blois. Florentine ambassador Petrucci wrote on 14 February that 'today the Queen Mother [Catherine] went to Chenonceau to meet the Queen of Navarre. Embraces and salutations were exchanged . . . and the Queen of Navarre asked at once for something to eat. Immediately afterward the two queens retired into a room alone'.

Jeanne's letters to the son she had left behind are revealing and sometimes appealing ones. She took to her prospective daughter-in-law: 'If she embraces our religion I may say that we are the happiest persons in the world'. Jeanne's thirteen-year-old daughter, Catherine de Bourbon, added her mite: 'I have seen Madame [Margot] and found her very beautiful. . . . She was kind to me and gave me a little dog I like very much'.

But Jeanne's initial attempts at optimism did not last. She suspected that Catherine and her son the king were trying to play her for a fool, and she was probably right. A Huguenot contemporary describes Charles IX lavishing attention on Jeanne in public but then asking his mother in private if he was not playing his part well: 'Leave it to me and I will deliver them into your net'.

An ardent Catholic had been advising Catherine on how to handle Jeanne: 'As one woman to another, make her mad while staying calm yourself'. Petrucci described one long and fraught bout of negotiations, in which Catherine had suggested they allow their differences to be settled by deputies, and Jeanne retorted that she trusted nobody but herself. 'This is no small break in the negotiations because *Navarra* is so obstinate . . . and no real results can be obtained without her agreement'.

On 8 March Jeanne sent a long and agitated letter to her son: 'I am in agony, in such extreme suffering that if I had not been prepared, it would overcome me. . . . I am not free to talk with either the King of Madame [Margot], only with the Queen Mother, who goads me [*me traite a la fourche*]. . . . She treats me so shamefully that you might say that the patience I manage to maintain surpasses that of Griselda herself. . . . I have come this far on the sole understanding that the Queen and I would negotiate and be able to agree. But all she does is mock me'.

Even Margot was not as she had been represented: 'She replied that when these negotiations begun we well knew she was devout in her religion. I told her that those who made the first overtures to us represented the matter very differently'.

Another letter to one of Jeanne's advisers three days later was even more agitated. 'I assure you I often remember your warning not to get angry'. She was fighting to keep her son away from the court while matters were still this unsettled, fighting to convince the sceptical French courtiers that he was as committed as she to the reformed religion.

'As for the beauty of Madame Marguerite [Margot], I admit she has a good figure, but it is too tightly corseted. Her face is spoiled by too much makeup, which displeases me'. The corruption of the French court was a recurrent theme. Everyone was aware of the possibility of espionage and deceit. Jeanne swore holes were drilled in the walls of her apartment by spies.

Jeanne d'Albret put her faith in the support of the English, claiming Queen Elizabeth would make a treaty with France only if the crown behaved properly over the Navarre marriage. But if it was important for Jeanne to feel the weight of international Protestant opinion behind her, then international Protestantism also needed this alliance.

Acting as England's ambassador in France, Francis Walsingham found himself in a very special relationship to Jeanne. On 29 March he was writing to Cecil of how, 'with the consent of the Queen-Mother, she had sent for us as the ministers and ambassadors of a Christian princess, whom she had sundry causes to honour, to confer with us . . . touching certain difficulties'.

Jeanne wished to confer with her coreligionists on some knotty points of doctrine concerning the marriage of a Catholic and a Protestant and also on the central issues of the two continuing still their separate religions. Her advisers urged her to stand firm on some points, but, nevertheless, it remained vital that the marriage should go ahead. 'Upon the success of the Navarre marriage depends the enterprise of Flanders', wrote Walsingham.

Toward the end of March, King Charles gave ground: as long as Henri of Navarre would come to Paris for the wedding, he would yield on all other points. Even the ministers to whom Jeanne appealed, asking if the marriage could be legal if it were not performed before a Calvinist congregation, declared that 'considering the urgent necessity of the case', then, yes, it was.

Jeanne wrote encouragingly to Henri of how he should behave at the French court: 'Be gracious, but speak boldly, even when you are taken aside by the King, for note that the impression you make on arrival will remain. . . . [T]ry to train your hair to stand up and be sure there are no lice in it'. ('Your sister has a very annoying cough, which keeps her in bed. She drinks donkey's milk and calls the little ass her brother', Jeanne added, charmingly.)

On 4 April the official decision was made to proceed, and the next day Jeanne d'Albret wrote to Queen Elizabeth: 'I would not, therefore, Madame, lose time in informing you of the event, so that I may rejoice with you. . . . I entreat you, Madame, to pardon the boldness which your goodness inspires, if I venture very earnestly to desire that I may soon have occasion to congratulate you on a similar event personal to yourself'.

The marriage contract signed on 11 April made mention of no religious issues but only of the inheritance of various lands. This was based on a French conviction that Henri, if not Jeanne herself, would soon be returning to the Roman church. The bishop of Mâcon saw it as Catherine's victory: 'The Queen Mother has chosen the best possible way. . . . [S]he has abased the haughtiness of the Queen of Navarre, overcome her instability, and made her accept conditions. . . . [W]e will soon see the Prince [Henri] returning to the bosom of Holy Church'.

JEANNE, EXHAUSTED, SET OUT FOR Vendôme to rest, but soon the need to prepare for the forthcoming marriage sent her back to Paris. As Anne d'Este wrote to her mother, Renée of Ferrara, 'The Queen of Navarre is here, not in good health but very courageous. She is wearing more pearls than ever'. Jeanne herself wrote to an absent Catherine late in May that 'I have seen your Tuileries fountains, when M. de Retz invited me to a private supper. I have found many things for our wedding in this city during my excursions with him. I am in good form awaiting your arrival'. This last was not true.

Jeanne d'Albret's health had been poor since childhood and growing worse: the chest problems from which she suffered were almost certainly a sign of tuberculosis. On 4 June, returning from a shopping trip, she felt tired and feverish. She took to her bed, and two days later rewrote her will. Catherine de Medici, Margot, and even Anjou came to visit her, but she seemed resigned to her fate. She had, after all, found this life very trying, *fort ennuyeuse*.

Protestant chroniclers provided long hagiographic descriptions of her heroic last days: 'As soon as the pain increased she did not lose courage, showing an admirable confidence in the last fight and preparing herself gladly for death'. Like Katherine of Aragon, albeit from the other side of the religious divide, she urged that her daughter should 'stand firm and constant in God's service despite her extreme youth', and this instruction Catherine de Bourbon (like Mary Tudor before her) most faithfully obeyed.

Jeanne's penultimate days were spent listening to expositions of scriptures and reading Psalm 31 and the Gospel of Saint John. The Calvinist ministers around her recorded with admiration and relief that she showed no concern for the worldly wedding arrangements that had been occupying her so completely. 'O my saviour, hasten to deliver my spirit from the miseries of this life', she prayed, 'and from the prison of this suffering body, that I may offend thee no more, and enter joyfully into that rest which thou hast promised and that my soul so longs for.

'Tell my son that I desire him, as the last expression of my heart, to per-severe in the faith in which he has been brought up'.

On 9 June 1572 she died. A suggestion that Catherine de Medici had poisoned her with a pair of perfumed gloves first appeared in 1574, in a vicious published attack on Catherine, but that was with the hindsight of what came next. It was not—even had Jeanne's state of health not made a natural death likely—mentioned by any strict contemporaries. But it was true that Jeanne's death, wrote the Venetian ambassador Cavalli, 'is causing the greatest possible setback to Huguenot affairs'.

The papal envoy praised God for the death of 'such an important enemy of His Holy Church', while the Spanish ambassador heard from home that 'all Madrid rejoices that the Devil has got her, at last!' But perhaps Jeanne d'Albret would prove lucky to have escaped the events of the next three months.

CATHERINE DE MEDICI'S ENERGIES WERE now devoted to weaning her son Charles IX from his dependence on Admiral de Coligny, which she feared would lead the country into a war with Spain. She declared that she (with Anjou) would retire to her estates in the country—or even back to Florence, some said. Charles backed down (more frightened, recalled one observer, of his mother and brother than of the Huguenots). Amid scenes of 'mingled violence and tender reproach', he begged his mother not to retire from public life. An emergency council meeting on 10 August voted overwhelmingly for peace. But when the admiral warned that Catherine might regret what she had done, it must have sounded like a threat.

Catherine and Anjou decided that Coligny was too inimical an influence and had to be gotten out of the way. Or so the *Mémoires* (produced by his son twenty years later) of the fanatically Catholic Maréchal de Tavannes, one of Catherine's advisers, declared, adding, however, that 'this design was not imparted to the King'. But, typical of her practicality, Catherine had first to finish with the wedding and its festivities.

After attending his mother's funeral at Vendôme, Henri of Navarre had come on to Paris. Perhaps recalling his youth at the French court, he seemed to be getting on well with Charles as they all waited through the summer heat in a city increasingly filling up with wedding guests, with peasants from the surrounding countryside driven out of their homes by drought and famine, and with Huguenots.

Catherine de Medici (who had been away visiting her daughter Claude) returned to find Catholic preachers fulminating from the pulpits and stirring up hatred of the Protestant visitors. She also found a Spanish ambassador demanding furiously why three thousand Huguenot troops had taken up station near the Netherlands border. It was clearer than ever to Catherine that Coligny had to be neutralised.

First, however, there was that wedding. The day 16 August saw a betrothal ceremony at the Louvre, and two days later came the actual marriage. As had been agreed by Jeanne d'Albret, Henri of Navarre would not attend the nuptial Mass; instead, he was represented by the bride's brother Anjou. One other hurdle had to be overcome—the assent of the bride herself.

When back in April Catherine de Medici had asked her daughter for her formal consent, Margot recalled later in her memoirs, 'I had no will, no choice but her own'. She begged Catherine, however, to keep in mind the strong Catholic faith that made her reluctant to marry a heretic.

She was, moreover, as many a royal bride—a Margaret Tudor or a Katherine of Aragon—must have been, justifiably and prophetically anxious about an alliance that would, if things went wrong, place her on the opposite side of her family in a conflict.

Now, dressed in blue with 'all the jewels of the Crown', Margot took refuge in a kind of passive resistance, going through the motions as she knelt beside Henri, but making no answer when the cardinal asked whether she took Henri as her husband. Finally, Charles IX stepped forward and pushed her head down as though she were nodding agreement. (Later she would use this lack of consent as grounds for an annulment, shades of Jeanne d'Albret and the Cleves match, some thirty years before.) There were to be four days of parties, with the king's masked ball boasting, as centrepiece, a *pantomime tournoi* that saw Charles and his brothers first dispatching Navarre and his companions to hell and then rescuing them again.

By 22 August, the festivities were at an end. As Admiral de Coligny walked back to his lodging from a council meeting at the Louvre, business having resumed that morning, he found a binding on his shoe come loose and bent over to adjust it. Just as he did so came the sound of a shot, but the bullet meant to kill him broke his arm and almost tore off a finger instead.

Catherine de Medici had just sat down to dinner with Anjou when the news was brought to her, and not even the watching Spanish ambassador could tell from her impassive face that it was not the assassination attempt but its failure that spelled disaster for her. Charles IX was on the tennis court when word came; finding himself confronted by his new brother-in-law, Henri of Navarre, and other senior Huguenots, he promised a full investigation and ordered that the citizens should not take up arms.

When Charles went to visit Coligny that afternoon, Catherine and Anjou went with him, but Coligny indicated that he had words for the king's ears alone. As Anjou put it later, 'The Queen my mother has since acknowledged that never had she found herself in a more critical position'. They could not discover what Coligny had said, but it was clear on the journey back to the Louvre that Charles was furiously angry with them.

No wonder Anjou, visiting his mother early the next morning, found she had not slept. They were desperate, he himself said later, to 'finish the Admiral by whatever means we could find. And since we could no longer use stratagem, it had to be done openly, but for this purpose it was necessary to bring the King around to our resolution'.

In the streets, people were crying out against the king and Catherine de Medici too, not for suspicion of the attempted murder, but for allowing themselves to be surrounded by Huguenots. The Huguenots were already armed, having intended to leave directly from the wedding for the fight in the Low Countries. Many Catholics now decided that they too needed to be prepared.

Opinions—contemporary and modern—vary wildly on who was to blame for the attempted assassination of Coligny. The Venetian ambassador wrote that 'everyone supposed it had been done by order of the duc of Guise to avenge his family, because the window from which the shot was fired belonged to his mother's house'. But later he changed his mind, having learned from various conversations that 'from start to finish the whole thing was the work of the queen. She conceived it, plotted it, and put it into execution, with no help from anyone but her son the duke of Anjou'.

Catherine's own daughter Margot seemed to agree: at first the Guises were blamed, but then it was revealed to Charles that his brother and mother 'had their shares in it'. At the lowest, Catherine de Medici and her sons (and the royal council with them) came to support the idea of Coligny's assassination once it had been introduced, but it is unclear whether the Guise family was their evil geniuses or their scapegoats. Was Catherine Machiavellian enough even to reflect that if the Guises suffered all the blame of these events, then she would be rid not only of the Huguenot-Bourbon threat but also of the other great noble house that challenged her position as the power behind the throne?

On the evening of 23 August, Catherine sent one of her supporters to the king to tell him not only that his mother and brother had been aware of the attempt on Coligny's life, but that the entire royal family was now in danger. Charles was told also that the Huguenots were planning an attack that very night.

Now Catherine herself entered the fray, urging again and again that the Huguenots had brought nothing but trouble. Though he at first refused to believe, finally the feeble young king was won over. 'Then kill them all', he is said to have cried. 'All', that is, of the senior Huguenots on a list Catherine had drawn up and that he now ratified, not all the Huguenots in Paris, or indeed in France.

At 3:00 a.m. the bell of the Palais de Justice was to toll to signal the start of the attack. By that time the militiamen had been alerted, all exits from the city closed, and chained barges linked across the Seine. The Duc de Guise himself led the party that went to Coligny's house, stabbed the admiral to death, and threw his body out of the window.

It was obvious from the first that no one was so grand as to be immune from this violence. The new bride Margot had been in her mother's apartments—together with her sister Claude, now arrived in Paris for the wedding—when it became obvious some sort of preparations were being made. But 'as for me no one told me anything about this', she wrote in her *Mémoires*. 'The Huguenots suspected me because I was a Catholic, and the Catholics because I had married the King of Navarre'.

> I was at the *coucher* of the Queen my mother, sitting on a chest with my sister of Lorraine [Claude], who was very depressed, when my mother noticed me and sent me to bed. . . . My sister said that it was not right to send me away like that to be sacrificed and that, if they [the Huguenots] discovered anything, no doubt they would avenge themselves on me. My mother replied that, God willing, I would come to no harm, but in any case I must go, for fear of awakening their suspicions. . . . I left the room bewildered and dazed without knowing what it was that I feared.

In the quarters where the Protestant royal party lodged, her new husband, Henri of Navarre, sent Margot to bed.

Woken by someone banging at the door and crying out for her husband, she found it was a stranger, one of Henri's gentlemen, wounded, and pursued by four archers. 'To save himself, he flung himself on my bed, and I, with that man holding me, rolled into the passage and he after me, still hugging my body. I did not know who he was nor whether he meant to outrage me nor whether it was him or myself whom the archers were pursuing. We both screamed and were equally terrified'. The captain of the guards arrived just in time to grant Margot the man's life before escorting her to Claude's apartment, where she 'arrived more dead than alive', ordering the man's wounds tended and changing her own bloodied shift.

But if none were too high to be troubled, none were so low as to be spared. The Huguenots—all too easily recognisable by their black and white clothes—were slaughtered. Violence against women featured heavily in the dreadful tales: pregnant women with their wombs ripped out, baskets of small children flung into the Seine.*

Protestant and admittedly partisan sources have one woman leaping out of a window to avoid capture and breaking both her legs in the fall, dragged through the streets by her hair, and having her hands slashed off at the wrists for the sake of her gold bracelets. Another woman, about to go into labour, was stabbed in the abdomen and hurled into the street below, where she died along with the child, its head already protruding from her body. The killers then looted the house. The Duc de Guise himself was so appalled by the scale of the killing (and by the fact that Catherine was according him the blame) that he could be seen defending Huguenots in the streets and opening his house to give them sanctuary.

The Spanish ambassador saw the mounting pile of bodies: 'While I write, they are casting them out naked and dragging them through the streets, pillaging their houses and sparing not a babe. Blessed be to God, who has converted the Princes of France to His purpose. May He inspire their hearts to go on as they have begun!' Priests encouraged the bloodshed, but of the three or four thousand killed in the capital alone, not all were necessarily Huguenots. Some were killed in personal vendettas rather than for their religious faith, as the orgy of bloodletting took on its own dreadful momentum.

The high-profile victims on the list compiled by Catherine de Medici and Charles IX were largely killed within the first two hours, but the flame once kindled could not be put out. This was something the royal group had not foreseen. That afternoon Charles sent orders for the killing to cease, but he was ignored.

It was another three days before Paris was quiet, and by then, despite fresh orders from the king, the violence had spread to the provinces. It would be October before the storm cleared southern France, and across the country, though estimates vary wildly, some suggest as many as thirty

---

* In this too the massacre was a precursor of 1789, which saw intensely sexualised violence directed against, for example, the Princesse de Lamballe.

thousand dead. The royal family had stayed sheltering inside the Louvre while the slaughter was going on; later (according to two sources), Catherine would recover enough, on being presented with the head from Admiral de Coligny's disfigured and emasculated body, to have it embalmed and sent as a gift to the pope.

THERE COULD, FROM THIS, BE no going back. 'You must clearly see that you cannot govern too wisely with kindness and diffidence', Anne de Beaujeu had said three quarters of a century before. A solitary act of aggression had served, in the end, as a magnifying glass through which irreconcilable religious conflicts could be seen in all their stark brutality. (Modern parallels can be found all too easily.)

The French ambassador to Spain reported that Philip literally danced for joy when he heard the news. He certainly wrote to congratulate Catherine de Medici on 'this glorious event', admitting to the French ambassador that 'he owed his Low Countries of Flanders' to the French action. (In the Netherlands, the Spanish general Alba's actions were becoming ever more brutal: that October, he allowed his men to sack and massacre the town of Mechelen, where Margaret of Austria had once lived in luxury.) The pope ordered *Te Deum* sung, until he was informed that the massacre had never been intended and that the original assassination attempt had been a political rather than primarily a religious story.

By contrast, the queen of England was appalled. As Elizabeth wrote to Walsingham, the murder of the supposed Huguenot conspirators, without 'answer by law', was bad enough: 'We do hear it marvellously evil taken and as a thing of a terrible and dangerous example. . . . But when more added unto it—that women, children, maids, young infants and sucking babes were at the same time murdered and cast into the river . . . this increased our grief and sorrow'.

When the English queen at last consented to receive the French ambassador Fénelon, not a courtier would speak to or look at him as he approached the presence chamber. There, so the story goes, he found the queen, her ladies, and her privy councillors all dressed in mourning black. What the queen said to Fénelon was mild compared to the reproaches of the councillors. Cecil told him it was the greatest crime since the Crucifixion. No one on the English side, now, could think of a marriage with the French royal family. If the French king had been 'Author and doer of this Act, shame and confusion light upon him', Leicester wrote to Walsingham. And the same would be true of his mother, naturally.

The other marriage that had sparked the dreadful affair was a done deal. Henri of Navarre (and his cousin Condé) had been taken from the apartment where Margot was so rudely surprised and brought to the king, who assured them of their safety. Margot claimed she was asked by her mother whether the marriage had indeed been consummated, since if not it could be dissolved, but Margot, fearing Henri's life would be in danger, refused to comply with the clear suggestion and said it had. The two Huguenot princes had, however, formally to be received back into the Catholic Church. Catherine, perhaps overstrained, burst into rude laughter as they made the sign of the cross before the altar. Henri had, moreover, to return Béarn to Catholicism. Jeanne d'Albret was truly dead.

But Catherine de Medici too had lost—lost reputation. She soon realised how much blame she would have to shoulder for the affair. Pamphlets against Catherine attacked the rule of women along with her other supposed iniquities; others harked back to her Florentine roots and recalled that Machiavelli's *The Prince* had been dedicated to her father.*

Her ambassador to Venice wrote that the massacre not only of the Huguenot leaders 'but against so many poor and innocent people' meant that the Venetians (though themselves Catholic) nonetheless 'cannot be satisfied with any excuse, attributing everything that has been done to you alone and Monsieur d'Anjou'.

She had, moreover, lost the chance of peace in France: Huguenots, believing the whole marriage had been a trap, now had stark choices, driven now, as Elizabeth of England said, 'to fly or die'. Those still standing out in La Rochelle called on the protection of Elizabeth, now their 'natural sovereign princess for all eternity'. As royalist forces embarked on a long and bitter siege, even the La Rochellais women mustered on the walls to throw rocks at them.

In fact, Elizabeth's support of the continental Protestants remained partial and hesitant for some time to come. (It was 1585 before she was finally persuaded to send an army to the support of the Dutch Protestants.) Elizabeth even—not without lengthy comment about the strangeness of the request—agreed to stand godmother to the daughter Charles IX's wife bore him that autumn. She found it politic now to seem to believe French assurances that the king had merely acted against a Huguenot plot and that what followed had been a tragic accident. But talk of her possible marriage to Catherine's youngest son, Alençon, was off—for the moment, anyway.

---

* Twenty years later, Christopher Marlowe's play *The Massacre of Paris* cast her as a stage villain: 'Tush, all shall die unless I have my will: / For while she lives, Catherine will be queen'.

Like her enemy and ally Catherine de Medici, Elizabeth Tudor (and Mary Tudor before her) had been forged by fear. It was one reason they and Mary Stuart—the child who grew up as darling of the French court—would never be sisters in any real way.

Another queen had lost here. Amid all the fallout of the massacre, one thing that could be seen was a new consensus among Elizabeth's ministers as to the danger represented by the Scots queen, Mary. Back in March 1571, Mary's agent the Bishop of Ross had written that the Queen of Scots' life had been in great danger, with Cecil and others urging she should be put to death.

Now Elizabeth's councillors were almost united in believing that Mary (so recently the Catholic focus of internal rebellion) should be excluded from the succession, if not actually killed. It would be another fifteen years before the tussle between Elizabeth Tudor and Mary Stuart reached its climax, but the end was already plain to see.

PART VII
1572 On

And nothing is firm or lasting in the gifts of Fortune;
today you see those raised high by Fortune who, two
days later, are brought down hard.

—ANNE OF FRANCE (ANNE DE BEAUJEU),
LESSONS FOR MY DAUGHTER (1517–1521)

43

TURNING POINTS
England and France, 1572–1587

❋

The early to mid-1570s represented a turning point in the history of women's rule in Europe. The question of Queen Elizabeth's marriage had retreated somewhat, only to have one last resurgence before finally it went away. The 'princely pleasures' of Elizabeth's 1575 visit to Leicester's Kenilworth signalled the last gasp of his long courtship, as well as promoting his bid to be allowed to help the beleaguered Netherlands Protestants. Elizabeth Tudor had, after all, turned forty—old for childbearing by the standards of the day—and her councillors must have been resigning themselves to her determined virginity.

But an heir, however important, was not the only point of a royal marriage. The increase in Catholic activity on the continent could leave England only more anxious for allies. Indeed, the mid-1570s saw the start of the great Catholic infiltration of England itself and Philip of Spain eyeing opportunities in Ireland. And there had long been that idea of an alliance with a son of Catherine de Medici.

For a time after the Massacre of Saint Bartholomew's Day—amid the massacre of her reputation—Catherine was preoccupied with the election of her favourite son, Henri, Duc d'Anjou, to the vacant throne of Poland (shades of Louise of Savoy and the election to the Holy Roman Empire), a throne he would, of course, abandon when that of France fell into vacancy. Her dying son, Charles IX, as he became ever more feeble, accused her: 'Madame, you are the cause of everything! Everything!' But nonetheless, on his deathbed, he ordered a new document to be drawn up, securing the regency to his mother until Henri could return from Poland. Charles died on 30 May 1574, holding her hand. As Catherine later said, 'After God, he recognised no one but me'.

The accession of her best-beloved Henri to the throne of France was at once a triumph and a problem for Catherine. She wrote that if she lost him,

too, 'I would have myself buried alive' and that his return 'will bring me joy
and contentment on contentment', while he wrote that he was her 'devoted
servant'. The secretary of the English ambassador, in the first days of the new
king's reign, wrote that Catherine's authority 'was as ample as ever'. But not everyone agreed. When Henri's dawdling journey home finally brought him back
to France, Catherine found a young man whose ideas did not always match her
own. She advised that in his new role as Henri III, he should show who had the
upper hand: he promptly put an end to the practice by which state papers might
be shown first to her, though mother and son still held joint audiences, and observers could still report that the Queen Mother 'commandeth very much'.

   The religious divisions showed no sign of abating. As Henri III's younger
brother François, the Duc d'Alençon toyed with joining the Huguenots,
Henri of Navarre escaped from the French court and back to his own lands
in the Southwest, where he abjured the Catholic religion to which he had
been forced to convert after Saint Bartholomew's Day. The Huguenots were
acting with virtual autonomy in several of the southern provinces of France,
and it was Catherine de Medici who, after a fragile peace was signed, had to
carry the king's message into what was effectively enemy territory. She was
still needed, but also marginalised by the very dissents within her family.*

   Henri's accession left his brother François—long at odds with his family, long debating the idea of marriage as a way to bolster his position—
more disaffected than ever.† In 1578 he allied with rebels in the Netherlands,
accepting from the Protestants there the title of 'Defender of the Liberties
of the Low Countries against Spanish Tyranny'.

   Elizabeth of England had in fact spent much energy patching up relations between the Dutch Protestants and the said Spanish tyrant, and her
first reaction was to send a message of solidarity to King Philip. The right
of monarchy always weighed with her more strongly than bonds of faith.
But in the long term, for the English, the important thing was to be on good
terms with anyone who held the harbours just across the sea. For Alençon,
of course, the important thing was to get English men and money. And in
any game of alliances, marriage was still the best piece anyone could play.

   But this last move in her long mating game was not wholly political, at
least on Elizabeth Tudor's side. The year 1579 saw first Alençon's personal
envoy, Jean de Simier, and then Alençon himself arrive to conduct an over-
heated courtship, acted out on all sides with a kind of delighted fantasy.

---

* Henri of Navarre, however, said to her, perhaps perceptively, 'This trouble pleases you and
  feeds you—if you were at rest you would not know how to continue to live'.
† Alençon, confusingly, had himself become Duc d'Anjou when Henri succeeded to the throne.
  For clarity's sake, however, I shall continue to refer to him as Alençon.

(Catherine de Medici talked of visiting England, to sort this thing out, another of those meetings doomed never to occur.) An on-off game for several years, it culminated in Elizabeth's publicly telling Alençon she would marry him, only to change her mind the next day.

In the spring of 1582, Alençon finally set out again for the Netherlands, with a hefty subsidy of English money. When he died in 1584, Elizabeth would write to Catherine de Medici that even her grief as a mother could not be greater: 'Madame, if you were able to see the image of my heart, you would see the portrait of a body without a soul'. Nonetheless, the start of the 1580s had effectively marked Queen Elizabeth's recasting of herself as the perpetual virgin. She would increasingly be figured as Diana, the ferociously chaste huntress.

The remaining female rulers continued to be, to some degree, aware of their gender as a potential bond between them. In 1578 Catherine de Medici was reported praising Elizabeth Tudor's Christian love of peace: 'For her part, she also was a woman, and as became her sex, desired nothing more than a general quietness'. Her communication with Elizabeth Tudor had often figured herself as a parent writing to a child (just as Elizabeth's letters to Mary Stuart had done). In June 1572 Catherine had told Elizabeth that 'I love you as a mother loves her daughter', and the maternal rhetoric resumed, in light of the possible Alençon marriage, quite soon after the Massacre of Saint Bartholomew's Day.

Catherine also sponsored the 1570s *Discourse on the Legitimate Succession of Women*, a defence of female sovereignty published in France by the Scot David Chambers. Brantôme would write of a private conversation in which she deplored the Salic Law and wished that her daughter Margot might inherit the kingdom 'by her just rights, as other kingdoms also fall to the distaff', since she 'is just as capable of governing, or more so, than many men and kings whom I know'. Sisterhood was, too, still an ideal to which Mary, Queen of Scots, never ceased appealing. But it had long ceased to have any reality in the relationship of Elizabeth and Mary.*

---

* Elizabeth in these latter years also entered into correspondence with Safiye Sultan, Albanian-born consort to the Ottoman ruler Murad III, who, on his death in 1595, promoted their son Mehmed III to the throne and herself exercised such power the English ambassador could report that Mehmed was 'wholly led by the old Sultana'. Often Murad, whose own communication with Elizabeth was beset with difficulties of status, found letters from his consort a useful way to approach one he saw as being of the weaker sex. Actively promoting a rapport with England, Safiye described Elizabeth ('most rare among womankind and the world') as following in the steps of the Virgin Mary. The two exchanged gifts. Safiye sent Elizabeth 'a robe, a sash, two gold-embroidered bath towels, three handkerchiefs, and a ruby and pearl tiara'. Elizabeth sent her a carriage in which, to the horror of the locals, Safiye used to leave the harem and travel through the streets. Joint military action between Murad and Elizabeth was even discussed, just as it had been between Murad's grandfather Suleiman and Louise of Savoy. Was Louise another outsider willing to step outside the club of European male rulers in her need for allies?

44

PRISE

FOTHERINGHAY, 1587

✳

Anyone who has ever been near a chessboard knows that if you manage to threaten your opponent's king, you have to give a chivalrous warning: 'Check'. Learning to play chess in the latter part of the twentieth century, I was taught a partial survival of an older tradition, that if you manage to get into a position where your next move would let you take the other player's queen, then you have also, by the same token, to give a warning: 'Prise'. Prise, as in *en prise*, in a position to be taken. Up for grabs, one might say.

In one sense, of course, Mary Stuart had been *en prise* from the moment she put herself into Elizabeth Tudor's hands. But the danger would be that her actions—her very existence—caused Elizabeth herself to feel the same vulnerability.

Mary's plotting had never ceased. As the 1570s turned to the 1580s, with the overthrow and execution of the last of her enemies, the Earl of Morton, in Scotland, Mary had even hoped she might soon be back in that country, perhaps ruling jointly with her son, James VI, perhaps even with Elizabeth's agreement. But while nothing came of that, she, or those who supported her, had never ceased to eye the other, the English, throne. And there would soon be no distinction made between Mary Stuart herself and those who perceived themselves as acting in her cause.

In 1584, after the assassination of William of Orange in the Netherlands and after several Catholic plots against Elizabeth herself, had come the Bond of Association. The signatories swore not only to defend Queen Elizabeth but also to kill anyone who attempted to harm her—and anyone 'for whom' such an attempt was made. (Mary herself offered to sign it, ironically.)

An act passed by Parliament the following spring modified some of the bond's more draconian elements, requiring at least a trial for the accused.

But the same month, James VI in Scotland informed his mother, Mary, that considering her captivity, he had no option other than that 'of declining to associate himself with her in the sovereignty of Scotland, or to treat her otherwise than as Queen-Mother'. Elizabeth, by contrast, his envoy assured her, could rely on James's affection for her 'as though he were her natural son'. (Their letters continued to employ the rhetoric of parent and child; Elizabeth was, of course, James's godmother, an important bond in the sixteenth century.)

Mary reacted with a surge of distress. 'I pray you to note I am your true and only Queen', she wrote to her son. 'Do not insult me further with this title of Queen Mother. . . . [T]here is neither King nor Queen in Scotland except me'. To Elizabeth, she protested, 'Without him I am, and shall be of right, as long as I live, his Queen and Sovereign. . . . [B]ut without me, he is too insignificant to think of soaring'. She was ignored, and when a year later James VI signed his own treaty with England, she ceased to be valuable even as a pawn one side or the other might wish to play.

But if Mary Stuart's life ceased to have value for others, so it now had only a conditional value for herself. She had no reason not to lend herself to another plot. Instigated by the young Catholic hothead Anthony Babington, it was in fact well known also to Elizabeth's spymaster Walsingham, and a tool ready to his hand, a matter that, as he wrote to Leicester, if it be 'well handled, it will break the neck of all dangerous practices'. And of practitioners, too.

There could be no doubt Mary was guilty, yet when they came to accuse her in August 1586, she was still protesting that she had always shown herself Elizabeth Tudor's 'good sister and friend'. In October the case was tried at the castle of Fotheringhay where Mary was being held. There Mary, after protesting that as a queen the commissioners had no right to try her, continued implausibly to protest her innocence: 'I would never make shipwreck of my soul by conspiring the destruction of my dearest sister'.

Crocodile tears? Yet it seems almost as if she did still half believe. No wonder Elizabeth herself seemed almost puzzled. To Mary's gaoler, she spat that he should 'let your wicked mistress know how with hearty sorrow her vile deserts compels these orders, and bid her from me ask God's forgiveness'. But Elizabeth also swore that 'if the case stood between her and myself only, if it had pleased God to have made us both milkmaids with pails on our arms, so that the matter should have rested between us two; and that I knew she did and would seek my destruction still, yet could I not consent to her death'.

The guilty sentence was made public on 4 December, Queen Elizabeth's proclamation declaring that 'we were greatly and deeply grieved in our mind to think or imagine that any such unnatural and monstrous fact should be either devised or willingly assented to against us by her, being a princess born, and of our sex and blood'. But Elizabeth had still to sign the warrant for the penalty required by the act: execution.

In December the council was forced reluctantly to deliver to Elizabeth a letter from Mary herself, begging her cousin to 'favour your equal', a letter that, in its requests about the fate of her servants and the disposal of her body, was calculated to bring home the full enormity of the prospective death.

'Do not accuse me of presumption', Mary wrote, 'if, on the eve of leaving this world and preparing myself for a better one, I remind you that one day you will have to answer for your charge . . . and that my blood and the misery of my country are remembered'. She signed herself, 'Your sister and cousin, wrongfully a prisoner, *Marie, Royne*'.

Several years before, she had expressed to Elizabeth her readiness to shed her blood, told the Spanish ambassador Mendoza that she hoped God would accept her death as an offering 'freely made by me for the maintenance of His church'. But that readiness did not mean Elizabeth was to be allowed to forget one jot of the horror of what she was doing.

Leicester wrote to Walsingham, 'There is a letter from the Scottish Queen, that hath wrought tears, but I trust shall do no further herein: albeit, the delay is too dangerous'. Elizabeth kept to herself as the new year came in, but antiquarian William Camden reported that she could be heard murmuring, 'Strike, or be stricken, strike, or be stricken'. It was her kinsman Lord Howard of Effingham who finally, on 1 February, persuaded her to end this excruciating delay. She signed the warrant for Mary's execution, handing it over with just enough vagary as to allow her later to claim she had never meant for it to be acted upon. Her councillors, however, under Cecil's leadership, agreed to take upon themselves the responsibility for the warrant's being put into effect.

Machiavelli had advised his prince that crime, when necessary, should be delegated to others: here and elsewhere Elizabeth seemed to have learned his lessons, as well as those of Anne de Beaujeu. Elizabeth's motto was *Video et taceo* (I see, but say nothing). Or, as Anne de Beaujeu had written, 'You should have eyes to notice everything yet to see nothing, ears to hear everything yet to know nothing, and a tongue to answer everyone yet to say nothing prejudicial to anyone'. Least of all anything prejudicial to your own sovereignty.

ON 7 FEBRUARY MARY WAS told she would be executed the next morning. She would die, she wrote, as a good Scotswoman and a good Frenchwoman—that odd dual role again—but above all as a good Catholic. Her
rule on earth had been a disaster, redeemed only (in the traditional, the
consort's, model of a queen's role) by whatever successes her son, James,
could win. But she had found her role as a martyr in heaven.

The scene of her execution is well known, in all its horror and pathos. A
report sent to Cecil described how the executioners helped her women strip
her of her ornaments and outer clothes and how she herself helped them
make speed, 'as if she longed to be gone'. She had pleaded with Elizabeth
that her servants should be allowed to be with her at the end: 'by the honour and dignity we have both held, and of our sex in common'. Briefly, the
nobles escorting Mary to her death tried to ban her women from accompanying her, but her frantic remonstrances prevailed.

> All this time they were pulling off her apparel, she never changed her
> countenance, but with smiling cheer she uttered these words, 'that she
> never had such grooms to make her unready, and that she never put off
> her clothes before such a company'. . . . [G]roping for the block, she laid
> down her head, putting her chin over the block with both hands, which,
> holding there still, had been cut off had they not been espied. . . . Then
> she, lying very still upon the block, one of the executioners holding her
> slightly with one of his hands, she endured two strokes of the other exe-
> cutioner with an axe, she making very small noise or none at all, and not
> stirring any part of her from the place where she lay: and so the execu-
> tioner cut off her head, saving one little gristle, which being cut asunder,
> he lift up her head to the view of all the assembly and bade 'God save the
> Queen'.

Her lips, Cecil's correspondent wrote, 'stirred up and down a quarter of an
hour' after she was dead.

Now she was dead, of course, she could safely be hailed as a Catholic heroine by the continental powers. Catherine de Medici told her ambassador, 'I am most grieved that you have been unable to do more for the
poor Queen of Scotland. It has never been the case that one queen should
have jurisdiction over another having placed herself into her hands for her
safety'. (Shades of Jeanne d'Albret?) Philip of Spain too wrote to his ambassador Mendoza that 'you cannot imagine the pity I feel for the Queen of
Scots', but the fact was that he could now continue preparations for his great

enterprise of England, his Armada, without having to question whether he really wished to place a queen committed to France on England's throne.

When the news was brought to Elizabeth herself early the next day, she 'gave herself over to grief', as Camden put it, a hysterical and histrionic paroxysm, meant to convince a watching Europe of her innocence, but doubtless springing from a real and complex cocktail of emotions.

It is perhaps not too overdramatic to say that Elizabeth Tudor knew the sisterhood of queens had also died that day. Could it all have gone differently, looking back to the beginning? Could Elizabeth have in effect mentored Mary Stuart? Probably not: their religion, with all its implications for the rights to the English throne, was in the way. It would be overly simplistic to say that religion ended any real possibility of sisterhood among Europe's powerful women. (There were, after all, plenty of powerful women within Catholic Europe among whom the game might still be played.) But perhaps it had always been a fragile plant, capable of flowering only in very particular conditions. And toward the end of the sixteenth century, the climate was growing cold.

POSTSCRIPT

✳

For myself, I was never so much enticed with the glorious name of a king or royal authority of a queen as delighted that God hath made me his instrument. . . . There will never queen sit in my seat with more zeal to my country, care to my subjects, and that will sooner with willingness venture her life for your good and safety, than myself.

—ELIZABETH TUDOR,
THE 'GOLDEN SPEECH',
30 NOVEMBER 1601

FOR ELIZABETH TUDOR, THE EIGHTEEN months after Mary Stuart's death represented something of another turning point. The Armada victory in the summer of 1588 might have owed more to good luck and bad weather than to leadership, and in a sense it represented what she had always dreaded, a military crisis in which, as a woman, she could not take direct command. Yet the speech she made to her troops at Tilbury, with the Armada ships in the Channel and Margaret of Parma's son planning an invasion from the Netherlands, became the most iconic of her career: 'I know I have the body but of a weak and feeble woman, but I have the heart and stomach of a king and of a king of England too—and take foul scorn that Parma or any prince of Europe should dare to invade the borders of my realm. To the which rather than any dishonour shall grow by me, I myself will venter my royal blood; I myself will be your general'.

As so often before, she was playing on her femininity—her vulnerability—and making it into a strength. A text underneath a contemporary painting in a Norfolk church has a variant on Elizabeth's words that tackles the gender issue more aggressively: 'The enemy may challenge my sex for that I am a woman, so may I likewise charge their mould, for they are but men'.

317

She made a point of leaving her ladies behind and rode through the troops with the sword of state carried before her—'sometimes like a Woman, and anon, with the countenance and pace of a Soldier', as Camden put it two decades later. Yet Leicester, in the days before Tilbury, had told her that her person was 'the most sacred and dainty thing we have in this world to care for, a man must tremble when he thinks of it'. She was at once appealing to her subjects' chivalry and impressing them with her potency.

If this were a great failure of the peace for which she and her sister queens had so often striven, it allowed her to take unto herself the persona of the warrior, for which male rulers had chiefly been admired.*

Yet the last years of the 1580s marked, for Queen Elizabeth I, the start of a 'second reign' by no means as successful as what had gone before. And on the wider stage, the 1570s and 1580s saw an epic battle between Catholics and Protestants played across northern Europe—dividing France, threatening England, confirming Spain in its crusading Catholicism, and stretching long tentacles out across the seas.

Elizabeth's longtime favourite and supporter the Earl of Leicester died within weeks of the Armada victory, to her great and solitary grief. She would lose another important councillor in each of the following few years. When William Cecil, by far the longest survivor, finally died in 1598, he left a son, Robert, to follow him as first minister, but Leicester was succeeded as her prime favourite by his stepson the Earl of Essex—and this was a relationship that threw a profoundly unflattering light on her woman's rule.

Long indulged by Elizabeth, Essex's final descent into open rebellion was marked by a young and militaristic man's disdain for an old woman. 'The Queen's conditions are as crooked as her carcase', he was reported to have said once, unforgivably. During a decade of economic hardship and uncertainty about the future, Elizabeth's court in the 1590s was rocked by a series of sexual scandals that not only reflected badly on her authority but also evoked the old stereotype of a woman ruler as surrounded by licentiousness.

Indeed, advancing age brought no halt to the slurs on Elizabeth's own reputation: it was in the 1580s that Catholic polemicist Nicholas Sanders brought out his scurrilous history of Anne Boleyn, a way of visiting the perceived sins of the mother on the daughter, and in the 1590s that Elizabeth's infamous interrogator Richard Topcliffe could fantasise aloud about having

---

* Her Netherlands allies, creating medals that depicted sunken Spanish ships, reportedly added the inscription 'Done by a female leader'.

felt her legs and her belly. When, after her death, Robert Cecil wrote that the queen had been 'more than a man and, in troth, sometimes less than a woman', it was the reverse side of the coin to the idea of a ruler's being above gender that had once empowered Elizabeth's female sovereignty.

Elizabeth continued to be addressed in terms of courtly love, but her looks had long faded. Anne de Beaujeu had warned her daughter that over forty, no clothes can make the wrinkles on one's face disappear. And when Cecil—a loyal servant but one anxious to secure both his own future and the succession—entered into correspondence with James VI of Scotland, he stressed the need for secrecy on the grounds of Elizabeth's age and infirmity, 'joined to the jealousy of her sex'. Even Elizabeth herself, taxing a Venetian envoy with the fact that Venice had failed to keep an ambassador at her court, asked bitterly if 'my sex hath brought me this demerit?' Her gender, she had to tell the man angrily, 'cannot diminish my prestige'.

IN THOSE LAST YEARS OF Elizabeth Tudor's life, even after Mary Stuart's death, there were several women among the leading candidates to succeed to her throne. Philip of Spain insisted that the chief Catholic claimant was his daughter the Spanish Infanta; when in 1601 Cecil had a list of claimants prepared, James VI of Scotland, in first place, was followed by Arbella Stuart (daughter to Lord Darnley's younger brother) in second, and James should arguably have been disqualified by reason of his foreign birth. But to the crowd of careful international observers, Arbella was interesting chiefly insofar as she might be married to a man who could thus absorb her claim: anyone from Robert Cecil himself to one of Margaret of Parma's grandsons.

The trouble was (as the watching envoys reported) that England, for the moment, had had enough of queens. As a Catholic commentator on the succession publishing as 'Doleman' put it: a woman 'ought not to be preferred, before so many men . . . and that it were much to have three women to reign in England one after the other, whereas in the space of above a thousand years before them, there had no reigned so many of that sex'.

In the end, by almost universal agreement, Elizabeth was succeeded by a man, Mary Stuart's Protestant son, James VI and (later) I. The proclamation made clear that he owed the throne to his female lineage, being descended 'from the body of Margaret [Tudor] . . . and of Elizabeth of York'. Yet James was a man whose own imaginative concept of the monarchy was cast in wholly patriarchal terms. Kings are 'compared to fathers of families', he told the English Parliament, 'for a king is truly *parens patriae*, the politique father of his people'.

James had, after all, been tutored in youth by a man, George Buchanan, a Protestant who had played a leading part in blackening Mary's reputation. Buchanan wrote that it was as unbecoming for a woman 'to pronounce Judgement, to levy Forces, to conduct an Army' as it was for a man to spin wool or to perform 'the other Services of the Weaker Sex'. This was to be the theme of writing on (or rather against) female succession in the decades ahead.

IF ELIZABETH WAS ONE OF the two giant figures left standing at the end of the sixteenth century, the other, of course, was Catherine de Medici. One of the reasons Catherine had been so appalled by Mary Stuart's death was the impetus her martyrdom would give to the Catholic League led by the Guises, who had effectively replaced the Huguenots as the threatening rebel force within the land.* When in 1588 the Guises did indeed assail Paris and make an attempt to kidnap her son Henri III, it was again Catherine who had to deal with them, first clambering over the barricades across the city and then remaining behind to liaise with the leaguers, while her son fled. But Catherine's 'authority and credit' with her son were now all but destroyed.

When her son on his own impulse ordered the assassination of the latest Duc de Guise, two days before Christmas of 1588, Catherine said he was 'headed towards ruin'. She was right—it was just seven months later that this last surviving (but childless) son was himself murdered by a Dominican friar, outraged that Henri III had allied himself with the Protestant Henri of Navarre. But Catherine had not lived to see Jeanne d'Albret's son, whose marriage had been the trigger for the Saint Bartholomew's Day Massacre, declared Henri IV of France. She died barely a fortnight after the Guise assassination, and it was Henri IV who would give her epitaph. 'What could the poor woman do', he asked, 'with five children in her arms after the death of her husband, and with two families in France—ours and the Guise—attempting to encroach on the Crown? Was she not forced to play strange parts to deceive the one and other and yet, as she did, to protect her children, who reigned in succession by the wisdom of a woman so able? I wonder she did not do worse!'

In 1593 Henri IV was received back into the church of Rome, having famously if apocryphally declared that Paris was worth a Mass. What would

---

* The Duchesse de Montpensier (daughter of François, the Duc de Guise murdered in 1563, and thus first cousin to Mary Stuart) was particularly rabid, carrying always at her belt a pair of scissors with which she threatened to tonsure the king and confine him in a convent.

Jeanne d'Albret have said? Henri's own assassination in 1610 would bring another woman, his wife, Marie de Medici—Catherine de Medici's kinswoman as well as her successor—into power as regent of France. But Marie's attempts at rule never amounted to successful control of the country.

THE CLOSING YEARS OF THE sixteenth century and the first years of the seventeenth saw some continued instances of female rule. Philip of Spain made his daughter the Infanta Isabella, with her husband, joint ruler of the Spanish Netherlands, a rule that ushered in the Netherlands' Golden Age. Queen Elizabeth 'says she wants to consider me as her daughter; just imagine how much profit I would get from such a mother!', said the Infanta ambiguously. But the most famous female ruler of the seventeenth century, Christina of Sweden, would resign her throne, writing that 'no woman is fit to govern' (a sentiment later echoed by Queen Victoria's belief that 'we women . . . are not fitted to reign'). Appropriate, perhaps, that the dream of woman's rule, which had progressed northward through the sixteenth century, should die in the Baltic Sea.

From a northern European perspective, at least, it is tempting to ask whether the end of the sixteenth century did not usher in a reduction in female autonomy—a reduction in the number of women to rule their country, a hushing of the gynocratic debate as to whether a girl should not be educated as well as a boy. Now the Amazon queen, in Shakespeare's *A Midsummer Night's Dream* and elsewhere, was featured as tamed by man and marriage.

It is true that the Counter Reformation had found one of its best weapons in a renewed and refreshed cult of the Virgin Mary, the Queen of Heaven. The Jesuits promoted the use of the rosary (and within it the Hail Mary), restored shrines, and encouraged confraternities devoted to the Mother of God. Mary was, after all, declared the true heroine of Lepanto, the great naval battle that in 1571 saw a Holy League organised by the pope and led by Spain defeat the Turks. The pope had declared the battle day, 7 October, as the Feast of Our Lady of Victory. But the Jesuits—who in their early days had relied so much upon the support of noblewomen—preferred now to turn to less controversial, male, patrons. Female religious orders had flourished during this period and would continue to do so, but increasingly, the women who had joined them would find themselves enclosed.

Not that things were any better for women in the Protestant community—far from it. The Protestants (and their largely married clergy) had long counterpoised the ideal of the family, with the father at its head, against the Catholic ideal of virginity. This left little room for the concept of the virginal woman warrior. In its early days, the Protestant Reformation had seemed to offer opportunities for women. But now, again, these seemed to be dwindling away.

A century after the death of Elizabeth I, England had once again a woman on the throne—another whose elder sister had held it before her. But Queen Anne's elder sister, Mary, declared that 'women should not meddle in government'. In theory, Mary reigned jointly with her husband, William—in fact, she ceded all control to him—and though Queen Anne by contrast relegated her husband, George of Denmark, to a background role, both Stuart sisters reigned over a nation that allowed the monarch far less power than Elizabeth had enjoyed.

On the continent, individual women had of course continued to play an important role. The Habsburg Dynasty in particular maintained its practice of using female relatives in a regent's role; in France Louis XIV's mother and regent, Anne of Austria (born a Habsburg), was just one important figure. Nonetheless, in the mid-eighteenth century, the power held by Maria Theresa—Habsburg sovereign of Austria and Hungary, whose success in engineering her husband's election as Holy Roman Emperor gave her the title of 'Empress'—represented something of a rebirth.* So too, of course, did that of the empresses who ruled Russia for much of the eighteenth century: Catherine I, Anna, Elizabeth, and Catherine II—Catherine 'the Great'. But they were operating within a very different political system and playing by different rules.

BOTH ELIZABETH TUDOR AND CATHERINE de Medici were chess players, like Isabella of Castile and Anne de Beaujeu, Margaret of Austria and Louise of Savoy. (Though Mary, Queen of Scots, played, she is not particularly associated with the game.) Catherine, indeed—who would have learned her game in Italy and promoted it when she came to France—was said to have sought to match herself against the great Italian champion Paolo Boi. Elizabeth, who had played against her great tutor Roger Ascham, was sufficiently aware of the symbolism of the game to have rewarded Sir Charles Blount,

---

* Maria Theresa dictated an autobiographical account of her proceedings entitled—in a phrase reminiscent of Anne de Beaujeu!—*Instructions Drawn Up from Motherly Solicitude for the Special Benefit of My Posterity*. Advising her son that 'a mediocre peace is always better than a fortunate war', she nonetheless celebrated the recapture of Prague in 1743 with a spectacle known as the Ladies' Carousel, at which she engaged in a jousting contest with another noblewoman.

after a successful joust, with 'a Queen at Chesse of gold richly enameled', which he would wear tied about his arm.

But female participation in the game was itself in decline by the turn of the seventeenth century. Those myriad medieval pictures of a man and a woman playing together dwindled away; by 1694 Thomas Hyde in his study of chess lamented that in a game of battle, to call the most active piece a queen was surely 'inappropriate'.

AND YET, AND YET . . . A tradition of female rule as strong as that seen in the sixteenth century cannot (however it may subsequently be overlooked) ever really go away. From now on, in the Western world, the tally card would record that it had been possible for women to control countries and that a number of them had done so very successfully. From now on, no one could say that was an impossibility.

Many of the battles these women fought are still relevant. Almost thirty years ago, Antonia Fraser, in her groundbreaking book *Boadicea's Chariot*, traced the line of 'warrior queens' from the ancient world to the Iron Lady. She identified several tropes of female leadership—the Chaste Syndrome and the Voracity Syndrome, the role of a woman as Holy (Armed) Figurehead or as Peacemaker—and traced them from Celtic mythology and the Roman Empire to the female leaders of her own day: Golda Meir, Margaret Thatcher, Indira Gandhi.

The women who ruled sixteenth-century Europe fitted Fraser's patterns almost precisely, from the doublethink that reclassified a successful woman as an honorary man to the number of them who reached power by what she called the Appendage Syndrome—as widow, mother, sister of a powerful male. Any look at the newspapers makes clear how well these tropes still work today.

The battles these queens and regents fought are relevant whenever it comes to the questions of women assuming power and questions over whether women participating in public life might wield that power in a different way. None of these questions are yet wholly answered, but they are being asked with new urgency. I write at a moment when in America a woman prepares to contest the world's most powerful office and when in Europe Theresa May, Britain's second female Prime Minister, enters negotiations with Scotland's First Minister Nicola Sturgeon and German Chancellor Angela Merkel. You might say the Age of Queens has come again—but the fact that it can do so is in part these earlier women's legacy.

Now say, have women worth? or have they none?
Or had they some, but with our Queen is't gone?
Nay Masculines, you have thus taxt us long,
But she, though dead, will vindicate our wrong.
Let such as say our sex is void of Reason,
Know tis a slander now, but once was treason.

—ANNE BRADSTREET, *IN HONOUR OF THAT HIGH
AND MIGHTY PRINCESS QUEEN ELIZABETH
OF HAPPY MEMORY* (1643)

ACKNOWLEDGMENTS

This book might never have reached its present form without the help of one person in particular, my old friend (and unofficial editor!) Margaret Gaskin, who, as so often before, came to my rescue and spent many hours helping me to mould a viable form out of some very challenging raw material. Her abilities make up for my deficiencies—thank you, Margaret. There is someone else I've had occasion to thank on every book I've done, the historian Alison Weir, for the unflagging support and enthusiasm that never fail her friends.

A number of other historians have been kind enough to help me, by reading material or by answering queries. I owe an immense debt to the kindness of Elena Woodacre at the University of Winchester, who organised a positive team of academic specialists to read parts of the text and ensure this generalist's book has as few errors as possible. I am indebted to Jonathan Spangler, Lucinda Dean, Cathleen Sarti, Rocio Martinez Lopez, Estelle Paranque, and Una McIlvenna as well as to Aislinn Muller. I am also very grateful to Carole Levin at the University of Nebraska–Lincoln, whose own work has been a source of inspiration and who supplied me with the *New York Times* quote that is the key to my Preface. Thanks, too, to Tracy Borman, Linda Porter, and Nicola Tallis, as well as to Sara Wolfson and Louise Wilkinson for their work in organising the conference Premodern Queenship and Diplomacy in Europe, held at Canterbury Christ Church University in September 2014, which I found of the greatest assistance. Needless to say, any mistakes that remain in the book are my own responsibility entirely.

I want also to thank my agents, Peter Robinson in the United Kingdom and George Lucas in the United States, and, at Basic Books, my publisher Lara Heimert and associate editor Leah Stecher for their acuteness and commitment, and Annette Wenda for her gentle but eagle-eyed editing. To all these and more, I only hope the book is worthy.

NOTES AND FURTHER READING

This book owes a particular debt to three others in particular—besides, of course, Garrett Mattingly's *The Defeat of the Spanish Armada* (Jonathan Cape, 1959) mentioned in the Preface. My awareness of the role played in the sixteenth century by women ruling beyond Britain's shores was heightened by William Monter's *The Rise of the Female Kings in Europe, 1300–1800* (Yale University Press, 2012), as too was my awareness that this was a subject our Anglocentric popular history has been slow to address. I had long been interested in the concept of inheritance from mother to daughter and was thrilled, halfway through my research, to discover that Sharon L. Jansen, in *The Monstrous Regiment of Women: Female Rulers in Early Modern Europe* (Palgrave Macmillan, 2002), had done so much to explore the field. I envisage a somewhat different pattern from Jansen, who traces coeval lines of inheritance through the royal families of four different territories, but hers is an infinitely valuable body of work and itself a formidable legacy.

The same must, of course, be said of Antonia Fraser's groundbreaking *Boadicea's Chariot: The Warrior Queens* (Weidenfeld & Nicolson, 1988), which I reread as I was finishing this book, admiring once again the dazzling virtuosity with which she explores patterns of female leadership from ancient history through to the modern day. I first met Lady Antonia many years ago, not in the context of any historical work but as joint spectators—sufferers—of a freezing springtime cricket match. I was grateful then for her generous offer of a sip from her warming hip flask; I am infinitely more grateful today.

It would seem ungracious, too, not to make a more general acknowledgment of academic work now done in this field, notably through the Palgrave Macmillan series Queenship and Power, edited by Carole Levin and Charles Beem, a series of which Sharon L. Jansen's book is one of the fruits. Other particularly relevant titles in the series include Beem's own *The Lioness Roared: The Problems of Female Rule in English History* (2008) and Elena Woodacre's *Royal Mothers and Their Ruling Children: Wielding Political Authority from Antiquity to the Early Modern Era* (2015), but everything they issue makes a valuable contribution to this ever-fertile field. Among a host of other books to address the subject, I should like to single out one further example, in particular, *A History of Women's Political Thought in Europe, 1400–1700* (Cambridge University Press, 2009), by Jacqueline Broad and Karen Green.

I should conversely also like to remind the general reader of the work being done in a very different context—on the Internet. The particular contribution made here is to set the sixteenth-century rulers in the wider context of powerful women across the world and down the centuries: among the exact contemporaries of 'my' women rulers, I shall always be sorry that the Rajput Rani, who rode into battle on her own war elephant, is outside the scope of this study.

Preface

My conception of the changes in the game of chess was formed by Marilyn Yalom's *Birth of the Chess Queen* (Pandora Press, 2004).

A wealth of information on sixteenth-century contributions to the gynocracy debate can be found in the notes to Sharon L. Jansen's book above, pages 229–231 in particular.

Part I. 1474–1513

I have previously written about the English experience of these years in *Blood Sisters: The Women Behind the Wars of the Roses* (HarperPress, 2012). For Margaret Tudor (and her successors in Scotland), see Linda Porter's compelling *Crown of Thistles: The Fatal Inheritance of Mary Queen of Scots* (Macmillan, 2013), while Margaret and her sister, Mary, are the subjects of Maria Perry's *Sisters to the King* (Andre Deutsch, 1998).

The standard biography in English of Isabella of Castile is Peggy K. Liss's *Isabel the Queen: Life and Times* (Oxford University Press, 1992). See also Barbara F. Weissberger's article in Anne J. Cruz and Mihoko Suzuki, eds., *The Rule of Women in Early Modern Europe* (University of Illinois Press, 2009). Julia Fox has written an important dual biography, *Sister Queens: Katherine of Aragon and Juana, Queen of Castile* (Weidenfeld & Nicolson, 2011). Katherine has also been the subject of a number of individual biographies, notably Giles Tremlett's *Catherine of Aragon: Henry's Spanish Queen* (Faber and Faber, 2010) and Patrick Williams's *Katharine of Aragon* (Amberley, 2013).

Margaret of Austria has been the subject of three comparatively modern biographies in English: Eleanor E. Tremayne's *The First Governess of the Netherlands: Margaret of Austria* (Methuen, 1908); Jane de Iongh's *Margaret of Austria: Regent of the Netherlands*, translated by M. D. Herter Norton (Jonathan Cape, 1954); and Shirley Harrold Bonner's *Fortune, Misfortune, Fortifies One: Margaret of Austria, Ruler of the Low Countries, 1507–1530* (Amazon, 1981). For Charles Brandon, see Steven Gunn, *Charles Brandon: Henry VIII's Closest Friend* (Amberley, 2015). Margaret's correspondence is published in Ghislaine de Boom, *Correspondance de Marguerite d'Autriche . . .* (Brussels, 1935). See also André J. G. Le Glay, *Correspondance de l'Empereur Maximilien I et de Marguerite d'Autriche* (Paris, 1839).

Many of the royal women of France lack a solo biography in English, but Pauline Matarasso's *Queen's Mate: Three Women of Power in France on the Eve of the Renaissance* (Routledge, 2001) is an authoritative consideration of Anne de Beaujeu, Anne of Brittany, and (in her earlier years) Louise of Savoy. For Louise's later life, see Dorothy Moulton Mayer, *The Great Regent: Louise of Savoy, 1476–1531* (Weidenfeld & Nicolson, 1966). *Anne of France: Lessons for My Daughter*, by Anne de Beaujeu, has been translated and edited by Sharon L. Jansen (L D. S. Brewer, 2004). Louise of Savoy's *Journal*, edited by M. Petitot in *Collection complete des mémoires relatifs a l'histoire de France* (Paris, 1826), can be found online.

I must also make special acknowledgment of *Marguerite of Navarre*, by Patricia F. Cholakian and Rouben C. Cholakian (Columbia University Press, 2006), for the development of the idea that passages in the *Heptameron* are autobiographical (see below). The translation I used is Marguerite of Navarre, *The Heptameron*, translated by P. A. Chilton (Penguin, 1984). See also *Lettres de Marguerite d'Angoulême*, edited by F. Génin (Paris, 1841); *Nouvelles lettres*, edited by F. Génin (Paris, 1842); and Pierre Jourda, *Marguerite d'Angoulême, Duchess d'Alençon, Reine de Navarre* (Paris, 1930). Brantôme's work on Marguerite is in Brantôme, Seigneur de Pierre de Bordeilles, *Oeuvres completes* (Paris, 1864–1882).

45 two long letters, signed simply 'M': The versions in the British Library's Cotton MS (Titus B. i. ff 142) are in the handwriting of Sir Richard Wingfield, the ambassador sent to the Netherlands to negotiate the proposed marriage between Margaret of Austria's nephew Charles and Henry VIII's younger sister, Mary. These are in English, presumably translated by Wingfield from the original French, and the British Library will admit only that 'M' can 'probably' be identified as Margaret. From the internal evidence, however—the places, the occasions, the long interviews with the king—it is hard to see who else 'M' was likely to be. Wingfield had, moreover, endorsed the letters as having been written from 'Loivain', Louvain, Margaret's territory, and concerning 'Secret matters of the Duke of Suffolk'. See also John Gough Nichols, ed., *The Chronicle of Calais in the Reigns of Henry VII and Henry VIII to the Year 1540*, Camden Society, vol. 35 (London 1846).

47 Heptameron . . . to some degree autobiographical: See Cholakian and Cholakian, *Marguerite of Navarre*, 21–38. Earlier writers touch on the possibility of an entanglement between Marguerite and Bonnivet, in terms, however, of their own day. Francis Hackett in his 1934 biography of Francis I writes that Bonnivet watched Marguerite 'with guarded avidity while she, the regulator of nuns, tingled with his attention. She invited it, as Francis did his own form of violence, by the way she suffered and endured it'. Hackett, like Louise of Savoy's biographer Mayer, also subscribed to the theory that Louise, 'the crafty and experienced matron', had fostered the affair, since Bonnivet could give Marguerite a child her husband couldn't. For sexual mores, and a possible autobiographical element, in Marguerite's writings, see also Broad and Green, *History of Women's Political Thought in Europe*, 70–71, 79–89. Chilton, introducing *The Heptameron*, notes that 'in periods when women show signs of assertiveness there is a corresponding preoccupation with violence against them': Marguerite may have been responding to a generally aggressive clime.

Part II. 1514–1521

In addition to the biographies cited above, see Antonia Fraser, *The Six Wives of Henry VIII* (Weidenfeld & Nicolson, 1992); David Starkey, *Six Wives: The Queens of Henry VIII* (Chatto & Windus, 2003); and Alison Weir, *The Six Wives of Henry VIII* (Bodley Head, 1991). Also see Glenn Richardson, *The Field of Cloth of Gold* (Yale University Press, 2013).

PART III. 1522–1536

The enigma that is Anne Boleyn has generated a huge volume of literature, though the single most comprehensive and authoritative biography remains Eric Ives's *The Life and Death of Anne Boleyn* (Blackwell, 2004). More controversial views can be found in *Anne Boleyn: Fatal Attractions* (Yale University Press, 2010), by G. W. Bernard, chief exponent of the theory that Anne was to some degree at least guilty, and Retha M. Warnicke's *The Rise and Fall of Anne Boleyn: Family Politics at the Court of Henry VIII* (Cambridge University Press, 1989). Alison Weir's *The Lady in the Tower: The Fall of Anne Boleyn* (Jonathan Cape, 2009) is a riveting forensic analysis of the circumstances leading up to Anne's execution, while Tracy Borman's *Thomas Cromwell: The Untold Story of Henry VIII's Most Faithful Servant* (Hodder & Stoughton, 2014) gives the other side of the story, and Suzannah Lipscomb's *1536: The Year That Changed Henry VIII* (Lion, 2009) examines the year of her fall. I also found fascinating Nicola Shulman's *Graven with Diamonds* (Short Books, 2011), in which Thomas Wyatt serves as a prism through which to observe the court culture that saw Anne's downfall.

For the great religious struggle of which Anne Boleyn's story was but a part, see Diarmaid MacCulloch's great *Reformation: Europe's House Divided, 1490–1700* (Allen Lane, 2003).

121 **brother did not want her to return:** It was possibly on her demoralised journey home that Marguerite wrote to her brother an undated, cryptic, and desperate letter. She seems frantic to know whether François will send for her, tortured by the thought of what he may do, afraid he may 'abandon the right path'—or afraid of what he may require her to do, by way of 'proof of surrender'. The letter—which Marguerite begs her brother to burn—breathes either the shame she seems so often to have felt or a terrified awareness of the need for secrecy. Her great nineteenth-century editor Génin was in no doubt of what François was demanding, to her horror—that she make their relationship a physically, as well as emotionally, incestuous one. But it is hard now to see what in the letter compels such an extreme reading, which indeed hardly fits with Marguerite's reiterated offers to come to her brother, instantly. (Incest was, moreover, an absolutely favourite bugbear for writers of the first half of the nineteenth century.) Barbara Stephenson in *The Power and Patronage of Marguerite of Navarre* (Ashgate, 2004), 119, argues convincingly that the letter may have been written by another 'Marguerite'.

126 **Henry VIII's letters to Anne:** There are quite literally as many different versions as there are writers on the subject of the chronology of Henry's letters, but I dwell too briefly on the subject to feel the need here to add to them. I find persuasive Eric Ives's theory as to which constitute the first three letters in the sequence, though otherwise I would differ slightly from his timetable.

166 **if the recollections . . . are accurate:** A letter supposedly from Jeanne is quoted in full by Nancy Lyman Roelker, *Queen of Navarre: Jeanne d'Albret* (Harvard University Press, 1968), 127:

> I am writing to tell you that up to now I have followed in the footsteps of the deceased Queen, my most honoured mother—whom God forgive—in the matter of hesitation between the two religions. The said Queen was warned by her late brother the King, François I . . . not to get new doctrines in her head so that from then on she confined

herself to amusing stories. Besides, I well remember how long ago, the late King [of Navarre], my most honoured father . . . surprised the late Queen when she was praying in her rooms with the ministers Roussel and Farel, and how with great annoyance he slapped her right cheek and forbade her sharply to meddle in matters of doctrine. He shook a stick at me which cost me many bitter tears and has kept me fearful and compliant until after they had both died.

Unfortunately, there have been questions as to the letter's authenticity. See Broad and Green, *History of Women's Political Thought in Europe*, 111–112.

171 **witchcraft or satanic practices:** See Diarmaid MacCulloch, *Reformation*, 561–570, for the role the fear of witchcraft played in the century, and perhaps in the decline of women's power at the end of it. It has been said that the 'Age of Queens' also birthed the great age of the witch hunt. Between 1400 and 1800, forty to fifty thousand people died in Europe and colonial North America on charges of witchcraft, the number mounting from 1560, when the burnings of heretics as such slowed. Witchcraft was seen as a natural successor to heresy, with the difference that it was particularly (though far from exclusively) associated with women. The *Malleus Maleficarum* (Hammer of Witches), published in 1487, specifically asserted that witches were more likely to be women, a 1484 papal bull gave approval to antiwitch activities, in 1532 Charles V's *Lex Carolina* gave the death penalty to both heretics and witches, and a crusade against witches was part of the Spanish attempt to impose order on the Low Countries in the 1560s.

PART IV. 1537–1553

For the biography of Mary of Hungary, see Jane de Iongh, *Mary of Hungary: Second Regent of the Netherlands*, translated by M. D. Herter Norton (Faber & Faber, 1959); for that of Marie de Guise, see Rosalind K. Marshall, *Mary of Guise* (Collins, 1977). The most recent biography of Mary Tudor is Anna Whitelock's powerful *Mary Tudor: England's First Queen* (Bloomsbury, 2009), following Linda Porter's *Mary Tudor: The First Queen* (Portrait, 2007) and Judith Mary Richards's *Mary Tudor* (Routledge, 2008). The main biographical study of Jeanne d'Albret in English is still Roelker's *Queen of Navarre*.

PART V. 1553–1560

I have written twice before about the reign of Elizabeth I, in *Elizabeth & Leicester* (Bantam, 2007) and *Arbella: England's Lost Queen* (Bantam, 2003). The bibliographies of those books provide a more extensive list of reading and reference, but there are books not then available of which I have since had the benefit. To Alison Weir's *Elizabeth the Queen* (Jonathan Cape, 1998) and Anne Somerset's *Elizabeth I* (Weidenfeld & Nicolson, 1991) has now been added Lisa Hilton's *Elizabeth: Renaissance Prince* (Weidenfeld & Nicolson, 2014), the European perspective of which I found particularly valuable. John Guy's *My Heart Is My Own* (HarperCollins, 2004) remains the outstanding biography of Mary, Queen of Scots.

To R. J. Knecht's *Catherine de' Medici* (Routledge, 1998) and Leonie Frieda's *Catherine de Medici* (Weidenfeld & Nicolson, 2003) has now been added Nancy Goldstone's

The Rival Queens: Catherine de' Medici, Her Daughter Marguerite de Valois, and the Betrayal That Ignited a Kingdom (Weidenfeld & Nicolson, 2015). Several of the French primary sources are now available online: *Lettres de Catherine de Médicis* (Paris, 1880), *Mémoires et poésies de Jeanne d'Albret* (Paris, 1893), *N. de Bordenave histoire de Béarn et Navarre* (Paris, 1873), and *Mémoires et lettres de Marguerite de Valois* (Paris, 1842).

While Christina of Denmark must join the long line of European women of whom there is no current biography in English, Julia Cartwright's biography *Christina of Denmark: Duchess of Milan and Lorraine, 1522–1590* (New York, 1913) is online.

Academic work I found particularly valuable included *High and Mighty Queens of Early Modern England: Realities and Representations*, edited by Carole Levin, Debra Barrett-Graves, and Jo Eldridge Carney (Palgrave Macmillan, 2003); Rayne Allinson's *A Monarchy of Letters: Royal Correspondence and English Diplomacy in the Reign of Elizabeth* (Palgrave Macmillan, 2012); and Cruz and Suzuki, *Rule of Women in Early Modern Europe*, especially articles by Carole Levin on Elizabeth, by Mary C. Ekman on Jeanne d'Albret, and by Mihoko Suzuki on Elizabeth and Catherine de Medici. See also Susan Doran's essay on the same subject in Glenn Richardson, ed., *The Contending Kingdoms: England and France, 1420–1700* (Ashgate, 2008).

POSTSCRIPT

322 **dwindling away:** To be reborn in England, in another time of crisis—the Civil War. Antonia Fraser's *The Weaker Vessel: Woman's Lot in Seventeenth-Century England* (Weidenfeld, 1984) details the importance of women's efforts on both sides. As Diarmaid MacCulloch notes in *Reformation*, 'Female self assertion was possible in periods of uncertainty and crisis. . . . When times quietened, there was a gradual reining-in of possibilities for women, together with a rewriting of history' (657).

For more on the gynocracy debate and its relevance for women today, as well as some influential women only touched upon in this book, please visit the website gameofqueensbook.com.

ILLUSTRATION CREDITS

✻

Game of Chess, 1555, Anguissola, Sofonisba (c.1532–1625): Museum Narodowe, Poznan, Poland/Bridgeman Images.

Isabella of Castile, Ms 604/1339 f.64v, King Ferdinand II of Aragon and Isabella of Castile, from the 'Devotionary of Queen Juana the Mad', c.1482 (vellum): Musee Conde, Chantilly, France/Bridgeman Images.

Anne de Beaujeu, detail of the right leaf of the Triptych of the Virgin in glory, 1498–1499, by Jean Hey or Hay (ca.1475–ca.1505), known as the Master of Moulins, sacristy of the church of Notre-Dame in Moulins, France: DeAgostini/Getty Images.

The Field of the Cloth of Gold: Wikimedia Commons.

Margaret of Austria, c.1490 (oil on oak panel), Master of Moulins (Jean Hey), (fl.c.1483–c.1529): Metropolitan Museum of Art, New York, USA/Bridgeman Images.

Manuscript miniature showing French queen Louise of Savoy: PVDE/Bridgeman Images.

Marguerite of Navarre, c.1527, by Jean Clouet (c.1485–1541), found in the collection of Walker Art Gallery: Fine Art Images/Heritage Images/Getty Images.

Margaret Tudor: Sir Francis Ogilvy/The National Library of Scotland.

Anne Boleyn, 1534 (oil on panel), English School: Hever Castle, Kent, UK/Bridgeman Images.

Katherine of Aragon: Universal History Archive/Getty Images.

Elizabeth I when a Princess, c.1546, attributed to William Scrots (1537–1553): Royal Collection Trust/© Her Majesty Queen Elizabeth II 2016.

Queen Mary I (1516–1558) 1554 (oil on panel), Mor, Anthonis vanDashorst (Antonio Moro) (c.1519–1576/77): Prado, Madrid, Spain/Bridgeman Images.

An Allegory of Tudor Succession: The Family of Henry VIII: Wikimedia Commons.

Mary of Guise (1515–1560), 1537, found in the collection of the National Gallery of Scotland, Edinburgh: Fine Art Images/Heritage Images/Getty Images.

Mary of Austria (a.k.a. Mary of Hungary), c.1520 (oil on vellum on panel), Maler, Hans or Johan (fl.1510–1523): Society of Antiquaries of London, UK/Bridgeman Images.

Margaret of Parma: Stedelijk Museum 'Het Prinsenhof', Delft, Netherlands/Lessing Images.

Jeanne d'Albret: Peter Horree/Alamy Stock Photo.

Catherine de Medici (1519–1589) (oil on panel), French School: Musee Conde, Chantilly, France/Bridgeman Images.

François Dubois (1529–1584), St. Bartholomew's Night, August 24, 1572: DEA/G. DAGLI ORTI/De Agostini/Getty Images.

Elizabeth I: His Grace the Duke of Bedford and the Trustees of the Bedford Estates, from the Woburn Abbey Collection.

Portrait of Mary, Queen of Scots, by François Clouet (1510–1572): World History Archive/Alamy Stock Photo.

INDEX

✳

Abarca, Pedro, 23
Act in Restraint of Appeals, 161–162
Act of Supremacy, 163
Adrian VI, Pope, 111
Agrippa, Cornelius, 4
Agrippa, Thomas, 208
Ahasuerus, King, 171
Alba, Duke of, 286–287, 292
Albany, John Stuart, 2nd Duke of, xix–xx
    Margaret Tudor and, 109, 113–114
    political role, 53–54, 72–77, 79,
      110–111, 164
Alençon, Charles, Duc d', 43, 48, 66, 68,
    117, 119–120
Alençon, François, Duc d', 292, 301, 305,
    310–311, 310n
Ales, Alexander, 155, 172, 174
Alessandro de Medici, 134, 320
Alfonso, 10
ancestors, power of, 143, 159, 170
Anglo-French Wars, 102, 110, 116, 118
Angoulême, Charles d', xviii, 18–19, 27
Angus, Archibald Douglas, 6th Earl of,
    xix, 76
    family life, 79–80, 108–109, 114–115, 132
    marriage, 72, 77
    political role, 72–73, 74, 114
Anjou, Henri, Duc de. See Henri III of
    France, King
Anne Boleyn, xvi, xxii, xxiii, 66, 87, 91,
    100
    Claude of France and, 66n
    death, 169, 174, 188

downfall, 172–175
Henry VIII of England and, 5, 6, 44,
    48n, 107–108, 111–112, 125–131, 126n,
    140–143, 147–148, 156–163, 169–175,
    197n
influences, xviii, xxviii, 161
jewels, 112, 128
Katherine of Aragon and, 9, 112,
    162–163, 176, 215
legacy, xxvii, 215
Margaret of Austria and, 3–9, 44, 61,
    125–126, 127, 157
marriage, 130, 162, 174, 197n
political role, 107–108
religion and, 155–157
sex and, 8, 112–113, 172–174
Wolsey and, 102–103, 111–112, 128,
    129–131, 142, 143, 158
Anne de Beaujeu (Anne of France), xviii,
    xxviii, xxix, 25, 28n, 189n
    with chess, game of, 13, 322
    counsel of, 13–14, 27, 57, 76, 105, 113,
    126, 136, 143, 169, 170, 173, 187, 263n,
    304, 307, 314, 319
    court, with standards and ethics at, 4,
    5–6, 20, 42
    death, 102
    legacy, 12–14, 18, 19, 96
    Louise of Savoy and, 15, 17–18, 27, 42
    Margaret of Austria and, 15, 16, 17, 18,
    20, 42
    military and, 17
    political role, 66–67

Anne d'Este, 287, 298
Anne of Austria, 322
Anne of Brittany, xviii, xxix, 19–20, 23n,
    27, 28, 29, 51
  death, 59–60
  Roman Catholic Church and, 99
Anne of Cleves, xxii, 181, 183, 194n
Anne of France. See Anne de Beaujeu
Anne of Great Britain, Queen, 322
Antoine de Bourbon, xix
  marriage, 202–203, 237–238, 237n, 268
  political role, 236, 238n, 251, 252,
    253–254, 255–257, 295
Antoinette de Bourbon, 184–185, 187, 200
Appendage Syndrome, 323
apples, symbolism, 161
Arande, Michel de, 102
Aristotle, xxix, 213
Armagnac, Cardinal d', 270–271
Arnolfini portrait, 5, 6
Arran, James Hamilton, 2nd Earl of, xx,
  38, 186, 187, 222, 223
  with marriage, 240
  political role, 246, 247
Arthur Stewart, Prince, 38
Arthur Tudor, Prince of Wales, xxi,
  30–31, 32, 38, 130, 141
Ascham, Roger, 206, 322
Ashley, Kat, 206
Askew, Anne, 197n
astrology, 19n
Augustine. See Saint Augustine
'Auld Alliance,' 50, 71, 184
Aylmer, John, 230–231, 239, 239n, 241

Babington, Anthony, 313
Bacon, Lady Anne, 220
banquet food, 91–92
Barton, Elizabeth, 197n
Beaton, Cardinal, 186, 187
Becon, Thomas, 230
Beggars' Summons, 245
Berquin, Louis de, 136, 137, 155
Beza, Theodore, 251

Bible, the, 118, 129, 131, 155, 215, 240
Blount, Charles, 322–323
Blount, Elizabeth, 80, 83, 176
Boadicea's Chariot (Fraser), 323
Boccaccio, 47
body politic. See Elizabeth I of England,
  Queen
Boethius, 18
Boi, Paolo, 322
Boleyn, George, 87, 172, 173–174
Boleyn, Mary, 66, 108, 125–127, 126n, 130
Boleyn, Thomas, 6–7, 8, 61, 88, 100, 147
Bond of Association (1584), 312
Bonnivet (Guillaume Gouffier), xviii, 48,
  82, 86, 91, 101, 117
Book of Martyrs (Foxe), 230
The Book of the City of Ladies (Christine
  de Pizan), xxviii–xxix, 12
The Book of the Courtier (Castiglione),
  1, 14, 42, 145, 179
Bordenave, Nicolas de, 192, 254, 254n
Bothwell, James Hepburn, 4th Earl of,
  xx, xxi, 284n
  marriage, 282–283, 290
  political role, 277, 279, 281, 283–284
Bothwell, Patrick Hepburn, 1st Earl of, 32
Bourbon, Charles, Duc de, 97, 102, 110,
  116
Bourbon, Nicolas, 155
Bradstreet, Anne, 323–324
Brandon, Charles. See Suffolk,
  1st Duke of
Brandon, Frances, 207
Brantôme, Seigneur de, 48, 69, 154, 193,
  238, 311
Breton, Nicholas, xxv
Briconnet, Guillaume, Bishop of Meaux,
  101–102
Brittany, Duke of. See François III
Bryan, Francis, 129
Buchanan, George, 320
Burghley, William Cecil, 1st Baron, xxiii
  political role, 240, 242, 255, 259, 261,
    262, 290, 297, 304, 314, 318, 319

Randolph and, 275–276
Throckmorton and, 263, 275
Burgundy, 9n
Butler, James. *See* Ormonde, 9th Earl of

Calvin, John, 195, 195n, 228, 238
  Calvinism, xxiii, 216, 255, 272
  political role, 251, 254, 270
  on women with power, 240
Cambrai, 40n
  See also League of Cambrai; peace
Campeggio, Cardinal, 140–141, 142, 143,
  147
Carey, William, 125
Castiglione, Baldassare, 1, 14, 42, 145, 179
Caterina Sforza, xxix–xxx, 133n
Catherine de Medici, xviii–xix, xx, 177,
  185, 199
  with chess, game of, 322
  early life, 134–135, 151–153
  with Edict of Romorantin (1560), 252
  family life, 201–202, 232, 235–236, 275
  jewels, 165, 258
  marriage, 165, 189–190
  Mary, Queen of Scots, and, 200–201
  Massacre of Saint Bartholomew's Day
    and, 293–306
  Petite Bande and, 189
  political role, 233, 235, 236, 251–257,
    264–266, 268–273, 283, 288–293,
    309–311, 320
  religion and, 286
Catherine I of Russia, 322
Catherine II 'the Great' of Russia, 322
Catherine of Portugal, Queen, xvii, 36n,
  129, 225n
Cavalli, Ambassador, 299
Cavendish, George, 83, 111, 112, 142
Caxton, William, xxv, 209
Cecil, Robert, 318, 319
Cecil, William. *See* Burghley, 1st Baron
chalcedony, 6
Chambers, David, 311
chansons, 6, 198

Chapuys, Eustace, 183
  political role, 157, 158, 160–161, 163, 170,
    171, 175
  religion and, 172
Charlemagne, 15n
Charles IX of France, King, xix, 293, 309
  early life, 252, 253
  political role, 264, 266, 270, 294–295,
    296, 299–301, 303
Charles of Austria, Archduke, 264
Charles 'the Bold,' 15
Charles V, Holy Roman Emperor,
    xvi–xvii, xxi, 3, 24, 118
  death, 234
  family life, 153, 154, 167–168
  life before accession, 36, 44, 45, 60,
    62–63
  Margaret of Austria and, 95, 97–98,
    119, 140, 144, 149–150
  Margaret of Parma and, 134
  marriage, 123–124, 132
  Placarten, 286
  political role, 68, 81–82, 84, 85, 86,
    88–89, 93, 96, 97, 98, 98n, 99, 102,
    109–110, 119, 121–123, 130, 135, 138,
    146–147, 151–153, 158, 160–161, 170,
    188–189, 190, 195, 204, 223–225,
    223n, 226, 285
Charles VIII of France, King, xvi, xviii,
    13, 16, 17, 27
  death, 28
  Margaret of Austria and, 19–20, 24,
    25
Charlotte of France, Princess, 116–117
Charlotte of Savoy, 13, 17
Chastelard, 264–265
chess, game of, 131, 131n
  en prise and, 312
  queen with power in, xxv–xxvi,
    xxv(n)–xxvi(n)
  women players, 6, 13, 322–323
The Chesse Play (Breton), xxv
Chievres, William de Croy, Sieur de,
  62, 63

children, 28–29
  in captivity, 122, 147, 150, 152, 269
  illegitimacy, 37–38, 163, 170, 176,
      181–182, 204, 233
  legitimacy, 141n
  orphans, 48n
  at play, 6n
  political role, 162–163
  sex and, 18, 31, 191
Christian III of Denmark, King, xvii, 61,
    133–134, 235n
Christina of Denmark, xvii, 188
  early life, 134, 167
  political role, 227, 233–235, 235n
Christina of Sweden, 321
Christine de Pizan, xxviii–xxix, 12, 18
Clarencius, Susan, 229
Claude of France, Queen, 29, 43, 99
  Anne Boleyn and, 66n
  death, 116–117
  marriage, 59–60, 69–70, 116
  political role, 69, 87, 89–93
Claude of Lorraine, 302–303
Clement VII, Pope, 125, 130, 131, 134
Cleves, Duke of, 191, 192, 193, 194, 202
Clifford, Margaret, 261n
Coligny, Admiral Gaspard de
  Catherine de Medici and, 299–304
  death, 304
  political role, 236, 269, 288, 289,
      294–295
Collectanea satis copiosa, 157
colors, symbolism, 4, 16, 232n
Columbus, Christopher, 22
Commentary on the True and False
    Religion (Zwingli), 118
Concordat of Bologna, 68
Concordia de Segovia, 11n–12n
Condé, Prince de, 251, 252, 253, 255, 268
  political role, 272, 288–289
  Protestantism and, 269
conjugal love, 10, 24, 113, 161, 203
Conspiracy of Amboise, 251
Cordatus, Conrad, 167

Cortés, Hernán, 5
Cosimo de Medici, 134
Council of Trent, 195, 256
Council of Troubles, 286–287
Couronne Margaritique (Lemaire), 23
court
  of Margaret of Austria, 3–9, 44, 133
  politics, 1, 14, 42, 145, 179
  standards and ethics at, 4, 5–6, 8, 20,
      42
  strategies at, 13–14
courtly love, 89, 265
  Anne Boleyn and, 8–9, 125–126, 127,
      131, 175
  sex and, 8, 42, 48, 112–113, 127–128,
      172–174, 189, 287
Cranmer, Thomas, 156–157, 161–162, 174,
    227
Cromwell, Thomas, xxii, 159, 163, 171, 172,
    175, 183

Dacre, Thomas Fiennes, 9th Baron of,
    75, 76, 80, 109
dance, 83, 92, 92n
Darnley, Henry Stuart, Lord, xx, xxi,
    238n, 267
  death, 280, 281, 290
  family life, 279–280
  marriage, 274–277
  with Rizzio, murder of, 277–278
Dauphin of France, 82, 94, 96, 100, 109,
    170, 176
David (Michelangelo), 134
De Carles, Lancelot, 4, 8, 108, 159, 172
De Cessolis, Jacobus, xxv, 209
De Cordoba, Martin, 11
De Feria, Ambassador, 229–230, 240,
    243
De La Pommeraye, Gilles, 159–160
De Noailles, Ambassador, 228
De Quadra, Ambassador, 243, 263
De Silva, Guzman, 282
Deborah (biblical figure), 240
Decameron (Boccaccio), 47

The Defeat of the Spanish Armada (Mattingly), xxviii
Defence of Good Women (Elyot), 208
dentistry, 37, 37n
Descurra, Juan Martinez, 191, 193, 270
Devereux, Robert. *See* Essex, 2nd Earl of
diamonds, 46, 52, 61, 77, 113, 128
Diane de Poitiers, 189, 189n, 201–202
Diet of Augsburg (1530), 151
Discourse on the Legitimate Succession of Women (Chambers), 311
Dissolution of the Monasteries, xxii, 172, 220
Don Carlos, Prince of Asturias, 258, 264
Don John of Austria, 287n
Don Juan Manuel de la Cerda, 62
Dorothea of Denmark, 134, 235n
Douglas, Archibald. *See* Angus, 6th Earl of
Douglas, Lady Margaret, xix, xx, 161n, 261n, 267
  in captivity, 176n
  legitimacy and, 141n
  with succession and, 220
Douglas, William. *See* Morton, 6th Earl of
dramatis personae
  England, xxi–xxiii
  France, xviii–xix
  reformers, xxiii–xxiv
  Scotland, xix–xxi
  Spain and Habsburg Empire, xvi–xvii
Drummond, Lord, 72
Du Bois, Simon, 151
Du Croc, Ambassador, 282
Dudley, Amy, xxiii, 243, 244, 265
Dudley, Guildford, 207
Dudley, John, 205, 207, 212
Dudley, Robert, 1st Earl of Leicester, xxiii
  death, 318
  Elizabeth I of England and, 242–244, 263–264, 263n, 266, 278, 293, 318
    Mary, Queen of Scotts, and, 264, 265–266, 278
    political role, 240, 267, 275, 304, 313, 314
    Randolph and, 276, 277
Duprat, Chancellor, 68n

Edict of Amboise (1563), 270
Edict of Romorantin (1560), 252
education. *See* women
The Education of a Christian Woman (Vives), 113
Edward IV of England, King, 15
Edward VI of England, King, xxii
  death, 211
  early life, 181, 182, 187, 211, 228
  family life, 198, 206
  Protestantism and, 204–205, 207
Eleanor of Aquitaine, 125, 127
Eleanor of Austria, xvii, 60, 121, 168, 224
  death, 225
  marriage, 61, 61n, 102, 129, 147, 151
  political role, 132–133, 150, 160, 189
Eleonore de Roye, 251, 252
Elisabeth of Valois
  death, 289–290
  political role, 201, 235, 256, 258, 271, 272
Elizabeth I of England, Queen, 173n, 225, 324
  background, xvii, xx, xxi, xxii, xxiii, xxiv, xxvii, xxviii, xxx
  as body politic, 239
  in captivity, 218
  with chess, game of, 322–323
  criticism of, 239–240, 239n
  diplomacy, 239
  Dudley, Robert, and, 242–244, 263–264, 263n, 266, 278, 293, 318
  early life, 162, 170, 171, 172, 181, 183, 197, 201
  education, 182
  family life, 151, 198, 212, 213
  illegitimacy of, 181–182, 233

Elizabeth I of England, Queen (*continued*)
  legacy, 317–320, 318n
  with marriage, 218, 227, 240–242, 244,
    262–264, 266–267, 278, 292, 294,
    309, 311
  Mary I of England and, 226–231, 241
  Mary, Queen of Scots and, 258–267,
    275–276, 278–279, 281, 284,
    290–292, 306, 311–316
  Massacre of Saint Bartholomew's Day
    and, 304
  military and, xxix, 27n, 317–318
  political role, 234, 238, 246–247,
    259–261, 288–289, 298, 310
  religion and, 155, 205, 207, 215, 238, 251,
    254–255, 286
  with sexism, 239–240
  Seymour, Thomas, and, 205–206
  speeches, xxix, 317
  with succession, 215, 217–218, 220,
    229–230, 231, 261n, 262
  at Tilbury, xxix, 27n
  virginity and, 241–243, 311n
Elizabeth II of England, Queen, 124n
Elizabeth of Austria, 293
Elizabeth of York, xxi, xxvii, 31, 32, 44
  death, 33
  political role, 30, 54, 319
Elizabeth Tudor. *See* Elizabeth I of
  England, Queen
Elizabeth Woodville, 171n
Elyot, Sir Thomas, 208
England, dramatis personae, xxi–xxiii
Enrique IV of Castile, 10
Enseignements (*Lessons for my daughter*)
  (Anne de Beaujeu), 13–14, 27, 57,
  105, 307
Erasmus, Desiderius, 5, 45, 76, 99, 166,
  197
Eric of Sweden, 240
Essex, Robert Devereux, 2nd Earl of, 318
ethics. *See* court
Evil May Day, 78–79

falconry, 78, 154
The Family of Henry VIII (painting), 198
Farnese, Alexander. *See* Parma, Duke of
Farnese, Ottavio. *See* Parma, Duke of
fashion, 4–5, 60, 75, 91, 92, 162
fasting, 117
female leadership, tropes, 323
femme sole, 213n
Fénelon, Bertrand, 304
Ferdinand I, Holy Roman Emperor, xvii,
  124
  early life, 36n, 133
  family life, 188
  political role, 240
  religion and, 167
Ferdinand II of Aragon, xxi, 24, 33, 35
  Concordia de Segovia and, 11n–12n
  death, 78, 81
  League of Cambrai and, 40
  marriage, xvi, 10–11
  political role, 36, 37, 39, 41, 60, 77–78
finances, 77, 79, 84, 85n, 110, 199
First War of Religion, 257, 261
*The First Blast of the Trumpet Against
  the Monstrous Regiment of Women*
  (Knox), xxiv, 230
Fitzroy, Henry. *See* Richmond, Duke of
Fitzwilliam, William, 96
Fleuranges, Seigneur de, 59, 64, 85, 95
Flodden, xxviii, 50–55
Foix, Françoise de, 126n, 127n
food, 91–92, 117, 161
Foxe, John, 155, 229, 230
France, dramatis personae, xviii–xix
François I of France, King, xviii, xxi, 19,
  27, 28, 29, 95
  in captivity, 117–122, 136
  death, 198–199, 202
  early life, 42, 43, 66
  family life, 165, 189, 190–193, 196
  Henry VIII of England and, 87–94,
  160
  marriage, 59–60, 116, 147, 151
  with mistresses, 126n, 127n

political role, 64–70, 73–74, 82–86,
96, 99, 101, 102, 116, 135–136,
146–147, 150, 166, 170, 184, 193–195
religion and, 164
François II of France, King, xix, xx, 247
death, 253, 259
early life, 190, 201, 235, 252
marriage, 232–233, 245
Fraser, Antonia, 323
Frederick 'the Wise' of Saxony, 85
French Wars of Religion (1562–1598), 257,
261, 269, 288–289
Fuensalida, Ambassador, 24

Game of Chess (De Cessolis), xxv, 209
Gandhi, Indira, 323
Gardiner, Bishop, 217
George of Denmark, Prince, 322
Gié, Seigneur de, 28, 29
Gilby, Anthony, 230
Giles. See Saint Giles
Giustinian, Ambassador, 76, 77, 83, 86
A Glasse of the Truth (pamphlet), 215–216
gold, 45, 83, 84, 91, 95, 186, 212
'Golden Speech' (Elizabeth I of
England), 317
Goodman, Christopher, 230
Gordon, George. See Huntly, 4th Earl of
Gouffier, Artus, xviii
Gouffier, Guillaume. See Bonnivet
Grenville, Cardinal, 287
Grey, Elizabeth, 44
Grey, Jane. See Lady Jane Grey
Grey, Lady Katherine, 261, 261n
Guevara, Don Diego, 5
Guise family
Anthony, 184, 185
Charles, xix
Claude, 184, 185
Francis, xix, 257, 261, 269
Henri, xix
Louis, 223
See also Marie de Guise

Habsburg Empire, 19, 29, 98, 98n
dramatis personae, xvi–xvii
inbreeding, 61n
legacy, xxvi–xxvii
Hall, Edward, 44
Hamilton, James. See Arran, 2nd Earl of
healing touch, of monarch, 214n
Heath, Nicholas, Archbishop, 242
Heilly, Anne d', 127n
Henri II of France, King, xix, 185
death, 236
early life, 82, 170
family life, 199, 200, 201–202, 232, 233
marriage, 165, 189–190
political role, 94, 96, 100, 109, 177, 217,
229, 236
Henri II of Navarre, King, 135, 135n, 190,
191–192, 237
Henri III of France, King, xix
political role, 266, 289, 309–310, 310n,
320
religion and, 164
Henri IV of France, King, xix, 150
early life, 236–237, 257, 268, 287–288
marriage, 300
political role, 272, 273, 289, 291, 295,
297–298, 299, 302, 305, 310, 310n,
320–321
Henri of Navarre. See Henri IV of
France, King
Henry I of England, King, 216n
Henry IV of England, King, 171n
Henry Tudor, Prince, 39
Henry VII of England, King, xxi, xxvii,
68, 198
death, 38–39
Margaret of Austria and, 36–37, 40
political role, 21, 31, 32, 33, 43, 213
Henry VIII of England, King, xvii, xix,
xxi, xxii, xxviii, 31, 32, 43n
Act of Supremacy and, 163
Anne Boleyn and, 5, 6, 44, 48n, 107–
108, 111–112, 125–131, 126n, 140–143,
147–148, 156–163, 169–175, 197n

Henry VIII of England, King (*continued*)
  Anne of Cleves and, 181, 183
  Boleyn, Mary, and, 66, 108, 125–127,
    126n, 130
  death, 198
  family life, 181–183, 198
  François I of France and, 87–94, 160
  Jane Seymour and, 171, 175
  Katherine Howard and, 181, 183
  Katherine of Aragon and, 6, 33–34,
    38–40, 44, 50, 71, 76–77, 79, 80,
    108, 113, 125, 126, 127, 129–131,
    140–143, 147–148, 157–158, 160,
    162–163, 169
  Katherine Parr and, 197
  Margaret Tudor and, 73, 74–75, 76,
    77, 80, 109, 115
  marriages, 33, 38–39, 44, 128, 129–131,
    140–143, 147–148, 157–158, 162, 169,
    174, 175, 181, 188, 197n
  military and, 43, 44
  Order of the Golden Fleece and, 62
  political role, 6–7, 38, 41, 43, 44–47,
    52, 54, 67, 78, 79, 83, 86, 97, 110, 114,
    123–124, 147, 187
  religion and, 156–157, 183
Hepburn, James. *See* Bothwell,
    4th Earl of
Hepburn, Patrick. *See* Bothwell,
    1st Earl of
Heptameron (Marguerite of Navarre),
    xviii, 47–49, 68, 101
heresy
  heretics, burning of, 227–228
  Placarten and, 286
Holy Roman Emperor. *See* titles
hospitals, 12, 48n
Howard family, 6, 7, 111
Howard of Effingham, William Howard,
    1st Baron, 234
Howard, Thomas. *See* Norfolk, Duke of
Huguenots. *See* Protestantism
Huntly, George Gordon, 4th Earl of, 261
Hussey, John, 174

Hyde, Thomas, 323

illegitimacy. *See* children
'Illuminati,' 118
*In Honour of that High and Mighty
    Princess Queen Elizabeth of Happy
    Memory* (Bradstreet), 323–324
inbreeding, 13, 29, 61n
independence, widows with, 4
indulgences, 85, 85n
Inquisition, 22, 118, 271
insanity, 12, 24, 26n, 35, 37
*Instructions Drawn Up from Motherly
    Solicitude for the Special Benefit of
    My Posterity* (Maria Theresa), 322n
Isabeau of Bavaria, 12
Isabella Clara Eugenia, 319, 321
Isabella of Aragon, Queen of Portugal,
    23
Isabella of Austria, xvii, 61, 133–134
Isabella of Castile, xvi, xxi, xxv, xxviii
  with chess, game of, 322
  Concordia de Segovia and, 11n–12n
  death, 34, 35
  influence, 51, 131n, 241
  legacy, 10–12, 14, 22, 39n, 213, 214, 217,
    241
  Margaret of Austria and, 15, 23–24, 35
  military and, 12
  political role, 141
Isabella of Hungary, 133n
Isabella of Portugal, 123–124, 132
Isaiah (biblical figure), 240
Islam, 22, 137
Italian Wars, 69, 95–97, 116, 130, 188, 234
Ivan the Terrible, 242

Jacquetta of Luxembourg, 171n
James II of Scotland, King, xix, xx
James IV of Scotland, King, xix, 77
  death, 52–53
  dentistry and, 37, 37n
  marriage, 31–32, 33, 37–38, 51–52
  political role, 38, 51, 52

James V of Scotland, King, xix, xx,
    183
  in captivity, 132
  death, 186
  early life, 53–54, 72, 73–74
  marriage, 184, 185–186
  political role, 110, 114–115
James VI of Scotland and I of England,
    King, xxi
  early life, 279–280, 282, 284
  political role, 312–313, 319–320
Jane Grey. See Lady Jane Grey
Jane Seymour, xxii, 171, 175, 181, 198,
    204
Jardin de nobles doncellas (De Cordoba),
    11
jasper, 6
Jean of Navarre, 150
Jeanne d'Albret, xix, 136, 236, 254n
  in captivity, 289
  death, 299
  early life, 190–191, 237
  finances, 199
  marriages, 191–195, 202–203, 237–238,
    237n, 268
  political role, 192–193, 237–238,
    238n, 251, 252, 254–257, 268–273,
    287–289, 291, 294–298, 300
Jeanne of France, 17, 28, 29, 141
Jerome. See Saint Jerome
Jesuits, 225n, 286, 309, 319
jewels, 74, 114
  Anne Boleyn, 112, 128
  Catherine de Medici, 165, 258
  Katherine of Aragon, 160
  Margaret of Austria, 47, 97
  Margaret Tudor, 52, 74, 77, 80
  Mary, Queen of Scots, 232, 258,
    262
  Wolsey, 93
  See also diamonds; pearls
Jews, 22, 171
Joan of Navarre, Queen, 171n
Joao of Portugal, 225n

Journal (Louise of Savoy), 19, 19n, 42n,
    59, 66, 67
jousting, 32, 44, 45, 64, 110, 126, 322n
Juan, Prince of Asturias, xvi, 11, 12, 21,
    23, 24
Juana 'La Beltraneja,' 11, 131n
Juana of Austria, Princess of Portugal,
    225, 225n
Juana 'the Mad' of Castile, xvi, xvii, 11, 21,
    23, 225n
  confinement, forced, 35–36, 36n
  insanity and, 24, 26n, 35, 37
  political role, 35–36, 37, 98n
Julius II, Pope, 41

Katherine Howard, 181, 183
Katherine of Aragon, xxi, xxii, xxviii, 11,
    21, 23, 183
  Anne Boleyn and, 9, 112, 162–163, 176,
    215
  death, 169–170, 171
  Henry VIII of England and, 6,
    33–34, 38–40, 44, 50, 71, 76–77, 79,
    80, 108, 113, 125, 126, 127, 129–131,
    140–143, 147–148, 157–158, 160,
    162–163, 169
  jewels, 160
  marriages, 30, 33–34, 38–39, 44, 128,
    129–131, 140–143, 147–148, 157–158,
    162, 169
  military and, 51
  political role, 37, 39–40, 50–54, 71, 75,
    76–78, 82, 83, 87–91, 93, 109–111,
    123, 124, 161
  speech, 51
  as widow, 31, 33
Katherine Parr, 151, 183
  as author, 197
  death, 205–206
Kennedy, Janet, 38
keyboards, 6
Keyle, Robert, 263
kingship, sword and, 10, 214
Kirkaldy of Grange, 282

Knox, John, xxiv, 230, 230n, 244
    influence, 245–246, 260, 264–265
    with sexism, 239–240, 274, 284

La Brosse, Jacques de, 187
La Tour d'Auvergne family, 189n
Ladies' Carousel, 322n
'Ladies' Peace' of Cambrai. *See* peace
Lady Jane Grey, xxii
    death, 218
    with succession, 207–208, 211–212,
        220, 261n
Lafayette, Aymee de, 190
Lamballe, Marie-Louise Thérèse,
        Princesse de, 303n
land
    Roman Catholic Church with, 220
    taxes, 36
Langley, Bonaventure, 54
laws
    Act of Supremacy and, 163
    Salic Law, xxvii, 12, 13, 136, 214n, 311
    succession, 124n, 163, 176, 181, 198, 262
    Treason Act of 1534, 173
League of Cambrai, 40–41
Lefèvre d'Etaples, Jacques, 155
legitimacy. *See* children
Leicester, 1st Earl of. *See* Dudley, Robert
Lemaire, Jean, 23, 23n, 40
Lennox, Matthew Stuart, 4th Earl of,
        222, 274–275, 281
Leo X, Pope, 68, 134, 135
Lepanto, battle of (1571), 321
Leslie, John, 32n
Lessons for my daughter. See
        Enseignements
Lewis, C. S., 125n
Liber Regalis, 213
Longueville, Louis, 185
Lorenzo de Medici, 27, 134
Louis II of Hungary, King, 133
Louis of Nassau, 286
Louis XI of France, King, xviii, 13, 15, 17
Louis XII of France, King, xviii, xxi

    death, 64–65, 71
    as Duc d'Orléans, 17, 18, 27, 28
    marriage, 29, 60–61, 64
    political role, 38, 43, 60, 64, 66–70
Louis XIV of France, King, 322
Louise of Savoy, xviii, xxix, 25, 184, 189n
    Anne de Beaujeu and, 15, 17–18, 27, 42
    Anne of Brittany and, 29
    with chess, game of, 322
    death, 151
    family life, 117, 190
    Journal of, 19, 19n, 42n, 59, 66, 67
    'Ladies' Peace' of Cambrai and, xxvii,
        137–138, 140, 143–148
    political role, 43, 74, 83, 85–88, 90–97,
        99, 100, 116–121, 137–138, 140,
        143–144, 150, 163, 311n
    Roman Catholic Church and, 99, 102,
        118
    as widow, 27–28
love, 131, 131n
    See also conjugal love; courtly love
Loyola, Ignatius, 286
Luther, Martin, xxiii, 84–85, 98–99, 167
    influence, 166–167
    Lutheranism and, 137, 164, 216
    Mass and, 166n
    Protestant Reformation and, 118
Lyon Herald, 72

Machiavelli, Niccolò, xviii, xxviii, xxix–
        xxx, 14, 43, 59, 144, 305, 314
Mad War, 18
Madeleine of Valois, 184, 185
Maitland, William, 259–261, 262, 264,
        265, 280
Malory, Sir Thomas, 242
'Malus Intercursus,' 40
Manuel I of Portugal, King, 23, 23n, 61n,
        129
mappa mundi, 5
Margaret Beaufort, xxvii, 30, 31, 50, 68
    influence, 72, 77
    political role, 213

Margaret of Anjou, 50, 97, 213

Margaret of Austria, xvi, xvii, xviii, xxii, xxviii, xxix
  Anne Boleyn and, 3–9, 44, 61, 125–126, 127, 157
  Anne de Beaujeu and, 15, 16, 17, 18, 20, 42
  Charles V and, 95, 97–98, 119, 140, 144, 149–150
  Charles VIII and, 19–20, 24, 25
  with chess, game of, 6, 322
  court of, 3–9, 44, 133
  death, 140
  family life, 121, 134
  finances, 84, 110
  Isabella of Castile and, 15, 23–24, 35
  jewels, 47, 97
  'Ladies' Peace' of Cambrai and, xxvii, 137–138, 140, 143–148
  marriage and, 9n, 19, 21–27, 45–47
  political role, 35–38, 40–42, 44–47, 59–63, 81, 82, 84–86, 88–89, 93, 95–99, 110–111, 118–119, 137–140, 149–150, 163, 244
  portraits, 4, 5
  as widow, 4–5, 26–27, 29

Margaret of Parma, xvii, 134, 153
  family life, 285n
  political role, 227, 285–287, 287n

Margaret of York, 15, 16, 21, 36, 99

Margaret Tudor, xix, xx, xxi, xxviii
  family life, 108–109, 113, 114–115, 141n, 161n, 184, 186
  finances, 77, 79
  jewels, 52, 74, 77, 80
  marriages, 31–33, 37–38, 51–52, 72, 77, 80, 130, 132
  political role, 38, 51–55, 71–76, 78, 79, 108, 110–111, 113–115, 132, 220
  power and, 73–75, 79, 183

Margot de Valois
  marriage, 300
  political role, 291, 294, 296, 298, 301–303, 305

Marguerite of Navarre (Marguerite d'Angoulême), xviii, xix, 19, 27, 55
  as author, xviii, 47–49, 68, 101, 151, 197, 198
  death, 203
  early life, 42–43
  family life, 150, 189, 190–194, 198–199, 202–203
  influence, 127, 161
  marriages, 43, 66, 135
  political role, 59, 68, 69, 70, 87, 92, 93, 116–121, 135–137, 145, 150–151, 160–161, 165, 185, 194n, 195–196, 238
  religion and, 155–156, 164–166
  Roman Catholic Church and, 99–100, 102, 137

Maria of Aragon, Queen of Portugal, 11, 23n

Maria Theresa, Empress, 322, 322n

Marie de Guise (Mary of Lorraine), xx, 184, 197, 200, 235, 239
  death, 247, 252, 259
  marriage, 185–186
  political role, 187, 206n, 222–223, 232, 245–247, 270

Marie de Medici, 321

Marignano, 69, 97, 184

Marillac, Ambassador, 194n

Marlowe, Christopher, 305n

Martyr, Peter, 51

martyrs, 197n, 227, 230

Mary II of England, Queen, 322

Mary of Burgundy, xvi, 15–16, 84, 150

Mary of Hungary, xvii, xxix, 61
  death, 234
  early life, 133
  family life, 168, 188
  political role, 133, 153–154, 167, 189, 204–206, 223–225, 285
  religion and, 166–167

Mary of Lorraine. See Marie de Guise

Mary, Queen of Scots (Mary Stuart), xix, xx, xxi, xxiii, xxiv, xxviii, 72n, 284n

Mary, Queen of Scots (Mary Stuart)
    (*continued*)
    in captivity, 282–283, 284, 290–291,
        313–315
    death, 315, 317
    Dudley, Robert, and, 264, 265–266,
        278
    early life, 186–188, 199–202, 222–223
    Elizabeth I of England and, 258–267,
        275–276, 278–279, 281, 284,
        290–292, 306, 311–316
    family life, 235, 279–280
    jewels, 232, 258, 262
    with marriage, 232–233, 232n, 245,
        262–267, 274–278, 281–283, 290
    political role, 199–201, 223, 247, 251,
        253, 257, 274–284
    religion and, 259
    with Ridolfi Plot (1571), 292
    Roman Catholic Church and, 264
Mary Tudor (Mary I of England), xvii,
        xxii, 39, 306
    Anne Boleyn and, 162–163, 171, 215
    coronation, 213–214
    criticism of, 239
    death, 230, 234
    early life, 76–77, 82, 83, 113, 163, 197
    Elizabeth of England and, 226–231,
        241
    family life, 158, 163, 182, 197–198
    illegitimacy of, 163, 170, 176, 181–182,
        204
    marriage, 216–219, 241
    military and, 218
    political role, 94, 96, 100, 109, 114, 123,
        124, 128–129, 183, 206n, 222, 238n,
        278
    Roman Catholic Church and, 204–
        206, 214–215, 219, 220, 227–228, 230
    succession, 211–221
Mary Tudor, Queen of France, xxii, 130
    death, 161n
    early years, 31
    marriages, xxi, 61, 64, 65–66

    political role, 60, 61, 65, 76, 79, 83, 87,
        92, 261n
Mass, 6, 166n, 205
massacres, 305n
    Massacre of Saint Bartholomew's
        Day, xxvi, 293–306, 309, 320
    Massacre of Vassy, 257, 261, 269
    sexual violence with, 303n
    of Waldensian sect, 195
The Massacre of Paris (Marlowe),
        305n
Matilda, Empress, 213, 216n
Mattingly, Garrett, xxviii
Maximilian I, Holy Roman Emperor,
        xvi, 3, 15, 16, 19, 77, 95n
    death, 84
    family life, 133
    League of Cambrai and, 40
    political role, 21, 24, 36, 38, 41, 43,
        60–63, 81–82, 98, 293n
Mehmed III, Sultan, 311n
Meir, Golda, 323
Melanchthon, Philip, 164
Melville, Sir James, 266
Mémoires (Jeanne d'Albret), 254n, 288
Mendoza, Inigo de, 128, 129, 141, 143–144,
        315
merchants, with social mobility, 6
Michelangelo, 134
Michieli, Ambassador, 230
A Midsummer Night's Dream
        (Shakespeare), 319
military
    Anne de Beaujeu and, 17
    Elizabeth I of England and, xxix, 27n,
        317–318
    Henry VIII of England and, 43, 44
    Isabella of Castile and, 12
    Katherine of Aragon and, 51
    Mary I of England, 218
'Mirror of Naples' diamond, 61
The Mirror of Glass of a Sinful Soul
        (Marguerite of Navarre), 151, 166,
        197

mobility
merchants with social mobility, 6
mobile hospitals, 12
monarch, healing touch of, 214n
monasteries, xxii, 99, 172, 220
Montezuma, 5
Montmorency, Constable, 117, 120, 193, 202, 235, 236
Montpensier, Catherine de Lorraine, Duchesse de, 320n
Moors, 11, 22
Moray, James Stewart, 1st Earl of, xx, 259, 275
More, Thomas, 31, 130–131
Morte d'Arthur (Malory), 242
Morton, William Douglas, 6th Earl of, 275, 283, 312
Murad III, Sultan, 311n
music, 6, 96, 182, 266

Naturelli, Ambassador, 85–86
"Le Navire" (Marguerite of Navarre), 198
New York Times, xxx
Norfolk, Thomas Howard, Duke of, 174, 176n, 247, 290–291
Norris, Sir Henry, 172–173, 291

The Obedience of the Christian Man and How Christian Rulers Ought to Govern (Tyndale), 156
On the Nobility and Excellence of the Feminine Sex (Agrippa, C.), 4
Order of the Garter, 44, 114
Order of the Golden Fleece, 62
Orléans, Louis, Duc d'. See Louis XII of France
Ormonde, James Butler, 9th Earl of, 103, 111
orphans, 48n
Ottoman Empire, 119, 133, 139–140, 153, 311n
Ovid, 18
Oysel, Sieur d', 223, 245

paintings. See portraits
Paraphrases upon the New Testament (Erasmus), 197
Parker, Matthew, 173, 173n
Parma, Alexander Farnese, Duke of, xvii, 285n, 287n
Parma, Ottavio Farnese, Duke of, 285n
Paul III, Pope, 166, 195
peace
'Ladies' Peace' of Cambrai, xxvii, 137–138, 140, 143–148, 189
Margaret of Austria and, 119
Maria Theresa on, 322n
Treaty of Arras, 16
Treaty of Perpetual Peace, 31, 38, 52
Women's International Peace Conference (1915), xxvii(n)
pearls, 26, 52, 77, 212, 290, 298, 311n
Percy, Henry, 112
Petite Bande, 189
Petrucci, Ambassador, 295–296
Philibert II, Duke of Savoy, xvi, 25–26, 63, 150
Philiberte of Savoy, 68
Philip I of Castile (Philip of Burgundy), xvi, xvii, 16, 21, 24, 35, 36, 37
Philip II of Spain, King, xvii, xxii, 240, 256
death, 235
family life, 271, 272–273, 289–290
marriages, 216–219, 235, 241, 258
political role, 190, 220, 223n, 224–229, 233–234, 238n, 269, 285–286, 304, 315–316
Philip the Good, 5
Philippa of Gueldres, 184, 185
Pickering, Sir William, 240
Pius IV, Pope, 271
Pius V, Pope, 291
'Placard Affair' (1534), 165
Placarten, 286
plague, 29, 79
Plato, 196
play, children at, 6n

Pole, Margaret, 183
Pole, Reginald, 220
Polignac, Jean de, 18
portraits
    Arnolfini, 5
    The Family of Henry VIII, 198
    Margaret of Austria, 4, 5
power, xxix, 4, 79, 176, 183
    of ancestors, 143, 159, 170
    Appendage Syndrome and, 323
    chess with queen and, xxv–xxvi,
        xxv(n)–xxvi(n)
    sex and, 243
    sexism with, 230, 239, 240, 274, 284
    usurped, 73–75
    women with power limited by law,
        xxvii, 12, 13, 136, 214n, 311
Prayers or Meditations (Katherine Parr),
    197
Princess of Wales. *See* titles
The Prince (Machiavelli), xviii, xxviii, 14,
    305
en prise, chess and, 312
Les Prisons (Marguerite of Navarre), 151
Protestantism
    Conspiracy of Amboise, 251
    Huguenots, 255, 261, 268, 270, 273,
        287, 301–303, 305, 310, 320
    Luther and, xxiii, 118
    persecution of, 195
    Reformation, xix, 197n
    role of, 204–205, 207, 216, 259, 269, 286
    Roman Catholic Church and, 251–257
    spread of, 236, 238
Psalms or Prayers (Katherine Parr), 197
Purgatory, 85n

queen, chess and power of, xxv–xxvi,
    xxv(n)–xxvi(n)

Randolph, Thomas, 260, 261, 266, 274
    Cecil, William, and, 275–276
    Dudley, Robert, and, 276, 277
Reformation. *See* Protestantism

reformers, dramatis personae, xxiii–xxiv
religion, 118
    dissent, 136, 137
    First War of Religion, 257, 261
    with heretics, burning of, 227–228
    Islam, 22, 137
    religious toleration, xxvi, 133n, 251, 255,
        256, 288
    riots, 246
    role of, xxvi, 155–157, 164–167, 172, 183,
        205, 207, 215, 238, 246, 251, 254–255,
        257, 259, 261, 286
    See also French Wars of Religion;
        Protestantism; Roman Catholic
        Church
Renaissance, 125n, 134, 167, 189
Renard, Simon, 213, 215
René of Savoy, 25
Renée of France, 59, 60, 68, 99, 287, 298
Reyes de Aragon (Abarca), 23
Richard III of England, King, 15
Richmond, Henry Fitzroy, Duke of, 83,
    124, 176, 176n
Ridolfi Plot (1571), 292
riots
    religion, 246
    taxes, 188–189
Rizzio, David, xx, 277–278, 280
Robsart, Amy. *See* Dudley, Amy
Roman Catholic Church, 15n, 41, 43, 95n
    Act in Restraint of Appeals, 161–162
    Concordat of Bologna and, 68
    Council of Trent, 195, 256
    indulgences and, 85, 85n
    influence, 118, 125
    Inquisition and, 22, 118, 271
    Jesuits, 225n, 286, 309, 319
    with land, 220
    with legitimacy, 141n
    Luther and, 85
    Mass, 6, 166n, 205
    with massacres, 195
    'Placard Affair,' and, 165
    Protestantism and, 251–257

reform, 99–100, 245

role of, 11, 68, 94, 96, 99–100, 102, 109, 111, 114, 118, 123–125, 128–131, 134, 135, 137, 140–141, 143, 151–153, 183, 204–206, 206n, 214–215, 219, 220, 222, 227–228, 230, 238n, 259, 264, 269–271, 278, 286

  with Rome, sack of, 130, 134

  virginity and, 242

Ronsard, Pierre de, 249

Ross, Alexander, Duke of, 71, 75–76

Rough Wooing, 187, 199

Roussel, Gerard, 164

Russia, chess in, xxv(n)–xxvi(n)

Sadler, Sir Ralph, 183, 187, 246

Safiye Sultan, 311n

Saint Augustine, 20, 242

Saint Giles, 246

Saint Jerome, 242

Saint Teresa of Avila, 166n, 176

Saint-Gelais brothers, 19

Saint-Gelais, Jean de, 13

Salic Law, xxvii, 12, 13, 136, 214n, 311

Sanchez, Mateo, 225n

Sanders, Nicholas, 318

'Scachs d'Amor, Chess Game of Love' (poem), 131, 131n

Schmalkaldic League, 151

Scotland, dramatis personae, xix–xxi

sex

  children and, 18, 31, 191

  conjugal love, 10, 24, 113, 161, 203

  courtly love and, 8, 42, 48, 112–113, 127–128, 172–174, 189, 287

  manipulation through, 42, 44, 243

  power and, 243

  sexism, xxvii, xxx, 4, 12n, 224, 230, 239–240, 239n, 274, 284

  sexual misbehaviour, 172–174

  violence, 48, 303n

Seymour, Edward. See Somerset, 1st Duke of

Seymour, Thomas, 205–206, 244

Shakespeare, William, 319

Siege of Vienna (1529), 152–153

silver, 6, 80, 83, 90, 95, 117, 145

Simier, Jean de, 310

Skip, John, 156

smallpox, 262, 263

Smeaton, Mark, 172, 173, 174

social mobility, merchants with, 6

Solway Moss, battle of (1542), 186

Somerset, Edward Seymour, 1st Duke of, 204–205

Soranzo, Michele, 233, 235

Southwell, Sir Richard, 212

Spain, dramatis personae, xvi–xvii

speeches

  Elizabeth I of England, xxix, 317

  Katherine of Aragon, 51

Spinola, Baptista, 211

Stafford, Thomas, 228

standards. See court

Stephen of England, King, 213

Stewart, Henry, 115, 132, 183

Stewart, James. See Moray, 1st Earl of

Stewart, Lady Janet, 79

Strozzi, Clarice, 135

Stuart, Arbella, 261n, 319

Stuart, Henry. See Darnley, Lord

Stuart, John. See Albany, 2nd Duke of

Stuart, Mary. See Mary, Queen of Scots

Stuart, Matthew. See Lennox, 4th Earl of

succession

  laws, 124n, 163, 176, 181, 198, 262

  War of the Castilian Succession, 11

  women with, 72, 207–208, 211–221, 216n, 229–230, 231, 241, 261n, 262, 311

Suffolk, Charles Brandon, 1st Duke of, xxi, 32, 44, 45–47, 76

  family life, 77

  on Louise of Savoy, 67

  marriage, 65, 66, 130

  political role, 91, 244

Suleiman the Magnificent, Sultan, 119, 133, 311n

Suzanne, Duchess of Bourbon, 96–97,
    102
sword, kingship and, 10, 214
symbolism
    apples, 161
    colors, 4, 16, 232n
    healing touch of monarch, 214n
    sword and kingship, 10
    widows, 71

taxes
    land, 36
    riots, 188–189
Teresa of Avila. *See* Saint Teresa of Avila
Testard, Robinet, 19
Thatcher, Margaret, 323
Throckmorton, Sir Nicholas
    Cecil, William, and, 263, 275
    political role, 236, 243, 254, 255, 259,
        275
*The Tied-Up Dutch Provinces Before Duke
    Alba* (painting), 287
Tiepolo, Ambassador, 234
Tilbury, xxix, 27n
titles
    femme sole, 213n
    Holy Roman Emperor as, 15n, 95n
    succession laws with Princess of
        Wales, 124n
toleration. *See* religion
Topcliffe, Richard, 318–319
Torquemada, Tomás de, 22
Tower of London, 3, 158, 173, 174
trade
    illegal, 155
    'Malus Intercursus,' 40
    merchants, with social mobility, 6
    trade guilds, 68
    wool, 206
Traheron, Bartholomew, 230
Treason Act of 1534, 173
Treaties of Greenwich, 187
Treaty of Arras (1482), 16
Treaty of Blois (1572), 292

Treaty of Cateau-Cambrésis (1559),
    234–235
Treaty of Edinburgh (1560), 247
Treaty of Madrid (1526), 121
Treaty of Mechelen (1513), 41
Treaty of Perpetual Peace (1502), 31, 38,
    52
Treaty of St Germain (1570), 291
Treaty of Westminster (1527), 129
Très Riches Heures du Duc de Berry, 3–5
Trivulzio, Marshal, 67
True Cross, 29
Tyndale, William, 156

Ubaldini, Petruccio, 242
universal religious toleration, 133n

Van Eyck, Jan, 5
Vienna, violence in, 152–153
violence
    Council of Troubles, 286–287
    Evil May Day, 78–79
    sexual, 48, 303n
    Siege of Vienna, 152–153
    See also massacres; riots
virginity. *See* Elizabeth I of England,
    Queen
Vita Mariae Angliae Reginae
    (Wingfield), 211
Vives, Juan Luis, 113

Waldensian sect, massacre of, 195
Walsingham, Francis, 292, 297, 304, 313,
    314
War of the Castilian Succession, 11
War of the Holy League, 41, 43–44
Wars of the Roses, xxi, 50
The Way of Perfection (Saint Teresa of
    Avila), 176
Weston, Sir Francis, 173
widows, 5, 26–28, 29, 31, 33, 76
    with independence, 4
    role reversals, 13
    symbolism, 71

William I 'the Conqueror' of England,
King, 213
William III of England, King, 322
William of Orange, 285–286, 287, 293, 312
Wingfield, Robert, 211
witchcraft, 171n, 279
Wolsey, Thomas, Cardinal, xxii, 38, 65
    Anne Boleyn and, 102–103, 111–112,
        128, 129–131, 142, 143, 158
    downfall, 147, 175
    jewels, 93
    Margaret of Austria and, 119, 137
    political role, 78–79, 82–83, 88, 89,
        93–94, 96, 109, 110, 111, 114, 119, 147,
        159
    rise of, 78
women, xxiv
    chess, women players, 6, 13, 322–323
    education, 4, 22, 27, 113, 124, 182, 201

female leadership, tropes, 323
    with power limited by law, xxvii, 12, 13,
        136, 214n, 311
    role of, 11, 163
    sexism, xxvii, xxx, 4, 12n, 224, 230,
        239–240, 239n, 274, 284
    with succession, 72, 207–208, 211–221,
        216n, 229–230, 231, 241, 261n, 262,
        311
    widows, 4
Women's International Peace
    Conference (1915), xxvii(n)
wool trade, 206
Worcester, Elizabeth Somerset, Lady,
    172
Wriothesley, Charles, 174
Wyatt, Sir Thomas, 112–113, 173, 217–218

Zwingli, Ulrich, 118, 166n

© Oliver Edwards

Sarah Gristwood is a regular contributor to many London publications as well as a commentator on royal and historical affairs. The author of several previous books, including *Blood Sisters*, Gristwood splits her time between London and Kent, United Kingdom.